THE ANZUS CRISIS, NUCLEAR VISITING AND DETERRENCE

Cambridge Studies in International Relations is a joint initiative of Cambridge University Press and the British International Studies Association (BISA). The series will include a wide range of material, from undergraduate textbooks and surveys to research-based monographs and collaborative volumes. The aim of the series is to publish the best new scholarship in International Studies from Europe, North America and the rest of the world.

CAMBRIDGE STUDIES IN INTERNATIONAL RELATIONS

THE ANZUS CRISIS, NUCLEAR VISITING AND DETERRENCE

MICHAEL C. PUGH

Lecturer in International Relations, Centre for International Policy Studies, Department of Politics, University of Southampton

WITHDRAWN

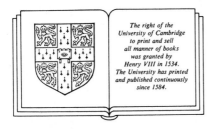

The right of the
University of Cambridge
to print and sell
all manner of books
was granted by
Henry VIII in 1534.
The University has printed
and published continuously
since 1584.

CAMBRIDGE UNIVERSITY PRESS
Cambridge
New York   Port Chester   Melbourne   Sydney

Published by the Press Syndicate of the University of Cambridge
The Pitt Building, Trumpington Street, Cambridge CB2 1RP
40 West 20th Street, New York, NY 10011, USA
10 Stamford Road, Oakleigh, Melbourne 3166, Australia

First published 1989

Printed in Great Britain by The University Press, Cambridge

British Library cataloguing in publication data

Pugh, Michael C.
The ANZUS crisis, nuclear visiting and deterrence. –
(Cambridge studies in international relations; 4)
1. New Zealand. Defence. Policies of government
I. Title
355′.0335′931

Library of Congress cataloguing in publication data

Pugh, Michael C. (Michael Charles), 1944–
The ANZUS crisis, nuclear visiting and deterrence/Michael C. Pugh.
    p.   cm. – (Cambridge studies in international relations: 4)
Bibliography.
Includes index.
ISBN 0-521-34355-0
1. New Zealand – Military policy.
2. Nuclear weapons – Government policy – New Zealand.
3. Nuclear warships – Government policy – New Zealand.
4. Australia – Military policy.
5. United States – Military policy.
6. Deterrence (Strategy)
I. Title.   II. Series.
UA874.3.P84 1989   89-6916 CIP

ISBN 0 521 34355 0

For Margaret, Ingrid and Evan

'Oh, I want for one moment to make our undiscovered country leap into the eyes of the world.'

Katherine Mansfield, journal entry, 1916.

CONTENTS

TABLES

PREFACE

In the mid-1980s, the spectacle of New Zealand withdrawing the customary warship visiting privileges of its powerful ally, the United States, and then absorbing reprisals, commanded world-wide attention. New Zealand is a small and vulnerable country in the international system, and its ban on nuclear ship visits was portrayed by sympathizers as a clash between David and Goliath. By contrast, hostile observers depicted the ban as preposterous grandstanding by a socialist government under the sway of misguided or even malevolent pacifists determined that their country should opt out of alliance responsibilities. Neither picture is accurate.

The alliance conflict and the media caricatures captured my interest and research began with the aim of writing a balanced interpretation of the ANZUS crisis in the context of changing security concerns in the South-West Pacific. In addition, it became evident that the subject could not be divorced from general problems associated with the visits of nuclear-powered and nuclear-armed platforms. In Washington, heightened sensitivity to anti-nuclearism led the Reagan Administration to demonstrate that a 'public good' would not be supplied to allies who restricted its distribution. Nuclear visiting, like basing, is one of the tangible means by which the assumed 'good' of nuclear deterrence is maintained and distributed. In April 1988 as this book was nearing completion it became abundantly clear from a political crisis in Denmark over the access of nuclear-capable warships that the problem was a general and continuing one. This issue, nuclear visiting, places the crisis in other contexts: the management of the Western Alliance and the perceived roles of nuclear deployments and nuclear deterrence in international relations.

It is with pleasure and gratitude that I acknowledge the financial assistance of the British Academy and Nuffield Foundation. Their support enabled me to conduct interviews in the United States, Australia and New Zealand, and to study documents in distant libraries. The University of Southampton kindly granted a sabbatical term for this purpose. Special thanks are due to Steve Smith, Peter Nailor and the CUP-BISA editorial team for their suggestions in regard to publication.

Many people helped me by their diligence in seeking out material, and with their conversation and hospitality.

In Australia: Don Aitken, Desmond Ball, Richard Bolt, Gary Brown, Joan Coxsedge MP, Karl Jackson Davies, Faith Doherty, Greg Fry, Paul Gilding, Peter Jones, Bill Lesley, Christopher Oates, Judy and Bruce Parr, Cynthia Southbown, Peter Stephens, Sen. Jo Vallentine, Derek Woolmer.

In New Zealand: Susan and Zoltán Apathy, Hon. Michael Bassett, Katie and John Boanas, Hon. Helen Clark, Kevin Clements, Hon. Paul M. Cleveland, Kath and Graeme Dunstall, Nicky Hager, John Henderson, Richard Hill, Richard Kennaway, Charlotte Macdonald, Ian McGibbon, Hon. Jim K. McLay, Denis McLean, Stuart McMillan, Merwyn Norrish, Hon. Frank O'Flynn, Hon. Geoffrey Palmer, Hon. Richard Prebble, Fran Wilde MP, Owen Wilkes, Peter Wills.

In the United States: David S. Addington, Dora Alves, Eugene J. Carroll, Lawrence J. Cavaiola, Eileen Connolly, Hon. Karl Jackson, Susan Keogh-Fisher, Gene La Rocque, Michael MccGwire, Simon Murdoch, Bernard F. Oppel, Ronald O'Rourke, Stanley Roth, Rt. Hon. Wallace R. Rowling, Russ Surber, Jack Talmadge, Hon. Paul C. Warnke, Lt. Col. John Williams.

My colleagues David Braddock, Alex Danchev, John Simpson and Frank Wareing, made sensible suggestions at an early stage. The overall interpretation is of course my own.

The staffs of the following libraries and institutions gave every assistance: Library of Congress; Foreign Affairs and National Defense Division, Congressional Research Service; US Senate Library; Australian National Library; Australian Parliamentary Library Defence Group; Research School of Pacific Studies, Australian National University; New Zealand National Archives; NZLP Head Office; General Assembly Library (whose Chief Clerk kindly gave permission for access to parliamentary submissions); University of Canterbury Library (and Kevin Clements for permission to examine Defence Enquiry submissions); British Library of Political and Economic Science; Defence Arms Control Unit, MoD, London; Institute of Commonwealth Studies (especially Tom Millar); International Institute for Strategic Studies; Icelandic Commission on Security in International Affairs (especially Gunnar Gunnarsson); Danish Commission on Security and Disarmament Affairs (especially Henrik Holtermann);

Norwegian Institute of International Affairs (especially Johan Jørgen Holst); Netherlands Institute of International Relations, Clingendael; the New Zealand and Australian High Commissions in London; and the London Embassies of Denmark, Japan, Spain and the United States.

Members of my family 'down-under' were very supportive, and I am particularly indebted to my stepfather Les Antill who was a model research assistant in Auckland. Ingrid and Evan were extraordinarily tolerant towards their preoccupied father. I thank them and my wife Margaret who worked long hours on the typescript and never ceased to be encouraging.

LIST OF ABBREVIATIONS

ABCA	America, Britain, Canada, Australia (Armies Programme)
AAEC	Australian Atomic Energy Commission
ABM	Anti-Ballistic Missile
ADF	Australian Defence Force
ALP	Australian Labor Party
Anzac	Australia and New Zealand, or residents of (orig. Australian and New Zealand Army Corps)
ANZCC	Australia and New Zealand Consultative Committee
ANZMIS	Australia and New Zealand Military Intelligence, Singapore
ANZUS	Australia, New Zealand, United States
ASEAN	Association of South-East Asian Nations
ASROC	Anti-Submarine Rocket
AWACS	Airborne Warning and Control System
C^3I	Command, Control, Communications, Intelligence
CIA	Central Intelligence Agency
CIC	Commander-in-Chief
CINCPAC	Commander-in-Chief, Pacific
CND	Campaign for Nuclear Disarmament
CTB	Comprehensive Test Ban Treaty
DIA	Defense Intelligence Agency
DoD	Department of Defence (Australia), Defense (US)
DSD	Defence Signals Directorate (Australia)
EC	European Community
EEZ	Exclusive Economic Zone
EO	Executive Order (US)
FOL	Federation of Labour (NZ)
GAO	General Accounting Office (US)
GCHQ	Government Communications Headquarters (UK)
GCSB	Government Communications Security Bureau (NZ)
HF-DF	High Frequency-Direction Finding

HMAS	Her Majesty's Australian Ship
HMNZS	Her Majesty's New Zealand Ship
HMS	Her Majesty's Ship
ICBM	Intercontinental Ballistic Missile
INF	Intermediate-range Nuclear Forces
JAEC	Joint Atomic Energy Committee (US)
kt	kiloton
LORAN	Long-Range Aid to Navigation (LORAN-C used for submarine navigation)
MARSAR	Maritime Surveillance Arrangement
MoD	Ministry of Defence (NZ/UK)
MoU	Memorandum of Understanding
mt	megaton
NATO	North Atlantic Treaty Organization
NCND	Neither Confirm Nor Deny
NDP	Nuclear Disarmament Party (A)
NFIP	Nuclear-Free and Independent Pacific
NFZ	Nuclear-Free Zone
nm	nautical mile
NPT	Non-Proliferation Treaty
NRC	Nuclear Regulatory Commission (US)
NSA	National Security Agency (US)
NSC	National Security Council (US)
NSF	National Science Foundation (US)
NSW	New South Wales
NUWAX	Nuclear Weapons Accident Exercise
NZ	New Zealand
NZAEC	New Zealand Atomic Energy Committee
NZLP	New Zealand Labour Party
PAL	Permissive Action Link
PMA	Peace Movement Aotearoa (formerly PMNZ)
PND	People for Nuclear Disarmament (A)
R & R	Rest and Recreation
RAAF	Royal Australian Air Force
RAF	Royal Air Force
RDF	Rapid Deployment Force
RAN	Royal Australian Navy
RN	Royal Navy
RNZAF	Royal New Zealand Air Force
RNZN	Royal New Zealand Navy
RSA	Returned Servicemen's/Soldiers' Association (NZ/A)
SANA	Scientists Against Nuclear Arms

SDI	Strategic Defense Initiative
SEATO	South-East Asia Treaty Organization
SIGINT	Signals Intelligence
SLBM	Submarine-Launched Ballistic Missile
SLCM	Sea-Launched Cruise Missile
SLOC	Sea Lanes of Communication
SPF	South Pacific Forum
SPNFZ	South Pacific Nuclear-Free Zone
SSBN	Strategic Nuclear-Powered Ballistic Missile Submarine
SUBROC	Submarine Rocket
TLAM/N	Tomahawk Land-Attack Missile/Nuclear
UKUSA	UK–US Security Agreement
UN	United Nations
UNCLOS	UN Convention on the Law of the Sea
US	United States
USAF	United States Air Force
USN	United States Navy
USPACOM	US Pacific Command
USIA/S	United States Information Agency/Service
USS	United States Ship
USSR	Union of Soviet Socialist Republics
VLF	Very Low Frequency
WA	Western Australia

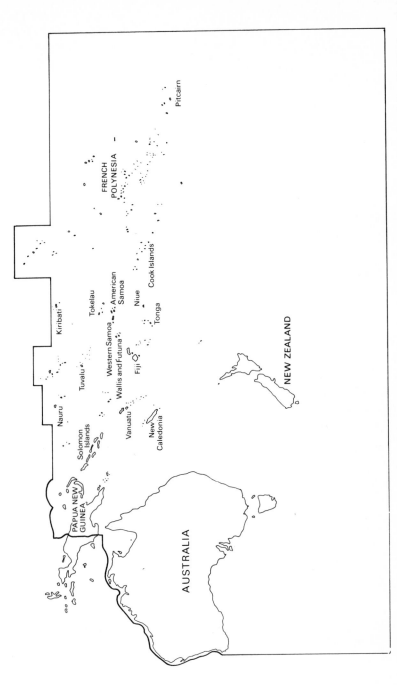

The South Pacific Nuclear Free Zone (Australian islands in the Indian Ocean, which are also part of the South Pacific Nuclear Free Zone, are not shown). Source: attachment to Annex 1 to the South Pacific Nuclear Free Zone Treaty.

1 INTRODUCTION: THE REVOLT OF AN UNDERLING

This is a study about conflicts of interest relating to some of the most pressing international issues of our time, most notably the salience of global nuclear deterrence. The focus is the ANZUS crisis of 1984–7: the collapse of the tripartite alliance relationship between the United States, Australia and New Zealand. With the enactment of the Nuclear Free Zone, Disarmament, and Arms Control Bill in June 1987, New Zealand became the only country in the world which has attempted to legislate disengagement from nuclear deterrence, incorporating a prohibition on visits by nuclear-propelled or armed warships and aircraft. This chapter begins with an outline of the crisis and an introduction to the issue of nuclear visiting. It then relates the ANZUS crisis to dynamic elements in international relations, namely alliance management, regionalism, nuclearism and the behaviour of small powers.

THE CRISIS

The immediate occasion of the crisis was the New Zealand Government's refusal, publicly announced on 4 February 1985, to accept a proposed visit by the USS *Buchanan*, a conventionally-powered, nuclear-capable destroyer. In July 1984 the New Zealand Labour Party (NZLP) had won a general election with a mandate to ban nuclear ship visits. After a six month period of grace, the US naval authorities decided to test the New Zealand Government's exclusion policy by requesting a March berth for the USS *Buchanan*. The New Zealand Cabinet finally turned down the request because it could not credibly assure the public that the ship would arrive without nuclear weapons.

This troublesome behaviour of an underling, which had hitherto been counted upon to make strenuous sacrifices for collective security, caused pain and bewilderment among allies. 'I must confess,' said

1

Admiral William Crowe, 'it is boggling my mind'.[1] Crowe, the US Commander-in-Chief Pacific (CINCPAC), joined a chorus of Washington officials in denouncing the ban. New Zealand was accused of undermining the ANZUS Pact, destroying the security equilibrium in the South Pacific and presenting opportunities to the Soviet Union. US policy-makers thus elevated the revolt to an issue of global significance, warning of a ripple effect which threatened the security of the whole Western Alliance structure. They feared that the New Zealand's action would inspire other allies to follow suit.

US officials also pointed out the impracticability of conforming to New Zealand's policy. Nuclear capability is so integral to the US Navy (USN) that forces cannot be subdivided into conventional and nuclear-armed vessels. Furthermore, 'on operational and security grounds', the US had long-standing rules, in common with other nuclear navies, to neither confirm nor deny (NCND) the presence of nuclear weapons on ships. Nor, in the USN's view, would it be acceptable for a foreign government to make its own assessment of a vessel's status.

The ANZUS Treaty of 1951 (reproduced in appendix 1) makes no mention of nuclear weaponry or unconditional access to ports, and the New Zealand Government argued that it was entitled to disengage from nuclear deterrence whilst remaining an active member of the Western Alliance. To meet US requirements the Cabinet made efforts to reach a compromise, and delayed the first parliamentary reading of the Nuclear Free Zone Bill until over two years after taking office.

This study is not preoccupied with establishing responsibility for the disaggregation of ANZUS. Such exercises have limited intellectual value. But there is no doubt that US measures to punish New Zealand were widely perceived outside Washington as an over-reaction. The reprisals clearly mobilized opinion in New Zealand behind the Lange Government though, in fact, the US response amounted only to a partial freeze on military co-operation and intelligence sharing. For domestic reasons US congressmen also urged the Administration to restrict New Zealand trade. Although Defense Secretary Caspar Weinberger and Navy Secretary John Lehman supported this, the Administration recoiled from economic measures.

However, the US did withdraw its security commitment to New Zealand in August 1986. This ended trilateral security co-operation, though the treaty framework was retained in case a future New Zealand Government should recant. The suspension was easily arranged because, unlike NATO, ANZUS has no earmarked forces or integrated military structure. Bilateral US–Australian and trans-Tasman defence co-operation continued. Although Prime Minister

Bob Hawke had sent a disapproving letter to Lange in January 1985, Australian policy towards New Zealand differed crucially from the American. The Australian Government did not regard support for nuclear deterrence as the basis for a viable alliance relationship. By contrast, the United Kingdom Government followed the US in suspending naval visits, explained that it could no longer offer security to New Zealand, and exerted diplomatic and political pressure on the Lange Government.

Reprisals are difficult to justify when directed against an ally. US policy-makers probably regarded New Zealand as a soft target. Unlike Australia, which has strategic value and residual rights over important US installations, New Zealand could exercise little clout. Observers have noted that the Reagan Administration tended to reserve disciplinary action for low risk 'targets of convenience' such as Grenada.[2] Further, any dispute with New Zealand affected a strategically marginal situation. Similar action against Norway, Greece or Japan would be much riskier. However, New Zealanders had little to lose from defence reprisals, and US 'heavy-handedness' only served to give New Zealand's policy 'undreamed of publicity'.[3]

To explain the crisis, commentators have emphasized the coincidence of an anti-nuclear government in Wellington and Reaganism in Washington.[4] Obviously this meant pronounced divergence of policy. Concepts of strategic fundamentalism and the notion of a Manichaean struggle with the Soviet Union infused policy-making in Washington. Military power, and alliance support for it, would be the chief arbiter of international security, and national security was a zero-sum game in which the US could win only at the expense of its adversary. As regards alliance management, the Reaganites seem to have assumed that US leadership would be accepted because a strong President and a powerful United States would be irresistible.[5] By contrast, the Labour Government in Wellington could hardly have ignored the political strength of anti-nuclearism which held that US policies were destabilizing.

Yet however much importance one attaches to the advent of particular governments, divergence in the alliance had been growing over many years. As suggested in chapter 2, both the ANZUS Treaty and the relationship were based only loosely on strategic denial of threats. One historical perspective suggests that the alliance was overdue for major surgery or even the mortuary. Nevertheless, during the crisis all parties hoped to keep ANZUS breathing. In the future, the US might prefer an unsatisfactory alliance with New Zealand to none at all, and New Zealand might welcome renewed military

3

co-operation with the US. The history of nuclear ship bans indicates that they have often been revoked or softened. But it is doubtful whether the trilateral relationship has been preserved merely by the Treaty being kept intact. The spirit itself may have expired.

NUCLEAR VISITING

The ANZUS crisis cannot be divorced from one of the practical manifestations of nuclearism, port visits by nuclear-capable or nuclear-propelled warships. 'Nuclear visiting' is the shorthand term used here to mean the temporary presence of such vessels in territorial waters or of nuclear-capable aircraft on airfields. Of course, virtually anything afloat or airborne is capable of carrying explosive nuclear devices. For our purposes, nuclear-capable warships may be defined as vessels fitted with fire control and launch systems, including aircraft, for delivering nuclear-tipped missiles, depth-charges or bombs. 'Nuclear-armed' refers to platforms carrying nuclear weapons, albeit in an unarmed, safety state. ANZUS being essentially a maritime alliance, this study focusses largely on the issue of warship visits. Unless designated for quick reaction alert duties, or transporting nuclear material from one base to another, allied military aircraft are not normally nuclear armed, and can reach nuclear stockpiles in a matter of hours. Indeed, nuclear-armed aircraft parked on British and American bases in Europe are probably unnecessary in peacetime because a period of tension would precede any crisis in which nuclear weapons were likely to be used. Significantly, the USAF is hardly concerned about NCND, and remained aloof from the controversy with New Zealand, though the Military Airlift Command flies regularly to Christchurch.

Obviously, nuclear propulsion can be considered as a matter distinct from the strategic and disarmament issues associated with nuclear weaponry. In fact, as shown in chapter 6, an important contrast between Australian and New Zealand opinion is that Australians are more uneasy about the nuclear-fuel cycle than about nuclear deterrence. Australia's uranium exports give the country a particular interest in, and international responsibility for, civil uses of nuclear material. In New Zealand the balance tilts more towards concern about the nuclear arms race and the intrusion of superpower militarism in the South-West Pacific.

But the overlap between the two sets of issues is sufficiently large to warrant consideration of reactors as well as weapons. First, about 70 per cent of the USN's major combatants in the Pacific are nuclear propelled. From what is known of nuclear weapon deployments at sea, it is a safe bet that any vessel powered by reactors also carries nuclear weapons. For this reason an attempt by Lange to distinguish between them for banning purposes was difficult to sustain. Second, reactors were excluded from several countries for liability reasons in the 1960s and 1970s and this affected military co-operation. When the suspension of reactor visits was lifted in New Zealand, in 1976, it gave an impetus to debate about alliance requirements and visits by nuclear-capable vessels. Third, by the 1980s interest in reactor safety had broadened to embrace environmental risks associated with nuclear weapons. In this way environmentalism had an impact on discussion of defence co-operation and nuclear strategy. Thus, it would be artificial to exclude consideration of nuclear-powered vessels.

The term 'visiting' excludes continuous passage and overflights, but includes diplomatic or ceremonial visits, and operational visits for goodwill, crew rest, exercises, replenishment or repairs. The temporary nature is the subject of some controversy. Most visiting lasts for less than a week, requires diplomatic clearance and is subject to rules laid down by the host as to number of vessels and duration of visits. But the concept of visiting is stretched when airfields or shore-based facilities offer permanent communication and logistic functions for visitors, some of which return frequently. Darwin, used by US Air Force (USAF) B-52s, and Cockburn Sound in Western Australia, fall into this grey area. However, even this level of visiting can be distinguished from 'homeporting', the basing of particular units at headquarters to which they return after operations.[6]

Technical advances in propulsion and seagoing replenishment can reduce the frequency of shore servicing needed by individual vessels. But without port visits, sustained operations in distant waters are hardly possible. And without the routine deployment of sea power, deterrent postures may be weakened. Visits are also valuable for showing the flag, influencing perceptions of the military balance, offering assurance and support to friendly countries, declaring an interest in stability and generating prestige. Significantly, however, the secretive and self-sustaining deployment of ballistic missile submarines (SSBNs), the backbone of the West's nuclear deterrent forces, is an exception to the pattern. For security reasons SSBNs do not visit foreign ports. It was perhaps fanciful for New Zealand anti-nuclear activists to argue that the US transfer of SSBNs to Bangor (Washington) and the deployment of Trident in the Pacific and Indian Oceans were reasons why the US wanted port visits.[7]

The Reagan Administration certainly re-emphasized nuclear deterrence at sea and aimed to increase naval strength from 479 ships, when Carter left office, to some 600. Ironically, Lehman argued that brittle relations with allies justified the increased sea-based deterrent because it involved less reliance on foreign political favours than forward territorial defence. Spreading nuclear capability much more widely throughout the fleet formed an integral part of the naval expansion programme. Long-range sea-launched cruise missiles (SLCMs), first deployed in the Pacific in June 1984, hold pride of place in the arsenal. Commodore Roger Bacon, Director of the USN's Strategic and Theater Nuclear Warfare Division, asserted that the Tomahawk missile would enable the US to expand its range of escalation control options without resort to central strategic systems; though independent analysts, such as Desmond Ball, vigorously contest this, and also point out that SLCMs are beyond arms control and that their warhead status presents a problem of verification.[8]

By the middle of the 1990s, the plan is to have 758 of the land-attack version (TLAM/N), with 200 kt nuclear warheads and a range of 1,500 nm, deployed on 190 submarines and ships. The USN's attack submarines will all be fitted with nuclear TLAM/N or SUBROC anti-submarine rockets. All the aircraft carriers are capable of carrying nuclear bombs and depth-charges. Of the other surface combatants, only the Oliver Hazard Perry (FFG-7) class of frigates is not nuclear capable. The rest are, or will be, fitted with TLAM/N, Terrier surface-to-air-missiles, or ASROC anti-submarine rockets, all of which have nuclear variants (see appendix 2). The USN was reliably estimated to have 3,700 nuclear warheads available in 1987, in addition to SSBN missiles.[9]

The United States is the power most often affected by queries about nuclear visits to allies and non-aligned states. As discussed in chapter 4 a formula of 'constructive ambiguity' based on NCND has been designed, officially to withhold information from adversaries. But it can be useful to secure access to friendly and allied ports in states where anti-nuclear sentiment is strong. Perhaps the best-known compromise is in the exchange of notes under the 1960 security treaty between Japan and the United States. Accordingly, the US is not supposed to deploy 'major changes' in equipment into Japan. However, revelations that warships do carry nuclear weapons into Japanese ports have encouraged the view that the US and Japan have devised 'a convention of duplicity' for keeping the domestic populace in the dark whilst protecting military collaboration.

Other allies have declaratory policies against nuclear armaments but

6

do not challenge nuclear-capable visitors. The declared assumption by governments that US vessels in particular conform to the rules seems unconvincing given the degree of nuclear and conventional mixing in the US fleet. Indeed if the USN did abide by the local non-nuclear strictures it would confirm to an adversary that the vessels are not nuclear armed. Soviet intelligence gatherers probably take a more cynical view. Yet when states announce a more positive ban, such as India's requirement in 1971 for a specification that vessels are not carrying nuclear weapons, then visits cease in order to protect NCND, so significant is it considered to be as a universal doctrine.

The Royal Navy (RN) abides by NCND and has experienced problems, notably over the dry-docking of the carrier HMS *Invincible* in Sydney in 1983 and visits to Denmark and Malta in 1988. There is no official information on the UK's nuclear inventory. Speculators claim that in addition to the four Polaris submarines, the three RN carriers can transport nuclear depth-charges and free-fall bombs for use by Sea Harrier fighter-bombers and Sea King helicopters. It is thought that the twelve type-42 destroyers are not likely to have nuclear arms in peacetime but can carry Lynx helicopters to deliver nuclear depth-charges in wartime. The eight type-22 frigates are said to be capable of peacetime carriage of nuclear depth-charges. Four auxiliaries are also perhaps capable of unloading from combat vessels. The RN's nuclear inventory had been guessed at about 50 until conjecture by William Arkin and others, published in 1988, suggested that as many as 198 tactical nuclear warheads may be available for surface ships.[10]

Neither France nor China appear to have been affected as visitors, though they have cavilled at being visited. China appeared to support New Zealand's ban and cancelled a projected visit by three USN destroyers to Shanghai in May 1985. Subsequently China agreed to a formula which allowed British vessels to visit.

The Soviet Navy puts a high premium on access to foreign ports, and it is convenient to deal with Soviet visiting at this point by way of comparison with American problems. Whereas overseas port calls enable the Western powers to maximize economy of force, they are valuable to the Soviet Union as a means of alleviating the inflexibility of dispersal. With the naval expansion of the 1960s and an emphasis on building up the Far East bastions, the quest for shore facilities en route between east and west became more pressing. Showing the flag was also part of Admiral Gorshkov's strategy to cultivate sympathy for the Soviet Union. Occasionally Soviet vessels have visited for mine clearing, for example in the southern approaches to the Suez Canal in 1974. Other visits occur in association with manoeuvres such as the first global exercise, *Okean*, in 1970. Detailed centralized control over visit protocol suggests that, unlike those made by the USN, visits are not for rest and recreation, but are vital ingredients of sea power in countering the West.[11]

Soviet vessels made few visits outside Eastern Europe prior to Stalin's death, and between 1953 and 1966 only 37 port visits occurred, mainly to Western Europe and North America. In the next decade the number quadrupled, with a significant shift to the Mediterranean. Egypt, Tunisia and Syria were among those which granted facilities. The period 1967–76 showed an increase in visits to developing countries of the Indian Ocean (see appendix 3), but no diplomatic port visits in South-East Asia and only six in the Pacific.[12] Nevertheless, the extension to the Indian Ocean changed the strategic environment for Australia, prompting the Canberra Government into building up the Cockburn Sound naval base. Soviet opportunities in the Pacific increased significantly only in 1979 after the Soviet Navy gained access to Vietnam for operational purposes. Twenty or more vessels a day are believed to operate from Cam Ranh Bay. Although in theory the Soviet Navy could be ejected, this seems unlikely while Vietnam needs Soviet economic and military support. But in the South Pacific visits are rare, and even the Soviet fishing fleet has often been denied servicing facilities.

As Donald Daniel shows, a large number of Soviet naval platforms, many of small capacity, can deliver tactical nuclear weapons and distribution is widespread. Excluding mines and air-launched missiles, the Soviet Navy deploys about 2,000 weapons with ranges of between 20 and 450 nm. Up to 50 per cent of the cruise missiles spread around submarines and surface ships might have both nuclear and conventional warheads.[13]

Yet, there is no known instance of a Soviet vessel being refused port access on account of its armament or propulsion. Developing states have tended to offer ports as a reward for Soviet help in an hour of need and as a result of mutual political interests between host and visitor. For example, Vietnam made access available after being attacked by China. However, the Soviet Union has not been able to rely on third world countries and has sustained losses in Albania, Egypt and Somalia. Once challenged, Moscow avoids undue aggravation, and when the situation escalates 'to the seemingly low threshold of Soviet tolerance, Moscow is willing to cut its losses'.[14]

It should be noted that for all major naval powers the maritime environment may become increasingly restrictive, as reflected in the UN Convention on the Law of the Sea (UNCLOS). Notwithstanding the view of some diplomats that UNCLOS permitted military exercises and weapon testing in foreign exclusive economic zones (EEZs), rights applicable to the high seas cannot be presumed to apply to EEZs. Leading academic authorities anticipate psychological obstacles to the activities of foreign warships in economic zones and territorial waters.[15] Proposals for peace zones in the Indian Ocean and South-East Asia, and the creation of the South Pacific and New Zealand nuclear-free zones, lend further weight to the enclosure thesis. On the other hand, it is argued that there is not much change in the flexibility of ships as peacetime instruments of foreign policy, though decisions about their use outside areas of vital and sovereign interest are likely to be increasingly sensitive and difficult.[16] The determining factors are changes in the distribution of power and divergent security perceptions of the kind which have produced stress even between allies as sympathetic as the United States, Australia and New Zealand.

Indeed, the ANZUS crisis and the issue of nuclear visiting exemplify four broad themes in international relations which recur throughout this study.

ALLIANCE MANAGEMENT

Most obviously, the crisis highlighted problems in the management of the Western Alliance. To encapsulate their view of alliance relations during the dispute, strategic fundamentalists in Washington commonly employ two metaphors. First, the Western Alliance represents a 'seamless web' of nuclear deterrence against the Soviet Union. According to the US official academic, Dora Alves, ANZUS is the Pacific counterpart of NATO in the shield of deterrence.[17] In this study, analysis of the ANZUS relationship will suggest that such a characterization is questionable. US management of the crisis was all the more problematic, relative to disputes in NATO, because of disproportionate stakes in the relationship and a clear-cut US hegemony. Second, New Zealand's anti-nuclearism was known as 'Kiwi disease'. The analogies had an internal logic. If the alliance were seamless, then clearly no discontinuities or particularisms could prevent the spread of pathogens. Rephrased for metaphorical consistency, a fly damaging the outskirts of the spider's web would inspire other flies to struggle and unravel the entire structure.

Yet if the unravelling of a web occurs, it is also logical to examine the activities of the spider at the centre. It is commonly acknowledged that Reaganism generated objectivization of the threat among the populations of allied countries. The notion of New Zealand as an exemplary

9

case underestimates the extent to which national idiosyncrasies inhibit élites from importing radical foreign models, especially from small and remote states. Further, the fundamentalist conception tends to equate military–technical co-operation, which may indeed encourage a seamless view, with political-security interests. In the ANZUS crisis the effect was to define 'ally' according to collaboration in nuclear deployments and acceptance that visiting vessels might be carrying nuclear weapons. But democratic alliances co-opt national differences for common security goals, and disagreement about the means is tolerated to a degree, as any comparison between British, French and Norwegian policy suggests. And, as Ian Clark remarks, the Western Alliance is endowed with flexibility to grow in some directions (incorporating a militarized Japan for example), whilst shrinking in others.[18]

To promote the notion of a seamless web is perhaps a useful device to encourage greater alliance cohesion. To proceed in international relations as if it exists, seems not merely simplistic but a challenge to democratic pluralism. US officials never denied that New Zealand had a sovereign right to dissent, but argued that on nuclear matters it either toed the line or forfeited any claims under ANZUS. Shared democratic goals did not suffice to contain the disagreement, and reprisals stood in marked contrast to America's economic deals with other 'troublesome' allies, such as Greece, and the 'arms for hostages' bargaining with Iran.

Evidence suggests that the seamless web notion formed part of a wider belief. Early in 1985 the Republican-dominated Senate Foreign Relations Committee provided a platform from which officials appealed for a consensus on foreign policy. Former Secretary of State, Cyrus Vance, queried whether the unanimity demanded by Reaganites was either possible or democratically desirable; it would be tantamount to giving the Administration a blank cheque.[19] In reality, Reagan's licence enabled subordinates to operate with scant regard for democratic process anyway. Also, the Administration invoked dreams of organic alliance behaviour whilst managing foreign policy in a style which strained alliance support. James Schlesinger, Secretary of Defense under President Nixon, advised the Senators that in a changing world the US should desist from insisting on alliance conformity. But at the very moment that the New Zealand Cabinet was meeting to discuss the USS *Buchanan*, Weinberger was testifying that the Administration had 'strengthened its ties with our friends and our allies around the world in pursuing a strategy of global deterrence – the same strategy pursued by previous administrations running all the way back to World War II'.[20] The next chapter examines the extent to which ANZUS fitted into this programme and indicates that Weinberger not only discounted the problems of alliance management but played fast and loose with the history of containment.

GLOBALISM AND REGIONALISM

A second theme relates to fragmentation in the international system, and the contrast between the global perspectives of US policy-makers and the regional concerns of the Anzacs. The dislocation of ANZUS owed much to the attenuation of mutual interests over a long period and to a growth in regional consciousness. Writing in 1986, the French geographer, Joël Bonnemaison, found that Australia and New Zealand lie at the furthest frontiers of the capitalist 'West' but hold ambivalent attitudes towards the Anglo-Celtic cultures from which they spring. Australia has a multi-cultural outlook and is an increasingly significant regional power, though critics argue that it displays more subservience to the US and less regional consciousness than New Zealand. At the turn of the century New Zealand refused to be absorbed into the Australian Commonwealth and asserted its separateness from Australia. Increasingly, the Maori population and Island immigrants have given New Zealand a distinctive connection to Pacific concerns. Bonnemaison noted that the North Island is in effect a Polynesian frontier, 'un engagement vers . . . le grand silence du Pacifique'.[21] Many Anzacs prefer to stand aloof from northern hemisphere tensions, and regional states are persuaded that the global rivalry of the superpowers has a negative impact on their own security preoccupations.

Regional implications of the ANZUS crisis are discussed in chapter 8. We should note, however, that successive Anzac governments have perceived no direct and immediate threats to their defence areas. There is little temptation for any state to invade or otherwise subdue them, and only the United States and Soviet Union have the capability. New Zealand is surrounded by the world's largest moat and is admirably suited to the posture of a pre-emptive cringe. Australians are more inclined to envisage threats of maritime interdiction and to place importance on the central strategic balance. Nevertheless, Australian parliamentary inquiries have identified poor relations between the superpowers as the most serious threat to Australia's well-being and the Hawke Government has regarded nuclear arms racing and nuclear war-fighting strategies as trends to be opposed or disengaged from.[22] Both countries have given a higher priority to regional and

11

national defence than to contingency planning for conflicts involving the United States.

Three years before Reagan came to power, Stanley Hoffman deplored an international system in which every local crisis threatened to drag in the superpowers. He recommended that US foreign policy should demote the contest with communism as the yardstick for world order, and should respect friendly states which saw limited value in coupling to the east–west balance.[23] But to American strategic fundamentalists, Western security depended upon the holistic approach. Globalism appealed particularly to the naval subculture in the Pentagon, for which, also, the Pacific was a focus for naval supremacy doctrines. Admiral Worth Bagley claimed that by the late 1970s regionalism had been rendered irrelevant and that nuclear technology had established global continuities of defence lines.[24] Although this may be true of nuclear targeting, officials in the 1980s could sustain an optimistic globalism only by discounting centrifugal shifts in the international system, and by ignoring those limits to American power detected by academics such as Paul Kennedy in *The Rise and Fall of the Great Powers* (1988).

There was no shortage of comment about change in the Pacific. The analyst, Ross Terrill, advised a congressional committee in 1981 that the greater instability of Asia, compared with Europe, lay in demographic factors and economic, racial and cultural fragmentation rather than military force which Europe had in greater abundance. There were fewer US bases than in the 1960s and widespread doubts about the validity of existing security arrangements in the Philippines, Australia and New Zealand. Furthermore, multipolarity had diminished traditional ties as keys to security. Thus, noted Terrill, Australian and New Zealand security resided less in ANZUS than in cordial relations between China, Japan and the United States.[25] This is not to say that the whole Pacific Basin functions as a regional subsystem. Subsystems have been defined as 'clusters of actors, issues and actions' which have distinctive geographical, economic and political proximities.[26] The strategically significant northerly rim, from Alaska to South-East Asia, embraces countries which have little in common. The superpowers have metropolitan orientations elsewhere, and the security problems are diverse, ranging from insurgency in the Philippines to the Sino-Vietnam territorial disputes. US and Soviet spheres of influence are less clearly demarcated than in Europe, and there is no regional arms control forum and no confidence-building régime comparable to the 1986 Stockholm Agreement.

Nevertheless, the South-West Pacific conforms in large part to the

12

requirements of a subsystem. It comprises Australia, New Zealand and an area bounded in the north by Papua New Guinea and the Tokelaus and in the west by the Cook Islands. Although, as Richard Herr argues, the institutions of regional co-operation are skeletal, Australia and New Zealand have been instrumental in sponsoring development and security, and the majority of the micro-states rely on the Anzacs for links to the rest of the international system.[27] Except for the US military facilities in Australia and potential fall back routes to the Indian Ocean, the area lacks military significance. It can hardly be spoken of as an internationally important strategic region. To argue that ANZUS, together with the Japanese security treaty, is the bedrock of US access to the Asian-Pacific land mass seems excessive and makes unwise presumptions about the willingness of the Anzacs to get involved on mainland Asia.[28]

NUCLEARISM AND ANTI-NUCLEARISM

A third leitmotif is the challenge to extended nuclear deterrence as a model of international security. Visits by nuclear-capable ships have been New Zealand's most tangible nuclear connection. But New Zealanders share the South Pacific consciousness which is closely identified with general anti-nuclearism. Commentators point out that the Pacific has borne the brunt of the nuclear age. Australia, Bikini, Enewetok, Johnston, Christmas Island and Moruroa* have all been used for tests, often with quite inadequate safeguards. Between 1946 and 1982 more than 150 nuclear devices were exploded in the Pacific area, and hundreds of drums of radioactive waste dumped on the ocean floor. In addition, numerous missile tests have occurred and US military installations alone house some 3,000 nuclear weapons.[29] Throughout the region support has been gathering since the 1970s for a Nuclear-Free and Independent Pacific (NFIP), a movement directed largely against the United States and France. Australia and New Zealand have made opposition to French colonialism and nuclear tests respectable, and taken a lead in creating the South Pacific Nuclear-Free Zone (SPNFZ).

New Zealand's defection from collaboration in nuclear deterrence could hardly be described as a body-blow to US strategic plans. Yet the Reagan Administration elevated the significance of nuclearism both operationally, by improving capability and elaborating war-fighting strategies, and politically by treating extended nuclear deterrence as

---

* The French military authorities called the atoll 'Mururoa', but the correct spelling, based on Mangarevan dialect, is 'Moruroa'.

the decisive element in alliance relations. In view of the difficulty in making nuclear weapons seem relevant to the South-West Pacific, the Administration relied on the argument that indivisible nuclear deterrence serves as a political construct and not merely as a technical fix. Admiral James Lyons, CINCPAC in 1986, argued that New Zealand had left a gap in deterrence. 'We never asked New Zealand to join our strategic nuclear policy,' he said, 'just to share the burdens.'[30] But this presumed that the Soviet Union would sail through the gap, a notion which hardly accorded with threat perceptions in the Anzac states.

Critics also condemned New Zealand for ignoring the 'realities' of nuclear deterrence in the international system, and for seeking to redefine ANZUS as a conventional alliance while benefiting from the peace established by the threat of mutual assured destruction.[31] But these critiques harboured their own assumptions about the validity of extended nuclear deterrence, the 'reality' of the seamless web, the regulatory function of the East–West polarity and the stabilizing effects of US strategic policy. Specifically, ANZUS may not be an obvious framework for meeting low-level security problems, and the prospect of US decision-makers putting Washington at risk for Wellington never struck the present writer as a likely contingency. More generally, there may be geographical and functional limits to the relevance of the balance of terror. Obviously, what McGeorge Bundy referred to as 'existential deterrence', or fear of what nuclear systems could do if activated, has universal significance. But declared strategies for organizing political relations, although they can impose a degree of structure and order on world affairs, can also be either disruptive or only marginally important. A weakness of extended deterrence in an era of superpower nuclear parity is that it causes disquiet among allies by failing to reassure or by seeming dangerous. Indeed Jean Chesneaux, Emeritus Professor of the Sorbonne and a critic of French nuclear testing in the Pacific, contends that world peace would be better served by 'region-centred political options'.[32]

Other scholars argue that the world is no less secure in the 1980s than in the 1950s or 1960s, and that fear of a nuclear war is a neurosis of élites. Popular majorities in allied countries have not felt strongly about nuclear weapons except when confronted with policies for their use.[33] However, if anti-nuclearism is a middle-class angst, then reactions to it by Reagan officials seem to have been equally neurotic. The nuclear paradigm effectively trapped strategic fundamentalists into making deployment of a weapon system the arbiter of an alliance relationship. The means of deterring the Soviet Union took precedence over common political goals.

14

On the other hand one cannot be certain that the New Zealand Labour Cabinet knew where its ban on nuclear visiting might lead. Did broadcasting it as a 'practical measure of nuclear disengagement' serve to rationalize a domestic requirement to halt disruptive naval visits? Evidence suggests that incrementalism rather than radicalism ruled the Labour leadership but that it genuinely tried to accommodate public security concerns. The policy gave rise to much misunderstanding. Critics too readily assumed that the New Zealand Government had 'almost wilfully' defected to the Soviet Union by succumbing to pacifism 'fostered largely by Moscow for its own subversive purposes'.[34] The conspiracy theory, however, ignored the historical and democratic forces which are discussed in chapter 6.

The anti-nuclearism was as much chauvinistic as ideological in spirit and reflected a 'small fry nationalism'. In his foreign affairs report of March 1986, Lange commented: 'Never before has this country been so much in the news around the world.' The controversies of 1985, which included the sinking of the *Rainbow Warrior* by French secret service agents, could only heighten the sense of nationhood.

SMALL POWERS IN THE INTERNATIONAL SYSTEM

A fourth theme, relevant to international relations theory, is New Zealand's conformity to a modified rational behaviour model of foreign policy. The country's nationalists had long argued that the superpowers were dangerously obsessed with delusions of competitive nuclear grandeur. Medium and small states offered the most hope for peace, 'if only they would be active, vocal and troublesome'.[35] Small states have low levels of overall participation in the international system. But they also adopt moral and normative positions and, in exhibiting a narrow range of concerns, persist with roles which mark them out. Having achieved renown for its anti-nuclearism, New Zealand is unlikely to yield ground.[36] Moreover, Lange discounted small power modesty when he maintained that New Zealand was acting in the interests of global welfare against an irrational drive by the superpowers for nuclear superiority. New Zealand's peripheral connection to nuclear strategy meant that Wellington was the place to start rolling back the tide of nuclearism, though to limit offence to the United States, Lange denied that New Zealand would inspire others.[37]

In fact the rational behaviour model has been qualified by the idea that small states ignore their limitations and undertake high-risk behaviour to assert independence and defy powerful states. Graham Allison's theory of bureaucratic determinism seems of limited rele-

15

vance to small states in view of such tendencies to incautious behaviour. According to Richard Falk, Professor of International Law and Practice at Princeton, powerful permanent bureaucracies resist any contrary political mandate of society' by diluting or disregarding what elected leaders seek if it does not suit an established consensus. This is especially true in nuclear matters, the heightened secrecy of which, in Falk's view, reduces citizens to impotence and is fundamentally incompatible with all forms of constitutionalism.[38] In New Zealand, however, security policy involves few experts or vested interests. Indeed, uncertainty about traditional security assumptions had prompted the Muldoon Government of 1981–4 to call for a public security debate and, following Labour's ban on nuclear visiting, ministers made a virtue out of democratic involvement in defence and security deliberations. Contrasted with more populous countries where policy-making remains largely protected from inconvenient aspects of democracy, security policy in New Zealand became democratized as well as politicized. In such circumstances, parties and pressure groups seem able to push small states into heroics.

SUMMARY

This study, then, links internal and external aspects of state behaviour and throws light on the stress in international relations between parochial perspectives and the conception of a seamless nuclear web. The earlier demise of US alliances, such as SEATO and the security treaty with Taiwan, had hardly been contested. But now, for the first time, an alliance was seriously disrupted as a consequence of a member disengaging from nuclear collaboration. In the process, New Zealand's revolt drew attention to the 'constructive ambiguity' which characterizes warship visits to other non-nuclear countries.

In preference to an artificial two-fold division of this study, the alliance crisis and nuclear visiting are interleaved where appropriate. Generally, the discussion progresses from historical developments in ANZUS to the breakdown in alliance relations and its consequences. The second chapter examines the ANZUS Treaty and the nature of the relationship up to the 1983 review. Defence integration and nuclear links in the alliance are treated separately in chapter 3. Chapter 4 deals with principles of nuclear visiting, including NCND, and examines the suspension of nuclear-powered visits enforced by New Zealand and Australia in the 1960s and 1970s. US policy-makers in 1984 seem to have been unaware that their predecessors in office had been through similar turmoil a decade before. The management of nuclear visiting in the context of environmental objections are discussed in chapter 5. Anzac domestic attitudes and security policies are analysed in chapter 6. The course of the diplomatic crisis, the failure of negotiations and the unravelling of tripartite security are covered in chapter 7. Discussion then turns, in chapter 8, to the ramifications of the crisis with emphasis on the future of ANZUS and security in the South Pacific. The concluding chapter considers the implications for the Western Alliance as a whole and the future of the neither-confirm-nor-deny policy.

The analysis proceeds from the premise enunciated by Steve Smith that we are 'in the business of dealing with competing theories and explanations'.[39] This work reflects preferences for certain explanatory theories, but recognizes that the international system does not conform to a ruthlessly logical pattern. However disapproving one might be of particular policies, one ought to acknowledge the role in international relations of ambiguity, compromise, contradiction and, for the sake of democracy, popular sentiments. Security itself is a matter of perception and hardly susceptible to precise objective measurement; it cannot therefore be reduced to zero-sum game. Indeed a broader conception of security can provide an intellectual framework distinct from traditional idealist or realist perceptions. As Barry Buzan emphasizes, the security paradigm is a quest for policies 'that can satisfy the legitimate concerns of states without at the same time amplifying the dynamics of insecurity among them'.[40] The point is equally valid for states within alliances, and we turn now to the historical dynamics and concerns of the ANZUS relationship.

2 THE ANZUS TREATY AND STRATEGIC DEVELOPMENTS

Although security relationships are not defined merely by written commitments, the ANZUS Treaty is the formal basis of the alliance. The signatories referred to its terms in justifying their varying policies. Indeed, there is general agreement among scholars that the Treaty was a 'bare and ambiguous framework' which allowed flexibility in the safeguarding of national security claims and, of course, in the interpretation of obligations.

The first part of this chapter shows that, in addition to a common commitment to anti-communism, the parties brought distinctive perspectives to the 1951 negotiations, perspectives which, duly modified over time, were to influence their responses during the later crisis. The Treaty was a political statement rather than a legal document. Accordingly, the second part of the chapter examines the extent to which, by 1984, security concerns had shifted in scope and emphasis away from the original framework of consensus reflected in the Treaty, to the point where an apparently minor crisis could damage it irreparably.

But even as an instrument of publicly visible foreign policy, the trilateral relationship rarely needed to withstand major pressures until the Vietnam War. The parties had little call to develop management skills and appear to have banked on cohesion stemming from shared Western values, a common language, and overwhelming public disinterest in defence. Policy-making élites seem to have been ill-prepared to cope with a gradual divergence in perceptions of the strategic role of the alliance. Commentators on the ANZUS dispute have been attentive to the nuclear issue and the policies of the Lange and Reagan Governments. But there is a case for arguing that the alliance had been atrophying by stealth for a decade before its dislocation after 1984.

Historically, the signatories had different security preoccupations which the Treaty was designed to encompass. Three facets are worthy of note. First, the Truman–Acheson conception of security arrangements in the Pacific was primarily concerned about the Asian offshore chain of islands. The early cold warriors also assigned to ANZUS a more detached and expedient role in containment than the critical construction for global deterrence subsequently placed on it by the Reagan Administration. Second, after the experience of Japanese bombing and submarine incursions, Australian leaders considered that their country was exposed to the risk of invasion. They were more persistent supplicants for security assistance than the New Zealanders. Australia nagged the United States and New Zealand into a formal security guarantee. Third, in so far as the Anzacs shared a security perception, it embraced conflicting hopes. They elicited help to deny the South-West Pacific to hostile forces and secure it as an Anglo-Anzac lake. But they were not completely convinced that the US would work in their interests.

STRATEGIC DENIAL

During the 1980s Australian and New Zealand policy-makers returned to the theme of strategic denial which had run intermittently through Anzac security history since before the First World War. Australia and New Zealand had a propensity to claim proprietary rights in the South-West Pacific in a kind of unwritten 'Tasman Doctrine'. In accord with it, the Hawke and Lange Governments exerted influence to prevent superpower rivalry infecting the region, though the former inclined more to the Reaganite view that regional strategic denial was part of a global web of Western deterrence. New Zealand politicians grew more concerned about the potential effects of globalism on regional tranquillity, particularly the escalation of nuclear arms racing at sea and the attendant prospect of increased demand on regional states for military support facilities. New Zealand's version of the 'Tasman Doctrine' in the 1980s would take the form of disengaging from nuclear deterrence.

From the late nineteenth century to the Second World War, Australia and New Zealand had often cavilled at the neglect by Britain of Imperial (or rather their own) claims in the region.[1] But they also sought security from the tyranny of isolation. To supplement the British presence they welcomed transient manifestation of American power, including a visit by the great American Fleet in 1908. However, protection was one thing, trespassing another. The Dominions expressed considerable apprehension in the late 1930s about US claims to islands for use as commercial air bases in the Central and South Pacific, some of which were under New Zealand sovereignty.[2]

Uncertainty about US motives helped draw Australian and New Zealand policy-makers into closer consultation. Until 1938 they had communicated with each other about defence and foreign affairs in London. Not until 1943 did they exchange permanent diplomatic representation in Canberra and Wellington. By then, of course, the Dominions had become informally allied with the United States.

Yet ambivalence towards the United States persisted into the Second World War. When Pacific Commands were formed Australia and New Zealand discovered, first, that their defence had not been provided for, and then in 1942, that their defence areas had been separated. In the Pacific War Council their representatives listened to what Britain and the US wanted to tell them and had virtually no influence, even on matters of direct concern. Vainly they sought a voice in post-war plans for Japan, and protested vigorously at not being consulted when Pacific security matters were discussed at the Cairo Conference in 1943. More alarm bells rang when the United States contemplated simply snapping up those islands on which it had built bases.[3] The Anzacs responded with the Canberra Agreement of 21 January 1944.

Australia had taken initiatives for a Pacific non-aggression pact in the 1930s and again took the lead in post-war planning. New Zealand tended to limp along behind. Dr H. V. Evatt, the acerbic Australian Minister for External Affairs, forged the Canberra Agreement as a statement of regional security principles. In a joint expression of 'Tasman Doctrine' the two countries asserted their common regional interests, proposed the maximum degree of unity in promoting them abroad, and warned other states off their patch. They would meet threats together and share in policing the area bounded by an arc of islands north and north-east of Australia to Western Samoa and the Cook Islands. They demanded a voice in post-war territorial settlements, and called for a Pacific conference. As a warning to the Americans, they denied that the use of wartime bases could justify claims to territorial sovereignty.[4]

Officials in Washington and London dismissed all this as pretentious posing. Cordell Hull, the US Secretary of State, killed any notion of an early Pacific conference and likened Evatt's diplomacy to that of Stalin. To forestall any further expressions of hubris, Admiral King, US Chief of Naval Operations, refused to allow the Anzacs to participate in further operations against Central Pacific islands. Neither Dominion participated in decisions about the surrender of Japan. As an official historian has remarked: 'Gratitude to the United States for its naval shield had not ended New Zealand's long held suspicions of American ambitions in the Pacific, and these were re-awakened.'[5]

For practical purposes the Canberra Agreement lapsed. When the Anzacs subsequently joined military operations abroad they did so as subordinates to Britain or the United States. But the Agreement signified a stab at independent action, was the first official indication that their priority lay in the Pacific rather than Europe, and reinforced the special relationship between them. In the 1980s all shades of opinion in New Zealand recognized that rebuilding a defence policy consensus hinged on stronger trans-Tasman co-operation.

But strategic denial did not signify isolationism. On the contrary, both post-war governments had strong internationalist leanings. As originally conceived by Evatt, regional security would supplement a global system. The two countries sought to promote policy not only through the Commonwealth, but also in combination with other small powers in the United Nations. Failing adequate international peace-making machinery, however, regional security required American collaboration. Percy Spender, Evatt's successor, argued with some understatement, 'the linking of England with Australia through the Indian Ocean is one of the most awkward of Imperial strategic problems.'[6] Yet it was difficult to elicit American interest in an area so strategically marginal. Australia and New Zealand would have to wait until the South Pacific fitted into a Washington framework of interests.

Evatt tried ensnaring US leaders into an insurance policy against some future menace from Japan, in view of American determination to strengthen Japan as a base and an ally. Spender anticipated that after the Vandenberg Resolution of 1948 and the negotiations for the defence of Western Europe, the North Atlantic Treaty might serve as a prototype for the Pacific. But these tactics failed. The US Secretary of State, Dean Acheson, declared in May 1949 that the North Atlantic Treaty 'was largely the product of a special set of circumstances . . . the logical culmination of a long series of developments'.[7]

The Truman Administration was only prepared to contemplate a security arrangement after Mao Zedong's victory in China and the attack on South Korea in 1950. By the end of 1950, Anzac support for American policies towards Korea and China paid off. Congress and the State Department grew more favourable to co-operation with the Anzacs. Cold war sentiments had also spread to Canberra and Wellington. New Zealand's Labour Prime Minister, Peter Fraser, had introduced peacetime national service and adopted a McCarthyite approach to left-wing dissent. His Minister in the United States, Carl Berendsen, became a convert to the new demonology. In an inflammatory dispatch of March 1950 Berendsen argued that another world catastrophe was on the horizon for which the Soviet Union was entirely responsible. Moscow had established full control over Eastern Europe and 'much of Asia'. It had fifth columnists in every country. New Zealand, he thought, would probably have to share in the defence of Japan and the Philippines as part of a global front against the spreading pestilence.[8]

But the ANZUS Treaty was hardly the child of necessity. Appraising the Pacific power balance, the New Zealand Chiefs of Staff concluded that on military grounds 'there are at present no reasons for an approach by New Zealand to the United States for the conclusion of a Pacific Pact'. Further, the disadvantages of becoming involved in a Pacific-wide arrangement would outweigh the advantage of any US guarantee to New Zealand.[9] Officials in Wellington were no more enthusiastic about treaty commitments north of the equator than officials in Washington were about commitments to the south. Dean Acheson and John Foster Dulles were plotting an offshore defence arc from the Aleutians and Japan to the Philippines, rather than a more extended perimeter.

The Australians had a keen awareness of their security needs under the false impression that they had been close to invasion by Japan. As Glen St J. Barclay points out, Spender, Minister for External Affairs in the Menzies Government, was obsessed with securing a binding US commitment linked to the Atlantic Treaty, even if it had to include Japan and the Philippines. He also wanted access to US strategic and political thinking, as well as compensation for serving NATO interests by providing forces to the Middle East. New Zealand would have settled for an American declaration of intent to assist in the short term (up to 1955) against the Soviet Union and its communist satellites, and in the longer term against 'Asian expansionism, whether communist or ultra nationalist'.[10]

THE TERMS

Signed on 1 September 1951, shortly before the Japanese Peace Treaty, the ANZUS Pact probably helped to reconcile public opinion to the lenient peace with Japan. But ANZUS was not a *quid pro quo* for Anzac acquiescence in the Peace Treaty. As J. G. Starke has argued, the major powers would have gone ahead with a lenient peace anyway. Even if there had been a restrictive peace, Australia and New Zealand would have agitated for security to ameliorate their isolation, so alarmingly exposed after the fall of Singapore in 1942.[11] Moreover, the United States would have pressed for military facilities in Australia and New Zealand eventually, with or without a Treaty.

In spite of panicky proposals for a comprehensive Pacific Pact in response to the outbreak of war in Korea, the Truman Administration had little inclination to allow the European security arrangement to act as a model. Article II of the ANZUS Treaty is identical with article 3 of the Atlantic Treaty, but this was a Vandenberg Resolution prerequisite for any US involvement in collective security. It required that the signatories 'separately and jointly by means of continuous and effective self-help and mutual aid will maintain and develop their individual and collective capacity to resist armed attack' (see appendix 1).

In 1985 the United States was to accuse New Zealand of breaching article II by refusing access for ships carrying nuclear weapons, thus making it impossible for the United States to fulfil its security obligations. However, the USN visited New Zealand, not for strategic or operational reasons but for goodwill and rest and recreation (R & R). Critics of the American interpretation argued that it was 'capricious and arbitrary . . . tantamount to saying that one party may demand of another any specific form of military co-operation as a condition of its continued participation in the security benefits'.[12] If New Zealand was not in serious breach of the Treaty, then the United States certainly contravened it by unilaterally suspending its security obligations.

Article IV, like article 5 of the North Atlantic Treaty, pledges action to meet the common danger with an additional proviso that action would occur in accordance with each party's constitutional processes. This held out the prospect that the United States would not be able to react in an emergency until Congress had given approval. The Truman administration was determined to avoid controversy with senators over constitutional powers, as had arisen in regard to the North Atlantic Treaty.[13] For a similar reason the phrase 'an armed attack against one or more . . . shall be considered an attack against them all' was diluted to the ANZUS signatories recognizing 'that an armed attack . . . on any of the Parties would be dangerous to its own peace and safety'. Unlike the North Atlantic Treaty there is no mention of the possibility of using armed force in fulfilment of obligations. This omission led critics to make unfavourable comparisons with the earlier treaty. But like apologists for the ANZUS wording, they miss the point that ANZUS was not meant to replicate NATO but to extend Monroe Doctrine to the Pacific. ANZUS was truly the outcome of an 'unusual constellation of circumstances'.[14]

In any event, as scholars have long recognized, a discretionary interpretation would be made for each contingency in the light of other commitments, though all parties would need to consider the political effects of any breach of faith. William Tow has suggested that article IV was devised to ensure that the United States would not be committed if its interests were marginal, and that 'New Zealanders have a healthy consideration for this reality'.[15] Certainly, the United States sought freedom of action to operate in areas of higher priority; the ANZUS Treaty omitted the provision in the North Atlantic Treaty (article 8) prohibiting engagements in conflict with the Treaty. In 1968 a congressional review of US commitments abroad recommended that ANZUS 'should be kept under continuous review to insure that contingencies which might arise under it are adequately provided for under other multilateral defense arrangements'.[16] Obviously, Australians and New Zealanders would not wish to be automatically committed to assist the United States either.

In the 1980s, Australian officials, parliamentarians and academics acknowledged that the threshold for US combat involvement could be quite high and referred to the 'uncertain and conditional' nature of the security guarantee. Contingency analysis by Ross Babbage suggests that a US response would be most probable if Australia sustained a direct isolated attack by the Soviet Union, and least probable in more likely low level threats.[17] However, as a Hawke Government review inferred in 1983, the United States would probably respond militarily if its key facilities located in Australia were in imminent danger, even in the absence of a treaty.

Malcolm Templeton also points out that the US had qualified its commitment without informing its partners. At the 1978 Special Disarmament Session of the UN Assembly the United States undertook not to use nuclear weapons against non-nuclear parties to the Non-Proliferation Treaty unless they were allied to a nuclear state. Thus the nuclear deterrent would not apply if Indonesia attacked Australia, unless supported in its attack by a nuclear power. This negative security guarantee has been characterized as making the ANZUS Treaty nuclear in parts.[18]

Article V is noteworthy for avoiding a definition of the Treaty's geographical scope; it merely refers to 'the Pacific Area'. The Reagan Administration regarded this as an advantage because it allowed the alliance to be relevant in changed international circumstances. As Barclay argues, the Pacific was always what the US wanted it to mean. But strains were bound to appear when the junior partners increasingly pursued their security goals regionally, whereas the Reagan Administration urged them to take on wider responsibilities.[19] Technically, the Treaty area includes the western littoral of Australia and Australian territory in the Indian Ocean but excludes the Indian Ocean as such.

Dulles had deliberately sought geographical imprecision. The Truman Administration was sensitive to the accusation that it had invited aggression by omitting Korea from the declared US defence perimeter. Also, the Americans did not relish guaranteeing the metropolitan areas of Australia and New Zealand without an Anzac commitment to defend US interests more distant than American Samoa.[20] Furthermore, article V covered threats to the signatories' armed forces because it was in Washington's interests to seek assistance for its forces scattered throughout the Pacific, notably in Japan, the Ryukyus and the Philippines.

The imprecision created uncertainty in the 1960s. Although China and communism were regarded as the main threats to Pacific security, Australia was also concerned about Indonesia's claim to Dutch West New Guinea (Irian) and the possibility of an attack on Australian New Guinea. In 1962 Australia received specific assurances from the US Secretary of State, Dean Rusk, that ANZUS covered such an eventuality. However, the United States remained neutral during the Irian crisis, and contrary to Australian wishes continued to provide Indonesia with military aid. Moreover, during Indonesia's attempt to destabilize Malaysia, a congressional delegation to South-East Asia grew alarmed that ANZUS might be activated. Although the 1964 ANZUS Council communiqué affirmed support for Malaysia, there is scholarly debate as to whether Washington was prepared to antagonize Indonesia by publicly extending ANZUS obligations to Anzac forces serving British interests in Borneo.[21] At no time has the US been obliged to choose between Indonesia and ANZUS, but it would no doubt wish to remain on good terms with Indonesia in view of its agreement for using the Straits of Sunda, Lombok and Ombai-Wetar.

Finally, although the ANZUS Treaty was improvised in a few days, it was to remain in force indefinitely, with no provision for review. Again Dulles had in mind the timeless Monroe Doctrine as a model.[22]

In recognizing, too, that ANZUS was partly about spheres of influence, Dulles aroused considerable anger in Britain. Churchill and Eden had angled for a Pacific NATO and regretted Britain's exclusion. Britain would be automatically involved if Australia and New Zealand were attacked. ANZUS, however, excluded Hong Kong and Singapore, and threatened to detract from Anzac contributions to the defence of Malaya and the Middle East. Indeed the Australian and New Zealand governments were sensitive to opposition criticism about Britain's exclusion, but Dulles expressly ruled out a commitment to protect British colonies.[23]

STRATEGIC DEVELOPMENTS

American perspectives emphasized the need to confront Soviet communism on the basis of limited military liability. Although stung by the failure of reliance on long-range, aid-dominated containment in Asia, Acheson and Dulles were careful not to allow the North Atlantic Treaty to become a blueprint. True, the planning paper, NSC 68, postulated that a defeat of free institutions anywhere was a defeat everywhere. Appearance might also suggest that the security treaties with the Philippines, Japan, Korea, Formosa and the South-East Asia Treaty Organisation (the last three modelled on ANZUS), formed a cohesive, interrelated structure. Yet Dulles made *ad hoc* arrangements for specific circumstances in what has been described as a crisis-ridden effort to make deterrence look credible. The treaties were 'anything but the manifestation of an overall strategy'.[24] SEATO, for example, was designed to hold the line in Indo-China with the US obligation confined to threats of communist aggression, so as to ensure that Americans would not be ensnared in local disputes.

ANZUS, as Starke has argued, reached the limits of the possible. The arrangement had more substance than the 1947 Rio Treaty which required the agreement of two thirds of the members before collective measures could be applied. But Dulles refused Spender's plea for machinery to liaise with NATO. The United States wanted to retain management controls. Indeed the most ardent post-war 'Asia Firsters', like MacArthur, were a species of unilateralist who regarded the Far East and Pacific as areas where the US could operate unchallenged and without messy allied consultations.

In fact, although Australia sought political influence in Washington and access to military planning and intelligence, the US Chiefs of Staff simply excluded the allies from decision-making. The annual ANZUS Council meeting would comprise foreign ministers rather than military chiefs. Military representatives would meet to recommend measures for mutual assistance and self-help, but the structure would be minimal. It entailed no deployment of forces abroad, no integrated force structures, no burdensome demands on military co-operation. ANZUS could almost be reduced to ship and aircraft visits; Dulles said there was no question of sending troops.[25]

The attraction for the United States hinged on the probably redundant obligation to defend Australia and New Zealand. As the New

Zealand Prime Minister remarked: 'I feel that Mr Dulles will also appreciate that – since the chances of an attack on New Zealand are remote, while the chances of trouble elsewhere are great – we are offering to others much more than we are asking others to give us.' And as Kim Beazley snr commented during the Australian debate on the Treaty in 1952, a conflict triggering American military support to Australia would be most likely to arise from a major threat to the United States when it might have other priorities.[26] Nevertheless, Australia and New Zealand had an alliance with the world's greatest power to shield them against remote contingencies. In return the Anzacs would continue to fight in Asia.

They would have been involved in South-East Asia anyway through the vestiges of imperialism: 'pulling our weight in the British boat' as New Zealand Prime Minister, Sidney Holland, put it. Their post-war involvement in South-East Asia had begun in 1948–9 with Common-wealth defence planning for Malaya. From 1949 Australians ran a signals intelligence (SIGINT) station in Singapore. Anzac combat forces participated in the Malayan emergency in 1955 and in Borneo against Indonesian aggression in 1965. These non-treaty commitments grew from historic concern with the strategic importance of Singapore in imperial security. Singapore was both a bridgehead and a key domino. According to Prime Minister Holland, it was the last place where the Anzacs could make a stand against communism. In Hol-land's fanciful analysis, 'the troubled area in the world – from Korea, to Japan, Formosa, Indo-China, Indonesia – is a succession of steps in the direction of New Zealand'.[27]

Anxiety about communism in South-East Asia prompted Australia and New Zealand to sign the Manila treaty and join the heterogenous members of SEATO in 1954, though with some diffidence about provoking China.[28] Under SEATO they dispatched forces to South Vietnam. Australia was anxious to get the US involved in South-East Asia, and President Johnson was keen for the rest of the 'free world' to show the flag in Vietnam. Australia sent military instructors shortly after the matter was raised at the 1962 ANZUS Council meeting. It also seems that Australia leaned on a somewhat reluctant New Zealand to enter the war as an ANZUS insurance premium. Public justification for involvement certainly included the insurance factor. It is no exaggeration to say that the relatively modest Anzac forces in Vietnam had greater political relevance for ANZUS than military significance for SEATO.[29]

International developments undermined the conventional wisdom of forward defence. In 1968 Britain announced an accelerated timetable for withdrawal of all its forces from South-East Asia and closure of the Singapore naval base. Washington unexpectedly announced peace talks with Vietnam and in 1969 President Nixon promulgated the Guam Doctrine. This fostered an agonizing reappraisal of Anzac security priorities. In a vaunted military tradition dating back to the Boer War, Vietnam was the only conflict which Australians and New Zealanders had helped to lose. It marked a retreat from forward defence and the belief in monolithic communism. In the atmosphere of disenchantment it seemed that ANZUS might go the same way as SEATO, which abandoned military planning in 1974. New Zealand advocates of non-alignment or qualified alignment, including academic luminaries, were paid the compliment of having their arguments countered by the Government.[30] Henceforth the Anzacs would cultivate interests 'closer to home in the Pacific' and question the efficacy of military force as the primary means of ensuring regional stability.

Apart from *ad hoc* contributions to international peacekeeping operations, the only forces retained overseas would be in Malaysia and Singapore under the Five Power Defence Agreements of 1971. Britain, Australia, New Zealand, Malaysia and Singapore were pledged to consult in the event of an attack on the peninsula. An exchange of notes provided the framework for a joint force, which included an integrated air-defence system, RAAF Mirages based at Butterworth, and a New Zealand infantry battalion in Singapore. But Australian ground forces withdrew by 1974 and the Royal Navy by 1975. The 1978 New Zealand *Defence Review* described retention of the battalion in Singapore as anachronistic, though plans to pull out were ditched following Vietnam's invasion of Kampuchea. Washington policy-makers valued this defence link with South-East Asia as a branch of containment and, according to Robert O'Neill, South-East Asian countries appreciated ANZUS as an indicator of continuing American interest in their security.[31]

After the Guam Doctrine Australia and New Zealand were more equivocal about the meaning of ANZUS. Although they continued to regard the relationship as the ultimate guarantee against external attack, they had to recognize that the United States would steer clear of regional wars. President Reagan's security adviser, William Clark, was to confirm that 'in contingencies not involving the Soviet Union, we hope to rely on friendly regional states to provide military forces'.[32] Australians seriously debated the acquisition of nuclear weapons, though Prime Minister Robert Menzies had ruled it out in 1957 as both too costly and an irresponsible contribution to proliferation. Australia ratified the Non-Proliferation Treaty in 1973, but defence planners did not completely abandon the idea of a nuclear force.[33]

Certainly the Whitlam Government of 1972–5 took a more independent stance, opposing the expansion of Diego Garcia and agitating for greater control over the US naval communications facility at North West Cape. In the same period the New Zealand Labour Government proposed that the ANZUS relationship should be reassessed and its defence aspects diluted. However, Whitlam ultimately backed the United States in discouraging such initiatives as threatening the fabric of military co-operation. With the erosion of assets after Vietnam and the demise of SEATO, the CINCPAC, Admiral Noel Gayler, indicated that his forces were operating at the margins of efficiency. Therefore military co-operation with allies would become more significant.[34]

The aggressively right-wing governments of Malcolm Fraser and Robert Muldoon, which took office in 1975, were more enthusiastic about the American connection. They encouraged increased defence support and voiced strident anti-Sovietism. They invited the US to maintain a forward posture and disapproved of the so-called 'swing strategy' whereby US Pacific forces would be depleted to reinforce Europe.[35] But Fraser and Muldoon did not completely reverse the independence of their predecessors. Vietnam had left lasting impressions and the Anzacs continued to develop defence postures based on a regional perspective. They expanded their role in underpinning regional institutions and increased aid for South Pacific states. Fraser admitted that US and Australian interests were not identical. Brian Talboys, Minister of Foreign Affairs in the Muldoon Government, spoke of a weakening rather than an enhancement of the alliance structure as a result of the Vietnam War: 'So if we have to stand on our own feet, we also have more freedom of action than we used to – more scope for pursuing our own interests for doing our own thing. That I believe is what New Zealanders want.'[36] He also cautioned against exaggerating the Soviet threat and singled out Australia as the most important ally. Both countries expressed hopes that the superpowers would exercise restraint and not extend their rivalry into the Indian Ocean and South Pacific.

By 1976 Australian officials also reached the conclusion that the two powers capable of launching an invasion (the US and USSR) were unlikely to do so. The 1976 defence white paper, *Australian Defence*, indicated that policy would no longer be based on the expectation that forces would be sent abroad to fight as part of some other nation's effort. Australia would therefore maintain a force adequate to deal with low level contingencies and to be capable of rapid expansion if needed. New Zealand followed suit in the *Defence Review* of 1978.

Uncertain about Carter's notion of US 'leadership without hegemony', Fraser and Muldoon noted in March 1977 that the futures of their countries were inextricably linked. Trans-Tasman defence consultations improved and a Defence Policy Group met for the first time in July 1977. The Anzacs agreed that in the event of a deterioration in the overall strategic circumstances affecting them they 'would wish to be prepared to give military support to each other as the situation required'; they would enhance their defence capabilities accordingly. However, they could not really recapture the spirit of the Canberra Agreement or adopt Professor Hedley Bull's suggestion of an Anzac Pact. The Australians did not share the New Zealand Government's view that they formed a single strategic entity. The Fraser Government interpreted ANZUS 'as conferring obligations on all parties to include the Indian Ocean' and Australia had become progressively subservient to nuclear deterrence strategies through bilateral defence agreements.[37]

In any event, by the middle of the 1970s, New Zealand's preoccupations were economic rather than military in character. Britain had joined the European Community at a time when over 80 per cent of cheese, butter, lamb and mutton exports were destined for the British market. Muldoon adopted the slogan 'Our foreign policy is trade', and agreed to allow Soviet fishing in New Zealand's EEZ. Crippled by oil price hikes, recession and protectionism, New Zealand shelved the spending plans foreshadowed in the 1966 *Defence Review* and warned that it could only contribute effectively to collective security if the economy could be sustained by fair access to the US market. Although the 1982 ANZUS Council agreed to work against the slide to protectionism, the United States resisted the temptation to pay much heed. Trade wars continued. As John Henderson argued, the more New Zealand sold to the United States the more likely it was to trigger protectionism.[38] The Anzacs and other regional states also regretted the US decision not to sign the UN Convention on the Law of the Sea which codified EEZs. Such conflict between economic and alliance interests was to re-emerge in 1986, this time straining the loyalty of Australian farmers to the ANZUS relationship.

Towards the end of the 1970s, the allies responded ambivalently to the frissons of superpower confrontation. Long before the Iranian revolution and the Soviet move into Afghanistan, the United States reverted to an assertive maritime role as Carter struggled to counter shrill warnings about the 'present danger' from domestic right-wing extremists. In 1977 talks with the Soviet Union on naval limitation in the Indian Ocean were called off, the USN presence increased, and penetration of the South Pacific by aid agencies and CIA-linked trade unions began. In 1978 the swing strategy and plans to reduce ground forces in Korea were abandoned, and a major ANZUS exercise, *Sandgroper*, was held in the Indian Ocean.[39] Although this reassured the Anzacs it again demonstrated how much regional strategic denial could be affected by US preoccupations.

One might imagine that the allies would find it easier to make common cause in the crisis atmosphere of 1979–80. Indeed Fraser described the invasion of landlocked Afghanistan, 5,000 miles away, as the most serious threat to Australia since the Second World War and sent a task force to the Indian Ocean. Muldoon went to the length of calling senior ministers together to discuss ANZUS, 'the first formal meeting for a long time on foreign policy'.[40]

But the Anzacs had reason to berate Washington officials after learning in the media that the United States had stretched the ANZUS security commitment to coincide with the US Pacific command area as far as Africa. Australian and New Zealand officials complained to a US General Accounting Office review body that they had 'minimal input in the American military decision-making process' and remarked that the Council meetings were usually 'a platform to announce predetermined courses of action'.[41]

Although the allies agreed at the 1980 ANZUS Council meeting to contribute, 'as resources permit', to deterrence of the Soviet Union in the Indian Ocean, the New Zealand Government downplayed the importance of the change. There was no question of rewriting the alliance and the ministers had merely agreed to explore the possibility of enhancing the effectiveness of the Treaty partners in the Indian Ocean. Whilst publicly echoing US global concerns in a minor key, New Zealand refused to jeopardize growing trade relations by imposing sanctions against Iran and the Soviet Union.[42]

Fraser offered the US naval homeporting at Cockburn Sound in Western Australia, but declined to participate in the US Rapid Deployment Force (RDF). In September 1981 an Australian parliamentary committee launched an inquiry into relations with the United States. Dominated by the political right, the committee's report, *The ANZUS Alliance* (1982), reflected widespread concern that reassertion of American power could strain Australian–US relations, especially if Washington expected Australia to become involved in extra-regional activity. Popular acceptance of the relationship would erode if Australian support for the US appeared to be mindless. Henry Albinski

31

advised that Australian governments should mollify domestic opinion and say no to the US occasionally, the better to 'follow an array of other American-related policies'.[43] Critics of the Hawke Government argue that it adopted such a tactic by promoting arms control measures contrary to US wishes.

In responding to the advent of Reaganism, the New Zealand National Government increasingly conveyed the impression that it was fighting off schizophrenia. It resisted American pressure to confront the Soviet Union, whilst emphasizing detrimental shifts in the balance of power in order to rebut domestic demands for neutralism and non-alignment. On the one hand, New Zealand officials argued, the country's interests could be thwarted almost anywhere in the world and so it would 'maintain armed force which can, if necessary, operate further afield than our own region'. On the other hand the force structure indicated a determination to achieve a degree of self-reliance for low level risks. New Zealand's lack of leverage in international affairs compelled it to seek security partners, but it would develop a clearer perception of its national interests and not simply pander to the whims of the United States. World tension was increasing dangerously, but New Zealand was not under threat.[44]

The evolution in New Zealand public attitudes on nuclear issues is discussed in chapter 6, but we might note here that by 1980 the defence establishment was giving greater attention to public concern about nuclear deterrence and warship visits. Nuclear weapons were said to have preserved peace and visits by US vessels were essential to this purpose. Yet ANZUS was not a nuclear alliance comparable to NATO and naval visits were not strategically significant or liable to turn visited ports into targets. Ignoring the adoption of nuclear war-fighting doctrines in the Pentagon, the National Government argued that 'only strategic weaponry ... would be involved in an ultimate confrontation between the United States and the Soviet Union'.[45] Such statements reflected uncertainty about the relevance of extended nuclear deterrence to the South-West Pacific.

Indeed for much of the post-Korea period US governments had paid scant regard to the South-West Pacific, relying implicitly on the stabilizing role of Australia and New Zealand. ANZUS was not among America's top ten commitments listed by the *New York Times* in 1963. The alliance was far from onerous and could be counted a net asset in support of US global objectives, requiring little attention until the 1970s after Australia and New Zealand had suspended visits by nuclear-powered warships.[46] Yet by the 1980s US declarations portrayed the alliance as critically important to Western security as a whole and a vital element in a system which had deterred aggression and underwritten regional stability for forty years.[47]

REVIEW IN THE 1980S

Allowing for rhetoric designed to make the Anzacs feel valued, the Pacific generally assumed increased importance for US policy from the late 1970s. This reflected the economic vitality of the North-Eastern rim, increased trade across the Pacific, the perceived thrust of Soviet military power, and an appreciation of the difficulty in securing sea lanes of communication (SLOCs) through the Pacific to the Indian Ocean and the Persian Gulf.

The Reagan Administration embarked on revitalizing Pacific alliance relations, partly to promote burden sharing and partly to present the Soviet Union with the threat of a two-front war. In this regard, the pivot for America's defence of Asia was always understood to be Japan, earlier highlighted in President Ford's New Pacific Doctrine of December 1975. Under Washington's tutelage Japan has become a significant military power, and there have been calls for a functional working relationship between the two hemispheres, in effect a JAN-ZUS.[48] Indeed Japan participated alongside the ANZUS countries in the 1980 Rim of the Pacific (*Rimpac*) naval exercise. But quite apart from historical distrust and in spite of the crucial trade between Japan and the Anzacs, their security interests are probably too diverse for them to form a strategic community.

Although the strategic balance has shifted against the United States in the Pacific as elsewhere, it does not necessarily signify a drastic diminution of Western security since Dulles was in his prime. South Vietnam was lost, along with the Cam Ranh Bay and Da Nang facilities. The Soviet naval build-up was observed with trepidation throughout the Pacific. But the security problem of Dulles' inner arc has been ameliorated by the disarray in communism, and by China's role as a counterbalance to Soviet and Vietnamese power. The second arc, from Taiwan to the Philippines and Singapore, has not been attacked, except from within by corruption and social injustice. Domestic unrest and a bid for sovereign control are the most potent threats to the US base facilities in the Philippines.

US policy-makers and opinion leaders inflated the Soviet threat as part of the war of words during the crisis with New Zealand. But in other contexts, testimonies have been reassuring and the inventories of Soviet capability put into perspective. Senator Phil Gramm (Texas) concluded: 'Despite this impressive buildup, the net political advan-

33

tage to the Soviets has been minimal, if nonexistent. The reason is that the U.S. is still perceived, and correctly, to be capable of projecting superior forces into the area'. Michael Armacost, Undersecretary of State for Political Affairs in the Reagan Administration, cautioned against obsession with Soviet prospects.[49] Indeed, perhaps there has been undue alarmism about Cam Ranh Bay. It is poorly serviced and would be vulnerable in wartime. From a New Zealand perspective the base is almost as distant from Wellington as it is from London, though with fewer obstacles in between.

In fact well-informed threat assessments in Australia and New Zealand stressed a much lower hierarchy of threats than direct Soviet pressure. The influential defence analyst, Paul Dibb, commented that there were 'few areas of the world, with the possible exception of Antarctica, that are of lower priority strategically for Moscow than the Southwest Pacific'.[50] An Australian parliamentary committee's report, *Threats to Australia's Security* (1981), found little evidence that the Soviet Union was in a position to concentrate its carrier force far from base in order to gain local air superiority over Australian beaches (pp. 28–9). A prolonged deterioration in superpower relations would have to develop for a Soviet threat to eventuate, and Japan, the only other power with short-term potential, would take at least five years to develop the capability to pose a threat (pp. 32–3).

Further, the prospect of a Chinese, communist-controlled Indonesia threatening Papua New Guinea or Australia had receded since it was judged the main danger in the 1960s.[51] Anzac relations with the Association of South-East Asian Nations (ASEAN) have grown warmer and even disapproval of Indonesia's human rights record has not been allowed to interfere with 'good neighbour' policies. Although concerned about the security of the Northern Pacific and the SLOCs connecting with the Gulf, the Anzacs had been cultivating relations with Indian Ocean littoral states and resisted being too closely identified with US military responses to complex political problems. According to Dibb, Australia was 'ill-advised to dissipate scarce defence resources in far-flung roles' and should resist any contribution to a US RDF or joint allied deployment for combat operations in Australia's neighbourhood.[52]

Obviously, ANZUS provided a *de facto* umbrella over the Pacific micro states for which Australia and New Zealand had legal and moral responsibility. In providing development assistance and military co-operation, the Anzac caretaker role has corresponded with US objectives to exclude hostile influences. However, the US notion that the ANZUS relationship grew increasingly important for local security reasons or even Pan-Pacific reasons is not entirely convincing. South Pacific countries have laid many of the destabilizing activities, from tuna poaching to unrest in New Caledonia, at the door of the United States and its allies.

From the mid–1970s, Australia and New Zealand preferred to keep superpower rivalry out of the region, and the general consensus among South Pacific Forum countries is that economic survival and internal political unrest are more relevant problems than any threat from Moscow. Thus, insofar as the United States promoted militarization, there has been friction over the means to achieve strategic denial. In 1982 Robert O'Neill advocated local groupings for limited purposes, relying on a series of discrete relationships to prevent escalation of local crises. With such a strategy, individual states could 'address their own particular security problems, be they regional or internal, and contribute to the stability of the global balance'. It is only fair to point out, however, that when New Zealand threatened to apply discretion to ANZUS, O'Neill resisted the case for subsystem dominance and, in line with American thinking, elevated global nuclear deterrence over 'particular security problems'.[53]

Indeed the Anzacs had to deal with the *idée fixe* among Reagan officials that ANZUS played a crucial role in Western defence as part of a seamless web of deterrence against the Soviet Union. Assistant Secretary of Defense for Asia and the Pacific, James Kelly, drew a girdle around the earth: 'A strong NATO strengthens deterrence globally to the advantage of ANZUS. But equally, the health of ANZUS is vital to the global Western alliance – especially given the increasingly important locations of both Australia and New Zealand.'[54] Some of this was for public consumption. During the crisis, a frustrated US official described New Zealand as 'a piss-ant little country south of nowheresville'.[55]

Nevertheless, so the Reagan Administration argued, the seamless web underpinned global nuclear deterrence. Kelly identified the ANZUS alliance with nuclearism:

> The worldwide fabric of deterrence on which our security against the greatest threat of all, nuclear war, is based, has worked for almost forty years, but we dare not take it for granted. Given the military capabilities of the Soviet Union, credible United States nuclear deterrent capability has become, of necessity, a key component of this worldwide fabric... Conventional and nuclear deterrence are not separable in U.S. forces, and the nature of U.S. deterrence responsibilities requires that they not be separated ... Over the years, ANZUS has undeniably been one of the keystones to our defense policy in the Pacific.[56]

Moreover a seamless web required discipline; the next worst thing to the Soviet threat was failure to demonstrate the will to resist it. There would be limits to pluralism. Allied support for nuclear deterrence became something of a loyalty test, and a determinant of US policy during the ANZUS crisis.

In the changed circumstances of the 1980s, the Reagan Administration adopted a concept of alliance relations which went well beyond 1950s containment. The cold war fought by Acheson and Dulles presumed a monolithic global threat of communism which could be met by expedient and limited security arrangements. Strategic fundamentalists of the 1980s also fought an ideological struggle against Marxist-Leninism, lacing it with Armageddon teleology. But they made few concessions to the limits of the US power and presumed a monolithic alliance would confront what was now popularly seen as a less certain, opportunist Soviet threat.[57]

By contrast, New Zealand officials portrayed ANZUS as unmilitaristic, drawing its strength from the broadest of shared interests. This interpretation became difficult to sustain. Strategic concepts advanced by the Pentagon appeared to contradict it, notably Weinberger's enunciation in 1981 of horizontal escalation whereby a Soviet attack in one part of the world might be met by US reactions elsewhere. Critics complained that the alliance could no longer be described as a regional security agreement if the United States regarded it 'as part of an entire conglomeration of nuclear weapons deterrence'.[58]

Successive Australian governments, including the Labor Government of 1983, conformed more closely to globalist considerations. ANZUS was said to contribute to the central balance of power in which, for the time being, mutual nuclear deterrence played an indispensable part. However, the Hawke Government fully endorsed the Palme Commission's Report as the basis for Australian arms control policy. Australia disapproved of war-fighting concepts and the bid for nuclear superiority favoured in the Reagan Administration. Nuclear deterrence must eventually be replaced, in the Australian view, though not by a destabilizing contravention of the ABM Treaty and SDI development. Australia's acquiescence in nuclear deterrence was qualified by promotion of the South Pacific Nuclear-Free Zone (SPNFZ), support for a verifiable nuclear freeze and strong pressure for a Comprehensive Test Ban Treaty (CTB). Notwithstanding a high degree of consensus about arms control policy, the Australian right-wing opposition parties declared that Hawke's qualified nuclearism put the two superpowers on the same moral level and damaged confidence in the West's system of security designed to restrict Soviet power.[59]

Shortly before the ANZUS crisis the Hawke Government also instigated the first governmental review of the alliance since 1951, unilaterally and then with the Treaty partners. Foreign Minister Hayden's statement to Parliament in September 1983 reaffirmed that, although the Treaty provided no guarantees, the alliance was 'fundamental to Australia's security and foreign and defence policies'. But Australia had not exercised its freedom and right to exert independence within the relationship.[60] In response to Australian pressure, the ANZUS Council of July 1983 agreed to strengthen the consultative process. The communiqué mentioned that the 'varying views and perspectives' did not affect the fundamental solidarity underlying the Treaty (see appendix 4). The 1983 review, however, forged 'solidarity' by failing to tackle sensitive issues. It contained more platitude than precision, and tolerable divergence did not extend to differences over nuclear ship visiting, or arms control.[61]

ALLIANCE IN SEARCH OF A PURPOSE

Subsequently it was politically convenient for US officials to argue that a left-wing New Zealand government's anti-nuclear stance brought two of the allies to the divorce court. The vulnerabilities were more profound than that. New Zealand's ban on nuclear visiting in 1984 was a manifestation of increasingly divergent views about strategic denial and reflected a long-term weakening of consensus about security. For New Zealand the alliance was worth keeping, but it lacked important attributes: a threat, a strategically significant area, a relevant strategy, and compensating economic privileges. The failure of imagined threats to materialize (from Japan, China, Indonesia, and the Soviet Union) also probably eroded the security consensus. Obviously one cannot be sure that because attacks do not eventuate a defensive alliance has deterred them. But it takes imaginative flair to assume, as Reagan officials did, that without ANZUS hostile powers would have filled 'a tempting security vacuum' in the South Pacific.[62] By the same token, the existence of SEATO did not deter North Vietnam. At best, perhaps, we might concede that 'the record of alliances as devices for containment is mixed and incomplete'.[63]

To critics the alliance relationship had become a relic of an obsolete cold war belief system, unlikely to survive in its old form beyond the 1980s. An analyst for Washington's Cato Institute argued that the growing divergence in the objectives and interests of the signatories had reached the point where ANZUS 'was in search of a purpose', though the members seemed reluctant to acknowledge it.[64]

None of the parties wanted to abandon the Treaty. Australian and New Zealand governments had recognized the value of a formal commitment to the West and a link with friends in the international system. Specifically, alliance membership was said to give the Anzacs a channel of communication to the highest levels of US government, thereby facilitating strategic dialogue. American officials laboured the point in dealing with the Lange Government's anti-nuclear stance. ANZUS was said to give New Zealand an ability to conduct a far more influential role in the system generally. Few if any nations the size of New Zealand had more or better influence, access and ability to make their voices heard.[65]

However, even if it can be shown that the alliance yielded privileged access in Washington, actual influence is more difficult to gauge. Following K. J. Holsti, some have argued that small allies like New Zealand have disproportionate influence for their size.[66] On the other hand we have seen evidence of lack of consultation about policy changes of direct interest to the Anzacs. Scholars have argued that Australia probably has less influence on nuclear issues than Belgium in NATO, and that trying to influence the United States is like trying to shift an elephant.[67]

There seems little doubt, as Coral Bell argues, that for much of the time the junior partners had a habit of compliance rather than one of risking dissent.[68] Whether this amounted to undue subservience is obviously a matter of dispute. O'Neill, Millar and Albinski were among those who testified to the Australian parliamentary committee which published The ANZUS Alliance that diplomatic constraints on Australia have not been significant and that the Anzacs happily relied on US strategic leadership anyway. A minority report by Labor and Democrat MPs argued, to the contrary, that Australian governments had failed to promote national interests. In New Zealand, Prime Minister Lange argued that the alliance mentality had led New Zealand governments to avoid thinking independently, with the result that they had evaded fundamental defence and security problems.[69] Anzacs of all political persuasion veered away from defining the relationship solely in terms of US hegemony.

New Zealand Labour leaders tried, unsuccessfully, to redefine the relationship in economic terms. American assertions that ANZUS already provided a framework for economic co-operation (and even for the stability which promoted the Pacific economic miracle) seem to border on the perverse for several reasons. First, the three members of

ANZUS sustained the lowest growth rates in the Pacific in the 1970s and 1980s. Second, the most spectacular economic growth has occurred among rim states where vested interests have experienced traumatic destabilization. Third, as we have seen, the relationship between alliance membership and economic benefits has been tenuous and at times conflictual. Fourth, since the 1970s Australian and New Zealand trade has increased with alleged 'threats', from Iran to the Soviet Union, while trade with the United States and other Western powers has declined or levelled off. As contended by Merwyn Norrish, permanent head of the New Zealand Foreign Affairs department, the change in trade patterns released the country, psychologically, from a foreign policy of dependency.[70]

In sum, the weakest partner came to regard the alliance as worthy but in need of reform, whereas the most powerful member accorded it greater significance than it had done in the past. The Reagan Administration was confronted with the prospect that Australia and New Zealand were becoming increasingly regionalist in sustaining national security interests. The Lange Government emphasized New Zealand's South Pacific identity, and clearly many New Zealanders viewed their harbours and surrounding seas with a Gaullist possessiveness. In the imagery projected by peace squadrons, sailing against nuclear vessels represented a confrontation with trespassers. Out of parochialism grew strategic denial with a vengeance. However, day-to-day defence co-operation had flourished between the professional élites of the alliance members, and the next chapter examines the military and nuclear linkages which existed outside the ANZUS Treaty.

3 DEFENCE CO-OPERATION AND NUCLEAR CONNECTIONS

Reporting on the 1983 review of ANZUS, the Australian Foreign Minister, Bill Hayden, recognized the distinction between the Treaty and the defence arrangements which had grown up between the partners, usually bilaterally, and often predating the formal alliance. Although often justified under the rubric of the Treaty, military co-operation was not devised in fulfilment of specific obligations. Recognition of this constituted an evolution in official Australian attitudes to the relationship towards greater pragmatism. During the heated row between New Zealand and the US, Hayden and Beazley encouraged a calmer discussion of the meaning of ANZUS. They downgraded the importance of the 'guarantee', and remarked that 'the day-to-day co-operation' gave Australia's alliance with the US its significance, compared to the less frequent or binding coincidence of strategic perceptions and interests.[1]

Even without ANZUS, of course, there would exist a high degree of bilateral military co-operation between Australia and New Zealand. As Desmond Ball notes, it reflects an inviolate concurrence of interests.[2] Regular ministerial discussions began in 1972, and these were augmented by the Australia New Zealand Consultative Committee (ANZCC), comprising the permanent secretaries of defence and the chiefs of staff. In 1969 the two governments made an arrangement for maximum self-sufficiency in production and maintenance of equipment. A fully-fledged logistics memorandum of understanding (MoU) of 1983 facilitated progress in several areas: small arms procurement; New Zealand servicing of engines for the RAN's guided-missile frigates; Australian repair of RNZN missiles and torpedoes; and enhancement of trans-Tasman defence communications.[3] In addition there are mutual training programmes and much personnel exchange.

But the main emphasis of this chapter is on the agreements, base facilities and visiting rights which have involved the Anzacs with the United States. Critics suggest that many of the connections are irrelevant to the regional and national security interests of the Anzacs, representing subservience to, and dependence upon, the Americans. There is obviously no clear cut distinction between national and mutual benefits, between defence co-operation serving regional and global security, or between conventional and nuclear-related functions. But it is quite clear that the globally important nuclear linkages were between the US and Australia, affecting the latter's political autonomy to a greater extent than New Zealand's.[4] Indeed, the willingness of the New Zealand and US governments to ditch much of their military co-operation betrays a degree of insouciance by both countries. In nuclear terms, New Zealand had little to disengage from, relative to Australia, though anti-nuclearists saw value in precluding future commitments.

CO-OPERATION AGREEMENTS

Broadly speaking, the ANZUS relationship hardly reflected pressing military or security exigencies, and defence co-operation entangled the parties almost surreptitiously. The Lange Government's persistence in excluding nuclear vessels in the knowledge that defence arrangements would suffer might even be considered a triumph of politicians over civil servants and the military. When jolted by the ANZUS crisis to review the military arrangements, bureaucrats in all three countries were only dimly aware of the scope of co-operation. The New Zealand MoD was unable to produce a definitive list of agreements, though it assumed the existence of about a hundred. Peace researchers obliged by producing their own lists.[5] An Australian inquiry revealed a heavy dependence on the United States for extra-regional intelligence data and assessments. Pentagon investigations disclosed that no-one knew the exact scope of the security relationship. US officials were reportedly astonished at the mass of agreements, some of dubious legality, and the limited degree to which co-operation was subject to civilian control. In all three capitals it was felt 'that there had been insufficient political direction in the development and management of ANZUS'.[6]

In fact the only agreement which falls directly under ANZUS is a secret maritime surveillance arrangement (MARSAR) whose existence was revealed in *The Dominion* (29 May 1985). In addition, the Radford-Collins Agreement of 1951, originally between the USN and the RAN, is believed to divide responsibility for tracking the Soviet Fleet and to co-ordinate the protection and control of friendly shipping. New Zealand joined in 1978 and assumed an area of responsibility in the

41

Pacific which the RNZAF patrols with P-3B Orions, warning Island states about poaching by US tuna boats. Under Radford-Collins, it is alleged that the Anzacs are expected to secure key domestic facilities for contingent allied use.[7]

Other routine agreements arose out of Anglo-US wartime co-operation, such as the ABCA Armies Programme for the promotion of standardization and economy in army equipment. New Zealand joined the US, UK, Canada, and Australia as an associate member in 1965. Similar arrangements exist for the other forces. The Air Standard-isation Co-ordinating Committee originated in 1947 to enhance US, UK and Canadian combined operations and provision of essential ser-vices. The RNZAF did not become a signatory until 1965. Again, New Zealand was a later adherent to interoperability in naval command, control and communications. And when, in 1970, New Zealand joined the non-atomic subcommittee of the Technical Co-operation Pro-gramme for co-ordinating defence research it was represented in Washington by Australia. Critics detected a nuclear war-fighting connection in this programme because it involved the Anzacs in research on Pacific storms and underwater disturbances which affect the detection of submarines. They argued that it was geared to locating submarines for kills using nuclear depth-charges in the deeper ocean basins.[8]

In addition to important local exercises in maritime surveillance and amphibious warfare, the Anzacs also exercised further afield in tasks which critics claimed were relevant more for attacks against mainland Asia than to the South-West Pacific. They included the two-yearly *Rimpac* exercise, the huge annual *Team Spirit* in Korea, and the air exercise, *Cope Thunder*, held seven times a year in the Philippines.

A plethora of arms purchase and logistic agreements date back to World War II when the Anzacs acquired much US weaponry. Re-equipment of their forces in the 1960s involved more American hardware and services. New Zealand became particularly reliant on the US for aircraft (Hercules, Orions, A-4 Skyhawks and Boeing 727s) and Bell helicopters. In 1962 Australia agreed to purchase three US destroyers and, for obscure reasons, Menzies plumped for F-111s rather than British TSR 2s for the RAAF. Subsequently, Australia agreed to buy two FFG-7 class frigates, and 75 F/A-18 Hornets for which Congress waived the $US50 million research and development component. Australian underwater detection systems and the Jin-dalee over-the-horizon radar have been assisted by US equipment, loans and technical advice.

Current at the time of the crisis were the logistic support MoUs of

1985 (Australia) and 1982 (New Zealand) which indicated the level of peacetime assistance which the allies could expect to receive for cash payments. The MoUs included host nation support clauses for the availability of pre-positioned weapon systems and munitions. The Muldoon Government confirmed that in time of international tension, as defined by the United States, New Zealand would facilitate repairs, logistic support, reloading and provisioning for US forces, including nuclear-armed ships and aircraft. Sensitive vigilantes regarded it as a green light for US military penetration.[9]

Intelligence sharing relies not on the existence of ANZUS, but on a supposed 1947 Security Agreement (UKUSA) which evolved from wartime arrangements. As Richelson and Ball have shown in *The Ties That Bind* (1985), UKUSA established the United States as the first party and others, Canada, Australia and New Zealand as second parties. Australia acted as proxy for New Zealand until the latter became a fully-fledged member in 1977. But as early as 1954, when a group of Americans led by Major-General Trudeau arrived in New Zealand to discuss intelligence procurement, 'a considerable amount of intelligence' had already been supplied to the CIA and American armed forces at their request.[10]

Governments neither confirm nor deny the existence of UKUSA, but Richelson and Ball examine the extent to which the national agencies for collection and assessment of domestic, military and foreign information became closely interwoven. Australia and the US probably demanded secure handling as the prerequisite for passing on material. With regard to signals intelligence (SIGINT), close relations developed between the US National Security Agency (NSA), Britain's Government Communications Headquarters (GCHQ), the Australian Defence Signals Directorate (DSD), and the New Zealand Government Communications Security Bureau (GCSB). According to Richelson and Ball, approximately 50 NSA operatives work in Australia, in addition to CIA, GCSB and other personnel. New Zealand's SIGINT station at Tangimoana was almost certainly established to common specifications with Australian DSD assistance. New Zealand officers work with the DSD in Melbourne, and ten were attached to an Australian-run intercept station in Singapore which was phased out in the 1970s. It is claimed that under a 1976 manning agreement a New Zealand officer was appointed to the Intelligence Center in Hawaii for training in intelligence assessment. Once again, however, New Zealand was often represented abroad by the DSD.[11]

Researchers surmise that the UKUSA agreement divides participants into spheres of responsibility for intelligence collection. The

Australian DSD monitors South-East Asia from Shoal Bay near Darwin and assists in other Asian work. At the New Zealand Defence HQ at Sembewang, Singapore, a small military intelligence group (ANZMIS) processes data collected by RAAF Orions and allegedly by photographers using a US Embassy launch to monitor Soviet naval traffic through the Malacca Straits. Material is sent to the Australian Joint Intelligence Organization in Melbourne.[12] No doubt Australia provides more intelligence about the region than the United States, but critics have been concerned about the possible use of SIGINT facilities in Australia in controversial events relating to surveillance work, including the Tonkin gulf incident and the capture of the USS *Pueblo* by North Korea.

NUCLEAR TESTS AND URANIUM

Australia slipped into a direct nuclear connection without undue consideration for strategic issues except as a byproduct of coupling Britain and the US to Australian security. In the development of nuclear weapons, Prime Ministers Robert Menzies of Australia and Sidney Holland of New Zealand discerned a close identity of strategic and political interests with Britain. As discussed in chapter 6, Holland quickly ran into domestic opposition to New Zealand's limited involvement in British tests in the Pacific. Menzies, however, had a compliant constituency and he more easily combined an obsequious attitude towards Britain with an imperial style at home. His failure to inform the rest of his Cabinet about Britain's request for testing, or to satisfy even the most elementary safeguards, stands in a class of presumption all on its own. Between October 1952 and October 1957 Australia hosted twelve British nuclear tests with an aggregate yield of about 120 kilotons. In addition, Britain continued with about 700 'minor' trials until 1963, several of which scattered more than 20 kilograms of plutonium over the Maralinga site in South Australia.

The Royal Commission of 1985, which reported on the tests, produced a catalogue of official deception and secrecy, cynicism about the effects on the Aboriginal life-style and lack of independent Australian control. Safety problems resulted in servicemen working without proper protection and Aborigines suffering radiation sickness. Low-level fallout from the third of seven tests at Maralinga drifted to the outskirts of Adelaide, 900 km to the south-east.[13] However, although Australia drove with scant care and attention into nuclear testing it has been able to drive out again. Vigorous government opposition to French underground tests, 8,000 km to the east of

Adelaide, is testimony to the new intolerance, and accusations of Anglo-Saxon hypocrisy are avoided by promoting a Comprehensive Test Ban (CTB) against US and British interests.

Uranium was mined in the 1940s and 1950s for British and US atomic weapons, but has been only an indirect strategic connection since a public inquiry of 1975–6 drew attention to the danger of diversion for use in weaponry. The inquiry concluded that Australia had a special responsibility to devise safeguards additional to those pertaining under the International Atomic Energy Agency and Euratom. Exports of uranium to non-signatories of the Non-Proliferation Treaty (NPT) should be prohibited, for the nuclear power industry was unintentionally contributing to a risk of nuclear war.[14] The Fraser Government permitted exports in 1977 but diluted the safeguards and also sold to France, though France had not signed the NPT and also continued testing at Moruroa.

To the fury of anti-nuclear activists and the ALP, Hawke lifted a Labor Government ban on sales to France as a budgetary measure in August 1986. Hawke noted that France had not stopped testing as a result of the sales ban and had bought uranium on the spot market. He also argued that strict safeguards prevented Australian uranium being used for weapons. Politically, Hawke's 'betrayal' led the ALP left to suspect subservience to mining interests and contributed to their disillusion with the Government's anti-nuclear posturing, even though Hawke reimposed the ban in February 1988 when evidence emerged of diversion to weapon use.[15]

FACILITIES

More strategically important are the US–Australian joint facilities. Of the 1,608 overseas bases and facilities with US jurisdiction, the US PACOM identified eleven in Australia serving the US armed forces.[16] Major territorial facilities were granted to the US much as nuclear test sites were granted to the British in the 1950s – without strategic debate and accompanied by official disinformation and evasion.[17] To avoid the stigma of 'security risk', the Whitlam Labor Government continued the policy of denying information to the Australian public which, it was privately admitted, the Soviet Union already knew. Whitlam pleaded with the ALP to accept the installations and he supported the addition of an Omega navigation station. Even so, there are reasons to suspect that alarm spread through the UKUSA intelligence communities about breaches of security, especially when Whitlam blew the gaffe on CIA control of the Pine

Gap facility and threatened to close it down. A former official has indicated that the CIA badgered other friendly security agencies with the idea that Whitlam was jeopardizing the Western security system, and a CIA task group in US Naval Intelligence is widely thought to have engaged in destabilizing the Government.[18]

No doubt Prime Minister Hawke was reminded of US sensitivities about the bases when he visited Washington in July 1983. Acting on an ALP pledge to provide more information about them, he made the blandest of parliamentary statements on 6 June 1984 after first clearing it with the US. The purpose of the statement, as Hayden explained, was to convince the public that the facilities enhanced security because of their deterrent and verification functions.[19] But the Government refused to be drawn into debate, presumably counting on majority support for the facilities and public disinterest in the security implications. Nevertheless, as Fedor Mediansky has argued, the facilities 'constitute some of the most far reaching and intractable problems in the management of the alliance'. They highlight divergence as well as convergence of strategic perspectives, problems of sovereignty and democratic control, and fuel a long-running domestic debate about the risks which make Australia the foremost, perhaps the only, nuclear target in the southern hemisphere.[20]

For detailed discussion of the facilities readers are referred to Desmond Ball's *A Suitable Piece of Real Estate* (1980). It will suffice here to outline the main nuclear-related functions of three in particular: North West Cape Naval Communications Station near Exmouth (WA), Pine Gap near Alice Springs, and Nurrungar near Woomera.

The USN station at North West Cape fulfilled a US requirement to communicate with Polaris SSBNs deployed in the Pacific. It is one of several VLF radio transmission stations for relaying communications, including fire orders, to submarines. The transaction of 9 May 1963, which granted the base, recalled the ANZUS Treaty, and the Australian Government presented it as an ANZUS facility. But an exchange of notes made it clear that its operations did not carry any degree of Australian control or guaranteed access, and of course New Zealand had no say.[21] Australia was thereby hooked directly and separately into US nuclear deterrence.

The Whitlam Government attempted to assert political rights after the transmitters had been used to communicate a nuclear alert to the US 7th Fleet during the Yom Kippur War. In 1974 the US agreed to a stronger Australian presence and promised 'full and timely information about strategic and operational developments relevant to the station and their significance for Australian national interests'.

However, access to certain communications rooms is supposedly denied and the RAN's facility restricted. In 1978 Australian Ministers were the last to hear that contracts had been let for a new global satellite communications terminal.[22]

North West Cape is said to have increased in significance in view of the US maritime forward offensive strategy, though it may now be superseded by upgraded stations in the US. The Hawke Government argued that it currently transmits to a range of 5,000 km, which falls short of the Sea of Japan and Sea of Okhotsk, and that the station was 'essentially limited to defence and deterrence purposes'.[23] But as scientists point out, technically North West Cape can reach further and can also communicate with attack submarines and surface vessels which could engage in nuclear war-fighting.[24]

Apparently concerned about the potential first strike role of Trident SSBNs, Hayden had said whilst in opposition that a future Labor government would demand a firm assurance that North West Cape would not initiate military action without Australian consent and that Australia would want a review if its function changed.[25] Indeed the 1983 review of ANZUS led to further concessions, giving the Australian Defence Attaché in Washington special access to the Pentagon. But critics pointed out that participation is not the same as control and there was no guarantee of US deference to Australia in a crisis.[26] No system short of overall Australian authority could ensure this and, for the credibility of US nuclear threats, allied involvement is probably not desirable anyway.

Unlike North West Cape's functions, which could be removed to Guam, Pine Gap has a role which can only be conducted from Australia. And, judged by the mystique surrounding it, Pine Gap station holds the key to world peace, or at any rate US security. Its highly visible radomes are completely vulnerable to external attack, but internal security is ferocious and Australians are excluded from the signals analysis section. Politicians of radical and voluble disposition allegedly emerge from briefings on the base impressed, silent and probably still ignorant of some of its functions. Pine Gap is estimated by some sources as more important to the US than the rest of the ANZUS relationship put together, a *casus belli* if ever it were imperilled.[27] Without it, perhaps a third of US surveillance would be blacked out.

Referred to as a joint defence space research facility, it is run by the CIA with extensive NSA participation, and according to Ball is a sister station to Menwith in Yorkshire. It receives data from satellites which monitor nuclear tests and missile telemetry, enabling the US to check

Soviet compliance with arms control agreements and receive earliest possible warning of nuclear attacks. Pine Gap's other main function is the vital SIGINT one, and there have been accusations, officially denied, that it routinely intercepts domestic and diplomatic communications. Critics argue that Pine Gap's subsidiary role in monitoring arms control and detecting illegal ABM radars is inseparable from provision of trajectory data for a first strike. Clearly, the arms control monitoring occupies only a fraction of the operators' time, and only the Partial Test Ban Treaty was in existence when the station was constructed.[28]

Nurrungar became operational in 1971, a year after Pine Gap, and has overlapping functions. It features a data link between the North American Air Command, Strategic Air Command and the US National Military Command System, and gives instant warning of ICBM and SLBM launches detected by satellites. For ICBM attacks this allows up to half an hour for checking false alarms or running away. The satellites also monitor compliance with test ban treaties. However, the system will be redundant for arms control if and when NAVSTAR satellites with improved sensors and direct satellite links to the US are fully deployed. Orbiting information for the new satellites is being provided by the Tranet Station at Smithfield in South Australia. Nurrungar's remaining use will be in obtaining war-fighting data supplied from new satellite sensors. In addition, Nurrungar has been placed under the control of the USAF Space Command which is deeply involved in the SDI. Andrew Mack's research indicates that the only justification for American assertions that Nurrungar will not have an SDI role is that future mobile ground terminals in the northern hemisphere will be less vulnerable and more capable for the purpose. Further ahead, data processing aboard satellites could eliminate the requirement for ground stations except as reserves.[29]

Regional high-frequency direction-finding (HF-DF) SIGINT is collated at the DSD headquarters in Melbourne. Information arrives from several HF-DF stations: Pearce (near Perth), Carbalah (Queensland) and Tangimoana in New Zealand. Data is supplied by direct satellite link to the USN's Ocean Surveillance Center at Makalapa, Hawaii, operated by the Naval Security Group of the NSA, and then on to Texas where, so researchers claim, it is transformed into targeting data for Tomahawk missiles.[30] Prime Minister Lange contends that Tangimoana, covering ship-to-shore and long-range air communications, is under complete New Zealand control. However, New Zealand has no control over how the USN uses the data, and critics say that it integrates New Zealand into US war-fighting strategy much more closely than ANZUS or ship visits. But in the absence of Soviet warships in the South Pacific its main role, according to Desmond Ball, is probably to monitor fishing trawlers.[31]

By contrast, the US Omega navigation station near Yarram, 180 km south-east of Melbourne, is part of an international network with a master station in Hawaii. Denial by the Australian authorities that it has military applications rings false. Omega is probably used by USAF and USN weapon platforms for accurate navigational positioning, though it is perhaps less capable and reliable than the LORAN-C system for updating inertial guidance on submarines.[32] Plans for a New Zealand installation were opposed by vigilantes and the US decided to locate it in Australia.

Black Birch transit circle observation near Blenheim, New Zealand, also has military and civilian roles. Completed in 1984 by the US Navy from its military construction budget, the observatory catalogues stars, determines satellite orbits and measures the earth's wobble. The only other stellar mapping stations are in the United States. The US Naval Observatory in Washington describes it as 'important for many DoD users, particularly strategic systems', and the data distribution list includes US sub-contractors on the Trident missile programme. The data will be freely available but is valuable for the stellar inertial guidance of Trident warheads and in precise positioning of launch sites. Critics believe that Black Birch entangles New Zealand in nuclear war-fighting, though they concede that astronomic data takes months to analyse and that the observatory would only be targeted through inadvertence.[33]

Indeed New Zealand is hardly worth expending a nuclear warhead upon, even as a time-slack target. By contrast Australia boasts ideal war-fighting or demonstration targets. The command, control and intelligence (C^3I) installations are 'soft' and exposed. Moreover, apart from the DSD headquarters in Melbourne and the naval facilities of Cockburn Sound, the nuclear-related bases are distant from the large population centres. It would be a saving grace, of course, if the Soviet Union has a similar targeting policy to the US for withholding attacks on C^3I stations. Their survival would be important for restraining submarine commanders and negotiating war termination. However, Soviet declarations and the advent of nuclear war-fighting doctrines, have led Ball to conclude that the bases would be targeted in the unlikely event of nuclear war.[34]

In 1981 the Fraser Government publicly conceded that key installations might be attacked in the course of a superpower conflict. But any increased risk was considered to be outweighed by contributions to the US nuclear deterrent upon which Australian security against the

Soviet Union depended. The Labor leaders, Hayden and Lionel Bowen, also announced that they were satisfied with the strategic value of Pine Gap and Nurrungar, though expressing reservations about North West Cape. As Foreign Minister, Hayden continued to argue that the early warning functions gave the US confidence and strategic advantage, and that Australia would suffer nuclear consequences from a superpower conflict whether it hosted the facilities or not.[35]

Belatedly, in 1987, the Australian DoD announced a new communications link to the facilities for domestic warning of nuclear attack. Detailed assessments of the nature and consequences of attacks were sent to individual states and the Northern Territory so that they might devise appropriate emergency plans. However, officials believe that the chances of strikes on the big coastal cities are remote, and nuclear-armed warships on visits would not tarry in Australian waters in the build-up to a nuclear war.[36]

Australia's bipartisan support for extended nuclear deterrence has remained firm for much of the 1980s, under the Hawke régime. The existence of the facilities was said to mean that the Soviet Union received a strong signal that an attack on Australia would trigger a US response. For domestic political reasons the Hawke Government has emphasized additional benefits from the facilities. Summoning the considerable rhetoric at his command, Hayden contended that they gave Australia 'moral standing in the position we intend to take more actively in the United Nations and other international fora in support of arms control'. Leverage could also be applied to push the United States in the direction which Australia wanted to go. In August 1984 Hayden warned that Australia would not countenance a first strike capability, and that if the US did not demonstrate a willingness to negotiate on arms control Australia might have to review some of its associations.[37] Hawke soft-pedalled furiously, though he himself had raised the issue of a comprehensive test ban (CTB) on his visit to Washington in June 1983. He had also spoken out against involvement of the facilities in SDI and had distanced Australia from aggressive naval strategies. In February 1985 the Cabinet had also obliged him to back out of his secret commitment to give logistic support for monitoring MX missile tests. None of this gave pleasure in Washington. But apart from blustering, the Hawke Government took no action to alarm the US intelligence agencies. Sharply divergent positions on arms control demonstrated Australia's lack of leverage.[38] In November 1987 the US and France were the only states to vote against an Australian CTB resolution in the UN.

VISITING RIGHTS

There can be little doubt that in a far-flung alliance visiting plays a key part in reinforcing common interests. The defence estab-lishments argue that visits signal to the international community that ANZUS is an obligation which the US is likely to support in the event of deteriorating strategic circumstances in the South-West Pacific. For their part, the hosts demonstrate support for the wider strategic interests of the Western Alliance. More directly, visiting can provide opportunities for exercising and an exchange of views for keeping up to date with military developments. With as many as 8,000 servicemen in a carrier group, local economies also benefit. In September 1986 the Tasmanian visit of the USS *Missouri* was anticipated to bring Hobart's shopkeepers $A250,000.[39]

For the visitor New Zealand and Australian ports offer the three Rs: replenishment, rest and recreation. In 1976, the CINCPAC Admiral Noel Gayler made it clear that visits to New Zealand were not for strategic reasons. Prime Minister Muldoon concurred: 'They will come here in the course of wide-ranging world cruises to let their crews ashore to meet our people and for you to meet them. . . . They will be here simply to further cement the good will between our peoples.' This confirms the view that the USN went beyond operational require-ments in sending nuclear-propelled vessels to New Zealand. Not one visit was operational, or provided for the express purpose of exercis-ing with New Zealand units.[40] The Australian authorities also acknowledge that in assessing port suitability they 'look principally to ports that are going to be attractive for R and R purposes'. Fremantle and Perth were said to be among the most popular R & R ports in the world, partly because of the 'friendly women'.[41]

This hardly makes them vital operational links in the US chain of Pacific defences. Crew comfort is undoubtedly important for man-power retention, but the USNs conditions of service proved a double-edged sword in securing acceptance of visits in the South-West Pacific in the 1980s. If visiting was of little strategic significance then, as far as New Zealand pressure groups were concerned, a ban on nuclear visiting would have no strategic significance for the alliance relation-ship. Alternatively, to argue, as US officials did in response to Wellington's ban of 1984, that such visits were also strategically vital, simply added to concern about the risk of accident and, in the case of Fraser's homeporting offer, of nuclear targeting.

A possible military objective is to familiarize crews with ports for use in wartime.[42] Even so, the truth is not enhanced by exaggeration. US

Assistant Secretary of Defense, James Kelly, argued that 'denial of access for nuclear-capable ships and aircraft . . . would greatly complicate, if not render unworkable, the USN's new forward deployment strategy'.[43] Not only do the Australian and New Zealand Governments have strong reservations about the strategy, but the USN's concept is strangely flawed if it can be wrecked by lack of R & R in Australia and New Zealand. Of course Australia would become more important if the US lost its forward bases. But the facilities which make the strategy 'workable' are in Japan, Taiwan, Hawaii, Guam, Diego Garcia and the Philippines. Only the last of these looks remotely like being denied to the US in the future.

It can be shown that in establishing visiting rights to the South-West Pacific after the Second World War the USN behaved in a rather casual and insensitive fashion, which New Zealand came to resent. The first peacetime visit of a US vessel to New Zealand was requested at only ten days' notice. However, the USS *Vincennes* which visited Auckland and Wellington in November 1945 was welcomed effusively by the Labour Prime Minister, Peter Fraser.[44] Nobody expected US warship visits to run into management problems, for the Americans appeared to be downgrading their presence in the South-West Pacific, retaining four air-sea rescue patrol craft and a few tugs based in American Samoa. Eight years passed before the next visit, by the carrier USS *Tarawa*, in May 1954.

However, the United States had sought an informal political understanding with the British Empire for a continuation of wartime visiting practices. No prior notice or application for diplomatic clearance would be necessary, arrangements being made at service level. Building on the sentiment for post-war co-operation against the Soviet Union expressed by Churchill at Fulton, Missouri, military planners pressed ahead. The agreement between General Spaatz and Air Chief Marshal Tedder for American use of air bases in the UK had a naval counterpart agreed between Admiral Sherman USN and Admiral Cunningham RN. The Americans casually raised the matter with the British Foreign Secretary, Ernest Bevin, in Paris in August 1946, indicating that naval arrangements, already a *fait accompli* as far as the USN and RN were concerned, should apply to all Commonwealth members. There would be no question of sharing bases or personnel because this would be 'liable to arouse international interests'. As well, the practice in some areas for American and British military aircraft to make reciprocal use of airfield facilities on an *ad hoc* basis would be extended to cover air bases on British and US territory throughout the world.

The Americans requested that the Dominions be excluded from the negotiations; they were simply expected to fall into line. Australia and New Zealand were presented with the visiting rights proposal towards the end of 1946, though the State Department wanted the arrangements to be entirely informal and kept off the record. Domestically, the Truman Administration had to tread warily in perpetuating wartime alliance arrangements. Internationally it did not want to raise issues of sovereignty, appear to be colluding with British imperialism, or give the Soviet Union reason to seek similar rights. Australia and New Zealand raised no objections. They were keen apparently to have visits which were not anticipated to be very frequent.[45]

Principles of visiting or staging were not discussed during negotiations leading to the ANZUS Treaty. Not until March 1954 did the US Air Attaché in Tokyo sound out Australian and New Zealand diplomats about regular quarterly visits, in this case by bombers from Clark Field in the Philippines for familiarization and goodwill purposes. The New Zealand air staff welcomed the suggestion but wanted visits restricted to no more than twice a year and a maximum of three aircraft in each flight because of the lack of facilities for extending hospitality.[46]

Ship visits increased markedly in the 1950s and the first US submarine visited Auckland in October 1956. New Zealand officials were given to understand that 'the USN finds NZ a pleasant place for shore leave and recreation', and that the increase in visits was 'part of a recruiting drive'. Several flotillas could be expected every year. However, clearance procedure caused a rumpus in 1957 when the USN sought confirmation of the post-war understanding. The British Admiralty produced a document issued by the US Chief of Naval Operations to all Fleet Commanders, dated 26 June 1947, which indicated that Canada, Australia and New Zealand required only service clearance. Unlike Australia, New Zealand had not abided by the spirit of the agreement, and had required each visit to secure diplomatic clearance and ministerial approval (with the exception of blanket clearance for Antarctic operations and special arrangements with the RAN). Confronted by an increasing number of American visits, New Zealand Ministers and senior officials were adamant that there should be no departure from this practice. A senior official noted: 'Whatever other British countries do I feel (& understand the Minister does also) that we should stick to our present arrangement of requiring clearance. Our problem is a special one & the number of vessels requires watching.'[47]

Why the right-wing Government of Sidney Holland should have seen it as a problem is not clear from the documents. If the USN took New Zealand's acquiescence for granted, perhaps this offended national sensibilities. Equally, New Zealand 'imperialists' may have resented a US challenge to the 'commonwealth preference' which reinforced New Zealand's British identity. Of course, the reciprocity principle hardly signified, given the potentially limited visiting by New Zealand vessels to US territory. New Zealand would be more host than hosted. But the most likely explanation is a practical one. Lack of facilities, the expense and the bureaucratic burden of visit management could have been problematic. In addition social and perhaps political difficulties might arise. New Zealanders had welcomed the 100,000 or so US troops stationed in the country during the war. But there had been friction and several riots, including a four-hour street battle caused by racist American servicemen in Wellington in 1943. Regular peacetime naval visits might pose unacceptable social problems for the small port populations, leading to curtailed sympathy for the Holland Government's cold war posture.

As far as is known, warship visit requests to Australia and New Zealand were always granted, except perhaps during the liability suspensions on nuclear-powered warships. But in New Zealand, the Prime Minister's office complained that the Americans were riding roughshod through the proper procedures. On several occasions the USN failed to ask the New Zealand naval staff for operational clearance while claiming to have already received it when applying for diplomatic approval.[48]

The hiatus in nuclear-powered visiting in the 1960s and 1970s is discussed in the next chapter. But visiting to Australia increased significantly after the revolution in Iran and the Soviet move into Afghanistan. Carter's call for forward defence of the Gulf and Indian Ocean brought forth Fraser's offer of Cockburn Sound as a US homeport to help contain Soviet activity. William Tow's notion that this complemented Washington's plans for an alternative supply route to Israel seems rather fantastic, more so than the contingency, suggested by John Dorrance, for a southern route to the Indian Ocean in the event of disruption to the Indonesian straits.[49] Both are probably wide of the mark. Cockburn Sound was a poor substitute for what the Pentagon wanted – an Australian contribution to the RDF. As Beazley pointed out from the opposition benches, Washington did not take the same frenetic view of occasional R & R visits.[50] Less a virtue than a convenience, even the convenience was doubtful. Cockburn Sound is just as far from the Persian Gulf as Subic Bay, and the US did not

Table 3.1. *Visits to Australian ports by vessels of the USN, 1980–1985* *(nuclear-powered in parentheses)*

1980	1981	1982	1983	1984	1985
47(11)	71(14)	72(10)	65(18)	53(7)	58(9)

Sources: *APD*, Senate, 34(1) 1, vol. S109, 8 May 1985, pp. 1576–81; 1985 figures from USIS, Canberra.

Table 3.2. *US warship days in Australian ports, 1976–1984*

1976	1977	1978	1979	1980	1981	1982	1983	1984
92	83	156	175	250	304	310	251	242

Source: Lyuba Zarsky, Peter Hayes and Walden Bello, 'Nuclear Accidents', *Current Affairs Bulletin*, June 1986, p. 8.

favour a huge investment in building up the Perth–Fremantle infra-structure.[51] Nevertheless, the increased frequency of port calls to Australia reflected new deployments to the Indian Ocean (tables 3.1 and 3.2)

Western Australia has hosted a disproportionate number of war-ships since 1980 (about 70 per cent) and opponents argue that the frequency constitutes *de facto* nuclear homeporting. About 25 per cent of the arrivals are nuclear powered and 80 per cent nuclear capable. Indeed the ALP Opposition desired to ban nuclear-armed ships altogether by seeking an extension of the US agreement that B-52s visiting Darwin would not be nuclear armed. But at the Canberra ANZUS Council meeting in June 1982, the American officials made it clear that there were no circumstances under which Australia could exercise the right to deny ships access. In talks with Deputy Secretary of State, Walter J. Stoessel, Hayden affirmed his support for visits for maintenance, essential repairs and shore leave. The ALP conference a fortnight later adopted a ban on the staging of operations involving nuclear weapons from Australian territory, including the 'staging of nuclear-armed warships in the context of a conflict in this area'. Beazley noted that Soviet targeting doctrine would take permanent homeporting facilities into account but not occasional visits.[52] Prime Minister Fraser ensured that the ANZUS Council communiqué con-tained an electoral embarrassment for the ALP. It confirmed:

> the high priority each partner placed upon a regular and comprehen-sive programme of naval visits to each other's ports, as well as to

55

friendly ports in the Asia/Pacific region generally. They recognise the importance of access by United States naval ships to the ports of its Treaty partners as a critical factor in its efforts to maintain strategic deterrence and in order to carry out its responsibilities under the terms of the Treaty. In this regard the Australian and New Zealand members declared their continued willingness to accept visits to their ports by United States naval vessels whether conventional or nuclear powered.[53]

After the election, Hawke told Parliament that although Labor supported a non-nuclear South Pacific, Australia did not wish to impede nuclear-powered ships or port calls. Despite protests and strikes by watersiders and other unionists, Hayden made a publicity call on the USS *Texas* in Brisbane, and the 1984 ALP national conference moderated its warship policy to a ban on homeporting.[54] US officials naturally assumed that the newly elected Labour Government in New Zealand would follow suit.

Between 1958 and 1985, New Zealand ports received 160 US Navy, 100 Royal Navy and 30 French Navy visits, mainly to Auckland and Wellington but also to Lyttelton, Dunedin, Whangarei, Tauranga, Napier and Nelson. It was widely believed that the Muldoon Government had encouraged USN visits to provoke anti-nuclear groups.[55] But in the Muldoon period, 1975–84, an average of four vessels a year visited, compared to an average of 13 a year in 1967–73, mainly destroyers in conjunction with the Vietnam War. The Muldoon visits were none the less provoking and, unlike the preceding period, included nuclear-powered vessels (see table 3.3). At least half were nuclear capable.

Table 3.3. *Visits to New Zealand ports by vessels of the USN, 1967–1984 (includes multiple port visits by individual warships; nuclear-powered in parentheses)*

1967	13	1976	2(2)
1968	14	1977	9
1969	26	1978	10(1)
1970	13	1979	12(1)
1971	18	1980	12(1)
1972	14	1981	10
1973	7	1982	2(1)
1974	1	1983	7(2)
1975	2	1984	8(1)

Source: Helen Clark, *Disarmament and Arms Control, Report of the Select Committee on Foreign Affairs and Defence*, Wellington, 1985.

It is difficult to believe, however, that occasional warship visits would cause the Soviet Union to target New Zealand. Even long range SLCMs would not be a strategic threat in New Zealand ports, and warships would join battle groups at sea during a period of tension. Although New Zealand is within range of land-based SS11 missiles, SLBMs and SS-NX-21 missiles on Soviet submarines, these would be engaged either against strategic land targets or strategically-armed US vessels. Soviet Air Force pilots would be unwise to set out on the long flight from Da Nang.[56] Critics argue that any US vessel capable of attacking a Soviet strategic platform in the vicinity would itself be a target (though Soviet strategic vessels are rarely in the South Pacific). Nevertheless, the point that by hosting US vessels New Zealand was supporting the structure of US nuclear deployment is incontrovertible.

Aircraft visits have had less of a political impact, but two controversies arose in regard to B-52s at Darwin, and Military Airlift Command flights to Christchurch. In response to Carter's post-Afghanistan call for help, Fraser announced in February 1980 that B-52 training and staging would be permitted at RAAF Darwin. Originally designed for high altitude bombing strikes, B-52s from Guam were switched to long-range ocean surveillance in the 1970s. Opponents of the plan called for assurances that the aircraft using Darwin would not be nuclear armed. The Fraser Government eventually released an official, unsigned note of 11 March 1981 which reiterated that operations were for sea surveillance in the Indian Ocean Area and for navigation training purposes only. Australia would have to agree before they could be used in support of 'any other category of operations'. From May 1981 operations occurred at a rate of one a month. Announcing an increase in flight frequency in 1982, the Australian DoD stated unequivocally that, as was the case with all the existing B–52 flights, 'the aircraft will be unarmed and will carry no bombs'.[57] The Hawke Government confirmed these visiting rights and the 'no bombs' declaration, but critics remain anxious that the US would get the restriction waived in an international crisis.

The significance of this B-52 agreement, however, is that it involved a breach of NCND. It was touted as a possible formula to overcome the USN's subsequent impasse with New Zealand.[58] But the USAF is more relaxed about the issue than the USN because nuclear weapons could be readily obtained from Diego, Korea or one of the Pacific bases.

Aircraft visits to New Zealand also became controversial, the more so, paradoxically, because flights were supposed to sustain the non-military United States Antarctic Program (colloquially known by its USN designation as Operation Deep Freeze). Although the Polar

Division of the US National Science Foundation (NSF) has budgetary and management authority, a Navy task group provides logistical and communications support on a reimbursible basis. The New Zealand–United States agreement of 1958 provided facilities for US Antarctic expeditions.[59]

However, the New Zealand MoD's explanation that the Harewood facility, adjacent to Christchurch civilian airport, is solely to support the Antarctic research programme stretches credibility. In reality its use by Navy, Marine, Army and USAF units has been much wider than that. The US Military Airlift Command began operating in 1962–3 to transport cargo for Deep Freeze and other US facilities in New Zealand. But of the 516 arrivals and departures from March 1986 to February 1987, 182 were neither directly nor solely to do with Antarctica. Twice a week, Starlifters and Galaxys were in transit between American Samoa, Honolulu or California, and Australia, mainly Richmond in NSW. As a director of the NSF commented, they were 'not in any way crucial to the efficiency of the [Antarctic] operation' and the small unit which serviced both those planes and the flights directly involved in Deep Freeze was 'of small consequence' and could be replaced by a commercial operation.[60]

As there are no special security precautions on the Harewood tarmac, aircraft are unlikely to be carrying anything more dangerous than intelligence material from Australia. The US Embassy Information Officer in Wellington allegedly breached NCND in his comment that 'If there was anything sinister about them, it would have come out years ago.'[61] Nevertheless, New Zealand has no jurisdiction over the base, and it was put on alert in October 1973 without the Government being informed. In official US documents it is treated as a military facility, requiring military security including the use of firepower in emergencies. It played an important role in the ANZUS *Triad* air exercise of October 1984, hosting an AWACs craft of the US Tactical Air Command. A presidential memorandum of 1976 noted that the DoD's logistical support for Deep Freeze 'gives the US an important flexibility and reach to operate in that area'.[62] In sum, the base may be dual purpose though 'scientific support' is the only publicly-acknowledged role.

BENEFITS AND DISTORTIONS

At the end of the Vietnam War, countries of the Pacific had taken a long, hard look at the operations of US bases. There were legitimate concerns about sovereignty and territorial jurisdiction.

However, by 1976, it was understood in the United States that modifications in the operation of bases in the region had restored the concept of mutual benefit, especially with regard to the critical North West Cape station and other C^3I capabilities offered by the allies.[63]

Quite apart from issues of extended nuclear deterrence, the defence establishments in Australia and New Zealand also emphasized the national benefits which accrued from the US military connection. Admittedly, no cost-benefit analysis can really measure the hidden and intangible gains of defence co-operation. In terms of strategy, however, the Anzacs had little or no say in the evolution of US thinking as it affected them. Nor did the working defence relationship necessarily accord with changing national strategic and political priorities.

In the first place, only after the middle of the 1970s did Australia and New Zealand take steps to extricate force structure planning from the constraints imposed by the need to act as adjuncts of American and British forces abroad. Secondly, US dominance of the intelligence domain and the possibility of distorted information has been the subject of concern. Since a memorandum signed by Eisenhower in 1953, information has been available to allies on a need to know basis and 'after determination that the furnishing of such information will result in a net advantage to the interests of the United States'. Consequently, according to Alan Renouf (former Head of Australian Foreign Affairs and Ambassador to the US) the flood of analysis 'inevitably tends to influence Australian policymakers towards the attitudes of the US'. Most of the information unpalatable to the US is withheld. New Zealand, the last stop down the line, was also vulnerable to pre-selection.[64] There seems little doubt that the US has been the main beneficiary from the communications and intelligence installations.

Moreover, Australian strategists in the post-Vietnam period maintained that Australian defence provision should not take immediate US support for granted and, whilst allowing for the necessary imports of sophisticated material, should minimize dependence on the US and also develop an independent intelligence gathering capability.[65] This did not, of course, signify to the Australians that there was anything wrong with the alliance as such, merely that distortions in defence posture had arisen. Beazley blamed Australian attitudes of subservience towards ANZUS 'which were essentially transferred from our previous approach to Empire defence'. Australia, he said, would overcome potential problems in regard to national sovereignty in the way the facilities were administered; they would serve approved purposes.[66]

But critics fear that Australia could still be involved in conflict without its consent. As a parliamentary committee noted, Australia had to allow for the 'possibility of institutionalized defence arrangements being altered imperceptibly by developments in military technology'.[67] There can be little doubt that the function of the facilities has changed over time in line with the US forward naval posture, warfighting concepts and the SDI programme. Andrew Mack suggests that any serious examination of functions would 'lead inevitably to the conclusion that they *are* part of a war-fighting system'.[68] In reality, as long as the US has jurisdiction over the multipurpose facilities, Australia has limited room to stand outside whatever strategy the US devises. Whatever Beazley might say about approved purposes and achieving ALP objectives through the ANZUS relationship, Australia is effectively hoist by its own Pine Gap.

Politicians across the Tasman sought rather more flexibility to specify the kind of strategic collaboration they wanted to be engaged in. They were assisted by New Zealand's far weaker nuclear connections and defence co-operation which sometimes relied on Australian representation. Attempts to improve the US military presence in New Zealand had been largely unsuccessful, one of the earliest abandoned plans being a 1959 proposal by military advisers at a SEATO meeting to site guided missiles in New Zealand and another a proposed Omega station.[69] Occasional visiting (about a fifth of the level received by Australia) was easier to challenge than permanent facilities. In fact, as the next chapter shows, warship visiting principles had been subject to unilateral change by the two host countries in the 1960s.

4 WARSHIP ACCESS AND THE ANZAC LIABILITY SUSPENSIONS

The ANZUS crisis was a political dispute over military co-operation and the next two chapters refer to principles which affect the particular form of co-operation and their specific application to Australia and New Zealand. Although the basing and visiting of aircraft caused controversy in relation to the staging of B-52s at Darwin and USAF shuttles to Christchurch, this discussion focusses on the rather more critical factors affecting warship access. In particular, as NCND is one of the conditions which nuclear navies insist upon when in foreign ports, the origins of and explanations for it will be considered here. Non-disclosure was to prove the stumbling block in New Zealand's bid to gain US and British acceptance that its ports and internal waters would be genuinely nuclear free.

The chapter then addresses the issue of port access for nuclear-propelled vessels which was disrupted in the 1960s and 1970s by problems over legal liability for accidents. The 'liability suspensions' operated by Australia and New Zealand had a lasting significance in the evolution of visit policy and the elaboration of ANZUS alliance requirements. Lifting the suspensions also added to the debate, discussed in chapter 5, about visit management and provision for dealing with nuclear hazards. To begin with, however, it is worth stressing that countries often restrict access by foreign warships to areas over which they can exercise control.

WARSHIP ACCESS

In spite of presumptive international law regarding freedom of the seas and the rights of innocent passage for warships in straits and territorial waters, states frequently operate restrictions. Canada, for example, has closed off the North-West Passage, and others impose conditions on transit through straits. France and the US have also declared danger zones on the high seas to facilitate nuclear tests in the Pacific. Ironically, New Zealand was among the countries which, at US insistence, conceded maritime rights to bring about a Law of the Sea which the US then refused to sign.

By contrast, the Soviet Union did adhere to UNCLOS, and in 1984 also produced a relatively liberal law which experts cite as something of a model for the theoretical construction of innocent passage and access. Passage is innocent if it is 'continuous and expeditious' and does not breach 'the peace, good order, or security of the USSR'. It allows for interruptions to movement as a consequence of insuperable force or distress, or to render assistance to others in distress.[1] Unfriendly actions, such as exercising or training with weapons, are prohibited. But there is still room for interpretation. In February 1988 provocatively 'innocent' passage by two US vessels in the Black Sea was described as 'dangerous manœuvring' by the Soviet Union, and it led to a diplomatic incident. For entry into ports and internal waters the Soviet Union follows the common practice of classifying visits into official and unofficial, requiring diplomatic clearance with a period of advance notice and limiting the number of warships and the length of sojourn. Basic information about vessel and crew is also a common requirement. Nevertheless, it is hardly possible to talk of an international régime for warship access to ports and internal waters.

Like the United Kingdom, Australia and New Zealand were content to establish procedures and naval protocol, comparable to Queen's Regulations and Admiralty Instructions, rather than enact legislation. They followed a liberal approach to access in furtherance of their traditional military relationships, though, as we have seen, New Zealand cavilled at American presumptions about post-war visiting arrangements. When there are no specific access provisions within an alliance or treaty framework, disagreement can arise as to whether the exclusion of certain vessels from internal waters represents a breach of obligations. In justifying its reprisals against New Zealand, the United States was to contend that New Zealand had violated 'a provision essential to the accomplishment of the object or purpose of the treaty'.[2] But the Lange Government claimed that it was merely exercising sovereign rights compatible not only with the Treaty but with accepted concepts of innocent passage in the territorial sea.

States commonly assert their sovereign right to restrict or exclude nuclear reactors, and there is no difficulty identifying nuclear-powered vessels. In the USN, for example, they are designated by the 'N' in their pennant numbers. As of 1988 some two dozen states have also had policies excluding nuclear weapons from territorial waters as well as territorial soil (see table 4.1). In addition, some interpretations

Table 4.1. *National prohibitions against nuclear weapons on soil and in territorial waters*

	Executive policy	Assembly resolution	Law	Bilateral agreement	Constitution
NATO					
Denmark	X	X			
Færoes		X			
Greenland		X			
Iceland[a]	X	X		X	
Norway	X				
Portugal	X				
Spain	X	X		X	
Other European					
Finland	X				
Malta	X				
Sweden	X				
Asia–Pacific etc.					
Belau[b]					X
China[c]	X				
Egypt	X				
Fed. States of Micronesia	X			X	
Fiji[d]	X				
India	X				
Japan[a]	X			X	
New Zealand			X		
Northern Marianas[e]	X			X	
Papua New Guinea	X				
Philippines[f]					X
Puerto Rico				X	
Seychelles	X				
Solomon Islands	X				
Sri Lanka	X				
Vanuatu		X			

Notes
[a] The US treaties with Japan and Iceland refer to major changes in equipment requiring prior consultation with the host government.
[b] Belau dropped its prohibition, and a referendum in September 1987 accepted the Compact of Free Association with the US which allows nuclear stationing. But in 1988 the change was declared unconstitutional and remains the subject of legal dispute.
[c] Prohibits foreign nuclear weapons.
[d] Fiji dropped its exclusion policy on 28 July 1983.
[e] A Northern Marianas prohibition of May 1985 exempted US nuclear materials related to foreign affairs and defence.
[f] The Philippines Constitution of 15 October 1986 has yet to be ratified.

Source: adapted from Alva M. Bowen and Ronald O'Rourke, 'Ports for the Fleet', *Proceedings/Naval Review*, vol. 112, May 1986, p. 149.

of the Treaty of Tlatelolco hold that nuclear weapons are banned from waters of the Latin American Nuclear-Free Zone. However, prohibitions on nuclear weapons have rarely been enforced, some have been abandoned, and many states listed in the table have received visits by nuclear-capable ships.

Non-aligned Sri Lanka (as Ceylon) may have been the first country to ban nuclear-armed ships and introduce an element of precision. Concerned about the intrusion of units of the US 7th fleet in the Indian Ocean, Prime Minister S. Bandaranaike announced on 23 January 1964 that:

> In pursuance of the policy of the Government of Ceylon to oppose the further spread of nuclear weapons and to support the creation of atom-free zones, my Government will, in future, deny entry into our seaports, airports and territorial waters of naval vessels and aircraft carrying nuclear weapons as well as those equipped for nuclear warfare.[3]

It is not clear how Sri Lanka enforced the policy, but in 1971 India followed with a ban which required specification that vessels were not carrying nuclear weapons. This was modified in 1972 to a request that host facilities would not be sought for such vessels. The US has not requested a visit since, and the issue was still under review in the 1980s.[4] In 1981 a left-wing government in the Seychelles also required prior assurance that foreign ships were not nuclear powered or armed. Both the Seychelles and Sri Lanka eased restrictions in 1983 after Reagan's roving ambassador, General Vernon Walters, made representations.[5] The exclusion policies of US allies are briefly surveyed in chapter 9 by way of comparison with New Zealand's prohibition.

NEITHER CONFIRM NOR DENY (NCND)

States which attempt to enforce the exclusion of nuclear weapons confront the problem that such weapons aboard vessels are not easily detected, and access to foreign warships is restricted by the rules of sovereignty. Nuclear navies keep outsiders guessing about the presence or absence of nuclear weapons on board ships, other than on purpose-built submarines for launching SLBMs.[6] In the United States, NCND applies to all services but is a particular analgesic of the USN and especially of its operations branches. Navy instructions state that 'it is the firm policy of the U.S. Government to neither confirm nor deny the presence of nuclear weapons or components on board any ship, station or aircraft'. When military authorities respond to enquiries 'such responses will not imply, speculate or otherwise disclose the presence or absence of nuclear warheads or other nuclear components'.[7]

The US armed forces claim that NCND originated in domestic security requirements, with a legal basis in the 1954 Atomic Energy Act as amended in 1958. An executive order of 13 January 1958, issued by the Assistant Secretary for International Security Affairs in the Department of Defense, amplified the Act and spelled out the policy.[8] Although the Act does not explicitly mention the location of nuclear material, the phrase 'restricted data' encompasses the 'utilization of atomic weapons'. The Joint Atomic Energy Committee (JAEC) and Department of Defense (DoD) can together decide to publish information on atomic weapons on condition that it is not transmitted to foreign governments – unless authorized by the President as being necessary to defence plans and training of personnel under the terms of an approved co-operation agreement. Such agreements have to involve security guarantees.[9] NCND is ultimately governed, then, by Presidential authority, though the President is obviously guided by advice from the DoD and National Security Council. At the time of the ANZUS crisis NCND was sustained by Executive Order 12356 on National Security Information, which superseded several orders dating back to Eisenhower. It states that non-disclosure of information on nuclear weapons' locations is justified if it 'reasonably could be expected to cause damage to the national security'.[10]

It is reasonable to speculate that the British NCND was not devised independently but replicates the US theology. The RN seems not to have encountered problems until 1983 when HMS *Invincible* tried to dock in Sydney. France appears not to have needed to devise an NCND formula until the Danish Folketing moved to tighten Denmark's access policy in 1988. But no doubt France would have adopted a non-disclosure stance in the unlikely event of New Zealand suspecting the presence of tactical nuclear weapons on the frigates and patrol vessels which visit New Zealand ports. Soviet comment has been oblique. When replying to inquiries about nuclear material aboard the Whiskey class submarine which grounded in Sweden in 1981, the Soviet Union said that it carried 'as do all other naval vessels at sea, the necessary weapons and ammunition'. This could be construed as meaning: 'if it is capable it does'.[11] However, apart from unscheduled calls, the Soviet vessels have less of a problem in that visits are generally confined to states where anti-nuclear sentiment hardly signifies.

The long-standing official explanation for its application to warships of the Western Alliance is that it contributes to deterrence by ensuring operational security. Soviet naval doctrine, argue US officials, put a premium on first use of nuclear weapons at sea, and 'it would be unreasonable for us to ease our adversaries' tracking and targeting problem by identifying which ships had greatest capability'.[12] NCND is thus presented as essential to keep adversaries guessing, a case underwritten by some scholars, who suggest that NCND decreases the temptation of the Soviet Union to use force.[13]

There is, of course, little tangible evidence for this, and the declared purpose of NCND rests on assertions which have the distinct advantage of being impossible to test adequately. Nor is there academic credibility in suggesting that some scholars might believe privately that NCND has little to do with security against adversaries. For alternative explanations, however, one can cite published testimonies about the historical purposes of NCND and consider the operational logic on its own terms.

Officials acknowledge that some US defence specialists consider that the reason for NCND was to cope with Japanese sensitivities and concerns expressed in Europe in 1958–64 when new missiles were being deployed.[14] This function was alleged when the validity of NCND was questioned in connection with the risks of stationing nuclear weapons abroad after Vietnam had been rapidly overrun. In 1975 the Joint Atomic Energy Committee indicated that refusal to reveal the number and location of nuclear weapons in the Pacific to protect Japan, Taiwan and Korea had been 'at the request of the nations where the weapons are deployed, since in most nations the existence of U.S. nuclear weapons within their borders is a difficult internal political issue'. The JAEC recognized a strong feeling in Congress that the Pacific deployments should be reviewed and reduced, and that the security classification was not in America's best interests.[15]

Morton Halperin (former Deputy Assistant of Defense for International Security Affairs), Senator Stuart Symington (Chairman of the Senate Subcommittee on Commitments), Admiral Gene La Rocque and Stanley Hoffman were among those who opposed forward deployment and non-disclosure. Halperin testified that the NCND was 'not, as is sometimes claimed, to keep the Russians or the Chinese guessing . . . Rather it is aimed at the publics in allied countries. Many governments are prepared to let the United States store nuclear weapons on their soil or to have ships with nuclear weapons call at their ports provided their people do not find out about it.' The deterrent effects of non-disclosure were uncertain, he added, because an adversary would not accept at face value a statement that weapons were deployed, or a denial. Further, this 'consorting with foreign governments to fool populations' inhibited discussion by the American public of US strategy, overseas deployments and foreign policy questions. As an example, Halperin cited controversy in the Administration about the removal of nuclear weapons from Okinawa, on its reversion to Japan, and the effect on US relations with China if they were transferred to Taiwan.[16] La Rocque and the 'peace admirals' in the Center for Defense Information have continued to argue that the policy was dictated by the need to avoid controversy in Japan and Western Europe, and that vessels do not habitually off-load nuclear weapons when entering ports.

In the 1980s NCND also played a role in confounding opposition to nuclear weapons in US ports. Democratic congressmen wrote to John Lehman arguing that the non-communicative policy conflicted with environmental requirements. Ronald Dellums, who conducted congressional hearings on homeporting in 1986 called it a 'bizarre and antiquated' policy, and considered that the population had a right to know if nuclear weapons were in their midst.[17] But the Navy had secured a ruling in the Court of Appeals, in *Weinberger v. Catholic Action of Hawaii* (1981), that it did not have to make public any environmental impact statements relating to construction of nuclear-capable facilities. The Court upheld the legal basis of NCND and ruled that consequently it could not be established whether the navy would put nuclear weapons in a particular nuclear-capable store. The USN's compliance with environmental laws was entirely beyond judicial oversight.[18]

Experts argue that the Soviet Union would experience targeting problems in maritime operations, and Donald Daniel has identified criteria which would make the early use of nuclear weapons at sea attractive to the Soviet Navy. In a purely conventional naval war the Soviet navy would be at a disadvantage, in protecting its own strategic nuclear and surface combatants from destruction, and in attempting to destroy the most feared elements of the enemy's forces. The relative efficiency of nuclear weapons, in producing shock waves and damaging US sonar systems, would offset Soviet disadvantages in conventional war. However, according to Daniel and others, Soviet naval planners would not be highly influential or decisive in the command structure, and Soviet leaders would not permit nuclear attacks at sea prior to nuclear strikes against land targets. Developments in Soviet military doctrine are biased in favour of prolonged conventional conflict in the belief that tactical nuclear attacks at sea would represent a precipice rather than a step.[19]

It would be logical, then, for Soviet forces to assume the worst and, in order to avoid nuclear escalation, attack non-nuclear surface vessels. In fact the USN has also claimed that NCND significantly complicates a potential enemy's tactical planning by 'forcing the enemy to treat all U.S. nuclear-capable platforms as if they were nuclear armed'.[20] In this case, the USN might consider openly declaring that even the non-nuclear-capable ships are nuclear armed. In a conflict likely to lead to the strategic level, NCND is premised on the idea that Soviet forces would target the most potent platforms. However, the major problem for the Soviet Union is not to assess which vessels are of high value but, as argued by Norman Friedman, to distinguish and target them within formations.[21] In determining high value targets, the Soviet Union no doubt considers that the US would not go to the expense of making vessels nuclear capable without carrying nuclear weapons as a matter of course. Publicly available information and Moscow's own intelligence is said to mean that 'if anyone knows which US ships are likely to be carrying nuclear weapons, it is the Soviets'.[22] The increased deployment of nuclear weapons at sea may also strain the credibility of the policy. The continued viability of non-disclosure in the light of dispersion, the New Zealand ban, arms control requirements and detection technology is discussed in chapter 9.

It is axiomatic that nuclear weaponry, which NCND protects, has more significant strategic implications than nuclear propulsion. Opposition to nuclear arms involves decisions about strategy and warfare; opposition to nuclear power entails judgements about technology and the environment. But, as suggested in chapter 1, the degree of overlap is considerable and both kinds of opposition have been dismissed as Luddite technophobia. In Australia and New Zealand, dispute about the carriage of nuclear weapons and NCND was initially encountered as a consequence of suspensions imposed on naval nuclear reactors.

THE LIABILITY SUSPENSIONS, 1964–1976

In the longer history of New Zealand ship visit policy several ironies stand out. Not only did the right-wing Holland Government express reservations about clearance for US Navy visits, but it was the Labour Government of Walter Nash which, in 1960, welcomed the first nuclear-powered visitor, the USS *Halibut*. Further, during the 1960s the National Government under Keith Holyoake, followed in 1971 by a conservative administration in Australia, stopped visits by nuclear-powered vessels in what might be termed the 'liability suspension'. This was not, as popularly believed, a ban instituted by the 1972–5 Labour Government in furtherance of its anti-nuclear stance,[23] though it had a significant impact on the evolution of anti-nuclear politics.

The issue arose in the 1960s because nuclear-powered vessels had become the subject of international dispute over accident indemnity. Within the United States provision had existed since 1957 for strict liability in regard to civilian reactors. The Price-Anderson Act set the maximum indemnity at $US560 million for payment of claims. Liability for civil reactors abroad was incorporated into the Atomic Energy Act of 1954, as extended to allow for operations of the nuclear-powered merchant ship *Savannah* which made its maiden voyage in 1962. Before the *Savannah* could put in at Southampton in 1964 the US and British Governments had to reach an agreement about liability for damage. Other ports, notably in Turkey and Japan, denied entry on liability grounds. Legal difficulties proved insuperable when the nuclear-powered German vessel the *Otto Hahn* sought a berth in the Port of London in 1971. The Japanese vessel *Mutsu*, built in 1972, had a disastrous career, being blockaded in August 1974 by some 300 fishing boats. It sprang a reactor leak and drifted in the Pacific for six weeks. The US 'atomic establishment' claimed that nuclear-powered civilian vessels had not proved commercially viable. In truth they could not trade like other ships because, as one editor remarked, 'they frighten the life out of people'.[24]

European states had drawn up international agreements, such as the 1960 Paris Convention on Third-Party Liability in the Field of Nuclear Energy, to deal with liability in regard to civil nuclear reactors. Belgium, India, Yugoslavia and other states had extended this in the 1962 Brussels Convention to absolute liability of operators of nuclear ships, including warships. It could not enter into force until a licensee state had signed. In 1975, West Germany indicated its willingness to sign the Brussels Convention to accept liability for the *Otto Hahn*.

The US State Department seemed to regard ratification of the Brussels Convention as the best means to ensure cover for American interests. But the JAEC and the DoD were adamant that warships should not be bound by international treaties. Rear Admiral Hyman Rickover (director of the USN nuclear propulsion program) argued: 'we simply cannot afford to subject what is now nearly a third of our major naval combatants to the dictates of international regulation under this convention . . . surely maintaining the sovereign status of these ships is more important to our national interests than solving the liability question for nuclear merchant ships.' He implied that the State Department's position, fostered by commercial interests, viewed ratification as the easiest solution to liability for merchant ships. Henry Kissinger at the State Department agreed that the Brussels Convention would certainly not be acceptable if it continued to include warships. 'It is my firm conviction that US nuclear-powered warship accident liability must be dealt with on a unilateral basis to protect the sovereignty of this most critical element of our national defense.'[25] Discussions with the British and West Germans took place in March 1975. The West Germans agreed not to sign the Brussels Convention but to incorporate its provisions into a national law, thereby avoiding the embarrassment of the Convention coming into force.[26]

Guided by Rickover, conversion of the USN to nuclear propulsion had proceeded in the face of congressional scepticism and economic restrictions. In the early 1970s, for example, delays occurred because of budget cuts, but Rickover insisted that there would be fuel and time savings. In addition, nuclear propulsion would increase the mobility of vessels and free them from the constraints of port calls. Rickover acknowledged that nuclear sea power might be second best, in strategic terms, to stationing forces overseas. Admiral Elmo Zumwalt, Chief of Naval Operations, actually used this as a selling point to a congressional committee. Nuclear power obviated reliance on overseas land bases.[27]

However, by 1981 Rickover considered that the benefits of longer range and time-saving were conditional on high crew morale. Because nuclear-powered vessels often operated in remote areas in difficult circumstances it was essential that the voluntary forces which manned the ships 'be allowed liberty in foreign ports where resupply and maintenance can also be performed'. Most operations were adequately supported by the availability of over 135 ports in more than 50 countries and dependencies. But the most troublesome area was the Indian Ocean where few countries accepted warships, and crews could be on station for up to eight months without a break. Securing port access, Rickover added, should be 'a matter of priority in our relations with friendly nations'.[28] Originally conceived as a programme which would reduce reliance on foreign facilities, conversion to nuclear power had aggravated the problem of port access for R & R.

By 1986 nuclear-powered vessels comprised about 40 per cent of the major combatants (about 70 per cent of the major combatants in the Pacific). In addition to the SSBNs, all but four of the attack submarines (due for retirement) were nuclear powered. Of the 14 aircraft carriers, the USS *Enterprise*, USS *Nimitz*, USS *Dwight D. Eisenhower* and USS

Carl Vinson were nuclear, plus three under construction (the USS *Theodore Roosevelt*, USS *Abraham Lincoln* and USS *George Washington*). Among the other ships, only nine cruisers were nuclear powered, the last funded in 1975. With Rickover's retirement in 1979 and the demise of the bid for an all-nuclear navy, only conventionally-powered cruisers are planned.[29] But the conversion process in the 1960s and 1970s had made port clearance for nuclear propulsion a pressing matter.

Hosts were demanding assurance of prompt compensation in the event of a nuclear reactor incident. Ambassador-at-Large Robert J. McCloskey indicated that he had been involved in negotiations with a number of foreign governments which had been reluctant to accept warships without liability assurances. And it had become a sticking point in renegotiating the Spanish Base Agreement. The Franco dictatorship had assisted the American authorities in coping with the aftermath of the Palomares incident of 1966, but insisted on guarantees for the future.[30] Governments around the world were impressed by a spate of accidents in the 1960s involving B-52 bombers and nuclear submarines. Although not necessarily caused by reactor failures, the USS *Thresher* had been lost off New England in 1963, the USS *Scorpion* off the Azores in 1968, and a Soviet submarine sank near Spain in 1970.

The safety aspect of visit management in the 1980s is dealt with in the next chapter, but states were alerted to hazards in the formative years of nuclear power. They gave liability as a reason for restricting port access. New Zealand and Australia were among them, and by the early 1970s there was hardly a port in the Pacific which would accept nuclear ships. Evidently, as early as 1965 the US Embassy in Canberra noted the Australian Government's extreme sensitivity to nuclear reactor safety and reluctance to accept visits. The US and British standard statements of assurance were not considered by Australia as sufficiently firm.[31] Apart from organizational designations the American and British statements are probably fairly similar (the latter is reproduced in appendix 5). The British statement promises that claims arising out of a nuclear incident will be dealt with through diplomatic channels in accordance with customary procedures for the settlement of international claims under generally accepted principles of law and equity.

In 1970 an interdepartmental committee on naval dockyard development in Australia recommended that Sydney be closed to nuclear-powered vessels because of collision risks and the large population surrounding the port. The following year the McMahon Government

71

requested Britain and the United States to refrain from proposing visits to Australia by nuclear-powered ships until environmental safety assessments had been made.[32] Until then, Australia had received 14 nuclear-powered visits. It seems, however, that the Holyoake Government in New Zealand had already suspended visits in the 1960s in view of the reluctance of insurance companies to accept risks. After the US carrier task group led by the USS *Enterprise* visited Wellington in 1964 there were no nuclear-powered visitors until 1976, and the Radiation Laboratory conducted no environmental monitoring between 1965 and 1977. The 1972 Labour Government of Norman Kirk thus inherited National's 'ban' on nuclear propulsion. It took the form of executive policy rather than a regulatory régime.[33]

Under the New Zealand Radiation Protection Act (1965) the Minister of Health's written consent was required before radioactive material could enter the country, but the Act did not come into force until detailed regulations were promulgated. The Labour Government laid down the detailed Radiation Protection Regulations in 1973 but they specifically exempted foreign warships from the legal provisions.[34] Thus the 'ban' continued as an executive suspension.

The Rowling Government, and the Whitlam Government in Australia, had additional reasons for persisting with restrictions into 1975. They were exploring a proposal for a nuclear weapons-free zone in the Pacific which broached the question of nuclear ship transit as well as nuclear tests by France. A delegation of American senators to the South Pacific certainly gained the impression that the Australian and New Zealand ship bans had been a way of highlighting objections to nuclear testing in what was regarded as a zone of peace.[35]

The United States responded to the nuclear power suspension with legislative and diplomatic activity. On the legislative front the United States was virtually forced by international concern to take action. US Public Law 93–513 was passed on 21 November 1974 and signed by President Ford on 6 December 1974. The need for such provision was made clear during hearings of the JAEC, which began in June 1972. Admiral Rickover and Admiral Elmo Zumwalt (Chief of Naval Operations) supported legislation, and Secretary for Defense James R. Schlesinger gave it his blessing. Described as 'long overdue, necessary and urgent', Public Law 93–513 was designed to recover access to foreign ports by the US Navy for 'efficient ship utilization and to provide a place for members of the crew to rest from their demanding duty'.[36] In view of the dénouement in Vietnam and the pending closure of bases in Thailand, the United States was doubly anxious to secure port visits.

The Law stated in part:

> That it is the policy of the United States that it will pay claims or judgments for bodily injury, death, or damage to or loss of real or personal injury, death or damage to or loss of real or personal property proven to have resulted from a nuclear incident involving the nuclear reactor of a United States warship: *Provided*, That the injury, death, damage, or loss was not caused by the act of an armed force engaged in combat or as a result of civil insurrection. The President may authorize, under such terms and conditions as he may direct, the payment of such claims or judgments from any contingency funds available to the Government or may certify such claims or judgments to the Congress for appropriation of the necessary funds.

Prospective claimants should note that Congress expressly avoided any dollar ceiling on the amount of liability, considering that this would act as a target. Nor, given an 'unparalleled safety record', did Congress establish special funds. It merely authorized the President to sanction the Secretary of the Navy to use existing contingency funds set aside in the DoD's budget. Congressional approval would be required to exceed the contingency money.

As critics indicated at the time, thyroid cases would not necessarily reveal themselves for thirty years and it would be necessary to prove that it had been radiation which caused injury. Doubts were expressed about whether psychological damage would be covered, who would do the medical monitoring and over what period, and by what means compensation would be assessed. Nor was it clear whether the DoD's contingency fund would suffice in the event of a major accident. Moreover, the Law had limited international value because it was a unilateral measure which could be repealed unilaterally.[37]

The British provision seems even less binding. In addition to the standard assurance presented when visit requests are made, it consists of a parliamentary written answer of 1976 which states that in the unlikely event of a reactor accident

> it would be our policy to pay compensation, subject to parliamentary approval of the necessary funds for personal property proved to have resulted from the accident. Certain exceptions would have to be made. For example, such compensation would not necessarily be paid for damage or injury arising in the course of any armed conflict or civil disturbance, nor would compensation be paid to a person, or his personal representatives or dependants, who intentionally caused the nuclear reactor accident which resulted in the damage for which compensation was sought.[38]

73

Neither the open-ended generosity of the British nor US Public Law 93–513 covered nuclear weapon accidents. In fact Schlesinger had requested amendments to the US Bill so as to underline the point that indemnity related to reactors only. Obviously this was a consequence of the policy of NCND, and provision was made to protect security information in the course of accident investigations. Nevertheless, in an exchange of notes attached to the Treaty of Friendship and Co-operation with Spain (1976), Ambassador McCloskey gave future unilateral assurances that the United States would endeavour to seek legislative authority to settle any further Spanish claims resulting from weapon incidents.[39]

The United States also had to make diplomatic exertions in the South Pacific because of the proposal for a nuclear-free zone. American representatives at the 1974 ANZUS Council meeting pointed out that the proposed SPNFZ could pose problems for transit, port visits and use of facilities for its increasingly nuclear-powered navy. In June 1975 the US laid down criteria for the acceptability of NFZs in an *aide-mémoire* to the Foreign Affairs Ministry in Canberra. Prior to the South Pacific Forum meeting the US also reiterated 'its objections to the nuclear-free zone proposal and its dissatisfaction that an Anzus ally should persist in a course which the US had declared harmful to its interests'. States were given an ultimatum – nuclear visiting or no security. Whitlam got cold feet and declined to co-sponsor the New Zealand–Fiji–Papua New Guinea nuclear-free zone resolution at the UN. He wrote to New Zealand Prime Minister Bill Rowling in October 1975 arguing that it 'could stir up controversy with the United States and raise questions about the ANZUS relationship'.[40]

Indeed the Americans put direct pressure on New Zealand to end its liability suspension, arguing that Public Law 93–513 had 'solved' the liability question and the 'ban' was inconsistent with ANZUS. Rowling revealed that the US had made representations and that as a consequence of the Public Law the Government would wish to review the situation. The Australian Defence Minister visited New Zealand to confer about restitution of nuclear-powered visits, and Rowling announced on 10 July 1975 that the Cabinet was re-examining its prohibition on nuclear-powered ships, though for the moment 'there are no plans for change'.[41] Doubts have been expressed about the determination of the Rowling Government to persist with the suspension, had it been re-elected in the November 1975 polls. Alerted to the possibility of backtracking, the Labour Party conference of May voted overwhelmingly for a prohibition on nuclear-armed as well as nuclear-powered vessels. Rowling left the platform smiling, and the Party's election manifesto made no reference to port visits but stated that the American alliance would be maintained.[42] Clearly, American pressure for a change in policy would have been difficult for a Labour Government to resist without general public support.

REINSTATEMENT

After the changes of government in Australia and New Zealand in November–December 1975, eight members of a subcommittee of the US House Armed Services Committee and four senators visited the South Pacific. On 14 January 1976 the congressmen had talks with Prime Minister Robert Muldoon, members of the Cabinet and officials. Muldoon left the talks to declare to waiting journalists that the ban on nuclear-powered ships was being lifted because the prohibition was inconsistent with New Zealand's obligations as a signatory to ANZUS. A few hours later the newly elected Fraser Government in Australia announced that it too was reviewing policy, having been told by the senators that the suspension was incompatible with ANZUS.[43] The CINCPAC, Admiral Noel Gayler, arrived in New Zealand in March 1976 to arrange visits by the nuclear-powered cruisers USS *Truxtun* and USS *Long Beach* for August and October, twelve years after the previous nuclear-powered visits to New Zealand and within a year of Muldoon's election triumph.

Reinstatement of nuclear-powered visits resulted from a coincidence of US pressure with the advent of right-wing governments in Canberra and Wellington. In a flush of euphoria, the Australian Deputy Secretary for Foreign Affairs advised the congressmen that the incoming Fraser Government would not merely support ANZUS, but further develop the alliance with the intention of using it as a vehicle for the solution of more 'global' problems, starting with power projection in the Indian Ocean. But as noted in chapter 2, in the post-Vietnam reappraisal of the strategic environment the Anzacs were slightly ambivalent about the US relationship. Fraser was content to say that lifting the suspension was required were Australia to remain an adequate and reliable ANZUS partner. Experts had assessed that the risks of mishap were low and hazards remote, and in any event Congress had accepted liability. In a pointed reference to US strategic indecision, Muldoon told the visiting congressmen that there was 'only one country in the world which will be in a position to exert positive leadership in the world for the next twenty-five years, and that is the United States. We believe that the alternative, if the United

States does not exhibit that leadership, will be world chaos.' The US delegation returned home under the impression that they had experienced a 'unique opportunity to literally be present at the rebirth of ANZUS'.[44]

Provision of accident cover had been a major preoccupation and Public Law 93–513 was a significant factor in lifting the suspension. In fact legal liability continued to give concern. New Zealand was anxious to secure assurances about indemnity for nuclear weapons. An approach to the US Ambassador in Wellington produced an *aide-mémoire*, dated 13 August 1976, similar to a settlement reached with Canada in 1968–9 covering liability for weapons as well as reactors. In the view of the New Zealand Ministry of Foreign Affairs this addition was 'as satisfactory as could be expected'. Australia took up the question, too, but was told that its Status of Forces Agreement (1963) with the US precluded it from qualifying.[45]

Both countries produced special regulations governing the entry to ports of nuclear-powered ships. The 1976 *New Zealand Code for Nuclear Powered Shipping* (AEC 500) included general precautions about movement and anchorages, and required Britain and the United States to certify that the operation of a ship would be in accordance with the standard statement of assurance. Air and sea monitoring continued to be undertaken by the National Radiation Laboratory. An interdepartmental committee, chaired by the Minister of Transport, met periodically to review berths in accordance with the code guidelines, and to consider requests from the Ministry of Foreign Affairs for warship visits. Diplomatic clearance was given to nuclear-powered vessels on a case by case basis, whereas conventionally-propelled ships had blanket annual clearance, though notification was still required.

The Australian regulations were tabled in the House of Representatives by Fraser on 4 June 1976, after the former Labor Government had established a DoD–Australian Atomic Energy Commission (AAEC) working party. An environmental impact statement remains classified, but the DoD–AAEC's public report, *Environmental Considerations of Visits of Nuclear Powered Warships to Australia* (May 1976), advised various safety measures. For security reasons Australian authorities would have no direct control over operating techniques or safety precautions carried out on board warships visiting Australian ports. Australian controls would be limited to approval of berths, conditions of entry and conditions outside the vessel. Berths would be approved by the AAEC, on the basis of criteria reviewed by the Ionizing Radiation Advisory Council and on recommendations of the Visiting Ships Panel (Nuclear) of the DoD. The Radiation Laboratory would conduct routine monitoring for radioactive discharge, in place of the *ad hoc* arrangement of the past. However, the guidelines relied heavily on the separate states to establish their own port safety schemes. In December 1982 the regulations were amended to allow Fremantle to host warships with reactors exceeding 100 megawatts in output, such as carriers of the Nimitz class.

Political principles, inherited and accepted by the Hawke Government, also date from 1976 and the lifting of the liability suspension. As amended in 1982 they state that:

(a) Visits will be for purposes such as crew rest and recreation and not for fuel handling or repair or reactor plant necessitating breach of reactor containment;

(b) Visits will be subject to satisfactory arrangements concerning liability and indemnity and to provision of adequate assurances relating to the operation and safety of the warships while they are in Australian waters;

(c) Movement of vessels must take place during daylight hours under conditions where visibility is not less than three quarters of a mile;

(d) Navigational controls on other shipping will be applied during the time that nuclear-powered ships are entering or leaving ports;

(e) There must be a capability to remove the vessel either under its own power or under tow to a designated safe anchorage or to a designated distance to sea within the time frame specified for the particular berth or anchorage and in any case within 24 hours, if an accident should occur; and

(f) An operating safety organisation competent to carry out a suitable radiation monitoring program and able to initiate actions and provide services necessary to safeguard the public in the event of a release of radioactivity following an accident must exist for the port being visited.[46]

However, these regulations and principles did not entirely restore public confidence and were not backed by safety schemes. Discussion about access, this time broadened to include nuclear weapons, was to be re-opened by a parliamentary inquiry in 1986.

REPERCUSSIONS

Indeed the suspension predicament had several lasting repercussions into the 1980s. First, the question of liability for reactor accidents became insuperably linked to the problem of carriage of nuclear weapons and thus to disquiet about the neither-confirm-nor-deny policy. In March 1975 Whitlam was asked to accept a visit to Fremantle by the nuclear-powered cruiser USS *Long Beach*. Whitlam parried by asking whether it would be loaded with nuclear weapons; if no assurance could be given it should stay away. The US Embassy replied with a neither-confirm-nor-deny pronouncement, arguing that 'cumulative denials could indirectly reveal location'. The New Zealand Labour Government had assumed that anything propelled by nuclear energy would be carrying nuclear weapons, but welcomed numerous conventionally-powered frigates and destroyers, some of which were nuclear capable.[47] Controversy had arisen in 1974, however, when Gene La Rocque testified before a US congressional committee that he had never known a conventionally-powered nuclear-capable vessel not to carry nuclear weapons. According to La Rocque: 'They do not off-load them when they go into foreign ports such as Japan or other countries. If they are capable of carrying them, they normally keep them aboard ship at all times except when the ship is in overhaul or in for major repair.'[48] This had caused unrest in Japan and was noted in New Zealand by Labour MPs who asked questions, unavailingly, as to whether particular vessels carried nuclear weapons.[49]

Second the suspension drew attention to nuclear escalation at sea. Both Anzac governments gave the trend to nuclear propulsion as a reason for reinstating visits. Critics also noted that since the first SSBN had put to sea in November 1960, the projected deployment of Trident missiles heralded a major escalation in the militarization of the Pacific. Refurbished Poseidon submarines were to be backfitted with Trident C4 and on station from October 1979. With their longer range it was unlikely that Trident submarines would travel back to Bangor, and critics feared that they would come to Australia and New Zealand if the US pressure to open up ports was successful. Subsequently, when the nuclear-powered submarine, USS *Queenfish*, arrived in 1984, peace activists suggested that it represented a softening up, preparatory to making facilities available for Trident submarines.[50]

Third, the issue gave renewed impetus to peace politics. The suspensions had been imposed by executive action without attracting public interest. Reinstatement, however, occurred at a time of profound disillusion with militarism as a result of the Vietnam experience. In Australia a small harbour protest greeted the first nuclear-powered submarine, the USS *Snook*, when it berthed at HMAS Stirling in Cockburn Sound in 1976. But Australian anti-nuclear opinion tended to focus on the uranium issue, whereas in New Zealand port protests directly challenged deployment of nuclear weaponry.

In 1975, in response to indications of American pressure for a resumption of nuclear-powered visits, the New Zealand Campaign for Nuclear Disarmament (CND), the Women's International League for Peace and Freedom and the UN Association petitioned Prime Minister Rowling for the 'ban' on nuclear-powered vessels to be extended to nuclear-capable ships and aircraft. In fact there is much evidence that the activists' distrust of the Labour leadership continued into the 1980s. An insistence on legislating a ban was designed to bind future governments of whatever complexion. After the anti-Vietnam war demonstrations, many protestors retired from political activism. Some, like the poet James K. Baxter, took to the bush as priests and commune gurus. But other divines, notably at St John's Theological College, Auckland, under the leadership of Revd George Armstrong, announced the formation of a small boat squadron to undertake symbolic blockades. As the historian of the Auckland peace squadron has noted, the ship issue slowly aroused a strong territorial sense among New Zealanders.[51] Muldoon played into their hands by inviting or accepting visit requests beyond a critical level. By the end of 1982 the hitherto fragmented peace groups began to develop greater co-ordination, and with a neighbourhood nuclear-free zone movement also gathering momentum, anti-nuclearism was poised to influence the middle ground.

Fourth, the liability suspension emphasized the contrast between the Australian and New Zealand political contexts. In Australia the Whitlam Labor Government felt constrained to bow to US pressure on the SPNFZ. If Washington insisted on unfettered ship visits as the *sine qua non* of ANZUS security, domestic opinion would not encourage continued or new restrictions on visiting. Like the ALP the NZLP also entered the wilderness in 1975. But in New Zealand the suspension had sown the seeds for strengthening legislative control rather than relying on an executive suspension.

When nuclear-powered visits resumed in August 1976, the Auckland Labour MP Richard Prebble, not one of the more dedicated anti-nuclearists, introduced a Nuclear Free Zone (New Zealand) Bill. Labour was reeling from the onslaught of Muldoon's authoritarian domestic policies. Given the undoubted popularity of action against

French nuclear testing, it seemed a promising political tactic to endorse the UN resolution for an SPNFZ and to prohibit nuclear-powered ships and nuclear weapons from entering New Zealand. The Bill made no mention of verification of nuclear-armed vessels and it was not raised in the debate. Prebble noted that Muldoon had lifted the suspension without consulting Parliament or his colleagues; others accused Muldoon of being a lackey of Washington. The Government responded that although the visits were only for good-will a ban was incompatible with ANZUS, and to prevent the issue being given an airing, the Government broke with custom by voting against the first reading of a private member's Bill.[52] By the 1978 election a ban on visits was part of Labour's manifesto, and although Prebble did not attempt another Bill until 1982, the legislative approach and renegotiation of ANZUS had gained respectability in the Party.

Fifth, the suspension of nuclear-propelled vessels had highlighted the security dilemma. What had begun as governmental concern about insurance liability became a question of obligations and a test of alliance loyalty. An editorial in the *Auckland Star* (15 April 1975) argued that the situation would have to be resolved: 'On the one hand stands our advocacy of a nuclear-free zone in the South Pacific and support for those seeking the same goal in the Indian Ocean. On the other there is the security we enjoy under the Anzus umbrella in return for obligations freely entered into.' Persuaded by the United States, the Muldoon Government contended that a restrictive visit policy would be incompatible with the ANZUS Treaty. The National Party argued that Labour 'must now say whether it wishes New Zealand to remain in the ANZUS treaty alliance'.[53] Nuclear visiting gave an impetus to views that the security relationship would need revision or aban-donment. CND, which had advocated a non-aligned foreign policy since 1963, was now in little doubt that New Zealand 'should get out of SEATO and ANZUS and proceed to develop a truly non-aligned stance, avoiding particularly the military systems of the Superpowers and other nuclear powers. We cannot do this if we allow ourselves to be used for the US's naval nuclear weapons systems.'[54]

Finally, the issue heightened environmental anxieties and drew attention to the possibility, however remote, of accidents involving radiated materials. There was concern not only about the adequacy of the US liability but also about the regulations and practices for admitting nuclear visitors to urban ports. Serious questions continued to be posed about the methodology of the accident model used by governments, and about risk calculations.

In the 1980s, environmental issues featured strongly in challenges to the rules governing port visits which had been established by 1976. As in the evolution of access policy, domestic demands for safeguarding national interests would have to be finely balanced against new external pressures on alliance co-operation.

5 NUCLEAR HAZARDS AND ENVIRONMENTAL SAFETY: ISSUES OF THE 1980s

Whereas the liability suspensions had been largely a matter of concern to bureaucrats, naval officers and insurance brokers, the reinstatement of nuclear-powered visits to Australia and New Zealand in 1976 activated a wider interest in naval visiting. Although the assurance of legal indemnity satisfied governments, it did little to calm public fears of reactor or weapon accidents in ports. Indeed the development of the US Navy's nuclear reactor programme, together with the dispersion of nuclear missiles, fostered concern among environmentalists as well as traditional nuclear disarmers. The risk of mishap had allegedly increased.

The current deployment of nuclear missiles in the USN was discussed in chapter 1. It should be recalled that over 80 per cent of the major combatants were categorized as nuclear capable. For convenience table 5.1 provides a summary of nuclear-powered, as well as nuclear-capable, vessels.

This chapter therefore examines controversies which affected the management of visits. Under pressure from port authorities, environmentalists and anti-nuclear groups, politicians and officials on both sides of the Tasman reconsidered the safety assessments which had underpinned the procedures and principles of 1976. The New Zealand Select Committee on Disarmament and Arms Control received submissions on the issue in 1983 and the Atomic Energy Committee began a review of its code in 1984. In Australia, serious practical issues of managing ship visits became apparent, and at the end of 1986 an Australian Senate committee commenced deliberations on accident contingencies and safety regulations. In fact, challenges to the status quo at official levels had occurred in Australia well before the Lange Government stopped nuclear visiting to New Zealand. The Victorian ban of 1982 and the HMS *Invincible* incident of 1983 are thus considered at the start of this chapter, followed by a discussion of environmentalism and the accident issues which have affected the management of nuclear visiting.

Table 5.1. *USN nuclear-powered and weapon-capable warships,*
1 April 1986

	total	nuclear-powered	nuclear-weapon-capable
Submarines			
ballistic missile	38	38 (100%)	38 (100%)
attack	101	97 (96%)	85 (84%)
Major surface combatants			
aircraft carriers	14	4 (29%)	14 (100%)
battleships	2	0 (0%)	2 (100%)
cruisers	31	9 (29%)	31 (100%)
destroyers	68	0 (0%)	68 (100%)
frigates	112	0 (0%)	65 (58%)
Total	366	148 (40%)	303 (83%)
Storage vessels			
SSBN supports	6	0 (0%)	6 (100%)
amphibious landing craft	62	0 (0%)	? ?
replenishment tenders	70	0 (0%)	? ?

Source: adapted from Ronald O'Rourke, 'Nuclear-Powered and
Nuclear-Weapons-Capable Ships In The U.S. Navy: An Aid To
Identification', Congressional Research Service, Library of Congress, Report
No. 86–659F, 1986, Washington, DC, p. 2.

VICTORIA'S BAN AND THE HMS *INVINCIBLE* AFFAIR

The first high-level challenges to nuclear visiting arose in
Australia when the federal authorities had to contend with state
governments which attempted to prevent visits or expressed disquiet
about the safeguards designed in Canberra. Premier Neville Wran had
stopped nuclear ships from calling at NSW for seven years without
telling anyone; so had Premier Don Dunstan of South Australia
though it had apparently made little difference. More seriously,
shortly before the Canberra ANZUS Council meeting of June 1982,
John Cain, whose position as Premier of Victoria owed something to
left-wing ALP support, announced that his government would not
permit nuclear-powered and armed warships in Victoria's harbours.
The ban would apply without qualification and was in line with
Victorian ALP policy since 1979. Cain implemented the decision by
letter to the Victorian port authorities. He also alerted the Americans,
and wrote to Prime Minister Fraser on 27 May 1982 as follows:

I look forward to your co-operation in assisting us in the maintenance of compliance with this policy. It would be appreciated if your Government could advise relevant foreign Governments, as appropriate, of my Government's policy in order to avoid misunderstanding. In each case of a proposed visit to Victoria by a naval vessel of a country controlling tactical nuclear weapons, it would also be appreciated if you could obtain from the relevant foreign government an assurance that no nuclear weapons are carried.

Fraser reminded Cain that the Commonwealth had ultimate power and responsibility for the entry of warships to Australian ports, though he recognized 'the importance of co-operation and harmony with the State Government concerned'.[1] Cain's effrontery also determined Fraser to encourage the US Deputy Secretary of State, Walter J. Stoessel, to accept the lengthy reference to ship visits in the ANZUS Council communiqué of 22 June. In addition, the US State Department remarked: 'Quite apart from the present dispute, it should be clear that access to allied ports and airfields for US ships and aircraft is critical to our efforts to maintain a strategic deterrence.' Washington officials issued a warning which was to become the standard response to New Zealand's bid to exclude vessels: 'It would be difficult, if not impossible for the US to carry out its responsibilities to assist effectively in the defence of its allies if it is denied the use of their ports.'[2]

Cain backed down on 17 June, after receiving an opinion from the Solicitor-General. Victoria's nuclear-free legislation would be confined to the civilian nuclear fuel cycle. But if the central government rode roughshod over the express wishes of the State, it should indicate its acceptance of responsibility for safeguarding the welfare of the people of Victoria. Fraser responded on 18 August by introducing the Defence (Visiting Warships) Bill to eliminate any uncertainty about the Commonwealth's exclusive authority. The Bill sought to formalize the provisions for authorizing visits and establish legal offences for obstruction. The federal regulations would be amended to specify that 'an operational safety organisation . . . must exist for every port being visited'. The Labor opposition ridiculed the Bill on the grounds that powers already existed under defence prerogatives in the constitution, and the legislation lapsed with Labor's victory in the 1983 federal election. For electoral reasons the federal ALP had backed away from opposing nuclear visits. Nevertheless, Victorian activists asserted that the federal powers should be challenged in court. They also demonstrated against visits to Port Phillip which resumed after a two year break. When the USS *Rathburne* arrived in June 1986, a serious fracas drew complaints of police brutality and condemnation of the Cain Cabinet for enforcing a policy which it had been elected to oppose.[3]

The second specific challenge to the status quo in Australia came towards the end of 1983 when the existing rules were unexpectedly put to the test by the RN's requirement to dry dock the light aircraft carrier, HMS *Invincible*, for propeller shaft repairs. Australia had made a clear and apparently rigid distinction between accepting berthed vessels with nuclear weapons on board and prohibiting nuclear weapons on Australian soil. But did a dry dock constitute Australian soil, and if the vessel carried nuclear weapons would dry docking contravene Australia's non-nuclear policy? The forensic niceties sorely tried the Hawke Government.

Initially, however, the RN task force comprising the carrier, two frigates and three auxiliaries, had arranged to call at New Zealand ports in November–December 1983, the first RN visit to New Zealand since 1979. It was part of a post-Falklands voyage with the declared purpose of demonstrating 'Britain's readiness to deploy naval forces worldwide'. The British High Commission in Wellington downplayed another objective, arms sales, and emphasized instead that the visit was in appreciation of the Muldoon Government's substitution of a New Zealand frigate for a British vessel in the Indian Ocean during the Falklands War. None of this mollified protestors who described the global voyage as a 'bizarre twitch' of the imperialist spirit. They noted Britain's decision to acquire 'first strike' Trident weapons and argued that the HMS *Invincible* would be carrying depth-charges as standard equipment.[4] New Zealand activists were keen to show that their anti-nuclearism was not just directed against the United States.

When the carrier was found to require dry docking it cut short its New Zealand stay and proceeded to Australia. There, the Navy Department made arrangements and set aside expenses for work at Garden Island, Sydney, during 19–22 December. Meanwhile the Australian Defence Minister, Percy Scholes, looked up the rules and advised Britain of Australia's long-standing policy against nuclear weapons on Australian soil. Regulations also stated that warships using dry docks in Australia had to disarm (because welding and cutting equipment increased the risk of fire or detonation). This could be waived in cases where it would be hazardous to move the ammunition; disassembly of triggering devices would be an alternative. The Australian DoD recognized that public perceptions of the relative safety of ammunition had to be considered as well as 'the possibility that industrial relations questions could arise if there were doubts about the risks entailed in having ammunition and other explosives on a ship being worked upon in dry dock'.[5]

The British presumably indicated that the status of the vessel's weaponry could not be revealed. Scholes explained that the ship could not be de-ammunitioned. A Sydney shop steward was quoted as saying that he understood the work was off because the vessel carried nuclear weapons. But the suspicion of conservative Australian politicians and the British MoD that the Hawke Government was held to ransom by trade unions offers an incomplete picture. The main problem lay with NCND policy and a literal interpretation of the regulations concerning the dry docking of warships. Perhaps a form of words could have been found to protect NCND. Nor is it clear why the RN did not utilize the task force supply ship for unloading ammunition.[6]

In the face of mounting right-wing criticism, the Attorney-General, Gareth Evans, identified the bipartisan strands in Australian policy as:

- no nuclear weapons on Australian soil, a policy consistent with the former Government's caveat on the stationing of USAF B-52s at Darwin;
- nuclear-powered vessels were allowed, subject to the 'stringent conditions' laid down in 1976;
- Australia did not ask foreign visitors to confirm or deny the presence of nuclear weapons on vessels or aircraft, again a bipartisan policy;
- conventionally armed ships had to de-ammunition before dry docking, subject to waiver or exemption (depending on the circumstances of the particular case);
- there was no established policy with regard to dry docking vessels which may or may not be armed with nuclear weapons;
- Australia would not in any way endanger the safety of the ship or crew by refusing to accommodate genuine needs which arose.[7]

Evans acknowledged the uncertainty about how the rules would apply in particular emergency cases. Indeed the NCND bind meant that the rules for nuclear weapon access affected all nuclear-capable vessels. In logic there could be no universal principle, worthy of the name, compatible with the three requirements of nuclear-free Australian soil, de-ammunitioning for dry docking and non-disclosure by the visitor.

The affair led to frantic diplomatic activity. Foreign Minister Hayden used a special telephone facility to contact the US Secretary of State George Shultz in Lisbon. Shultz reportedly told him to play down the controversy and 'nip in the bud' any misunderstanding generated in the public mind. A Cabinet meeting on 14 December identified the need to consult the allies about dry docking, and within hours Scholes held discussions with the American and British defence chiefs, Caspar Weinberger and Michael Heseltine. For the present, the Australians announced that 'for operational reasons' HMS *Invincible* did not require the docking facilities. There was no reason to believe that the Captain of the hapless ship had any doubts about the effectiveness or timeliness of any work which might have been performed.[8] This explanation seems perilously thin in view of the fact that the Captain then sought facilities in Singapore. It is a moot point what would have happened had the vessel been unable to proceed, given the opposition to emergency servicing subsequently declared by the left-wing trade union leader John Halfpenny.[9]

Eventually the Hawke Government avoided commitment to any course of action. The Australian DoD issued a statement on 26 February 1984, after consultation with British and US officials, which agreed that in future each request for dry docking would be 'considered on its own merits taking into account technical and safety factors and the strategic and operational circumstances obtaining at the time'. Both nuclear states also indicated their awareness of Australian concerns with respect to storage of nuclear weapons on Australian territory. Australia accepted the reasons for NCND but emphasized that Australian interests in safety were paramount.[10] However, this left open the probability that if an Australian Government could cope with adverse public reaction, nuclear-armed ships would be docked in emergencies. New Zealand's stance in 1984 would be less ambiguous – no weapons in ports or harbours.

Australia's position derived from an emphasis on technical safety factors. Although the dry dock issue was initially treated as a political defence of Australian policy on nuclear weapon access, as soon as the implications of NCND became apparent it was dealt with as a technical matter which could be resolved without disruption to strategic and alliance priorities. By contrast the evolving political attitudes in New Zealand would not be nipped in the bud by attending to regulations, for the anti-nuclearism there had more to do with disengagement from nuclear strategy. The HMS *Invincible* affair was significant, then, for three reasons. It was the first time that the problem of dry docking a nuclear-capable ship had arisen, obliging the Australian government to re-examine the application of the rules of access, and adding weight to the environmental concerns of state governments and opposition Labor spokesmen. A public inquiry into the hazards of nuclear visiting would be an astute approach to managing the political disquiet. Second, the incident appears to have been the first time that the RN confronted a challenge on the carriage of nuclear weapons and NCND. Third, the United States was moved to make a weighty political intervention during the affair to protect NCND and to reaffirm the linkage between ship access and ANZUS security obligations.

ENVIRONMENTALISM

A more general challenge to the existing régimes in Australia and New Zealand derived from environmentalism, which had made a significant political impact in the space of a decade. In 1974, for example, a campaign against nuclear power stations in New Zealand proved highly popular, though the decision not to build any was primarily influenced by power-demand projections. In the 1970s, the environment-conscious New Zealand Values Party attracted protest votes in elections, and although it failed to win any seats its 'green' platform was absorbed, albeit diluted, into the body politic. Petra Kelly of the West German Green Party struck a responsive chord on her Antipodean tour in 1984. Her New Zealand audiences needed little convincing that they had stewardship of a fertile garden, 'one of the most beautiful, unspoiled countries on earth', which should be kept that way by opting out of the West's economic strictures and militarism. As one observer put it: 'We are sensitive to any relationship or contact with foreign powers that may prove a danger to this natural heritage.' Opinion polls testify to high levels of support for maritime ecology issues.[11]

Australia, too, has its share of new Arcadians, and it seems likely that dissenting politics will take a stronger green direction than an anti-deterrence one. Labor politicians had cited world-wide concern about the nuclear cycle, and argued that European migrants viewed Australia as a sanctuary from nuclearism. As leader of the Opposition in Canberra, Whitlam had accepted the reinstatement of nuclear-powered visits in 1976, but voiced concern about the environmental question and the need for consultation with the governments of NSW and WA. Victoria's Nuclear Activities (Prohibitions) Act of June 1983 declared a need 'to protect the health, welfare and safety of the people of Victoria and to limit deterioration of the environment in which they dwell by prohibiting the establishment of nuclear activities and by regulating the possession of certain nuclear materials'.[12] Regularly conducted polls suggest that support for hosting nuclear-powered ships declined from 74 per cent in 1976 to 46 per cent in 1985, while over the same period opposition grew from 20 per cent to 44 per cent (see appendix 6). The Three Mile Island disaster of 1979 concentrated the minds of environmentalists as well as reactor engineers.

However, in seeking a compromise between helping allies and the paramount issue of the safety of Australian cities, the key objective for some critics was not to deny visits but to relocate them. They argued that Australia should be rigorous in exercising its sovereignty and not bow to alleged US pressure for big city attractions, especially as the USN did not subject its own populations in New York and Boston to nuclear-powered vessels.[13] According to US officials, however, no berth is used in a foreign port that would not be used in the US for the same purpose and type of ship. The criteria used by the USN in assessing port acceptability includes the size and manœuvrability of ships, not their mode of propulsion.[14] Nevertheless, in the United States the number of federal environmental laws had increased from three in 1965 to twenty-four by 1984, and environmental objections were raised by opponents of the USN's strategic homeporting plan for dispersing battleship task groups.

Reaching an independent assessment about accident risks is fraught with difficulty due to the paucity of reliable information about past accidents and about technical details of reactor and warhead design. In the case of zero-infinity risks, in which the contingency is remote but the payment of claims potentially ruinous, there is plenty of leeway for defence establishments and anti-nuclear lobbies to take up polar positions. Although it may be in the interests of one side to minimize and the other side to maximize the risks, both visitors and visited have a common interest in accident avoidance. Naval authorities have political and strategic grounds for wishing to avoid accidents which could result in being denied port and harbour facilities world-wide. Rickover had been extremely meticulous about quality control. But the nightmare of a reactor accident led him to fret that it could wreck the entire nuclear propulsion plan. Apparently he tried, unsuccessfully, to ban visits to heavily populated areas.[15] In regard to warheads, US Pacific and European Command instructions warn of the disastrous consequences of accidental or unauthorized detonation, including an 'adverse effect on overall nuclear posture and operational flexibility'.[16]

Anti-nuclearists, however, also focussed on environmental safety to direct public attention towards political and military relationships. Submissions to the Australian and New Zealand parliamentary inquiries were part of a consciousness-raising exercise, not so much because they wanted visits to be made safe but because they wanted them to cease. As the Australian Senator for Nuclear Disarmament, Jo Vallentine, argued: 'Nothing short of a ban on nuclear warship visits can ensure the protection of the people and the environment.'[17] In offering constructive suggestions for managing visits, groups such as the Australian People for Nuclear Disarmament (PND) perhaps anticipated that confronted with publicity and civil defence exercises, the general public would turn against visits altogether. The Auckland Regional Authority had issued a hazard warning in advance of a visit by the US submarine *Haddo* in January 1979, which can only have heightened public concern. At a minimum PND sought to redress the balance of interests which governed the entry of warships. Of course one cannot deny that anti-nuclear groups have genuine worries about the accidental release of radioactive materials. In fact they consider that the danger of a nuclear weapon accident is more immediate than that of a nuclear war.[18]

On the other hand, it must also be noted that the Australian parliamentary inquiry of 1986 was not empowered to consider the desirability of visits. Its terms of reference were limited to examining the 'adequacy of current contingency planning by Federal and State authorities to deal with the accidental release of radiation from visiting nuclear powered or armed vessels in Australian waters and ports'. Committee members thus deliberated on the premise that the hazards to be revealed in submissions would not be so great as to warrant a visit ban, though safety regulations and berth assessments might require amendment. In a highly 'political' submission the DoD noted that the Hawke Government considered the risks acceptable given the safety factors and existing arrangements. As critics commented, the authors of these arrangements, notably the DoD, could be said to have vested interests. Further, in the absence of indigenous expertise, Australian and New Zealand authorities were perforce obliged to rely on the word of overseas agencies: the United States Nuclear Regulatory Commission (NRC) and the UK's Atomic Energy Authority and Nuclear Powered Warships Safety Committee.[19]

Even so, committee members were keen to allay public anxiety on this score and requested independent authority for foreign assertions about safety. Senator David Hamer, a vigorous supporter of nuclear visiting, for example, was not satisfied with mere reliance on assurances by other countries. 'We ourselves', he said, 'will be trying to point out to our allies the significance for them of us getting this right. They cannot say that it is reasonably safe and we should just take their word for it ... if they are asking us to have a hundred megatons of nuclear weapons in our ports, we have to satisfy ourselves that there is no way that they will go off.'[20]

NUCLEAR REACTOR RISKS

With regard to nuclear reactors, government authorities had to respond to public concern about the methodology of risk calculation and the adequacy of safety precautions for three main types of hazard: radioactive waste disposal and coolant discharge in harbours; possible release of radioactive material from core cooling system failure or a power excursion accident; possible rupture of a containment vessel caused by external damage.

These matters had generated serious concern in the United States in the early 1970s, and questions had been raised in Congress about reactor integrity. Scientists testified in 1973 that experiments on pressure vessel failure had resulted in designs to withstand high levels of stress. A safety margin was added. This was based on probabilistic data which underpinned the 1975 Rasmussen Report and the NRC's methodology for risk analysis. Pressure vessel failure was considered to be an incredible event.[21] The US Navy's Nuclear Power Directorate also reported that in the period 1971–3 annual radioactivity discharged within twelve miles of shores from all nuclear-powered ships and their support facilities was less than 0.002 radioactivity-curies (excluding tritium, which is present in the environment). The total amount released each year, mostly at sea, from all US ships, tenders and shipyards was said to be less than 200 curies. Any accidental discharges of primary coolant had been quite drinkable. An official statement provided by the US to its allies said that USN reactors in service as of 1985 had accumulated over 2,700 reactor years of safe operation.[22]

The Australian authorities were informed by the nuclear allies that naval reactors are inherently self-regulating, and that runaway power excursions are virtually impossible. Multiple safety features were imperative because of combat risks, and naval reactors were built to withstand rapid transients of temperature and to cope with pressures which occur in manœuvring. Naval reactors were said to be subjected to more stringent quality assurance programmes than civilian reactors. Design standards were rigorous and drew upon the unmatched expertise of establishments such as the US Naval Materials Research Laboratories, Washington. Moreover, naval reactors are about a twentieth the size of large commercial plants, have a lower level of power output, and their control rod withdrawal rates are slower. In regard to operational safety, sea-based reactors ease off power about two miles offshore, operate at a fraction of capacity when in port and can be moved away from centres of population. In Australian ports, as elsewhere, extensive maintenance or fuel handling is not permitted and a procedure to dry dock would involve the shutdown of reactors. The Australian Atomic Energy Commission (AAEC) acknowledged, however, that it did not have sufficient details of operational procedures to take human errors into account, or the means of corroborating USN accident data.[23]

Critics have argued that with a world total of 376 marine reactors controlled by military authorities, without independent or international oversight, an immaculate operational record stretches the bounds of credulity. So does the US claim that the only accidents have been in the Soviet Navy (which had 135 nuclear-powered vessels in 1983).[24] The Royal Navy is said to have had various incidents in 16 years of reactor operation, including a confirmed minor failure in the electrical system on board HMS *Resolution* whilst docked in Scotland in January 1988.[25]

David Kaplan of the Center for Investigative Reporting in San Francisco maintains that the USN has sanitized, for public consumption, its own accident record. He noted some 37 marine power plant incidents since the 1950s, involving fires, floods, groundings, crashes, and breakdowns. Kaplan acknowledged that the causes of the loss of the US submarines, *Thresher* and *Scorpion*, could not be known for certain, but he cited naval authorities who believed that the disasters occurred as a result of emergency reactor shutdowns. More common were accidental discharges of reactor coolant in coastal waters. These included 25 incidents in Puget Sound, an increase in cobalt-60 radiation levels in mudflats near Holy Loch, Scotland, in 1965, and a discharge in Guam from the disabled submarine tender USS *Proteus* in 1975. Routine dumping at sea of solid radioactive waste had occurred, some of it blowing back on to the vessels. Although the USN no longer dumps at sea and is aware of the need to develop a publicly acceptable disposal programme, there is obviously a difficulty in disposing of decommissioned reactors. The problem is a general one which confronts the British MoD anew as it replaces Polaris submarines.[26] In addition to these, the AAEC listed various collisions – a tug causing superficial damage to a ballast tank on the USS *Thresher* in 1962; the submerged USS *Nautilus* colliding with the US carrier *Essex* in 1966, damaging the submarine's sail; and HMS *Renown* sustaining a damaged periscope from an encounter with a freighter in 1969.[27]

Kaplan's allegations were partially rebutted by Vincent C. Thomas, in *Sea Power*, September 1983. Thomas argued that the nuclear-propulsion programme had exceeded all expectations; there had been no loss of life directly resulting from an accident involving a reactor. An explosion in the US submarine *Triton* in October 1959, killing a man, resulted from a faulty air flask which had nothing to do with the reactor operation. Kaplan's 'collisions', argued Thomas, included tangling with whales and bumping the seabed. After the loss of the US submarines *Thresher* and *Scorpion*, Navy officials found no radioactivity consistent with a reactor accident. Bombs which exploded on the USS *Enterprise* flight deck in 1969 blasted down three decks, but did no damage to the reactor plants. The jamming of a mechanism when a spent cell was being lowered from the US submarine *Sand Lance* at Puget Sound in September 1979 could not be described as a reactor related incident. None of the leakages at Puget Sound would have required reporting to the NRC. Although in May 1968 Japanese scientists at Sasebo had found radiation levels up to 20 times higher than normal, allegedly spilled by the USS *Swordfish*, American checks failed to confirm this. Rickover implied that the Japanese scientists responsible for evaluating samples had falsified records.[28]

In the 1970s Australia and New Zealand had relied heavily on US data and had standardized their assessments on the 'reference accident' model. A reference accident was defined as a failure of the reactor primary coolant circuit, resulting in meltdown and the release of gaseous and volatile fission products to the reactor containment, followed by slow leakage to the environment. The AAEC considered that such a contained accident represented 'an upper limit of risk in terms of its probability and consequence'. A worse scenario would require coincidental high speed collision with partial containment loss, leading to rupture of the containment vessel and contamination of the sea. In accord with British estimates for their own nuclear-propelled vessels, the AAEC considered that a release of 50 per cent of iodine-131 into the atmosphere over twelve hours would then be feasible.[29]

Using US calculations, the Australian and New Zealand authorities put the probability of a reference accident at no greater than 1 in 10,000 per reactor per year; and for uncontained accidents no greater than 1 in 10 million. The odds against an accident in Australia or New Zealand were improved by the short duration of visits, on average four to five days. In the event of a reference accident, allowing for dockyard evacuation within two hours, the number of additional cancer deaths in the ensuing 30 years was estimated at generally less than five and certainly no greater than ten. Nevertheless the authorities appreciated that it would be prudent to make safety arrangements.[30]

Environmentalists challenged the conventional methodology on the grounds that the reference accident contingency had been exceeded at the Fermi research reactor in the United States in 1965. Also, an event with a calculated probability of 1 per 1,000,000 reactor years was said to have occurred twice within the space of a week at Salem in the United States.[31] Certainly, risk analyses for land-based reactors have become more pessimistic since the 1970s. Rasmussen had put the risk of a core meltdown at once per 20,000 reactor years. But in 1982 an Oak Ridge Study for the NRC, which took greater account of coincidental component and human error, reduced the timespan to 200–600 reactor years. W. Jackson Davis, of the Nuclear Policy Program, University of California, indicates that the modern accident history record computes to approximately one serious accident in 14.3 years throughout the world.[32]

Obviously, extrapolating civilian reactor analysis to naval reactors is unsatisfactory. While naval engineers assert that seaborne reactors have superior safety features, anti-nuclear activists claim that these are offset by thinner containment structures to minimize the weight problem, limitations of space affecting design safety, lack of public regulatory supervision, crew fatigue and the prospect of collisions. Moreover, the safety of a ship may require it to maintain power at sea when a land-based reactor would be shut down.

As for the Australian and New Zealand reactor safety regulations, critics noted that they made no provision for boarding foreign military vessels or inspecting records and equipment. Port authority regulations commonly require the vessel to be towed to a safe anchorage within twenty-four hours of an accident and evacuation of an area within 600 metres of the vessel. But if a reference accident were exceeded, such measures could increase the hazards to human life.[33] The reference accident model had determined that emergency planning zones should extend to less than five miles. But even firm advocates of nuclear visiting queried the adequacy of this if a collision resulted in a plume which could be a hazard for a distance of 50 miles. Nor had the AAEC made a study of coastal or harbour collision patterns.[34]

Australian federal regulations required states to produce comprehensive safety schemes. But by 1987 only Western Australia had a publicly available plan (but not for all ports). It dealt with agency responsibilities rather than the social consequences of an accident, and critics also argued that none of the designated WA 'safe anchorages' were sufficiently remote from residential areas. In Tasmania, the Gray Ministry gave security reasons for persistently refusing to make public its safety plan. South Australia's Premier, J. C. Bannon, considered the central government to be responsible for the safety of visiting warships and argued that, in view of the considerable harbour development, nuclear-powered ships should be kept out until the Commonwealth had reassessed the designated Adelaide berth. Victoria had no plan and there was some debate as to whether one existed for NSW.[35]

NUCLEAR WEAPON RISKS

Risk assessment of weapon accidents is also problematic. Much of the data relating to fires, weapon design, storage conditions, and handling is classified. A nuclear weapon accident is officially defined as 'an unexpected event involving nuclear weapons or radio-logical nuclear weapon components that might detonate, release radioactivity or cause a public hazard'. 'Incidents' are less serious. Shaun Gregory and Alistair Edwards provided a more refined categor-ization in 1988, and readers are referred to their list of 200 British, Soviet and American events.[36]

Several other sources indicate that mishaps may be more frequent than was assumed when Australia and New Zealand were concerned only about legal liability for reactor accidents in the 1960s and 1970s. Official statistics inadvertently released in the course of a Hawaii court action, *Lind v. Dept. of the Navy* (1980), revealed 381 incidents involving USN nuclear weapons between 1965 and 1977. Of the incidents, twelve were designated as 'significant'. In addition a more serious accident occurred in 1965 when an A-4E bomber carrying a B-43 war reserve bomb fell off a carrier in the Western Pacific. A second accident (involving destruction or serious damage to the weapon itself) remains classified. A Soviet Golf-class submarine which sank in the Pacific in 1968 is alleged to have lost nuclear torpedoes. The United States informed the Australian defence staff of 630 incidents and two accidents between 1965 and 1985, mainly sprinkler malfunctioning, but including paint scratches and flat tyres on nuclear weapon carriers. More than 60 of them involved weapons on surface ships in ports. Bombs carried by naval aircraft were frequently involved, and ASROC also appears to be accident prone (with about 90 incidents) because of frequent handling. None of the occurrences was said to pose a nuclear hazard. This conflicts, however, with an expert source cited by Davis to the effect that several incidents involved radioactive

95

release. Davis concluded that major accidents involving nuclear weapons or power were 'inevitable'.[37]

No accident has ever involved a nuclear yield, as far as is known. La Rocque claimed that when he was Captain of the USS *Providence* a fully automated nuclear warhead was almost fired during target practice, and that fellow officers had experienced similar frissons.[38] Nevertheless, a series of deliberate actions are necessary before a weapon becomes nuclear capable and arming mechanisms are stored separately from the weapons themselves. States ensure that nuclear weapons will not function when dropped, hit by fragments or set on fire. If one did explode, a resulting 'one-point accident' would not lead to a nuclear yield, though plutonium would be scattered in the immediate vicinity. It has been suggested, however, that permissive action links (PALs), normal on land-based warheads, should be extended to those carried at sea to prevent unauthorized use or accident. The USN rejected PALs on the grounds that nuclear weapons at sea were inherently secure from external threats. In the case of submarines, it was felt that communication of the enabling codes from control centres could not be assured.[39]

Among the potential port hazards cited by critics are the risk of terrorist attack, and drug or alcohol abuse by personnel certified to handle nuclear weapons. But the most frequently cited weapon accident scenario is that resulting from a major fire affecting the sensitized conventional explosive of a nuclear weapon. According to Davis further spreading as a result of incineration could not be ruled out, a possibility highlighted by the Soviet Yankee-II submarine fire off the Eastern US coast on 4 October 1986. In Sydney harbour a sub-critical reaction producing an oxidized plutonium cloud would probably cause between 33 and 11,000 latent cancer deaths within a 55 km radius, depending on prevailing conditions.[40]

With respect to safety procedures, hosts are assured that whenever foreign warships enter any port they are required under their own regulations to ensure that weapons are stowed in a safe condition. Nuclear weapons would be unarmed, though not necessarily removed from vessels, before entering port. Weapons are not handled in ports or put into a condition where inadvertent release is possible. Magazines have automatic spraying and flooding mechanisms, and crews are certified as trained in emergency procedures for nuclear accidents. In Australia warships are required to establish liaison with local fire fighting authorities to ensure that any assistance that might be required could be obtained rapidly.[41]

There seems a fair chance that, as permitted under the regulations, nuclear weapons are carried by visiting ships to Australia and were formerly carried to New Zealand. The terms of reference of the Australian Senate inquiry indicate as much. Senator Hamer, a former Admiral, acknowledged it at a Canberra hearing in March 1987, and serving Rear Admiral David Martin announced that some of the seven nuclear-capable ships, such as the USS *Missouri*, visiting for the RAN's 75th anniversary in October 1986 could be carrying nuclear weapons.[42] US vessels on extended deployments carry as close to a contingency wartime load of weapons as possible and the *Missouri* was said to be likely to be carrying nuclear Tomahawk missiles.[43] Warships visiting Australia, and formerly New Zealand, would be on Pacific exercises or long tours of duty in the Indian Ocean.

Yet none of the Australian and New Zealand emergency procedures were directed at weapon accidents. The authorities declared that because the risk was non-existent it would not be sensible to develop emergency plans. The AAEC had never been briefed to engage in monitoring or assessments for a weapon accident, though queries were raised by officials in early 1987. Other countries were said to be unlikely to have plans because weapons would not be primed when ships were in port.[44] A probable, though unstated, reason for what critics regarded as reckless negligence was that assessing particular vessels would imply a challenge to NCND.

It is clearly incorrect to assume that other countries make no provision for weapon accidents. The US and British armed forces certainly take the possibility seriously and the US held exercises (NUWAX) in 1979, 1981 and 1983. British accident training has involved the scattering of radioactive dust around the site of a simulated road accident and, possibly, rehearsals for a US bomb accident. The Nuclear Accident Response Organisation of the MoD, whose existence was first officially acknowledged in July 1987, can call on specially trained units in the armed forces, including the Naval Emergency Monitoring Organisation. The MoD also has contingency plans for public protection, though they are not made public.[45] Ties may have been strengthened with the US to maintain standards of protection for the transport of numbers of nuclear weapons for overhaul or redeployment. Britain and the United States have provided Australia with documents pertaining to naval accident procedures, and two Australian Air Force officers attended the 1983 NUWAX.[46] US Pacific Commanders are required to make detailed plans for dealing with nuclear weapon accidents in Australian ports in fulfilment of 'vigorous and aggressive programs' for preventing accidents and minimizing effects. In Europe, too, commanders involved in the storage or transport of weapons are expected to develop comprehensive nuclear accident information plans. Instructions include provision for briefings and liaison with host countries.[47] By contrast Australia and New Zealand made no provision.

Perhaps, so critics argued, US training and co-ordination with hosts have not developed very far because exercises abroad are seen as politically sensitive. It is largely left to the United States to maintain its own arrangements for seeking help in the event of a weapon accident. Navy Nuclear Accident Response Crisis Action Teams are stationed at overseas bases and travel aboard vessels, and procedures are detailed in a US Defense Nuclear Agency manual. In providing assistance in foreign territories, the USPACOM is expected to protect classified information and claim control over a radius of 600–700 metres surrounding a vessel. NCND is to be maintained in the event of an accident 'for the longest possible period consistent with public safety/alarm'. However, 'lack of confirmation . . . when the situation has clearly indicated to most observers that nuclear weapons are present, could be disastrous to the credibility of the DoD'.[48] In Europe NCND would be waived under certain conditions, with the concurrence of the host government, in order to reduce public alarm. But critics argued that, in view of the three day delay in notifying the Spanish government about the two H-bombs which burst at Palomares, there was no guarantee that early advice of an accident would be forthcoming.[49]

Australian environmental groups recommended extending the minimum emergency evacuation zone from 600 metres to 5 kilometres to allow for an uncontained reactor accident, the establishment of emergency evacuation and decontamination plans (to be regularly rehearsed), clarification of indemnity for clean-up operations and the assertion of Australian law and sovereignty within the accident area. Nuclear-capable warships should submit to on-board radiation monitoring and visits stopped altogether until safety procedures had been revised. The safety of Australians was said to 'run a distant second to the desire to reinforce the US alliance'. The political dimension had allowed risks to be downplayed or in the case of weapon accidents to be ignored.[50]

Some Australian officials predict that the rules for nuclear-propelled warships will be extended to nuclear-capable ones, but the extension will have to be managed in such a way as to preserve the requirements of NCND. Intrusive monitoring will be out of the question. What is certain, however, is that for the time being at least New Zealand is saved the additional efforts of monitoring, emergency standby provisions and disaster drills (over and above civil defence for natural calamities), which are part of the costs in managing nuclear warship visits.

Of course such management costs weighed less heavily in the New Zealand political debate than perceptions of the security problems associated with nuclear visiting. The management and safety issues are taken seriously, for cogent practical reasons, by authorities in countries visited by nuclear warships. In Australia and New Zealand the remoteness of a serious accident occurring had, it seems, led to a degree of laxity and confusion about safety precautions. It left the authorities vulnerable to challenges by environmentalists and peace groups. Even conservative politicians expressed disquiet about management, the more so, perhaps, to ensure that there should be no hurdles to continued warship access. Peace groups, by contrast, found these practical issues of the 1980s useful in raising questions about national interests and the wider security context. From discussion of the practical problems of visit management, our analysis now moves to the political dimension and the role of anti-nuclear politics in the ANZUS crisis.

6 ANTI-NUCLEAR POLITICS

The analysis so far has suggested that strategic drift in the ANZUS relationship and lack of political management was paralleled by flourishing defence co-operation, particularly between Australia and the US and between the Anzacs. Ironically, the alliance partners had originally had a minimalist conception of military commitments. Australian politicians, however, were disposed to accept nuclear connections as a way of tying Britain and the US into Australia's security concerns. We have seen how one of the components of defence co-operation, visiting rights and warship access, had been subject to strain as a consequence of technological developments in the USN. Strategic changes and the increased deployment of nuclear-powered warships became a matter of interest to Australian and New Zealand governments and then to environmentalists and peace campaigners.

This chapter contends that a key factor in the ANZUS crisis, the political effectiveness of anti-nuclear opinion in New Zealand, was more nationalistic than ideological in character. In the favourable conditions of strategic drift and attenuated connection with nuclear strategies, public opinion could outweigh the resistance of defence advisers and the ambivalence of the Labour leadership. US policy-makers misread the breadth of passive support for anti-nuclearism, and assumed that, as in Australia and Europe, activists would be kept in their place. At first sight, indeed, the effectiveness of the New Zealand peace movements is baffling.

The country's political culture is one in which conservative pragmatism is highly valued. Fears of a Russian threat and paranoia about communism have traditionally borne little relationship to the distance from any significant group of Russians or communists. The list of prime ministers, from William Massey onwards, is dotted with authoritarian figures who enlivened the political scene by manipulating red scares. Sidney Holland, a prominent member of the quasi-

100

fascist New Zealand Legion in the 1930s, may have been the only one who had once worked to abolish political parties, but others often acted as if there were some 'higher democracy'. Politically significant extremism has occurred on the right of the political spectrum and was sufficiently strong, in the form of the New Zealand Party, to split the right-wing vote in the 1984 general election. Vicious intolerances on 'liberal issues' are not unknown, and the term 'socialism' is virtually taboo. As well as overseeing the shift in security relations, the Lange Government abandoned any ideological pretensions by launching an economic strategy consistent with theories of unfettered capitalism. If the Americans could hardly understand the anti-nuclear complication, it seems unlikely that the Soviet Union could have managed to manipulate it.

But one should appreciate that the ANZUS debate occurred in the context of profound social change. Multi-culturalism had taken root in a society formerly dominated by British immigrants who identified closely with northern hemisphere issues. The idea of homogeneity has been in retreat since the 1970s and with it the assumption of consensus politics. This has made debate both more possible and conducive to a review of traditional links with the outside world.

One psychological explanation for anti-alliance sentiment has been that New Zealand (more so than Australia) was reluctant to break with Britain, but that oedipal fury over economic betrayal has been displaced on to the US.[1] This overlooks both the extent to which US policy in Vietnam was seen as a moral 'betrayal' and the extent to which discontent with the alliance quickened as a consequence of anti-nuclearism. In this regard official opposition to French nuclear testing gave direct action a cachet of distinction in New Zealand.

The New Zealand Labour Party (NZLP), in the political wilderness for much of the post-Korean War period, was amenable to a radical security policy orientation. This chapter draws attention, therefore, to the way in which peace politics moved to centre stage through the party system in New Zealand. In Australia, not only did anti-nuclear activists have to contend with a less congenial security environment and the hurdles of federal political organization, but also the problem of disassociation. For although the minority Democrat Party was converted wholesale to anti-nuclear and anti-ANZUS policies, the ALP's conservative Centre-Unity faction could cite electoral expediency for being cautious. Anti-nuclear forces in Australia had to set up their own single issue parliamentary party.

FALLOUT AND FIELD WORK

The first major impetus to anti-nuclear politics in New Zealand came in 1957 from British nuclear tests and concern about strontium 90 fallout. The Society of Friends was instrumental in organizing parliamentary petitions calling for suspension of the tests and an end to New Zealand's participation.[2] Prime Minister Holland stated that New Zealand had been assured that British scientists had 'mastered the fall-out problem' of the high air bursts over Christmas Island. As a dutiful daughter New Zealand had a close interest in the success of the tests because the 'Motherland' was vulnerable without a deterrent. Nevertheless, the National Government had to acknowledge a growing public opposition to the tests and, with an election approaching, Holland promised to seek assurances that tests were kept to the minimum consistent with defence requirements.[3] The Labour Party called for their suspension pending a treaty.

By the late 1950s a New Zealand Campaign for Nuclear Disarmament, modelled on the British organization, was also raising public awareness about tests in the Pacific, though it took a cautious line on the alliance relationship. Opposition to tests mounted after a Soviet 50 megaton explosion was measured in Auckland from two pressure waves travelling around the world in each direction, and a US test over Johnston Island in 1962 reddened the night sky over New Zealand. Hiroshima Day marches in the major cities became a highpoint in the New Zealand anti-nuclear calendar, equivalent to Palm Sunday rallies in Australia. In 1962 CND and NZLP also adopted the Australian Labor Party leader's proposal for a nuclear weapons-free southern hemisphere. The US indicated that such a zone might be incompatible with ANZUS, and CND hardened its policy to nonalignment. However, the zone concept was regarded by the public as some kind of protection against fallout not as a political formula which could affect alliance commitments.[4]

In response to continued public unease, Prime Minister Keith Holyoake stated on 31 May 1963 that the National Government wanted an end to nuclear tests, but that a Pacific zone was out of the question because the whole region was under the threat of Soviet power and Chinese communism. Holyoake emphasized, however, that 'New Zealand has no nuclear weapons, we have no intention of acquiring any, and there are no nuclear bases on New Zealand territory'.[5] The country was unlikely to be deeply involved in strategic nuclear basing anyway, but the statement showed a tactical awareness of the domestic climate. In the 1980s the National Party referred to this as equivalent to declaring New Zealand a nuclear-free zone.

After the Partial Test Ban Treaty of 1963, CND faded and peace activism was directed against the Vietnam War. Student radicals also led a campaign against defence installations. A government announcement in 1968 that a USN Omega station would be built in the South Island, triggered a broad-based protest centred on Christchurch. Radical left-wing students and researchers at Canterbury University played a significant role in publicizing the fact that Omega could communicate with Polaris submarines to update inertial navigation systems, thereby facilitating the plotting of missile trajectories. The Labour Party announced its opposition and, in May 1969, after demonstrations in Christchurch and Wellington, the Omega scheme was aborted. As indicated earlier, the US decided to locate the station in Victoria, though the Southern Alps were technically better suited. The issue, as described by Owen Wilkes, raised for the first time the notion of New Zealand being a target through the American alliance.[6]

Students also turned their attention to the Woodbourne USAF facility near Blenheim. There, atmospheric tests were monitored for developing methods of shielding communications from nuclear disturbance. Satellite surveillance made it obsolete, but vigilantes claim that their field work and protests were partly responsible for its closure in 1973. Similarly, researchers investigated the USAF Satellite Tracking Observatory on Canterbury University land at Mount John, near Lake Tekapo. They considered that Mount John gathered data necessary for intercepting hostile satellites. In March 1971 some 250 protesters fought a surrealistic pitched battle with police in the otherwise deserted New Zealand high country. Wilkes claims that this field trip forced the University to give up its title and the operation to close down in 1983, though other systems had made Mount John redundant anyway.

The New Zealand public had no opportunity to debate these installations. But in a small society it was difficult to avoid finding out what was going on. Protestors were often technically better informed than the government and may have influenced official perceptions about the level of American presence that would be feasible. The South Island campaigns were co-ordinated by the Committee Against Foreign Military Activities in New Zealand, which continued to campaign for the demilitarization of Deep Freeze. Christchurch already had a tradition as a centre of peace activism, and its blend of Christian dissent, research on defence technology and radical suspicion of the United States persisted into the 1980s.

The decision by France to transfer atmospheric testing to Moruroa in 1966 antagonized the wider public, including agricultural interests, as well as students and committed pacifists. Protest vessels sailed to the test area, marking a unique approach by New Zealand dissenters, involving careful planning and complex logistic arrangements. Although official monitoring revealed no dangerous increase in fallout levels on pasture, anger against France reached critical proportions in the 1970s. In 1973 the Kirk and Whitlam Governments took their historic legal actions against France in the International Court of Justice, and New Zealand also dispatched the frigate HMNZS *Otago* to the test exclusion zone with a cabinet minister aboard. Whitlam made an oiler available for refuelling. This may have been an absurd gesture, but it had the important domestic effect of making New Zealanders feel they had cut a dash in the world and it stamped an imprimatur on principled anti-nuclearism. As Kirk pointed out, the expedient course would have been to accept French tests and preserve access to European markets.[7]

THE MULDOON AND REAGAN FACTORS

Although Labour's resolution for an SPNFZ came before the UN in late 1975, the new Muldoon Government was markedly less enthusiastic and allowed the initiative to lapse. In retrospect, a senior National Party politician regarded this as a mistake; a more vigorous prosecution of an SPNFZ would have undercut the anti-nuclear movement, as Hawke's was later aimed to do in Australia.[8] Certainly the failure to make progress on arms control contributed to the pressure within the Labour Party for a local ban on warship visits.

In contrast to sporting contacts with South Africa and opposition to French nuclear testing, Muldoon's lifting of the liability suspension in 1976 may have roused little immediate unrest. But the mid-1970s were a crucial time for radical causes because the National Government menaced all kinds of dissent. Anti-nuclear politics survived partly because nuclear visiting changed the focus of pressure groups from matters they could do little about (French tests and an SPNFZ) to one in which they could take direct action. Nuclear weapons on board warships were the closest that New Zealanders came to the nuclear arms race. It was a logical focus for arms control agitation. Like the Vietnam War, it also focussed attention on the alliance relationship. Critics were concerned that renewed visiting was an anæsthetic for another base operation. They saw no other rationale for it,[9] though visits were probably linked to increased US deployments in the Indian Ocean.

Eight years after failing to get a first reading for his NFZ Bill, Labour MP Richard Prebble tried again, in April 1982. Prebble dropped the ban on nuclear-powered vessels in an effort to get bipartisan support. However, under clause 5 any person who had reason to suspect that a nuclear weapon had been brought in or was about to be brought in to the twelve mile zone could apply to the High Court for an injunction. This poorly-drafted measure simply ignored practical problems, yet there was a marked difference in the political atmosphere since the earlier Bill. In the first place Muldoon's working majority in parliament was down to one, and National's anti-nuclear MP, Marilyn Waring, regarded the Bill as a useful way of stimulating discussion on the issue. She voted against the Bill only when the National caucus agreed to establish a parliamentary committee to receive public submissions. Second, this time Labour's sincerity was not questioned, for the nuclear-visiting problem had little to do with ideology.[10]

The National Government had acknowledged the importance of disarmament and arms control by joining international demands for a comprehensive test ban, and lending New Zealand's expertise to the UN's Ad Hoc Seismic Group for establishing a global monitoring network.[11] But Muldoon held to the view that warship visits were essential to ANZUS. US officials subsequently suggested that Muldoon had failed to educate the public on the value of the alliance for nuclear deterrence. Such a task would have been a labour of Sisyphus, given New Zealand's tenuous connection to US nuclear strategy. Nor was it the Muldoon style to engage in measured debate.

The belief that it was vital to have a powerful ally was ultimately shaken by nationalism, and Muldoon played a significant part in this by reinforcing nativist fears of imported disorder. To say that his Government presided over a white terror against 'alien influences' in the media, churches, unions and opposition groups would be an exaggeration. But political intolerance flourished in a country where a comfortable standard of living was being undermined by a diminution of the British market for exports. By the time Labour gained office in 1984, the nativism which had been a means of internal control seems to have found an alternative outlet in reinforcing fears of an external nuclear threat.

Disengagement from nuclearism was not, then, a particular whim of the Labour Party but derived from currents of cultural and political independence. New Zealand's interests were seen as increasingly convergent with those of its Pacific neighbours who were struggling against neo-colonialism and 'nuclear imperialism'. Furthermore, America's enemies were categorized as New Zealand's enemies for no obvious reason. Some critics thought it amazing that the country had allowed itself to be 'so pitifully pushed around' for so long through fear of upsetting the United States. A dependent mentality was said to have prevented New Zealand reaching its potential 'as a unique nation that could take a creative lead in a very troubled world'. New Zealand's friends should fit in with New Zealand's policy for once.[12]

It hardly needs stressing that the advent of strategic fundamentalism in Washington created anxiety that nuclear war itself was the threat. There was also a 'ripple effect' from the European crisis over Intermediate Nuclear Force (INF) deployments as critics noted a parallel stimulus to the nuclear arms race in the Pacific. Australian and New Zealand critics were especially preoccupied by SLCMs visiting their ports, and by developments in US anti-submarine warfare which were said to threaten the stability of mutual deterrence.[13] The reality of nuclear stability may have been quite different, but local perceptions were not disabused during the crisis by misleading pronouncements from US congressmen to the effect that New Zealand was a target with or without port visits.[14]

For the most part, peace groups avoided anti-Americanism and certainly denied promoting it. But, obviously, those who incorporated their anti-nuclear views into a broad perspective of anti-imperialism and identified their cause with the struggles for the integrity of the Pacific nations were highly critical of US foreign policy. Labour Party conferences in the 1980s routinely condemned US intervention in Latin America. Citing the Grenada invasion and 'Contra thuggery' in Nicaragua, militants contended that New Zealand was guilty by association, tainted by Yank disease. 'We have allied ourselves', said Wilkes, 'with the one power most involved in all the repression and with the least interest in relieving it'. Others referred to the US as a 'nuke junky'. But pillars of moderation also found the utterances and actions of the Reagan Administration quite alarming.[15]

Anti-Reaganism did not, however, signify pro-Sovietism. Few New Zealand activists advocated unilateral nuclear disarmament by the West. The far right had no easy task proving Soviet manipulation of New Zealand anti-nuclear politics. Moscow was said to be inflaming fears of nuclear war through support to trade unions and the World Peace Council, which the United States regards as a Soviet front organization. But the Peace Council hardly became the vanguard of anti-nuclear politics. Hard left leaders in the New Zealand Federation of Labour (FOL) helped to establish the Pacific Trade Union Forum in 1980 which took a strong anti-nuclear line. Its links with Moscow were documented for a Hoover Institution Conference in Washington in

March 1987, entitled 'Red orchestra: Instruments of Soviet policy in the South-West Pacific', a right-wing examination of Soviet sub-version. True, waterfront workers and other unionists stopped work during visits by nuclear ships, but the closure of Wellington docks and disruption to inter-Island ferry services did not necessarily endear the unions to the public.[16] And there is no evidence that the New Zealand unions influenced the Government. Indeed the FOL had great difficulty influencing industrial relations policy, let alone foreign policy.

A few attending the 'Red Orchestra' conference, including several from Australia and New Zealand, were themselves subjected to taunts of enjoying American hospitality and having connections with a 'Rambo right'. Perhaps the subversion theories were not so much smears as wishful thinking for a simple explanation of New Zealand's 'defection'. The links they detected between New Zealand's anti-nuclearism and Moscow were too narrow to be credible. The peace movement was based primarily on the hundreds of middle-class affinity and neighbourhood groups.[17] Anti-nuclearists were them-selves concerned that the conservative defence establishment would not recognize foreign-inspired right-wing subversion which, in the New Zealand context, was said to be a more likely test of democracy. The Ministries of Defence and Foreign Affairs were described as out-posts of the US Embassy.[18]

Activists were also prone to regard New Zealand as less enthusias-tic about anti-nuclearism than European countries, partly because of the Anzac military tradition. On the other hand, dissenters could capitalize on the environmental movement and the disturbances sur-rounding the 1981 Springbok rugby tour, which had demonstrated that shifts in traditional attitudes were occurring.[19] One of the handful of left-wing Labour MPs, Helen Clark, expressed the con-fidence of a new generation:

> The establishment which fashioned our post-war security policies saw New Zealand's role as that of a small nation which by and large could only have an impact on world affairs through its contacts with large allies – primarily the United States and to a lesser extent the United Kingdom. They worked to ensure that New Zealand was close to the ear of the giants. They also seemed to assume that what was good for the giants was good for New Zealand ... Meantime New Zealand society has been undergoing changes which I believe are profound. We are no longer predominantly a settler society which looks back to and identifies with an old world in Europe and its tensions ... Many Pakeha are making the psychological adjust-ments to being the Pacific people which we must become. Some

107

fifty-eight percent of New Zealanders ... were not even born when
New Zealand made its post-war security arrangements.[20]

PROFILE OF ANTI-NUCLEAR ACTIVISM

There was no possibility of peace groups being orchestrated
from outside. They were too improvised, setting agendas for short-
term goals and disagreeing about alternative security policies.[21] As the
1986 Defence Committee of Enquiry into New Zealand security noted,
there are many gradations of 'nuclear free', ranging from no stationing
of nuclear weapons on national soil, to no military involvement with a
nuclear state. A common position seems to have been that adopted by
one of the Enquiry's members, the Quaker and Canterbury University
lecturer, Kevin Clements. He favoured membership of ANZUS if the
US accommodated New Zealand's stand on visits, but was willing to
abandon the alliance if it did not.[22] Many activists, however, preferred
getting out come what may.

The most striking features of New Zealand anti-nuclearism were the
effectiveness of decentralized organization and the high degree of
accessibility to politicians and decision-making bodies. The concept of
horizontal networking and avoidance of hierarchy were taken from
the United States but taken to greater lengths in this close-knit society.
Groups were autonomous but networks could quickly mobilize
support for events. CND was only one among many organizations,
but was instrumental in generating a major demonstration in Auckland within 48 hours of learning about the proposed visit of the USS
Buchanan. Similarly, the Foundation for Peace Studies, established in
1975, was particularly active in promoting peace education and in
changing the political climate by sponsoring well-publicized tours by
the 'mother' of the US nuclear-freeze movement, Helen Caldicott, and
the Princeton Professor of International Law, Richard Falk.

Nevertheless, there was a need for nationwide co-ordination of the
myriad groups. From February 1982, Peace Movement New Zealand
operated as a channel of communication and research. Re-named
Peace Movement Aotearoa (PMA) after the 1984 general election, it
had no authority over the 300 anti-nuclear groups in the country but
was accountable to them through annual workshops. In fact when
PMA moved in 1983 from Dunedin to a ramshackle headquarters
convenient to Parliament in Wellington, its magazine, *Peacelink*, continued to be produced in Dunedin and other centres. Some commentators continued to find New Zealand anti-nuclear politics fragmented
and lagging behind the European movements.[23] But they under-

estimated the significance of parochialism in the New Zealand context.

Even in cities and towns, neighbourhood groups could make large ripples in small ponds. This was particularly evident from the strong grassroots NFZ movement formed in 1980. Ironically the first local authority NFZ was the Auckland naval base suburb of Devonport in 1981, and by 1986 there were 104 zones, including the major cities and accounting for about 70 per cent of the population.[24]

Another, equally important, factor was the linkage between feminism and anti-nuclearism. Among the estimated 10,000 or so activists throughout the country, women played a disproportionately significant role because peace issues were a wide concern within the feminist movement. Moreover, both the Women's International League for Peace and Freedom and Peace Action Dunedin were activating women before Helen Caldicott's tour in April 1983. In addition to their own groups, women ran many of the neighbourhood organizations. Their campaigning contributed to the increasing political awareness of women and they reoriented pressure group politics to account for feminist concerns. Typically, they argued that defence issues had been controlled by a patriarchy which stressed technical issues rather than social values. Not surprisingly, women were particularly active in promoting anti-racism and anti-colonialism through groups, such as the Dunedin-based Te Whanau Matariki. This, in turn, linked activists to the Nuclear-Free and Independent Pacific movement (NFIP). Women like Hilda Halkyard Harawira were instrumental in making anti-nuclearism a priority within Maoridom, and making Pakehas more aware of Maori perspectives.[25]

Middle-class professional groups, formed mainly between 1980 and 1983, gave anti-nuclearism an element of respectability and prestige. In addition to local branches of International Physicians for the Prevention of Nuclear War and Scientists Against Nuclear Arms (SANA), there were organizations for engineers, psychologists, librarians and others. The physicians' group, representing about 10 per cent of the medical profession, were mostly 'older, conservative types' anxious to avoid politicking.[26] SANA, founded in May 1983, grew to a membership of about 300 and specialized in investigative reporting, making full use of the US and New Zealand freedom of information legislation.

The boating community adopted the idea of American Quakers who had protested in kayaks against military shipments to Pakistan from Baltimore and Philadelphia in 1971. But the tactics were extended into full-scale blockades which have never been successfully imitated elsewhere. In a succession of harbour demonstrations against nuclear visitors New Zealand squadrons in every port became increasingly proficient at interfering with navigation, their camaraderie enhanced by adventurous seamanship and brushes with the law. As a solicitor, David Lange defended a former cabinet minister who was arrested for protesting in his sloop against the USS *Long Beach* in October 1976. When the SUBROC-fitted nuclear submarine, USS *Pintado*, arrived in January 1978 it had to force a passage with the help of police launches, RNZN frigates and helicopter escorts. Over a hundred motley craft created chaos when the submarine USS *Haddo* visited Auckland a year later. A rural labourer managed to leap on to the *Haddo*'s hull where he did a dance of defiance which the media could hardly ignore. In August 1983 the destroyer USS *Texas* was forced to a standstill in Auckland Harbour, and its sojourns in Auckland and Wellington were marked by large street demonstrations. Three nuclear-powered visitors within ten months of the 1984 election ensured that the protest would maintain momentum.[27]

Among established institutions, the main churches supported the anti-nuclear trend. At the 1985 meeting of the National Council of Churches, delegates approved the document 'Nuclear Weapons and ANZUS' which backed the new Labour Government's policy 'as a clear signal to the nuclear powers that we do not accept their doctrines regarding nuclear war and will not be a party to them'. But the clerics failed to elucidate New Zealand's role within ANZUS.[28] Although several prominent retired civil sevants also supported disengagement, the 'retired servicemen anti-nuclear syndrome' did not feature as prominently as in Australia or the northern hemisphere. Retired military chiefs had spent their careers trying to engage more closely with the US and, like the executive of the Returned Servicemen's Association (RSA), they lined up with the status quo. But the RSA executive clearly did not speak for all its members, as evidenced by letters to the *RSA Review* and submissions to the public inquiries critical of the hierarchy's pro-nuclear stance.[29]

Pro-ANZUS groups were in some difficulty over whether to insist that nuclear deterrence was relevant to New Zealand security or to reassure their audiences that the nuclear connection was so slight as to be harmless. Even the idea that nuclear deterrence had kept peace between the military blocs took second place to the argument that an end to practical defence co-operation was too high a price to pay for keeping harbours nuclear free.[30] Traditionalists did not really organize themselves until after Labour's ban on the USS *Buchanan*. Seventeen distinguished retired service chiefs then published an open letter in

May 1985 countering the Government's dishonesty, as they saw it, in allowing the country to be protected by the American nuclear umbrella whilst refusing to pay the premiums. Servicemen reportedly comprised half the members of a Security and Defence Association, led by the manager of the Armed Forces Canteen Council. But there was no military coup. An ANZUS Group formed in Masterton in early 1986 sought to restore the alliance and delay the introduction of anti-nuclear legislation. It boasted the support of former Chief of Defence Staff, Sir Leonard Thornton, and was presided over by a former member of the Pests Destruction Council.[31]

Strategic conservatives could count on the sympathy of defence professionals, but even military experts conceded that US alliance leadership had caused problems. Air Marshal Sir Ewan Jamieson, who resigned as Chief of Defence Staff in disagreement with Labour's policies, conceded the nationalistic impulse and argued that the US should recognize the different perceptions of a small nation.[32] And two important Dunedin conferences in 1983, attended by officials, politicians, peace researchers and academics, revealed shifts in the traditional outlook. Although ANZUS membership was a focus of disagreement, all believed in a more independent stance which avoided involvement in nuclear arms racing. The permanent head of the MoD, Dennis McLean, denied that the alliance guaranteed protection or committed New Zealand to nuclear designs.[33]

Cracks in the old consensus were also reflected in the written submissions to public inquiries. Of the 150 submissions on nuclear legislation received by a parliamentary select committee in 1983, only two opposed a nuclear-visiting ban. Of the 1,236 submissions on the NFZ Bill introduced by Lange in 1985, only eleven were fundamentally opposed to it. The 1986 Defence Committee of Enquiry estimated that fewer than 500 of the 4,182 submissions it received explicitly called for withdrawal from ANZUS, and fewer than 1,000 explicitly supported the warship ban. But if one includes those submissions which expressed deep hostility to US policies in particular and to alliances and militarism in general, those which advocated civilian based defence, transarmament, non-alignment or neutrality, or expressed pride in New Zealand's stance, then the ratio in favour of greater independence or disengagement ran at about 6:1. Excluding newspaper coupons inserted by a right-wing group, this fell to about 5:1 after the chairman of the inquiry called for more pro-alliance submissions. It is, of course, to be expected that those most interested in achieving change would have a stronger motivation to make a submission. Anti-nuclear groups encouraged their

111

members to participate, though only about 50 submissions conformed to a model.[34]

THE ELECTORAL IMPACT

Yet peace movements could not have made much impact without an evolution in passive support among the public at large. New Zealand is one of the more frequently polled countries in the world and it is conceivable that the Soviet Union is deterred from attacking by three million centres of decision-making. Even allowing for the perils of interpreting polls, the trends are unmistakable. In 1978 a poll indicated that 61 per cent wanted ANZUS maintained or strengthened, whilst only 31.5 per cent rejected nuclear-armed ships in any circumstances and 39 per cent rejected nuclear-powered vessels.[35] By early 1984, 73 per cent of respondents approved a ban on nuclear-armed vessels. Subsequent polls suggested less enthusiasm for banning nuclear propulsion (about 50 per cent) but continued high support for banning nuclear-armed vessels (see appendix 6). Obliged to choose between visits and ANZUS, there was roughly an even split. Polls conducted for the Defence Committee of Enquiry are discussed in chapter 8, but we might note that by April–May 1986, 75 per cent favoured some form of nuclear disengagement. About 25 per cent preferred no alliance at all whereas 71 per cent favoured remaining in ANZUS, including those who wanted it denuclearized.

In this opinion shift, 1983 can reasonably be considered as a turning point. Helen Caldicott attracted huge audiences, and the NFZ movement spread to conservative rural communities. The mirrored concerns of cruise deployment in Europe reached a peak and more nuclear-capable ships arrived in New Zealand, including HMS *Invincible* at the end of the year. *Peacelink* reported in September 1983 that 'Peace has suddenly become hot political property, and all the parties are responding to the perceived political clout of the peace movement.'

Much of the running was made by the Social Credit Party, which favoured self-reliance in all things. As a minority party it could afford to be radical, and its leaders sensed the possibility of gaining marginal seats by appealing to the peace vote. They were more dogmatic than the Labour leadership about ANZUS; it was a useless piece of memorabilia and should be replaced by armed neutrality. In August 1983, the Social Credit leader, Bruce Beetham, introduced the Prohibition of Nuclear Vessels and Weapons Bill. Unlike Prebble's second Bill, the Beetham proposal reverted to banning nuclear power. It also required the New Zealand government to turn away a vessel if the

Captain adhered to NCND. Beetham challenged the Government to deny that visitors carried nuclear-attack weapons. The Minister of Defence, David Thomson, acknowledged that visitors 'may possibly' carry nuclear weapons and that although not specifically required under the treaty, 'such visits are in keeping with the spirit of ANZUS'. For his honesty he was labelled a puppet of the Pentagon.[36] Social Credit entered the 1984 election with legislation against nuclear visits as a high priority.

Other small parties also had stronger anti-ANZUS policies than Labour in the 1984 election. Militant Maoris described ANZUS as one of the many oppressions felt by the indigenous population. The Mana Motuhake Party, which came second to Labour in three Maori electorates in 1984, took an NFIP stance. But major responsibility for making the pre-emptive cringe strategy respectable goes to the New Zealand Party, formed in 1983. Bob Jones, a property tycoon who led this right-wing party of free marketeers, preferred demilitarization to nuclear disengagement. The New Zealand Party's election manifesto deplored the annual sum of $NZ700 million spent on defence, denied the Soviet Union was an enemy and advocated armed neutrality. It won applause from many in the peace movement. With uncanny presentiment, Jones suggested that there would be 'a Russian submarine scare' if New Zealand took steps in the direction he proposed.[37]

The governing National Party was in some disarray. Twenty-five years earlier a National MP had said that ANZUS enabled him to sleep peacefully 'in the full knowledge that if we are attacked there will immediately rush to our defence the most powerful nation on earth'.[38] Not many now retained that degree of confidence. Muldoon and the traditionalists went along with the Reagan Administration's arguments on ANZUS, nuclear deterrence and ship visits. But the majority were compromisers. Defence spokesman Doug Kidd and president Sue Wood recognized that it would be an election issue. They argued that ship visits should be subject to negotiation, rather than a unilateral ban, with priority given to the preservation of ANZUS. Nuclear states might be persuaded to adopt a code of behaviour: no strategic weapons in ports, tactical nuclear weapons to be disarmed in territorial waters and adherence to safety measures for nuclear-powered vessels.[39]

Others on the right opposed nuclear visiting as inconsistent with the renunciation of storage and manufacture of nuclear weapons. Wellington was declared an NFZ because conservative councillors voted for it. A small group of Nuclear-Free Nationals argued that no military alliance should compromise New Zealand's nuclear-free aspirations. Marilyn Waring indicated that she would not even trust easily-breached US assurances like that given to Australia for B-52s at Darwin. She wanted all nuclear-capable vessels kept out. At the 1983 Dunedin party conference, Waring used the phrase 'New Zealanders do not want to be defended, and in fact cannot be defended, by nuclear weapons'. It became a stock phrase in Lange's speeches.[40]

The Labour Party's nuclear policy developed in the 1970s and was pushed towards non-alignment by lack of progress in arms control. Pressure for unilateral action built up when the SPNFZ idea stalled, and from 1977 onwards the annual party conference voted against ANZUS. Although resolutions did not bind the leadership, structural and generational changes in the Party increasingly inhibited the freedom of MPs to ignore conference decisions. The 1979 conference established a Policy Council, of MPs and party delegates in equal measure, to choose between competing policy options. The 1981 election brought younger MPs into parliament including three women with strong anti-nuclear views, Helen Clark, Fran Wilde, and Margaret Shields. Clark served on the Party's National Executive, and Wilde was made Junior Whip. The 1984 election brought more tough anti-nuclearists into the caucus. Labour's leadership was thus confronted by party pressure for unilateral withdrawal from military commitments, but the need to reassure a predominantly pro-alliance electorate. Rowling and Frank O'Flynn framed a policy for the 1982 conference to the effect that if a ban on nuclear visiting were not respected by the US, there would be 'unilateral action'. This did not convince the delegates who voted overwhelmingly for withdrawal.[41]

The following year was a crucial one, for the NZLP needed to court uncommitted voters in the run up to the 1984 general election. David Lange, the new leader, wanted the option of accommodating the passage of warships. When this was howled down, he issued a statement on 6 July 1983 which addressed the problem of disclosure. Unless as Prime Minister he received assurance that ships and aircraft were not carrying weapons they would not be allowed in the twelve mile zone. No nuclear reactor would be allowed 'until strict safety conditions can be devised and enforced preventing any environmental hazard'. An SPNFZ should be made acceptable to nuclear powers by permitting transit of nuclear weapons. The Party's anti-nuclearists, many of whom played leading roles in the Wellington region's ginger group, Peace and Justice Forum, or in outside pressure groups, demanded categorical exclusion of nuclear-powered vessels and distrusted the formula of a prime minister being given private

114

assurances about weaponry.[42] Consequently the 1982 party conference voted for a proposal that New Zealand officials board vessels to check for nuclear weapons.

However, the leadership wrung a concession from delegates. Rowling had written a memo for the Policy Council in May 1983 laying out various alternatives on ANZUS and opting for a review of the relationship. A Labour government would call the bluff of those who said a visit ban would mean the end of ANZUS; the United States would not want to be seen bullying a small ally on a sensitive issue. The review was anticipated to establish the power of veto in alliance decisions and give greater emphasis to regional economic stability. It would also help determine the limits of US policy on an SPNFZ. Unlike the 1951 Treaty negotiations, New Zealand would drag Australia along. The rank and file swallowed it but insisted on the word 'renegotiation' rather than review.[43]

In June 1984, Prebble made a third attempt to introduce legislation, but with no provisions for enforcement. He referred to the controversy in Europe, the introduction of SLCMs to the Pacific and tension between the superpowers. New Zealand could take an initiative that 'would capture the imagination of the world'. Muldoon intervened to report that Weinberger had assured him that ANZUS would collapse if the Bill became law. Citing Hayden's photo session on the USS *Texas* in 1983 and the Australian ANZUS review, Muldoon and other National MPs encouraged the outside world to believe that any future Labour Cabinet would follow Hawke and admit vessels with nuclear weapons.[44] The debate ended in uproar when Waring was prevented from speaking, and her defection from the National caucus gave Muldoon reason to call an early election.

Peace Movement Aotearoa had already decided to give anti-nuclearism a political thrust in 1984 by tackling security and alliance issues. The focus culminated in the 'Beyond ANZUS Conference' in Wellington attended by over 500 delegates. They resolved to work for non-alignment and National's downfall. New pressure groups, such as Votes For Peace, came into existence to operate in marginal electorates, but were keen to influence conservative voters and not make life too easy for Labour. With the New Zealand Party urging withdrawal from ANZUS, Labour could escape with a middling policy of renegotiation. Basic requirements in negotiation would be an 'unconditional anti-nuclear stance' comprising a prohibition on nuclear warships, legislation to make New Zealand and its territorial waters nuclear free and an SPNFZ. Closer defence links would be forged with Australia.[45]

The 1984 election was fought on the economy and Muldoon's authoritarian style, but voters could be in no doubt that anti-nuclearism was an issue, even if they had illusions about the prospects for renegotiating ANZUS. Although 62 per cent of the electors cast votes for anti-nuclear parties, including 12 per cent for the New Zealand Party, it would be unsafe to make assumptions as to why they did so. Nevertheless, when subsequently asked how important the anti-nuclear issue had been in determining their vote, 41 per cent of respondents to an opinion poll said it had been very or fairly important, compared to 34 per cent who said unimportant.[46]

Anti-nuclear politics remained significant after the election. PMA was reasonably confident about the prospects for disengagement and made an accurate prediction. Either the US would have to search its Navy for an unambiguously non-nuclear vessel or try to force the issue by sending a nuclear-capable vessel and sticking by NCND, in which case the Government would not risk domestic unrest. Either way the ban would work.[47] But many believed that Labour could not be trusted without legislation, and that a law was crucial to hobble any future government. The Australian experience also taught the necessity of resisting pressure from a US administration anxious to squash a precedent.[48] Both within and without the Labour Party, anti-nuclearists agitated to keep the Government to its promises, made a concerted effort behind the scenes to ensure an unambiguous stance over the USS *Buchanan* and monitored US responses. But nuclear disengagement sentiment gained ground, at the expense of ANZUS, in the wake of US retaliation and the sinking in July 1985 of the Greenpeace protest vessel, *Rainbow Warrior*, in Auckland Harbour. The Party took a firmer position on regional security, seeking to revert to Tasman Doctrine and exclude, in collusion with Australia, all non-regional countries.

Although Lange himself held the foreign affairs portfolio, the new Cabinet's priority was economic restructuring. But it could not afford to compromise on nuclear policy too. No discerning political commentator could fail to notice that the ship ban was essential to satisfy the Party while fundamental economic changes occurred. Lange was personally opposed to nuclear weapons but dithered about offending the US. In a tactically wise move to avoid being stigmatized by the right, he also proclaimed that: 'Peace groups and I are like oil and water.'[49] The Cabinet timed the third reading of its Nuclear Free Bill partly to string activists along and partly to disconcert National. In the run up to the 1987 election press advertisements depicted a mushroom cloud with the caption: *'New Zealand banned it. Don't vote it back*

116

in.' In soliciting election funds, Lange wrote letters which reportedly asserted that a Labour victory at the next election was 'the only sure way of keeping New Zealand nuclear free'.[50] Lange had little incentive to marginalize the security issue as Hawke had done in Australia. It was National's Achilles' heel, and a pre-election intervention by three former military chiefs urging voters to vote for a return to ANZUS probably enhanced Labour's appeal as the anti-bomb party.

National wavered. Muldoon's successor as National Party leader, Jim McLay, had announced in May 1985 that 'while any ship visit request would be agreed to, I would not regard such visits as being the first items on my agenda. Attention must first be paid to ensuring the appropriate domestic climate.' The ban would have to continue for a cooling-off period, before the USN turned up as part of a multi-national flotilla.[51] The next party leader, Jim Bolger, adopted a low-key approach for the 1987 election. There was 'no need for nuclear weapons to be brought into New Zealand to secure peace in this part of the world, nor do I believe our allies want to bring them in.' National would amend the legislation to allow co-operation to continue whilst making it clear that New Zealand did not want weapons in its ports. The ban on nuclear-powered vessels would remain until a public inquiry had examined safety aspects.[52] From opposing quarters this seemed like a fudge. Anti-nuclear pressure groups argued that nuclear states simply ignored Norwegian-style declarations. A die-hard editorial in *The Press* (10 July 1987) regretted National's trimming to political winds and urged unquestioning acceptance of nuclear weapons. National's position was indeed queried when the US Republican counsel to the House Foreign Affairs Committee said, albeit in a personal capacity, that a return to ANZUS would require the same conditions as those pertaining to Australia and that the Treaty 'required there be no limit on weapons passing through local waters'.[53]

In the event ANZUS and nuclear visiting had a low priority for most 1987 voters, well below unemployment, the economy, crime and racial problems. Deprivation of American security benefits left the majority unruffled. Analysis of consistency voting in 1987 shows that party fortunes neatly reflected the fall-out of Labour's economic policies. More of the rich voted Labour; more of the poor abstained. But the nuclear issue had been the only thing left in Labour's programme to tempt party activists and canvassers out to drum up votes.[54] Labour's increased majority in 1987 testifies that nuclear disengagement had done it no harm domestically at all. What the anti-nuclear activists had succeeded in doing over the previous seven years was to move their

117

definition of 'nuclear free', an unambiguous ban on nuclear visiting, to the centre of the stage so that it would have to be taken into account in any new political consensus.

AUSTRALIAN CONTRASTS

Although unable to tap similar grassroots sentiment, Australian anti-nuclear activists also made a political impact. Peace movements had gone into a lull after the 1960s campaigns against conscription and the deployment of Australian forces in Vietnam. But the middle-class militancy which had spread among young people, professionals, and disaffected Liberal and Labor supporters, revived in response to Reaganism and the INF unrest in Europe. Among the impacts of anti-nuclearism we should include: the Victorian NFZ Bill passed in December 1982, with the Liberal Opposition not wishing to be seen voting against it; the HMS *Invincible* affair; the first nationally co-ordinated blockade of a uranium mine at Roxby Downs in August 1983; the mobilization of up to 250,000 Australians for the Palm Sunday rally in 1984 (including a police estimate of 150,000 in Sydney); and the election in 1984 of Jo Vallentine as a federal senator, standing on the issue of nuclear disarmament.[55] Anti-nuclear opinion in the ALP was sufficiently strong to force Hawke to back down from assisting the US in MX tests and, in February 1988, from continuing to supply France with uranium. Publicity was generated by temporary peace camps, notably outside Pine Gap where disturbances in 1987 led to Senator Vallentine's arrest and subsequent conviction for trespass.

Anxiety about Lehman's maritime strategy and the deployment of cruise and Trident missiles also fostered objections to nuclear visiting. Street demonstrations in WA greeted the arrival of the USS *Carl Vinson* carrier group in 1983. Directly inspired by the Auckland experiment, peace fleets operated in Sydney, Perth, Hobart and Queensland. The Sydney Peace Squadron attracted attention when it sailed round the USS *Missouri* at the RAN celebrations in 1986. Nor could the media ignore a surfer who intercepted the launch carrying Hawke across Sydney Harbour to the Opera House for the opening of Labor's 1987 election campaign. Whitlam, it was suggested, would have walked over.[56]

But this was small beer compared to blockades in New Zealand, and up to 1988 the overall political effect has been marginal. Indeed the contrasts between the Australian and New Zealand political contexts highlight the implausibility of the seamless web view of the Western Alliance. First, Australian anti-nuclearism is decentralized to the point of being dysfunctional. The size of the country inhibits pressure group co-ordination and, as the Quaker activist, Peter Jones, points out, there are different preoccupations in each state and territory. Victorian dissenters have a tradition of anti-uranium agitation. Tasmanians have been absorbed by conservation issues. Nuclear visiting affects WA much more than the east coast, and although NSW has the largest anti-nuclear movement it lacks a military focus.[57]

Many activists have a healthy suspicion of federal politics and political parties and have deliberately avoided the snares of élitism and distant hierarchical organization. But whereas horizontal networking operated effectively in compact New Zealand, in Australia it increased the scope for sectarianism. In fact there are two national co-ordinating bodies – the Coalition for a Nuclear-Free Australia and the Australian Coalition for Disarmament and Peace. The latter, comprising nuclear disarmament groups, trade unions and churches, organized a major disarmament conference in Melbourne in August 1985. But it projected the second characteristic of Australian anti-nuclear politics, a multi-focus approach. Instead of establishing priorities the participants decided to respond to issues as they arose, whether warship visits, Aboriginal land rights or independence for the Kanaks.[58] By contrast, New Zealand activists had focussed on nuclear disengagement and alliance relations.

If there is a common base for Australian anti-nuclearism it resides in the opposition to uranium mining, an assault on the starting point of the nuclear cycle. After the 1976 Ranger Report, the Movement Against Uranium Mining added proliferation of nuclear weapons to its existing concerns about safety hazards, environmental damage and the impact of mining on Aborigines. Yet, although a ban on mining is dear to anti-nuclear activists, not least the Victorian ALP Anti-Uranium Committee, Australia's role in nuclear deterrence hardly stands or falls by uranium production. For all the passion expended over the ALP's 1982 decision to continue mining to save jobs, a uranium ban would not fail the US nuclear loyalty test.[59]

More pertinent in this respect is the Melbourne-based Campaign Against Political Police which originated partly in protest against the effect of uranium legislation on civil liberties. At its broadest, this counter-security activity is directed against the 'recolonisation of Australia by US secret agencies'. But domestic political freedoms are the immediate concern.[60] Another anti-uranium overspill was the Nuclear-Free Zone Secretariat. It co-ordinates local councils in symbolic opposition to uranium mining and nuclear visiting, though few of the NFZs are likely candidates for visits.[61] But even if opposition to

119

mining and visiting becomes effective at state level, there is the bigger hurdle, as Premier Cain of Victoria was reminded, of federal government authority.

A third distinction in Australia is that opposition to the nuclear connection has had to overcome mainstream angst about national security. Whereas there had been increasing opposition to the nuclear fuel cycle, including naval reactors, opinion polls up to 1987 also showed that the majority of the population regarded the nuclear connection as enhancing Australia's defence. Opinion polls have their limitations. One in 1981 revealed that 47 per cent of those asked could not name any US facility but that 60 per cent approved of the US military presence. Nevertheless, even basing nuclear weapons in Australia had majority support in a 1982 survey – a result which would have been inconceivable in New Zealand. As for the alliance, over 70 per cent in polls in 1983 and 1984 thought the US connection was important to Australia's security and that the US could be trusted if Australia were threatened. Up to October 1982, polls suggested that as many as 58 per cent agreed that US naval vessels carrying nuclear weapons should be allowed to visit, with 39 per cent against. After New Zealand's ban in March 1985 an *Age* poll on US warships carrying nuclear weapons indicated that 65 per cent favoured visits and 27 per cent favoured exclusion (see appendix 6). As discussed below, polls in 1987 and 1988 indicate a subsequent anti-nuclear shift in opinion, but the circumstances differ from those which pertained in New Zealand in the early 1980s.

Explanations for the traditional strength of support for nuclear deterrence in Australia include the suggestion of media control and bias. For example, the left-wing Victorian MP, Joan Coxsedge, argues that the Australian media is dominated by Rupert Murdoch syndicates which voice uncritical support for US security policies.[62] Whilst true that no Australian metropolitan newspaper has objected to Australia's nuclear connection, the situation scarcely differed across the Tasman. The New Zealand media reported anti-nuclear stunts and opinion, but apart from one or two newspapers, such as the *Auckland Star*, editorial writers were no less supportive of the United States than they had been during the Vietnam War. Nearly all the big circulation dailies are in the Murdoch group; nuclear politics influenced the middle ground in spite of hostility in the fourth estate.

A second explanation for Australian caution concerns the country's social composition. The significant Irish-Catholic population has been a 'carrier of conservatism'. Also, strong racial prejudice, once reflected in a White Australia policy, became linked to anti-communism. A higher proportion of refugees from communism in Eastern Europe and Asia is said to contribute to Australia's greater conservatism, in contrast to New Zealand's more homogenous, and flighty, Anglo-Saxon population.[63] This seductive ethnic hypothesis needs qualification. The single largest group of migrants in the 1981 Australian census was born in Britain (37 per cent), followed by Italians (9 per cent), perhaps fleeing poverty rather than Togliatti, and then New Zealanders. Among the newer Asian immigrants, the Vietnamese might be expected to harbour mixed feelings about France and the US as well as bitterness towards Hanoi. In New Zealand's case it can be surmised, though not proven, that many British immigrants in the 1970s had a revulsion against 'Wilsonian socialism', trade union militancy and causes identified with the left in the northern hemisphere. New Zealand also welcomed Hungarians and Czechs. But any list of prominent New Zealand critics of the anti-nuclear and anti-alliance trends, in varying degrees of intensity and sophistication, would be headed by well-established Celts. Perhaps the forebears of David McIntyre, Jim McLay, Ewan Jamieson, Dennis McLean, and Geoff McDonald suffered the torments of Marxism on Clydeside. A sociological explanation, however, should certainly take account of the Pacific peoples. Maoris and other Polynesians in New Zealand comprise 12 per cent of the population and have oriented the country towards a greater interest in the emergent nationalism of the region.

In Australia, as Alan Renouf noted, policy-makers have had a long-standing obsession with security.[64] Japanese wartime raids did nothing to stifle this. Australians have traditionally held stronger threat perceptions than New Zealanders. The quest for great power protection was partly a function of geography as well as experience. In addition to the prospect of being cut off from the outside world by disruption to communications, the extensive coastline perimeter was difficult to protect from amphibious attack, and the Northern Territory lay open to the Asian hordes who are now being welcomed as immigrants and tourists. Australia is also just within bombing range of Da Nang.

It was the prime aim of People for Nuclear Disarmament (PND) to change these attitudes. Inaugurated in Melbourne in 1981, PND spread through Victoria and then to other states with a policy of multilateral nuclear disarmament, saving a unilateral ban on nuclear visiting and extrication of the bases from US strategic functions. In 1984 the NSW branch also adopted a policy of non-alignment.[65] As a pressure group claiming to represent some 500 organizations and 5,000 individual members, its most promising tactic seemed to be to

121

generate sufficient momentum to influence ALP policy. However, this highlights the final feature of the Australian situation – bipartisan support in Canberra for the nuclear link with the US.

Attempting to influence the ALP has proved difficult, partly because its right wing has a tradition of Catholic anti-communism. Only half its MPs and two cabinet ministers are in the Parliamentary Nuclear-Free Australia group. Also, in the critical 1982–4 period, Hawke supplanted Hayden as leader; Hawke's closeness to Reagan and Shultz put him beyond the pale for anti-nuclearists.[66] The ALP leadership was unlikely to forget the CIA's alarmism of the 1970s and, as discussed in chapter 3, Hayden himself decided not to antagonize the US on ship visits. In addition Hayden, Beazley and Lionel Bowen persuaded the 1982 ALP conference to accept a 'creative ANZUS policy', to displace the 'fawning manner' of conservative governments. It would be tough enough, they argued, selling an ANZUS review to the electorate; a policy of closing bases would provide Fraser's election campaign with first class propaganda. The same 'devastating electoral consequences' were cited at the 1986 conference. The Opposition would play the Soviet card.[67] Even Hawke's bipartisanship drew right-wing criticism for being ambiguous about the alliance. It could hardly fail, of course, to excite the wrath of Conservatives. The Catholic activist, B. A. Santamaria, the academic, Colin Rubenstein, and the journalist, Peter Samuel, lambasted the Hawke Government for not backing the US on Nicaragua, SDI and the SPNFZ. Hawke had undermined the alliance and given credibility to the view that nuclear weapons are inherently bad, thus sustaining 'Soviet proxies' in the peace movement.[68]

At federal level the main running on nuclear issues has been made by the Democrat Party. Formed in 1977 after a split from the Liberals over uranium mining, it has the same policies as PND and has increasingly developed an anti-alliance tone. But Democrat representation is restricted to the Senate where Don Chipp, the leader until June 1986, introduced anti-nuclear legislation on several occasions. One of his Bills sought to prohibit the passage of ships carrying nuclear weapons in Australian waters except for transit or emergencies. Masters would be required to produce cargo manifests and Australian officials would be required to search vessels for nuclear weapons.[69] But such efforts were doomed by the sovereign immunity of warships and ALP senators voting with conservatives.

As the historians of the Australian peace movement remark, dissenters have tended to vote Labor in elections for the House of Representatives to keep Liberal-National numbers down, but vote for

Democrats or protest parties in elections for the Senate.[70] Disgust with the ALP's betrayals, however, led to the formation of the Nuclear Disarmament Party (NDP) in Canberra in 1984. The NDP originated with People for Nuclear Disarmament but became a loose coalition of disarmers, traditional left-wing dissenters in Melbourne, Tasmanian environmentalists and youth populists in NSW. Its platform advocated a prohibition on foreign bases and nuclear weapons in Australian territory, and an end to uranium mining. Although the NDP was not really prepared for the general election of December 1984, it attracted media attention when a rock singer, Peter Garrett, and a former ALP senator, Jean Melzer, stood as candidates. It gained half a million votes, over 7 per cent of the national total, though won only one Senate seat. However, the NDP's first National Conference in April 1985 was rent by factional disputes about organization, leadership and future directions. Melzer, Garrett and Vallentine resigned in the belief that the pro-Moscow Socialist Workers Party had infiltrated the NDP. Vallentine took her seat as an independent and was re-elected in the 1987 election. Also in that election an NDP candidate was returned but disqualified, his place taken by a 'running mate' who eventually sat in the Senate as an independent anti-nuclear member. Together with the Democrats, anti-nuclearists hold the balance of power in the Senate, embarrassing Labor senators who feel obliged to vote for the Government and against their consciences on security matters.[71]

The NDP remains a single issue party. A future prospect for dissent is on the lines of a broader-based Green Party (or Rainbow Alliance), favoured by Vallentine, or as part of a new left-wing coalition. Manœuvres in 1986 to establish a radical group to the left of the ALP, uniting Aboriginal activists, left-wing unions, environmentalists and ethnic interests, were prompted both by the NDP's success and the limitations of single issue politics.[72] But any new coalition would probably suffer from the endemic Australian disease of debilitating factionalism. The New Zealand anti-nuclearists had a distinct advantage in being able to work through the existing party system and its relatively accessible politicians.

Yet it cannot be denied that a shift has occurred in Australian intellectual circles. Conventional wisdom has been challenged through peace research by the Victorian Association for Peace Studies, and the Peace Research Centre at ANU funded by the Hawke Government. Some writers, such as David Martin, have explored non-alignment as an appropriate direction for Australia to take. Dennis Phillips, an ex-patriate American academic, argued that Australia's independence had amounted to choosing dependence on the US and its dangerous nuclear strategies.[73] Such appeals are pitched at the same kind of patriotic sentiments which gave New Zealand anti-nuclearism its populist tinge. However, as the Melbourne PND convenor, Richard Bolt, argues, disarmers cannot simply call for nuclear disengagement. They have to address the insecurity fears of Australians.[74] In this respect conservative shifts in élite opinion have occurred, partly through research work associated with the Strategic and Defence Studies Centre at ANU. To some extent, as we shall see in chapter 8, reappraisal of Australian security problems has proceeded top down as much as bottom up.

Security fears have also been addressed by a change in the international environment. Six opinion polls, conducted by Frank Small Associates of Sydney between September 1987 and August 1988, have implied a strong swing to qualified alignment in an electorate apathetic about defence issues. The September poll indicated that 58% either wanted no alliance or a relationship without nuclear weapons; 38% preferred the status quo. In February 1988 only 24% supported nuclear-armed ship visits, whereas 50% opposed and 26% were undecided. In July 1988 51% opposed the US bases; 39% approved. A clear majority (66%) wanted them used as bargaining chips in trade talks with the US. Although Australia might be following New Zealand's lead, a more likely explanation, offered by Andrew Mack, is that a combination of generational change and lower threat perception is responsible.[75] Rather than a nuclear war scare providing an impetus, as in New Zealand, it seems that the softening in superpower relations has meant that Australians are disinclined to see a need for nuclear deterrence.

In terms of alliance discipline, the United States is in a dilemma. If an aggressive stance is adopted, some allies are frightened off; if common security with the Soviet Union is pursued, allied populations might drift into indifference. However, the contrasting international situations have also had contrasting domestic political effects. International confrontation engendered a sense of crisis in New Zealand and spurred anti-nuclear activists to bid for the commanding political heights. In Australia in the late 1980s anti-nuclear activists were bidding against each other for authority in the dissenting constituency. When security is not a burning issue mainstream parties may be less vulnerable to pressure for radical change in alliance relations.

In any event, the circumstances in New Zealand presented greater opportunities for anti-nuclear activists to build upon public unease about the manifestations of nuclear deterrence and turn it to political advantage. This does not mean that the New Zealand population believes it could survive the consequences of a northern hemisphere nuclear war. A poll in March 1985 indicated that 66 per cent thought otherwise. Studies of 'nuclear winter' effects have had considerable publicity.[76] Yet as David Campbell's analysis suggests, the ban on ship visits was understood to constitute action to reduce the perceived nuclear threat.[77] Whether or not one considers this to be hopelessly unrealistic and environmentally precious about the dangers of nuclear deterrence, fending off 'contamination' from nuclear visiting was a simpler proposition in New Zealand than in Australia where there were other forms of nuclear engagement. Whether Australian opinion will continue to shift on the lines of the 1988 polls, sufficient to affect federal politics, will depend more on internal reappraisals of the outside world than on any 'Kiwi disease' imported from across the Tasman.

Ultimately New Zealand anti-nuclearism was a statement about foreign policy and the country's role in international relations. In this regard, the dispute between the US and New Zealand over ship access revealed that the superpower had limited leverage over the underling. Indeed, for New Zealand activists who urged complete military disengagement Washington's stick was better than any carrot. The next chapter, then, discusses the policies and negotiating positions of the governments involved in the dispute.

7 FROM NEGOTIATION TO LEGISLATION

Responding to New Zealand's refusal to accept the USS *Buchanan*, Admiral William Crowe announced that 'New Zealand had increased the risk of nuclear war'.[1] US reprisals for this indiscretion did little obvious harm to New Zealand but gave an appearance of outrageous coercion. Although domestic imperatives and divergent security perceptions were already creating difficulties in the ANZUS alliance, the occasion of New Zealand's bid for nuclear disengagement, and the American reaction, blighted the prospects for any diplomatic compromise. This chapter deals with the crisis over the USS *Buchanan*, the US responses and the problems of Australian and British mediation. It suggests that the Labour Government attempted to steer between the Scylla of domestic pressure and the Charybdis of the Reagan Administration's nuclearism. Once it was clear that the US would not renegotiate the New Zealand corner of the ANZUS triangle, the Labour Cabinet attempted to permit a tactful warship visit. When this failed it explored ways of satisfying the US and British non-disclosure policy and adopted a minimalist stance in legislating a nuclear-free zone.

In defending American interests the Reagan Administration identified the health of the alliance with New Zealand accepting a nuclear-capable ship. The Administration's hidden agenda was to dissuade other states from redefining their alliance relationship in similar fashion. In particular, the Australian facilities were thought to be at risk. The Australian Government, itself, faced domestic embarrassment as a result of New Zealand's nuclear ban. But the Hawke Cabinet never considered that the alliance with New Zealand should be defined by a particular weapon system. By contrast, the Thatcher Government in London conformed closely to the US view of a global web of nuclear deterrence.

US officials seemed unprepared for the breach. Yet congressmen had returned from a Pacific tour in 1981, impressed by a great deal of 'nervousness and confusion' about the Reagan Administration's foreign policy. Although NZLP leaders had said that warm feelings towards the US made it impossible for any party to run an anti-American campaign in New Zealand, the American politicians were also left in no doubt about Labour's unalterable commitment to a nuclear-free zone.[2] But the US officials directly involved in managing the crisis seem to have been rather complacent, at least in public. Asked about the treaty relationship, Fred Iklé, Under-Secretary of Defense for International Security simply replied that it was of course sound. Richard Armitage, Deputy Assistant Secretary of Defense for East Asian and Pacific Affairs, argued that the United States supported independence and diversity among allies in the region and did so 'without demanding conformity'. In the State Department, Paul Wolfowitz, Assistant Secretary for East Asian and Pacific Affairs, expected the close relationship to continue 'with any Australian and New Zealand Government no matter what particular differences on specific issues might arise'.[3]

It would seem that desk officers were more concerned about the situation in the Philippines, and Japan's procrastination in rearming, than about strains in ANZUS. In 1982 Walter Stoessel, Deputy Secretary of State, and Eugene Rostow, leading light of the Committee on the Present Danger and head of the Arms Control and Disarmament Agency, had been to Canberra and Wellington to ensure that the US view on ship access and the need for SLCMs was appreciated. Subsequently, the Hawke Government had proved pliable. No-one, however, could have predicted the catalogue of false assumptions, lack of communication and diplomatic bungling which followed Labour's election in New Zealand. The burlesque undermined negotiations but also exposed and delineated fundamental differences in perception between two of the allies.

THE USS *BUCHANAN* TEST

An air of unreality pervaded the July 1984 ANZUS Council meeting in Wellington. Muldoon had persisted with it, though he had timed the general election for two days beforehand. The new Labour Cabinet was not represented. Like Fraser in 1982, Muldoon accepted, or encouraged, the inclusion of a commitment to ship visits in the final communiqué. Further, Secretary of State George Shultz observed that the 1983 ANZUS review had worked out satisfactorily and that the alliance was stronger than ever as far as Australia was concerned. The US would work with New Zealand in the same way. But this did not include renegotiation, for there was nothing to negotiate about. A thorough examination would lead people to the same conclusion reached the year before.[4] In the course of meetings with Shultz, Lange argued that ANZUS allowed discretionary nuclear protection and reiterated the case for denuclearization. This made no sense to the other two partners for whom nuclearization had been assumed rather than excluded, but Shultz agreed to a period of grace before planning ship visits. The parameters of US policy had been set, however. Nothing would change. Having just confined Australia to a minimal review, the United States was not about to look again more seriously. Nor would the Hawke Government welcome re-opening the issue and stirring up debate in the ALP.

In fact there was a general expectation in the US and Australia that Lange would 'do a Hawke'. Australian Foreign Minister Hayden had said at the ANZUS Council press conference that, on ship visits, the Hawke Government had 'made a rather unsteady start, but we established beyond any doubt what our position was within a few weeks'. Shultz counselled patience and gave Lange a crucial assurance that there would be no economic reprisals if they failed to resolve the matter. It seemed that Washington would act circumspectly. It also seems that Reagan's loyal, serious-minded Ambassador to Wellington, H. Monroe Browne, understated the strength of New Zealand opinion in his reports to the State Department.[5]

For its part, the New Zealand Government sent confusing signals to Washington. Its negotiating position required recognition of an 'unconditional' nuclear-free stance, the right to actively promote an SPNFZ, acceptance of absolute equality of partnership on all issues and the requirement that ANZUS decisions be unanimous. But what did an unconditional non-nuclear stance amount to? The NZLP and anti-nuclear groups feared that the Cabinet would compromise. Ambassador Browne later alleged that Lange had asked for six months' grace to get his colleagues to understand the need for ship visits. Lange vigorously denied it, but perhaps he had used an ambiguous form of words.[6] In October 1984 the largest allied air exercise held in the country, Triad 84, went ahead with nuclear-capable F-16s. It had been scheduled for two years but had been criticized by Lange as introducing the spectre of militarism into New Zealand.[7] An element of confusion in Wellington is explicable in part by the Cabinet's preoccupation with upheaval in the financial system, and in part by lack of experience. Following tradition, Lange took the foreign affairs portfolio, but he had been an MP only since 1977. The average age of Ministers was only 42. In mitigation the New Zealand Government could plead that it was learning the ropes.

Through the remainder of 1984 US officials relied on psychological pressure. Admiral Crowe remarked that New Zealand threatened his responsibilities under ANZUS, and Browne confirmed that there was nothing in the relationship to renegotiate.[8] Nevertheless, the US had little option but to concede New Zealand's right to negotiate ship visits. The International Security Policy branch of the Pentagon, staffed by Iklé, Richard Perle and other prominent ideologues, and the Naval branch under Lehman, were anxious that New Zealand should not get accustomed to being without port calls. The United States favoured the diversion of a vessel from the *Sea Eagle* ANZUS exercise planned for March 1985, though no visit to New Zealand had occurred after the two previous *Sea Eagle* exercises. Lange wanted more time, but asked for a list of vessels from which he could choose suitable visitors. To reassure sceptical supporters, the Government let it be known that it could tell which ships would be nuclear armed. In the absence of private US information, this meant relying on *Jane's* publications and knowledge of recent naval deployments.

The USN refused to be humbled in this way, so Lange asked for a ship to be nominated. Browne interpreted this to mean that a request would be granted, whereas Lange apparently assumed that the US would send an Oliver Hazard Perry destroyer, not specifically fitted for nuclear warhead delivery. But CINCPAC HQ in Hawaii, guided by Pentagon officials, determined on an unambiguously nuclear-capable ship in order to breach New Zealand's anti-nuclear stance. The New Zealand Chief of Staff, Jamieson, went to Hawaii and negotiated the USS *Buchanan*. Ways of permitting access without revealing information were discussed at length, and journalists have speculated that Jamieson was tipped off that the *Buchanan* would not carry nuclear weapons. Publicly, the USN's stance was quite straightforward: no confirmation or denial of status on its part, and no assessment, however ill-informed, by anyone else. In view of the New Zealand Government's proposal to make its own judgement, the *Buchanan* presented the Lange Government with a credibility problem.

Nor was its policy-making assisted by the tricky working relations between the Minister of Defence, Frank O'Flynn, and his officials. O'Flynn was openly disappointed about getting the defence job, and MoD personnel, including the defence attaché in Washington, were seemingly opposed to the policies of the Labour Government. MoD briefing papers took a contrary view of nuclear deterrence and contained stern warnings about likely US responses to nuclear disengagement. Some Labour politicians strongly believed that NZ officials were playing their own game. Departmental 'leaks' led eventually to questions about loyalty.[9] Alternatively, officials may have been working on instructions which had not been properly spelt out. There was a distinct lack of confidence between political masters and civil servants, though the Ministry of Foreign Affairs adapted to the new régime with greater finesse.

The formal *Buchanan* request of December 1984 was dealt with by Lange's deputy, the former law professor Geoffrey Palmer, while Lange visited the Tokelau Islands. Palmer announced on 13 January 1985 that nuclear-capable vessels which, in the context of their operations, conformed to the anti-nuclear policy would not necessarily be excluded. This alarmed the Party and anti-nuclear groups which had little faith in the Government's ability to resist US and bureaucratic pressures. The Government had kept the *Buchanan*'s identity secret, but a leak from the Prime Minister's Department alerted peace activists to the fact that it would be nuclear capable. They were determined that the Cabinet should declare 'certainty' rather than 'confidence' that a ship was nuclear free. The leaky conditions continued with the publication in Australia of a personal letter from Hawke to Lange. Hawke wanted clarification of the New Zealand position before he travelled to Washington in February, in view of Australia's need to assess the outlook for further intelligence co-operation. His missive included the statement: 'We cannot accept as a permanent arrangement that the ANZUS alliance has a different meaning and entails different obligations for different members.'[10] It created some resentment in New Zealand, adding to the growing tension.

By mid-January MPs were being deluged with thousands of petitions. Peace squadrons threatened direct action against any nuclear-capable ships. Key ministers changed course and Palmer, like Scholes at the time of the HMS *Invincible* incident, took a precise view, deciding that the *Buchanan*'s capability ruled it out. At a cabinet meeting on 28 January and a back-bench caucus on the 31st it was made abundantly clear to the now-returned Prime Minister that the vessel was unacceptable. Lange asked Ambassador Browne for another ship, but journalists had deduced that this might happen and publicized their hunch, thus scotching the possibility of a substitute. It seems unlikely, however, that the US would have co-operated anyway. Had the Reagan Administration been more sensitive to the Labour Government's restricted room for manœuvre it would have suggested a non-nuclear-capable vessel in the first place or held off for longer.

According to sources who were intimately involved in these events, Lange dithered about implementing the anti-nuclear policy, but was willing to explore various avenues until they were blocked. He personally believed that nuclear deterrence existed as an objective condition, but that it was being destabilized by new strategies and the arms race. Personal conviction aside, Lange had decided not to oppose routine warship visits but simply wanted to discover what was feasible and what was not. He had tried to dilute the visiting policy without success in the past, and distrust of compromise had grown. In the end 'it became clear to the PM that pushing for the *Buchanan* was like boarding the *Titanic*'.[11]

One can argue, then, that a prime factor in the dispute was lack of political direction from the top. Personal animosity developed towards Lange among US officials, almost to the point of believing that there would be no problem without him. He was regarded as unhelpful and unpredictable, and his penchant for press conference quips earned him a reputation in Washington for being an impulsive 'mouther'.[12] It is not obvious, however, what sort of pro-visit direction Lange could have given without committing political suicide and risking another 'Springbok tour'. The affair highlights the issue of how far governments and bureaucracies can or should protect security policy from the depredations of democratic expression. Public opinion is commonly volatile, uncomprehending and confused, whilst defence provision and foreign relationships are best served by continuities which outlast public whims. US officials believed that the Labour Cabinet could have ignored what they assumed was 'trendy' anti-nuclear pressure. Yet to be worthy of the democratic label, state policy should reflect to some degree social change as well as international developments. An élitist approach is less viable in a country with traditions of accessibility and intimacy between rulers and ruled, and where vested interests are not heavily shielded from scrutiny.

The Government presumably judged, also, that the consequences would not be sufficiently serious to damage national interests. As Shultz pointed out, the *Buchanan* incident indicated that only ships which could be identified as unambiguously non-nuclear 'could ever call in that nation again'.[13] This was exactly how New Zealand defined its nuclear disengagement. Moreover, the US defence-related reprisals which followed might have been devised to validate and sustain the case for qualified alignment.

US RESPONSES AND THE POLITICS OF REPRISALS

The fury which emanated from the United States resulted initially in reprisals affecting defence co-operation. Although subsequently justified as measured and systematic by US officials, the reprisals gave an impression of unco-ordinated, punitive and egregious petulance. Australia had to cancel *Sea Eagle* because the USN refused to participate, and New Zealand was excluded from other exercises, including *Team Spirit* in Korea. The US declined to attend military conferences in Australia, and Hawke cancelled the July 1985 ANZUS Council meeting because the US would not sit down with New Zealand representatives.[14] In Los Angeles at the end of February, a mere deputy-assistant secretary of state confronted Lange with a list of measures affecting intelligence work and military exercises.

In fact the freeze was partial. As suggested in chapter 3, security co-operation proved difficult to unravel and much of it involved agreements with powers outside ANZUS. Perhaps a New Zealand observer retained access to briefing papers on the ABCA armies' committee of the 'famous five'. Exchanges and military training proceeded on a case by case basis 'without predisposition to approve', but critical missions and training on US equipment were unaffected.[15] CIA, FBI, and Australian Security Intelligence material probably remained largely undisturbed, whereas US military intelligence and strategic assessments were curtailed by some 80 per cent. But the US was anxious not to take steps which could be construed as jeopardizing the safety of personnel or New Zealand's immediate security, and the Naval Data Center in Hawaii may have continued to supply Daily Estimated Position Locator reports.[16] New Zealand continued to supply Australia, and thus the USN, with data from Tangimoana. Whether the decision to curtail military intelligence was reached in concert with the other signatories to UKUSA is unknown, though Australia co-operated in sorting intelligence before forwarding to Wellington. Pacific Fleet HQ in Hawaii also asked the Australians to replace the New Zealanders in Singapore who monitored Soviet naval movements using US equipment.[17] As regards logistic supply, the MoU due for expiry in June 1987 was not renewed, though New Zealand qualified for rights normally accorded to non-allied friendly nations. At an early stage of the dispute the American DoD decided to keep the framework of support intact, though the signals received in New Zealand suggested that the US regarded defence co-operation as dispensable.[18]

Lack of trust deepened when Washington officials allowed or encouraged threats of economic reprisals to gain credence. New Zealand's economic vulnerability was discussed by a State Department official during congressional hearings on the crisis, Weinberger and Lehman advocated economic reprisals, and a New Zealand business mission returned from the US with dire warnings about the trade relationship.[19] Protectionist measures and dumping of agricultural produce had frequently antagonized the Anzacs in the past. In 1985 New Zealand's economic restructuring had already triggered a farming crisis. The US countervailing duty on lamb, announced in September, was higher than expected, but independent of the nuclear dispute. In fact trade with the US increased by nearly 50 per cent in the year ending June 1985, though US officials argued that New Zealand would eventually lose its privileged status in Washington. Actually the Reagan Administration never deviated from its promise to avoid economic sanctions; it even acted to restrain hot-heads on Capitol Hill. But the polemics were enough to heighten nationalism in New Zealand and contribute abroad to the impression of the US treating a friendly nation worse than an adversary.

As a better understanding of New Zealand's anti-nuclear politics penetrated Washington, the National Security Council instructed the US Information Agency (USIA, known abroad as Service) to lead a public relations campaign in New Zealand. But this also offended local sensibilities, especially when a USIS office was opened in Christchurch in 1986, home of Deep Freeze and anti-nuclear groups. Mindful of the extent to which the USIA had become politicized under Charles Z. Wick, Reagan's Hollywood colleague, a group called Nuclear-Free Kiwis monitored the campaign and the activities of groups on the 'loony right'. The vigilantes noted that the USIS organized and financed trips to the US by selected journalists, politicians and 'sound' public figures. But as the editor of The Press observed, New Zealand newspapers had consistently supported the American position, and journalists would recognize propaganda for what it was.[20]

The USIA also subsidized right-wing think-tanks, such as the ANZUS Project at the Georgetown University Center for Strategic Studies in Washington, DC. Described by Lange as a 'right-wing fundamentalist group', the ANZUS Project was set up shortly after the New Zealand election under the direction of Ray Cline, a former CIA chief. Such activity and predictions by Richard Falk and former CIA officials alerted New Zealanders to the possibility of destabilization. Labour Party supporters assumed that anti-Whitlam measures would be repeated to hinder Labour's re-election chances in 1987.[21]

Given the CIA's record in Australia, and in Indonesia during the last days of Suharto, plus evidence of US intimidation of Belau and interest in the first Fiji coup, it might be naïve to assume that the US did not at least consider covert operations against the Labour Government. Indications of activity were reported in the BBC's *Listener* (15 March 1984), after one of the principals of a Hawaii business company stood trial for tax fraud and tried to implicate the CIA. The company had an office in Auckland for a while and links with personnel of the notorious Nugan-Hand Bank which had laundered CIA money in Australia.[22]

Indeed the Maori loans scandal of 1986 resembled the CIA's approach to Australian Ministers with financial offers which were used to harm the Whitlam Government. In 1986, the permanent head of the Maori Affairs Department in Wellington was offered a large loan on easy terms to finance Maori development. Television journalists traced the loan-fixers to the same Hawaii business interests. Although the Lange Government found no hard evidence of US complicity, anti-nuclear activists argued that the scandal had all the hallmarks of a CIA operation to promote racial unrest and embarrass the Government. Paul Cleveland, who had replaced the hapless Browne as US Ambassador, denied it.[23]

In February 1986, the long-awaited submarine turned up, not in Cook Strait but off the Cook Islands. An RNZAF Orion became inadvertently engaged in identifying it, but the strongly pro-American, Cook Islands' Premier, Sir Thomas Davis, imposed a news blackout and Lange declined to divulge the submarine's nationality on the basis of MoD information. The opposition leader, Jim McLay, was given a confidential MoD briefing, but made no effort to raise a scare about New Zealand's vulnerability. Lange finally dismissed the vessel as a whale with flatulence. Detailed research into the incident led to the assumption that it conformed to well-established 'psy-op' procedures for US submarines engaged in covert activities. There was speculation that the 'whale' wanted to attract the attention of local fishermen, but not the scrutiny of the RNZAF.[24]

The most serious visible action taken by the Reagan Administration was its unilateral withdrawal from the security commitment to New Zealand. This had been promised as a reprisal for New Zealand legislating its nuclear-visiting ban, but Lange was so dilatory that the US moved first, leaving no adequate response when the Bill became law. Talks between Shultz and Hayden in San Francisco, on 10–11 August 1986, described as an ANZUS Council meeting, produced an exchange of letters affirming continuation of the relationship between the US and Australia. Both parties called upon New Zealand to restore access and agreed that the ban detracted from the Treaty requirement to enhance collective security. The US said that it could no longer honour its obligations to New Zealand and they were suspended 'pending adequate corrective measures'.[25]

Shultz had wanted a tough communiqué but avoided legalistic phrasing and stopped short of saying that New Zealand had contravened the Treaty. Reaganites had limited faith in the machinery of international law, having secured America's withdrawal from the International Court of Justice in the Nicaragua merits case after the illegal mining of Nicaraguan waters. Any steps under international treaty law would have created further antagonism, and generated controversy about NCND and the sovereign right of states to determine conditions of warship access.

Significantly, also, Reagan officials heeded Australian advice not to seek a new bilateral treaty but to keep ANZUS in place for the day when the National Party returned to power in New Zealand. It would have been quite a leap to push New Zealand into non-alignment and there were countervailing pressures against it, such as New Zealand's role in the Pacific islands. Nevertheless, the action confirmed suspicions in New Zealand that the country did not count for much in the US scheme of things. Reprisals also had an historical and symbolic significance, manifesting a change in the political relationship. Accordingly, the US reaction could only be justified by endowing the crisis with global significance.

Although the crisis drew a mild enough expression of regret from Reagan on 7 February 1985, his executives elevated New Zealand's defiance to an issue of apocalyptic proportions. They warned that New Zealand's challenge threatened the security of the entire Western Alliance, on the assumption that given a chance allies would opt out of the awkward parts of burden sharing. On several occasions Shultz reiterated the notion that New Zealand had walked off the job of deterring war:

> Even when one partner shirks its responsibilities, the health and unity of the entire alliance are placed in jeopardy . . . If one partner is unwilling to make these sacrifices, others will wonder why they should carry their share of the burden. The result may be the gradual erosion of popular commitment to the common cause.[26]

Even tentative disengagement, said James Kelly, Assistant Secretary of Defense, lowered the conflict threshold.[27]

Irate editorials in the American press urged firm retaliation and condemned New Zealanders as sanctimonious and hypocritical.[28] The language of officials was less sharp in public but did nothing to allay an impression of bullying. Weinberger and Perle threatened to make New Zealand 'pay dearly' so other allies would note that defiance was not cost free. In this, as Stephen Hoadley argues, official opinion in the US was divided only about the degree of severity of response.[29] State Department officials realized the danger of economic sanctions, whereas the Navy and ideologues in the International Security Policy section of the DoD urged a more publicly punitive reaction.

Obviously, much of the rhetoric was designed to exert psychological pressure on New Zealand. Yet reactions were dictated less by the strategic significance of the South Pacific than by the seamless web theology and an anxiety about the inspirational effect of Wellington's anti-nuclear stance. This misplaced fear is considered in chapter 9, but we should note that various countries were mentioned as the real targets of US reprisals, including Belgium and Denmark, 'with the hope that the Greeks will also get the message'.[30] In fact the Administration was primarily concerned about keeping Japan and Australia on the right lines and about anti-nuclearism at home.

The immediate operational implications concerned Navy Secretary John Lehman in particular. The Navy had suffered heavily in the 1970s, he said, from constraints on its nuclear warships. When the USS *Eisenhower* returned to Virginia in 1978, after 140 days without a port call, 85 per cent of the crew had resigned. A close associate of Iklé and Perle, Lehman also typified the fundamentalist approach to managing alliance opinion. If the US did not take a hard line, he argued, it would 'prove irresistible to other social democratic governments to indulge and buy off their extreme leftist factions at the expense of the US Navy'.[31] Lehman had another hidden agenda. Alongside his zeal for a 600 ship navy, SLCMs and a forward maritime posture, he promoted a strategic homeporting plan for dispersing battleship task groups around the US. It had to be fought through the Pentagon, where there was resistance to it on strategic grounds, through the General Accounting Office, which was unconvinced of the economic benefits, and in Congress, which wanted environmental reports on the proposed sites. To the astute Ronald Dellums, Chairman of the House Military Installations Subcommittee, it looked like a cynical attempt to spread the Navy's political influence.[32] The project led to an unseemly scramble by coastal cities to obtain a share of the expenditure, but by 1985 local authorities and anti-nuclear pressure groups in San Francisco and New York threatened to jeopardize the scheme. New Zealand's ban could not have come at a less convenient time for Lehman who naturally wanted the appropriations secured.

Homeporting featured in the display of congressional pique. Sanctionists developed a sudden interest in the South-West Pacific because they supported the Navy's plan for homeporting a battleship surface action group in New York. The Chairman of the Senate Sea Power Subcommittee, William Cohen, noted that in contrast to New Zealanders, New Yorkers recognized their responsibilities. Accusing New Zealand of appeasement, though without saying what demands were being appeased, he advanced a resolution which attracted 52 cosponsors. It recommended that the Administration explore the possibility of a bilateral treaty with Australia and restrict New Zealand trade.[33]

Few New Zealand commentators realized it, but much of the support for Cohen had more to do with Staten Island than Auckland Harbour. New York and New Jersey politicians had secured the battleship group for Staten Island in July 1983 after stiff competition from Boston and Baltimore. The New York Democrats, Samuel Stratton (member of the House Armed Services Committee) and Joseph Addabbo (Chairman of the Appropriations Committee and a leading critic of defence spending), along with Mayor Koch and Governor Mario Cuomo, had agitated for it. The New York home port would involve a capital expenditure of millions of dollars and up to $US3 million a year in taxes. But locals, supported by the Revd Jesse Jackson and Democratic congressmen, were nervous about SLCMs stationed opposite Brooklyn.[34] Among those who denigrated both this opposition and Lange's 'grandstanding' were Stratton, Gerald Solomon, William Carney, Benjamin Gilman and Guy Molinari. Molinari, whose constituency office was close to the proposed construction site, accused New Zealand of adding fuel to the fire in New York by setting a precedent. On his initiative 140 members of Congress sent a cable to the Speaker of the New Zealand Parliament urging a reconsideration of the ban.[35]

Other signatories represented traditionally isolationist agricultural communities. Not overly distressed about subsidized US wheat sales to the Soviet Union, they were particularly concerned about the USN's ability to operate globally. Representatives of mutton, wool and casein constituencies argued that a strong reaction was justified because 'this is a threat to the entire defense of the Western World'.[36] For good measure, a few mid-West senators wanted to include a ban on Australian products, such as uranium, because Australia was a country which worked hard 'to malign the use of nuclear weapons'. The Australian Ambassador worked hard writing to every congressman.[37] In fact the Administration also put out a restraining hand by encouraging J. Leach (Republican, Iowa) to trump Cohen's resolution for economic measures with another which referred to the New Zealand blood spilled in wars of democracy. The Leach Bill commended the President for rejecting economic sanctions, urged continued negotiations to resolve 'this temporary discord' and favoured endorsement of an SPNFZ if it allowed port visits. Subsequently, Leach thought the Administration's reprisals had gone too far.[38]

Nevertheless, the congressional anger prompted Stephen Solarz, Chairman of the House Subcommittee on East Asia and the Pacific, to instigate hearings. Solarz had visited New Zealand after Labour's election and understood some of the impetus behind the nuclear disengagement policy, but he voiced disquiet about its effect on continued support for the facilities in Australia. Other congressmen, including Stratton, also visited the South-West Pacific in January 1986. Some of them used such violent expressions about punishing New Zealand that an all-party Australian parliamentary committee had to explain that Australian opinion would not countenance vindictiveness.[39] During the Solarz hearings several witnesses, notably the academics Henry Albinski and William Tow, advised caution against mismanaging the crisis, given that New Zealand's ban made no strategic difference to US security. The Democrat leader, Walter Mondale, also urged dialogue rather than precipitate action. Others noted that the US would not dream of taking similar action against 'the Danish, the French, the Norwegians, all of whom have failed to come up with something'. To Solarz, US–Australian relations had paramount consideration, and in one of the saner comments to emerge in the politics of reprisals, he suggested that the US should heed Australian advice.[40]

AUSTRALIAN NEUTRALITY

US officials apparently anticipated Australian co-operation in teaching New Zealand the facts of life, but in September 1984 the Hawke Government made it clear that its disapproval of New Zealand's ban did not extend to acting as an emissary of the United States.[41] After Hawke's personal letter to Lange in January 1985, it was likely that further intervention would have been counter-productive anyway. Certainly Australia and the United States had a common interest in keeping the Treaty alive. The Liberal–Country Party Opposition urged a new bilateral treaty. But Hawke could not pursue this without debate and dissent within the ALP. Yet to have replaced the Treaty with an exchange of letters would have seemed like diluting the relationship. Hawke's overriding interest was to limit damage to his Government. He achieved this by remaining firmly committed to ANZUS, distancing Australia from New Zealand's policy sufficiently to satisfy the US, but without upsetting Anzac sentiment and co-operation. His worst moment arrived when the ALP revolted against his decision to allow the use of Sydney as a staging-post for monitoring MX missile splashdowns in the region. His personal friend, Shultz, allowed him to cancel the commitment as an affordable concession for the sake of more important interests.[42]

Australia's problems increased substantially when US reprisals threatened to affect defence co-operation, especially intelligence access. Some re-organization was unavoidable and, as Ross Babbage remarked, the crisis complicated US–Australian relations. Such was the mood in Washington that when Australian officials enquired whether the United States would co-operate on South Pacific defence arrangements if New Zealand were involved, they were told: 'we are not in a position to engage in the type of defence co-operation that would normally characterise an alliance relationship such as we have with Australia.'[43] But Australia secured New Zealand's recognition of the additional costs of duplicating military exercises and gained some compensation in joint procurement with New Zealand. Largely as rhetorical reassurance to the US and conservative opinion in Australia, Hayden emphasized on a visit to New Zealand in December 1986 that Australia could not be expected to substitute for the US in security matters. Subsequently he contended that the adjustment process had settled down and was working well.[44]

The implications of the crisis for Anzac security co-operation are discussed in the next chapter, but we can note here that Hayden and Beazley confirmed that co-operation with New Zealand remained a cardinal component of Australia's foreign policy. Far from being ostracized, New Zealand had become increasingly important in complementing the regional emphasis in Australian security. Hayden implicitly criticized the US zero-sum approach, and told Shultz that nuclear visiting was not a vital determinant as to whether any part of regional security would stand or fall.[45] Even the less critical Hawke made it clear that Australia was not in the business of wreaking vengeance on New Zealand. Asked about Lehman's bid to transfer Deep Freeze from Harewood to Hobart he went so far as to say: 'We regard New Zealand as a friend, and one friend shouldn't try to derive advantages from the temporary difficulty of the other.'[46] In sum, the Australians adopted an attitude of bemused tolerance towards New Zealand, and whereas the Reagan Administration regarded support for nuclear deterrence as the *sine qua non* of alliance membership, the Hawke Government considered that New Zealand's policy did not vitiate its value as an ally.

At the San Francisco suspension meeting of August 1986, Hayden reiterated Australia's disagreement with New Zealand policy and 'expressed understanding' of the action which the United States had taken. But the communiqué also noted that Australia retained its bilateral security relationship with New Zealand. In addition, Australia argued that economic protectionism, in which the US was a leading practitioner, seriously damaged Australian interests and impaired its ability to co-operate in ensuring regional stability. Ironically, New Zealand was dumped at the same time as the US Agricultural Department dumped wheat and sugar in the direction of the Soviet Union and China. This so infuriated the victims, Australian farmers, that they threatened to march on the US facilities demanding rent. In January 1987 the US dumped subsidized barley in Saudi Arabia, a leading Australian market. Australian producers estimated the loss at $A700 million and described the action as a 'complete disaster'. The President of the Farmers' Federation remarked that if the US was prepared 'to chop us off at the knees, all the security arrangements should be up for reappraisal'. Even fervent admirers of Reaganism conceded that the US had miscalculated badly. Hawke was critical but carefully avoided linking the issue to the facilities.[47]

The bulk of the Australian population continued to value the US connection. Although the warship ban was said to have given New Zealand the highest profile in Australia in living memory it remained influential only at the political margins. A poll in 1985 suggested that 59 per cent thought the ban unwise for New Zealand, against 33 per cent who considered it wise. At the same time, 35 per cent thought Australia should side with the US in the dispute, 22 per cent supported New Zealand and 37 per cent backed Hawke's neutrality.[48] Neither the Australian right nor the Reagan Administration appreciated Hawke's skill in limiting damage to national interests as perceived by the Australian majority.

Malcolm Fraser suggested an alternative source of mediation. Writing as a personal friend to the US Vice-president, George Bush, in March 1985, Fraser noted that US policy appeared coercive. The best approach was to persuade Britain to get heavily involved, because New Zealand felt closer to Britain than to any other country. 'British influence, properly used', he argued, 'can be pre-eminent in achieving a change of heart in New Zealand, and the tragedy is that that approach has not been adopted, low key, and long ago.'[49] By 1985 it was too late, and Fraser rather underestimated the social changes and perceptions across the Tasman which made British sway less powerful than in the past.

BRITISH INFLUENCE

As an ally of the ANZUS partners, also affected by New Zealand's ban, Britain took a keen interest in the clash. In February 1985 Thatcher joined Reagan in condemning New Zealand policy, and took the same stance on nuclear deterrence, alliance unity and NCND. Whether or not prevailed upon by Bush and Fraser, the British Government also declared a readiness to help resolve the difficulties. This amounted to exerting diplomatic pressure to dissuade the Lange Government from establishing a legal precedent. However, the succession of British officials and experts who visited Wellington, notably Sir Michael Armitage, Director of British Defence Intelligence, and John Stanley, Minister for the Armed Forces, made little headway.

Also, by some accounts, Admiral Sir John Fieldhouse's visit in February 1986 was rather unrewarding. Fieldhouse argued that New Zealand was weakening the fabric of opposition to communism and may well have explained the subversive threat posed by Soviet fishing trawlers and merchant ships. Cynics are said to have rumoured that New Zealand might have become the first country to sink a Soviet vessel in peacetime; a local pilot had recently tried to take a short cut with the passenger cruise vessel *Mikhail Lermontov* in the Marlborough Sounds. Yet the British Chief of Defence Staff had discussed 'all sorts of proposals' to cope with the NCND impasse.[50] By now, however, the Lange Government was publicly committed to avoiding a verbal formula which allowed business as usual. Fieldhouse pointed out that defence co-operation with Britain might be affected by legislation, including personnel exchange schemes. Clause 5 in the NFZ Bill made it an offence for New Zealand personnel to assist in the command of nuclear weapons. But Sir John's representations appeared to rub national sensitivities. Lange later remarked that if exchanges ended it would not be the end of the world. New Zealand was no longer a colony though the British had seen fit to send out an Admiral 'to lecture us'.[51] Evidently it could be claimed that on South Pacific security matters, the views in Wellington were at least as well informed as those in Whitehall.

In April 1986 the Baroness Young, Minister of State, arrived in Wellington with the unenviable task of convincing New Zealand that nuclear weapons were not imposed on allies, just that allies were expected to help maintain deterrence by hosting ships which might be carrying nuclear weapons.[52] Although her logic and phraseology closely resembled that employed by US officials, it would be a mistake to assume that British views were dictated from Washington. The ideology of the seamless nuclear web was equally entrenched in London.

Britain's main leverage related to access for New Zealand agricultural produce to the European Community (EC). New Zealanders had been acutely aware of this since the Chirac Government used economic sanctions to secure the repatriation of the agents who sank the British-registered *Rainbow Warrior*. The Thatcher Government rendered less support to New Zealand over this incident than might otherwise have been expected, largely because it supported French nuclear testing and appreciated the contributions of France to European security.[53]

Dairy quotas had been declining annually since 1973. But in April 1987 in the first bilateral visit by a British Foreign Secretary for 15 years, Sir Geoffrey Howe linked butter access to ship access. He stigmatized New Zealand policy as seeking 'a free lunch on the alliance' and warned that although Britain would honour its obligation to press New Zealand's case in the EC, the cause was less likely to prevail with NATO members because of the anti-nuclear policy. Naturally, European farmers and governments attempting to deal with their own expensively-supported over-production, had reason to query butter arriving from 12,000 miles away. But it was the Irish Republic, neither in NATO nor greatly exercised by nuclear visiting, which delayed agreement on access in 1986. France and Britain were the only NATO–EC countries pursuing a link between trade and nuclear weapons. Howe's comments merely stirred resentment, especially as he expressed the hope that the shadow over New Zealand–UK relations would shortly be lifted. A general election was due in a few months, and the British High Commissioner noted that the National Party's policy was more in agreement with what was generally accepted in the Western Alliance.[54]

Lange resisted the temptation to look a gift horse in the mouth. 'For anyone', he said, 'to come here and attempt to use the difficulties of the European market as a lever against New Zealand's anti-nuclear policy is to advance an argument which is unsustainable ... Such is its illogicality that it can only be construed as an attempt to intervene in New Zealand's domestic politics.' The reduction in quotas, he added, was the price New Zealand paid for European farm support. The anti-nuclear policy was irrelevant, but if Europe tried to take advantage of New Zealand's trade vulnerability, then the answer did not lie in greater submission.[55] Labour supporters were delighted by the impact of Howe's remarks. The *New Zealand Herald* (29 April 1987), one of the most conservative newspapers in the country and trenchantly critical of Labour's anti-nuclearism, now fulminated against Howe's 'veiled threats ... to withhold our pocket money'. New Zealand's policy was democratically made and neither the US nor the UK could teach New Zealand much about sacrifices for liberty. British diplomacy not only encountered suspicions that the Thatcher Government ran errands for the Reagan Administration, but that Britain was a 'gathering irrelevancy' because it laboured under the illusion that the Pacific was a watery replica of Europe.[56]

British mediation lacked the requisite degree of disinterest to be productive. In theory Britain was in a reasonable position to have helped ease New Zealand into a *modus vivendi* on ship visits. So long as HMS *Invincible* was not offered, it is conceivable that Lange would have risked accepting a British visit request in 1984. However, the ANZUS crisis provided a benchmark, not merely of divergence on nuclear issues, but of the increasingly disconnected security preoccupations of the two countries.

FINAL ACTS

Indeed, the absence of agents for mediation and arbitration was a striking feature of the crisis. In an alliance of only three powers, moderating influences were at a premium. Much of the diplomacy seemed to be conducted via the press and television. Lange accused the US of adopting the morality of totalitarianism, and Shultz refused to receive Ambassador Rowling. As late as the middle of 1987 diplomacy was still in abeyance.

Some advance in mutual understanding did occur. The idea in Washington that the New Zealand Government had become a prisoner of left-wing ideologues, gave way to the view that a job had to be done to educate New Zealanders to the 'realities of nuclear deterrence'.[57] The Cabinet in Wellington also began to grasp the importance of dealing with American sensibilities. If the US insisted that to be rescued by the cavalry you should be prepared to see the horses from time to time then this was understandable, though New Zealand had no requirement for the cavalry. If US policy was dictated by concern about a ripple effect, then, so Lange argued, New Zealand policy reflected a unique set of circumstances. Other countries 'must confront the nuclear problem in their own ways'. New Zealand could implement a small measure of arms control 'while in no way disturbing the balance of strategic interests elsewhere'.[58] If the US did not have one navy painted nuclear and another painted conventional, then New Zealand would accommodate the universality of NCND. If the US had an imperfect understanding of the Westminster system which allowed a government to repeal legislation within three months of taking office, then executive policy might suffice. When legislation became unavoidable, it would be made as palatable as possible. New Zealand would place limits on nuclear weapons in the immediate vicinity but the law would make no difference to the strategic operations of any nuclear navy.

But concessions did not wipe out the offence of symbolic disengagement from nuclear deterrence and the fact that reprisals were a warning to others could hardly convert New Zealanders to the American view. As Richard Kennaway notes, reprisals shifted the debate away from problems of visits to the problems of being allied to the United States.[59] Opinion hardened. Lange spoke of the Treaty being scrapped if it hindered New Zealand relations with the US, and at the 1985 NZLP conference Helen Clark told cheering delegates that the policy had given the people a new pride in being New Zealanders.[60] Labour could play the patriotic card against opponents. National's leader, Jim McLay, was accused of sending people on a 'bootlicking pilgrimage' to the US State Department to get help with the National Party election campaign. Actually they had warned the Americans that economic reprisals would make it impossible to reverse Labour's policy.[61] Then the *Rainbow Warrior* affair not only added a certain piquancy to relations with France, but demonstrated once again that a small sovereign state was being treated with arrogance by nuclear powers. Confrontation hardly damaged Labour's standing in the monthly polling surveys. By the beginning of 1986, after the first reading of the NFZ Bill, Labour's lead over National had stretched to 15 per cent.

Negotiations collapsed at a forty-minute 'High Noon' between Lange and Shultz in Manila in June 1986. Shultz clarified the dilemma: 'either we would conform to the law and render NCND useless; or we (or your Prime Minister) must deliberately flaunt the laws of New Zealand. I would point out that implicit in the neither confirm nor deny policy is a requirement for ambiguity about the nature of the armaments of our ships.' Therefore New Zealand would remain a friend but no longer an ally. Shultz rejected a proposal for private assurances about particular ships, allegedly on the grounds that even if New Zealand could keep requests and rejections secret, the US defense establishment leaked like a sieve. In any event anti-nuclearists regarded nods and winks as inherently unreliable. Palmer told Canadian officials that politically his Government could not modify the promise to assess itself whether vessels were nuclear armed or powered.[62] Reportedly, Shultz told Lange that from time to time allies must expect to host ships carrying nuclear weapons. Lange pounced on this 'revelation', leaked it and argued that the National Party's policy of restoring visits would inevitably mean nuclear weapons in New Zealand ports.[63]

The New Zealand Cabinet had delayed legal action as long as possible, perhaps hoping for tractability to emerge in Washington. Delay certainly allowed an assessment of the SPNFZ, agreed by the South Pacific Forum on 6 August 1985. But the Treaty of Rarotonga heightened concern in Washington about a spreading nuclear-free inkblot, even if it permitted signatories to decide their own policy about hosting nuclear warships and did not presume to curtail existing US operations. Delays in producing national legislation, however, looked to anti-nuclear groups like procrastination and lack of resolve in the face of US pressure. In September 1985, the Social Credit leader, Gary Knapp, reintroduced Prebble's third Bill to keep the Government honest. But by then the Government had begun drafting its own law in the light of provisions in the SPNFZ. The Labour majority on the parliamentary Select Committee on Foreign Affairs and Defence also recommended a Bill to give expression to public concern about the arms race.

When Palmer took the draft to the United States in September to talk over American objections, Shultz and Weinberger refused to consider it. Naturally, they wanted no part in a law which implied a degree of precision about the status of warships. In Australia, by contrast, Palmer seems to have found Hayden helpful in suggesting ways to make the legislation less offensive to the United States. Only on the eve of New Zealand's leap into the legislative dark did Weinberger take a peek at it.[64]

What he found in the Bill, presented to Parliament on 10 December, no more satisfied him than it did the anti-nuclear campaigners. Much of the Act implements the arms control measures to which New Zealand is already a party. But in establishing a national zone, clause 9 states that a prime minister may only grant approval for warship access 'if he is satisfied that the warships will not be carrying any nuclear explosive device upon their entry into the internal waters of New Zealand'. When considering visits he would have to regard all the relevant information and advice available to him, including that

145

relating to the strategic and security interests of New Zealand (see appendix 7). Clause 10 made the same provision for aircraft landing in New Zealand, but with an escape clause to allow blanket clearance for aircraft landing at Harewood. Other clauses prohibited the stationing or testing of nuclear devices in the zone, nuclear waste disposal and the entry of nuclear-powered vessels. The Bill laid down a maximum penalty of ten years' imprisonment for contravening the law, but proceedings subsequent to arrest required the consent of the Attorney General. At the committee stage, over 1,000 public submissions offered criticism on three main counts.

First, critics submitted that the integrity of the NFZ had been made synonymous with the integrity of prime ministers. A future government could maintain that the strategic and security interests of the country required a warship visit and 'could choose not to ask too many questions'. Therefore a prime minister should be required to state that he was satisfied 'beyond reasonable doubt' that nuclear weapons were absent. Alternatively, reliance on probability assessments ought to be replaced by a categorical ban on nuclear-capable ships. The Ministry of Foreign Affairs noted that banning delivery systems could seriously inhibit conventional, dual-capable systems. It had been the subject of extensive discussion in drafting the Treaty of Rarotonga, but had been left out of that too.[65]

Second, the banning provisions applied only to ports, harbours and fjords, and not to territorial waters or straits because, so officials argued, a more extensive ban would contravene freedom of the seas. Critics argued that New Zealand was entitled to consider that certain ship movements would be prejudicial to the state's peace, good order and security under article 19 of UNCLOS. Moreover, under article 23, New Zealand could impose conditions on freedom of passage including inspection of ships' documents and restriction to sea lanes, as already demanded by other states.[66]

Third, legal opinion argued that without full executive accountability an unsympathetic government could put the Act beyond judicial review. Officials pointed out, however, that the powers of the Attorney General were in fact exercised by the Solicitor General, a non-political office and therefore impartial. But it is also the case that the British constitutional tradition does not encourage courts to tangle with government, and the Lange Cabinet had no wish to allow a repetition of the legal challenge made by an individual to prevent extradition of the *Rainbow Warrior* saboteurs. In particular the Cabinet seemed willing to allay Washington's fears that NCND would be investigated in a court. Once negotiations with the US had failed, however, Lange countered domestic concerns by arguing that: 'If it is a law the courts can review it whether review is provided for or not.' He was certain that no case would succeed under Labour because of its anti-nuclear commitment.[67]

The parliamentary committee reported back on 16 October 1986 with only marginal changes to the Bill. It received a second reading in February 1987, and was passed into law by 39 votes to 29 on 4 June. Lange argued that it was the only means by which the public could be absolutely sure of disengagement from strategies of nuclear deterrence. But only a country outside the central strategic balance could have produced such a law. It was essentially a symbolic measure, which added to the sense that anti-nuclearism was part and parcel of the national identity. As National MPs pointed out, the legislation would make little difference to the condition of the world. It would not reduce nuclear arsenals, make New Zealand immune from attack or shut out the effects of nuclear war in the northern hemisphere. It was not intended as a model for others, so could only represent unilateral arms control by the unarmed.[68] The Act was a carefully tailored minimalist one to account for the strength of anti-nuclear feeling, whilst attending to some of the objections of the United States. Legal exclusion was said to be the only means by which the public could be certain of disengagement. But perhaps the greatest value of the law to anti-nuclearists was its signal to Washington that the possibility of New Zealand hosting bases in the future was now more remote than ever.

Ironically, the Bill threatened to create a problem regarding the Deep Freeze facility which, as noted in chapter 3, hosts Starlifter flights en route to and from Australia. The USAF seemed unconcerned about potential trouble over the military cargoes, but in October 1986 Lehman requested the National Science Foundation (NSF) to make contingency plans for a short-notice move to Hobart. This may have been a tactic to scare New Zealand away from legislation; Deep Freeze is worth about $NZ15 million to the Christchurch economy. But Lehman went so far as to antagonize the Australian Federal Government by holding direct talks with the Premier of Tasmania. Although in early 1987 Lehman predicted a move in about two years, the Reagan Administration never seriously entertained the idea. It was Lehman's farewell gesture before retiring in March.[69] A shift would have been costly, requiring congressional funding. It would have been irreversible, even if a National government overturns the ban on nuclear warships. And it would have been absurd to expect scientists to relocate facilities which support research in nuclear-free Antarctica, for purely nuclear reasons.

The New Zealand Government was meticulous about not challenging the flights, and agreed with Ambassador Cleveland that they should have blanket clearance under clause 10(3) without breaching NCND. Early in 1988 the NSF ended speculation by signing a major aircraft servicing contract with Air New Zealand. Nevertheless, as far as the US was concerned, the demilitarization of Harewood was not for discussion. Peace groups threatened to use the law to stop military flights and accused Lange of naïve trust in the Americans, given the US contingencies for airlifting nuclear weapons to countries like Iceland. But Lange argued that the aircraft would not be nuclear armed because this would contravene detailed arrangements worked out between the US and Australia.[70] If a case were brought under the Act, it would not get very far.

Washington's only response to the legal ban was the New Zealand Military Preference Elimination Act, removing New Zealand from the list of allies entitled to preferential treatment in military supply. Representative William Broomfield introduced it early in 1987, but the New Zealand National Party defence spokesman told Weinberger that it would damage National if passed before the 1987 general election. Frank Carlucci, Reagan's new National Security Adviser, wrote to Broomfield suggesting that it was the right bill at the wrong time. It should wait until New Zealand's legislation was passed because it was all the US had left to respond with.[71] In effect it made little practical difference because New Zealand had not received preference since the *Buchanan* incident, and it merely meant that any US offer of defence equipment would require the elapse of 30 rather than 15 days after notification to Congress.

No doubt, as senior New Zealand officers and MoD officials pointed out, reprisals have adversely affected the operational effectiveness of the armed forces. But they have not revolutionized the situation. New Zealand is heavily dependent on US equipment, which it imports to the tune of $US35–40 million a year. Spare parts, instruction and up-dating manuals now take longer to arrive. But arms procurement is not a major problem for a country which buys second-hand or off-the-shelf. Australia supplies most of the regional intelligence, and neutral global assessments of interest to New Zealand are available on the open market. Loss of trilateral training exercises was acknowledged as a serious blow by the *Review of Defence Policy* (1987). The RNZN had relied on exercising with the USN. This, and command staff experience, can only be partly made up by Australia. However, some of the air training exercises, for strikes deep into Soviet territory, for example, were hardly relevant to New Zealand's security situation.[72]

148

The damp squib response to New Zealand's legislation neatly symbolized the Reagan Administration's difficulty in openly punishing an ally, especially when the disagreement arose from democratically-expressed sentiment in a country of limited strategic consequence. Given the desire to prevent New Zealand's action becoming a model for others, American responses lacked the kind of subtlety which a delicate situation demanded and allowed. There is little firm evidence either that New Zealand's policy provided a model, or that reprisals provided an object lesson for other allies. The imperative to define the problem by requesting a nuclear-capable vessel in the first year of the Labour Government indicates hypersensitivity to anti-nuclearism. In this respect, damage to the alliance derived as much from US handling of the problem as New Zealand's quest for nuclear disengagement. As Lange remarked: 'It was only when nuclear weapons were excluded from New Zealand that it was revealed beyond doubt that they were the keystone on which the whole structure depended.'[73]

New Zealand has shouldered more than its share of collective security burdens in the twentieth century. It is also reasonable to argue that Wellington's intimate working knowledge of South Pacific security issues more than compensates the US for the loss of two or three R & R visits a year. Returning from a visit to the United States in June 1987 National's defence spokesman, Doug Kidd, reported a strong awareness in US official circles that they needed to conduct foreign policy in the Pacific 'on a somewhat more sophisticated and sensitive basis' than in the past.[74] Nevertheless, as Lange noted, the fact that two protagonists could take such different views of ANZUS raises questions as to how the alliance will be managed and the security of the South Pacific maintained in the future.[75] To a large extent, New Zealand's anti-nuclear policy represented a reassertion of Tasman Doctrine and strategic denial rather than a contribution to global arms control. It is now appropriate therefore to consider the regional implications of the crisis.

8 REGIONAL SECURITY AND THE FUTURE OF ANZUS

Navy Secretary John Lehman and other American officials were prepared to write off New Zealand as a participant in the Western Alliance. But the curtailment of military co-operation by the Lange Government certainly did not mean that New Zealand's fundamental orientation had changed. Only dogmatists would equate a ban on nuclear visiting with non-alignment. US ideologues also expressed dismay at deviant trends in Australian security policy. In this case they were confronted by a willingness in Australian official circles to entertain revisionist ideas. As the Wellington pressure group, Just Defence, discerned, 'Australia, in a strange reversal of the New Zealand situation, has a more independent thinking defence establishment and less independent thinking Government than us.'[1] In examining the regional ramifications of the ANZUS crisis, this chapter indicates that despite divergence in both concept and process, there was an element of parallelism in the Australian and New Zealand policy reviews. Moreover, the regional impact of the crisis needs to be considered with reference to sources of regional instability and the interests of South Pacific states, particularly their opposition to nuclearism. Developments in regional security also suggest that the disparities in the ANZUS relationship are likely to persist.

DEFENCE REVIEWS IN CANBERRA AND WELLINGTON

Whereas New Zealand had a defence review thrust upon it by the ANZUS crisis, developments in Australian defence policy had little to do with the dispute, but had similar sources in regional preoccupations and a quest for self-reliance. As noted earlier, the security consensus in Australia coalesced around the view that the American alliance deterred any aggression beyond Australia's capability to repel. But by the 1980s, experts of impeccably conservative credentials had realized that strategic policy and the structure of the Australian Defence Force (ADF) had become arthritic and incapable of effective independent defence.

The thorough examination of defence posture conducted during Hawke's term was fully in line with the findings of a parliamentary committee in the Fraser period. As noted in chapter 2, this committee's report, *Threats to Australia's Security* (1981), virtually ruled out the prospect of full-scale invasion from any source. Intermediate-level threats, such as lodgements, regional aggression or sea lane disruption, would require specialist forces by an aggressor. Australia was protected from lodgements by geography, surveillance capability and the ANZUS alliance, and would be able to internationalize any conflict affecting sea lanes. Low-level contingencies, from smuggling to attacks on isolated military facilities, were the most likely threats.

Under Labor, the Joint Committee on Foreign Affairs and Defence followed on with a report on *The Australian Defence Force: Its Structure and Capabilities* (1984). It suggested that the ADF's priority in an essentially benign strategic environment should be to deter threats to national security and provide a rapid response to low level threats. Any American support in a crisis 'should be regarded as a bonus to, rather than an anticipated central element of, Australia's response capacity' (p. xv). Australia's area of principal defence interest comprised national territory, maritime and air approaches and the potential basis and staging areas from which opposition forces might be launched (p. xvi). Actually, the Hawke Government obtained explicit agreement at the 1983 ANZUS Council meeting that Australia's prime defence role was to build self-defence capability within the regional context rather than as a potential part of some broader deployment.[2]

Such decisions and assessments paved the way for the more exhaustive analysis by Paul Dibb, acting as a consultant to Defence Minister Kim Beazley. Dibb was a former official of the Joint Intelligence Organization and an academic who, together with Desmond Ball, strongly influenced the development of Labor's defence policy. But in his *Review of Australia's Defence Capabilities* (1986), Dibb was also able to carry with him the Canberra bureaucracies and key military figures, including the Chief of the Defence Force, General Sir Phillip Bennett. Dibb's acumen was brought to bear on the 'definition of priorities and the application of strategic parameters' to the design of the ADF.[3]

This was long overdue, and Dibb spelt out the implications of the earlier surveys. First, strategic concepts based on overseas experience had little relevance to Australia and there was no requirement for Australia to become involved in ANZUS contingency planning for global war. Second, 'neither this possibility, nor other remote possibilities for calls of assistance under ANZUS, should influence the structure and equipment of the ADF' (p. 47). The ADF should be structured for layered defence of the regional strategic community, 5,400km from north to south and 7,200km from east to west. Third, the level of threat perception dictated a need for long-range surveillance and interdiction to deny an adversary the use of the sea-air gap to the north, counter-mine measures, new air bases in the north and mobile ground forces to protect installations and populations in remote parts of the country.

The main complaint of the defence hierarchy was that Dibb's 'strategy of denial' would force Australia into a reactive posture and would not suffice to win a war.[4] From the right, indeed, the Dibb report looked like a 'capitulation to leftist-pacifism' and a resort to isolationism. The parliamentary Opposition also called it a retreat into fortress Australia which would detach Australia from the US. In fact Admiral James Lyons, CIC Pacific Fleet, publicly criticized Dibb's 'insularity', and reports from Washington strongly suggested that 'rewriting ANZUS by Dibb' was unacceptable to Weinberger and Shultz.[5] The critics overlooked the bipartisan trends in defence thinking. Already, before Labor came into office, the glamour of blue-water forward defence had been stripped by the decision not to replace the carrier, HMAS *Melbourne*. Dibb's synergism defined a long-term conservative shift towards semi-detached alliance defence. As an editorial in *The Age* (20 March 1986) argued, the Dibb report was a comprehensive plan for achieving the self-reliance which had been recognized as necessary ten years previously.

Decentralizing the fleet, for example, was a manifestation of the structural change in Australian security which had been under consideration for some twenty years. In a Fleet Base Relocation Report of February 1987, Beazley noted that the historical reasons for locating the fleet on the east coast no longer applied (access to an industrial base, protection of the major cities and the equipping and training of expeditionary forces to support allied operations). The self-reliant posture required homeporting half of the fleet in WA, where it would be more readily available for defending the western approaches and the northern choke points. Also, development of wharves and facilities on the east coast at Jervis Bay in Commonwealth Territory would be undertaken to relieve congestion in Sydney Harbour. The Sydney Peace Squadron regarded this as a way of sweeping nuclear visits under the carpet, but it would appear that undercutting the objections to nuclear-armed visits in Sydney was a bonus rather than an imperative.[6]

Beazley's white paper, *The Defence of Australia* (1987), was based essentially on the Dibb report, but it tried to satisfy critics that layered defence did not preclude the possibility of offensive military operations in the region. Beazley was also at pains to point out the distinction between self-reliance and self-sufficiency. The alliance and the framework of regional connections provided the support which made greater self-reliance possible and, in the area of equipment and intelligence, gave Australia an edge over its neighbours. Commentators wondered whether the projected $A20–25 billion over 15 years would eventuate, given that Beazley had already retreated from Dibb's proposed annual growth rate of over three per cent. Treasurer Paul Keating's harsh mini-budget of May 1987 cut defence spending further and the economic outlook suggests that it will continue to be below three per cent of gross domestic product.[7] The overall effect is likely to increase Australian emphasis on the region as a contribution to global stability, but with a clearer perception of Australian interests.

The process was independent of the New Zealand dispute, in any case, but the disruptions of 1985 meant that Australia gave increased attention to New Zealand and to the problems of dependence on the United States. Dibb spurned involvement in US contingency planning, but drew attention to the scope for joint planning with New Zealand as a complementary focus of support in the South Pacific. New Zealand adds about 15 per cent to Australia's forces and can be expected to assist regional security in a sensitively calibrated way. Beazley's Statement on Defence of 1987 proposed to continue close defence co-operation, 'not only because of the old and close friendship ... but because such co-operation is important to Australia's own defence interests'. The ANZUS crisis may have pointed up the problems of excessive dependence on the US for satellite monitoring, though the decision to construct a new Australian-run DSD station the size of Pine Gap at Geraldton (WA) was essentially a response to new Soviet communication techniques. It will certainly simplify SIGINT collaboration with New Zealand which, in 1987, also announced a new station in Marlborough, to be compatible with the Geraldton facility.[8]

Also in February 1987, Beazley announced improved defence co-operation in the South Pacific, and increased RAAF surveillance and RAN visits to the islands lying across trade routes. Meanwhile, deployments to distant waters like the Sea of Japan would decline. The microstates would receive the same priority as South-East Asia had received in the past. Some grand designers envisage Canberra as the new political headquarters of the South Pacific, and the ANZUS crisis might have been expected to enhance their claim. But Australian officials have not sought to rival Wellington's pre-eminence in Polynesia.

New Zealand's disengagement was based on the premise that nuclear weapons were irrelevant to regional defence. It was far from clear, however, what defences were appropriate. The defence establishment hankered after the kind of decisive power which could only come from alliance with the United States. Yet the argument that Labour's policy had created a vacuum which would attract aggression seemed unconvincing. Nor was it the case, as military critics claimed, that New Zealand was left with a crude choice between commitment to the US or defenceless non-alignment.[9] Objectively speaking, of course, the retired defence chiefs could not escape some responsibility for the atrophied condition of the armed forces and paucity of regional strategic doctrine. The Lange Government inherited only two days' ammunition, vintage museum equipment, frigates designed for chasing submarines in the North Atlantic and a series of piecemeal decisions, including an eccentric proposal to acquire attack submarines. An independent naval commentator remarked that ANZUS membership 'was nothing more than an excuse to avoid addressing the real problems involved in defending this country'.[10]

This is not to say that Labour had a coherent defence policy either before or after the 1984 election. Inconsistencies continued, and unfavourable comparisons have been drawn between Wellington's defence review and the exercise conducted in Canberra. The process was more complex than in Australia, involving a major public inquiry. Other complications derived from Labour's desire to renegotiate ANZUS though the US had ruled out any change, the messy consequences of US reprisals and a defence bureaucracy which displayed a marked enthusiasm for rescuing the status quo ante. Critics made the cogent point that a change in defence arrangements preceded a policy review. Ramesh Thakur, for example, argued that the cart had been put before the horse and both had ended up directionless.[11]

But for many years New Zealand and Australia had increasingly pursued foreign policies which did not always coincide with American concerns. New Zealand's ban on nuclear visiting was partly a manifestation of a general change in foreign policy outlook. Further, one might legitimately consider the old régime flawed by a lack of political control over trilateral defence co-operation. If defence policy remained incoherent it was partly, as Malcolm Templeton argues, the result of low threat perception, low priority and the legacy of moral and physical dependence on the United States.[12]

Nevertheless, various documents taken together constitute an unmistakable policy thrust. They include a Cabinet position paper, the Defence Minister's annual reports, a discussion document, *The Defence Question* (1985), and the white paper itself, *Defence of New Zealand* (1987). The 1986 Ministry of Defence Report, for example, proposed increased self-reliance, closest possible co-operation with Australia and declared an intention to shape forces for assisting in the Pacific rather than as appendages to wars in distant lands. This more or less accorded with the findings of the Defence Committee of Enquiry set up to canvass the public's views on security questions. Parliamentary select committees had already drawn increasing numbers of public submissions, though under the National Government, the Committee on Disarmament and Arms Control met only four times and Muldoon tried to have it axed.[13] Reconstituted by Labour, its report of 1985, *Disarmament and Arms Control*, reflected the dynamic approach of the new chairperson, Helen Clark. But in the wake of the crisis, the Government recognized that the whole future of New Zealand's defence and security was such a matter of public interest that a wider-ranging inquiry, independent of Labour's majority, would be necessary.

Frank Corner, a former ambassador to the UN and the United States and former permanent head of Foreign Affairs, was appointed to the chair. His foil was the Quaker, Kevin Clements, who made it clear before being appointed to the Committee of Enquiry that his irreducible stance was no surrender of the Government's anti-nuclear position.[14] As indicated in chapter 6, the overwhelming majority of submissions were critical of traditional policies. Specially commissioned opinion polls reflected broad support for the Government's original intention to remain in ANZUS but without nuclear ship visits. About 75 per cent of respondents favoured some form of disengagement from nuclear strategies (see appendix 6), and four times as many were more worried about nuclear war than invasion. The importance of defence links with Australia came through consistently strongly, in spite of Australia's nuclear-related linkages. Given the lack of consensus about the priority between alliance membership and the visit ban, the Committee toyed with the notion of tactful ship visits, though the possibility had collapsed at the Shultz–Lange meeting in Manila.[15]

The Committee's report, *Defence and Security: What New Zealanders Want* (1986), contained a tendentious 'history' of foreign policy partly based on Corner's personal experience. The sweeping assertions had drawn objections from Clements, but several survived the drafting stage.[16] Moreover, the report failed to elucidate the claim that acceptance by allies of the possibility that warships are nuclear armed is 'the basis for the entire operation of the western alliance' (p. 87). Rather unexpectedly Clements went along with this, though he threatened to write a minority report if Corner persisted in advocating a 'tactful' visit policy.[17] Consequently, *Defence and Security* emphasized the major area of common ground, the importance of continued alignment with Australia. Although some of the interpretations led to an altercation between Lange and the Committee, in broad terms the report legitimated the Government's position.

The Government had made it clear that it would not necessarily implement the Committee's recommendations and, more than previous white papers, the *Defence of New Zealand* bore the stamp of political control. It was produced by a senior member of the Prime Minister's Department after holding lengthy consultations with the Defence Council and officials. It formally adopted the concept of the armed forces operating independently to counter low-level threats and to meet, with Australia, the defence needs of the region of immediate strategic concern (about 16 per cent of the globe). Consistent with this was the marked increase in training, exercising and EEZ surveillance in island territories. So, too, was the inevitable and long-foreshadowed announcement, postponed during the ANZUS crisis, to withdraw the battalion from Singapore.[18]

However, the review lacked analysis of force structure and attracted criticism for 'deceiving the public' about New Zealand's ability to maintain a credible defence force without access to American doctrine and technology.[19] True, the Government favoured replacing the Leander-class frigates with vessels designed for long-range, seakeeping endurance, featuring helicopter accommodation and surveillance facilities rather than complex weapon systems. A new navy tanker and air refuelling system would also improve reach. But endorsement of the previous government's $NZ140 million upgrading of avionics and weaponry for the RNZAF's Skyhawks, for compatibility with US forces, and acquisition of another elaborately equipped Orion for EEZ surveillance seem less consistent with the need for basic platforms. Moreover self-reliance would be governed by financial constraints. Defence spending increased in real terms by four per cent in 1985–6, including $NZ16 million for ammunition and improved forces' pay. But co-operation with Australia, savings on exercises with the US, and eventual savings on a proportion of the Singapore costs will help keep defence expenditure at about two per cent of GDP, similar to the proportion in Switzerland and higher than in Finland, Austria or Ireland.

In Corner's view this could only work by 'fiddling the threat'. The 1987 white paper noted the difficulty in imagining what concessions by New Zealand would be of sufficient importance to prompt hostilities or, one might add, so-called nuclear blackmail. The 1983 defence review had referred to the relevance of the Falklands War, but it is difficult to see where New Zealand's Argentina lurks. As the former Secretary of Defence, Sir Jack Hunn, argued, a Soviet armada would need to be many times larger than the British fleet in the Falklands, all to acquire 70 million sheep at the end of the journey. Perhaps, as Wilkes remarked, postulating potential military threats to New Zealand is an invitation to enter the realm of the absurd.[20]

However, the 1987 review prudently assumed that the South Pacific would not always be free of regional threats, or a serious deterioration in strategic circumstances. In particular New Zealand was vulnerable to disruptions in trade and communications. Proposals for civilian-based territorial defence, transarmament and guerrilla forces had been presented to the Enquiry. The Government dismissed them as underestimating pro-alliance sentiment, the financial costs of armed isolation and the need for offensive capabilities to fulfil constitutional obligations to safeguard the Tokelaus, Cook Islands and Niue. Indeed the Government agreed to bring the Ready Reaction Force up to strength.

Corner made a risible allegation that the country's defence policy had been hijacked by a minority of neutralists in the anti-nuclear movement.[21] But by no stretch of the imagination did the Government's policies constitute neutrality or non-alignment. After public debate about alternative defence postures, no revolution materialized. Only about 15 per cent of poll respondents favoured non-alignment or neutrality. The Government ignored them, as it ignored the NZLP's resolutions for a limit of 1.5 per cent of GDP on defence spending, and disowned radical proposals in the NZLP's submission to the Enquiry. Lange argued that New Zealand should seek out and make common cause with nations which shared unease at superpower confrontation, but this did not signify that New Zealand was drifting out of the Western camp.

The Prime Minister seemed keen to demonstrate his cold war credentials. Although Moscow had refrained from publicly exploiting the ANZUS rift, he reprimanded the Soviet Ambassador for misrepresentations of the crisis by TASS. He responded to a Soviet overture for information exchanges on shipping movements by telling the Soviets to keep their ships as far away as possible. New Zealand also expelled an alleged KGB agent fom the Embassy and the Soviet Foreign Minister Edvard Shevardnadze visited Australia in January 1987 without an invitation to stop over in Wellington.

Elements of bipartisanship, based on qualified alignment, emerged in 1987 when National adjusted its policy for the election. As Malcolm Templeton noted, there was a consensus that ships ought not to bring nuclear weapons into ports and strong reservations about nuclear-powered vessels. A credible national defence capability based increasingly on self-reliance and co-operation with Australia was widely supported, together with an emphasis on regional responsibility.[22]

The close relations between the Anzacs will be cemented anyway by the establishment of a free trade area by July 1990. Economic interpenetration has increased significantly, and New Zealand has improved its trade with Australia (its second largest customer) more rapidly than vice versa. Still, the prospect for a constitutional union remains remote while they are divided by assertive nationalisms. In a guest speech at the 1983 NZLP conference, Beazley gave an accurate picture of the relationships, noting that few countries were closer to each other, 'living in each other's pockets', asserting compatible but distinctive expressions of national identity.[23]

The ANZUS crisis intensified rather than upset these fundamental realities. Australia's defence posture with its emphasis on regional defence increased New Zealand's importance to the security of the region. The *Defence of Australia* (1987) emphasized the need for co-ordinated policies and compatibility of equipment. Although having different spheres of interest, Australia and New Zealand have worked together in the South Pacific Forum (SPF) on a range of issues – from fish poaching to unrest in Fiji. As Hayden remarked: 'Some of us do not always appreciate the scale of the contribution made by New Zealand to the welfare of the region we share. New Zealand has paid its dues.'[24]

The Australian parliamentary Opposition promised that unless New Zealand reinstated nuclear visiting a future right-wing government would downgrade trans-Tasman defence relations. But this has a hollow ring to it. There can be little doubt that they must remain close allies in spite of their differences on nuclear engagement. It is inconceivable that they would not provide mutual military assistance in the event of an attack on their territory. Far from discouraging closer relations the crisis speeded up the process of integration. The considerable potential for joint procurement was explored. New Zealand entered negotiations to buy four Australian-built light patrol vessels (against Labour Party hostility on grounds of cost), to add to the purchase of Steyr rifles and light field guns made under licence in Australia. A new Memorandum on Defence Communications and Electronics co-operation was completed. Common equipment maintenance, exercising, training and intelligence co-operation continued more or less as normal, and the crisis intensified the level of staff exchanges and joint contingency planning. After two visits to Wellington by Beazley, following the row with Washington, confidence about the Anzac link among officials on both sides of the Tasman had grown significantly. Hawke's visit to New Zealand in November 1987 confirmed that the ship issue had subsided and that upgrading the relationship had US knowledge and approval.[25]

Although Australia will continue to spend more on defence than New Zealand and have significantly different strategic requirements, it seems unlikely that New Zealand will default into a defenceless posture. New Zealand could never afford frontier technology anyway and had difficulties keeping up with its allies. Looking on the bright side, Jamieson suggested that the Australian defence establishment might be relieved that it no longer had to share the attention of the US with New Zealand. Consequently the relationships had become less, not more, complicated.[26]

REGIONAL SECURITY

The independent island states have either very limited or no defence forces, except Fiji which has too many. In the absence of a regional infrastructure for collective security, they lean on the Anzacs for military support, sometimes through exchanges of notes such as that between Australia and Papua New Guinea. In the past, some states sounded out the possibility of formal accession to the ANZUS Treaty.[27] But the ANZUS dispute appears to have had a muted impact on regional sensibilities. Although the staunchly pro-American rulers of Fiji, the Cook Islands and Tonga disapproved of New Zealand's policy, early concerns that the crisis was compromising island security have not developed into a significant issue, except perhaps in Fiji. The patrician leader of the Cook Islands, Sir Thomas Davis, a former US Army research scientist, was out of step with the rest of his Cabinet in embarrassing New Zealand. His dismissal in August 1987 led to the re-establishment of normal relations between Rarotonga and Wellington. Other governments have been reassured by the stronger mutual alignment of New Zealand and Australia with the region.[28]

Nor can it be said that Soviet potential for involvement in the region has burgeoned as a consequence of the crisis. The South Pacific was virtually a *tabula rasa* for Moscow. It had made only modest progress in establishing diplomatic relations, with Fiji (in 1974), with Papua New Guinea, Tonga and Western Samoa (in 1976) and with Vanuatu (in 1986). Regional states have often played the Soviet card, exaggerating Soviet contacts to gain greater consideration from the Anzacs. But Soviet trade is negligible, cultural and scientific exchange non-existent, offers to participate in hydrographic surveys had been turned down and the USSR had no residential embassies. In 1977 and 1980 Moscow made informal approaches to Tonga about port visits which were rebuffed. Vanuatu's offer in 1982 to host Soviet naval visits, which would have required non-nuclear declarations, were not followed up.

The flurry of Soviet diplomatic activity in the middle of the 1980s arose not from disarray in ANZUS but from regional discontent with traditional friends, particularly over fish poaching. Papua New Guinea, the Solomons and Kiribati have all seized American trawlers, and Kiribati tried to salvage its fragile economy by signing a fishing agreement with the Soviet Union. The agreement lapsed when Moscow found it too expensive, but in January 1987 Vanuatu allowed Soviet vessels to fish in its EEZ with provision for port calls for repairs and supplies.

No doubt the USSR would like ANZUS to collapse outright. It would indicate US inability to control its allies. But there is no practical way in which the Soviet Union can capitalize on the New Zealand ship ban, and it hardly represents a strategic windfall. Moscow's major potential gain would be the removal of US facilities in Australia. Even such a diminution of US assets would not necessarily add to the Soviet Union's readily exploitable power in the South Pacific. Soviet political and military interest in the region remains minimal, and island footholds would be of little strategic advantage so removed from Moscow's priority areas. As Jonathan Alford noted, islands are not swallowed up by major powers for the sake of it.[29]

In any event, the island peoples retain their basic political, religious and educational connections with the West and remain strongly anti-communist. Increased fishing and diplomatic activity does not amount to exploitable strategic advantage, as regional experts testify. The limited Soviet gains were related primarily to the insensitivity of the Western powers to regional aspirations. The refusal of the United States to sign UNCLOS and the SPNFZ and its support for French nuclear tests and colonial interests have been propaganda gifts for Moscow. 'By any rational and objective assessment,' in the expert judgements of Richard Herr and Robert Kiste, 'it is clear that France had created the greatest opportunities for Eastern bloc penetration.'[30]

Likewise, the tenuous links established by Libya in the region have arisen from impoverishment and the untidy legacies of colonialism. Vanuatuans, Kanaks and Melanesian guerrillas in Irian Jaya have received military training in Libya, and Maori and Aboriginal militants attended an anti-imperialism conference in Tripoli in 1986 when Qaddaffi showed interest in countering superpower influence in the region. The leader of nonaligned Vanuatu, Father Walter Lini, sent Qaddaffi a message of solidarity after the US attack on Tripoli and has made no secret of Vanuatu's need for economic subventions from all sources. Nevertheless, an insight team writing in *The Bulletin* (19 May 1987) concluded that whilst islands accept aid, Libyan influence is marginal and often short in delivery.

In monitoring the Vanuatu–Libya links, Australia provoked Lini's Government to ban visits by Australian warships and aircraft in retaliation for alleged interference by the Australian intelligence services. Lini received expressions of support from the Solomons and Papua New Guinea. Australia may have been anxious to demonstrate its commitment to Western security interests, the more so because of differences of opinion with traditional allies. An active policy also helps to forestall precipitate US intervention. Reagan's roving ambassador, General Vernon Walters, made much of the Libyan activity on a visit to Canberra, and there was some loose talk by Admiral Lyons about using the USN against Libya in the Pacific. By making a dramatic effort to consult New Zealand about Vanuatu in May 1987, and by closing the Libyan Bureau in Canberra, it is plausible that Hayden was demonstrating that the problem could be handled regionally.[31]

The scare illustrates the range and complexity of regional issues, and the fact that the main security concerns of the islands are the struggle for economic survival and a determination, particularly on the part of the Melanesians, not to be pushed around by the metropolitan powers and their agents. The main external causes of regional instability are perceived as the colonial oppression and nuclearism of familiar friends, rather than any unfamiliar devils from the socialist world. Pacific states are maturing rapidly, identifying with third world issues, and appreciating that their own national interests do not necessarily coincide with those of the Western powers.

In spite of the divergence and factionalism detected by commentators, there is a degree of rapport between states and leaders which has bolstered a growing confidence in exerting rights over EEZs and opposing nuclear proliferation and colonialism. The Forum states finally pressured the US to sign a treaty in April 1987 which promises to regulate the rapacious activities of the American Tuna Boats Association. And although the 1987 Forum meeting was overshadowed by disputes over the situations in Fiji and New Caledonia, it also sought to extend its membership to Micronesia and to increase its standing in the UN. It also agreed to an Australian proposal to improve intelligence links and counter-terrorism measures.

From time to time there has been friction between the islands and Australia and New Zealand, for example over immigration, aid levels and regional policy. In 1986 Australia reduced its aid to the South Pacific by nine per cent for the year, prompting the *Canberra Times* (11 November 1986) to comment that Australia could not complain if islands sought assistance elsewhere and moved into a different political orbit. In providing employment, development assistance, emergency provision, the education of élites and surveillance of the EEZs, the two wealthy states have to be acutely aware of the need to avoid accusations of neo-colonialism. This has made it more problematic for Australia and New Zealand to project influence as if buttressing Western interests.[32]

Widely recognized as the most potentially explosive situation is French colonial rule in New Caledonia and the Society Islands. Whether or not metropolitan control is doomed, as Jean Chesneaux suggests, it certainly creates difficulties for the Anzacs in their capacities as Western representatives in the region. They have been instrumental in restraining Melanesian impatience at French policy in New Caledonia, but have themselves frequently clashed with France. In addition to exchanging insults about the treatment of indigenous populations the Anzacs gained UN support at the end of 1986 to have New Caledonia reinscripted as a colonial territory. France suspended ministerial relations with Australia, and in January 1987 declared the Australian consul in Noumea *persona non grata*. Across the entire political spectrum in Australia this was regarded as more evidence of French arrogance in the region.[33]

Nor is it always politic for the Anzacs to be seen shoring up the strategic balance. Their problem is accentuated by a linkage in island perceptions between their third world consciousness and antinuclearism. Lini argued that colonialism and nuclearism in the Pacific are part of the same evil.[34] Indeed New Zealand's strong identification with island concerns about nuclearism, offending the United States in the process, may have done its standing in the region little harm.

Indigenous populations have genuine grievances. Nearly 200 devices have been exploded throughout the Pacific, over 50 in the

Marshall Islands. As an apologist for the Reagan Administration's policies has noted, the Marshallese are regarded in many quarters as martyrs of superpower rivalry and the US as an unreconstructed colonial power different from France only in its level of hypocritical rhetoric.[35] Entire populations have been evacuated from half a dozen islands in the US sphere of influence, and severe radioactive contamination has rendered several islands uninhabitable for all time. This has led to unrest in Belau, land claims in Ebeye and a state of emergency in 1986 on Kwajalein. Belau is the last UN trust territory and its 1981 constitution prohibits the testing, storage or disposal of nuclear weapons within its territorial jurisdiction. In 1987 the constitution was amended by executive action, under American duress, after nine referenda had failed to produce the 'right' pro-nuclear result. It is possible that the ANZUS crisis prompted the US to secure Belau's agreement in November 1985 to permit US vessels and aircraft to enter internal waters without compromising NCND. But the pressure was increasing in any event as a consequence of US contingency planning for alternative bases to the Philippines.[36]

The ANZUS crisis ought to have heightened awareness in the United States and Britain of the penalties of supporting French nuclear testing. As Rawdon Dalrymple (Australian Ambassador to the US) argued, anti-nuclear pressure in the South Pacific has very little to do with Soviet propaganda. Continued French testing was 'absolutely certain to prejudice the South Pacific people against the west'.[37] Although a scientific team, under French military guidance, gave Moruroa a clean bill of health in 1983, radioactive leakage from porous rocks is strongly suspected, and in March 1988 French officials hinted at a move to another atoll. France has refused to publish health statistics since 1966, but figures produced by the Danielssons show an abnormal increase in cancer-related cases. To most regional governments, as Chesneaux argues, it seems that France has used political control and considerable economic largesse to serve a nuclear strategy whose priorities are at the other end of the planet.[38] Western interests generally would be better served if France could be prevailed upon to test in Nevada.

Popular unrest is illustrated by the rise of the Nuclear-Free and Independent Pacific (NFIP) movement. It originated with the Young Women's Christian Movement in Suva after France decided to conduct tests on Moruroa. By the middle of the 1970s the Pacific Conference of Churches, imbued with liberation theology, had significantly boosted the popularity of anti-nuclearism. The fourth NFIP conference in 1983, attended by representatives from 33 countries,

163

confirmed a Pacific People's Charter expressing solidarity with indigenous people struggling to end all forms of oppression, including nuclear activity, throughout the Pacific. Catholic Action of Hawaii has also been instrumental in popularizing concern about the deployment of nuclear weapons in the Pacific.[39]

Even if popular anxiety about the potential for a nuclear conflict has been ill-founded, regional governments have been obliged to reflect anti-nuclearism, and would have done so with or without ripples from New Zealand. The collective measure to control nuclear activities by the creation of an SPNFZ is discussed shortly. A few states had taken separate steps which pre-dated New Zealand's visit ban.

Vanuatu had earlier used the device of requiring assurances that ships were not nuclear armed, and in February 1982 in the absence of assurances, cancelled a proposed visit by two US vessels. In 1983 a parliamentary resolution prohibited tests of nuclear devices and delivery systems, storage, transit, deployment or any form of presence of nuclear weapons, bases which aid the performance of nuclear delivery systems, and nuclear reactors, and all transit storage, release or dumping of radioactive material.[40]

In the Solomons a ministerial statement, placed before parliament in June 1983, indicated that the Government would 'exercise restraint' in allowing nuclear-powered or armed vessels within the 200 mile EEZ during peacetime. States would be obliged to inform the Solomon Islands Government 'in strict confidentiality' of the status of vessels wishing to enter waters and ports. In the event of war, access would be considered 'in the context of Solomon Islands security and safety'. Despite this, the frigate USS *Bronstein* visited in February 1984, though it was greeted by demonstrations and a dock union strike. The Solomons Government claimed that it had received verbal assurances from the US Ambassador in Port Moresby, but this was denied. Subsequently, the Foreign Minister announced a requirement for written assurance before making port calls or entering or transiting territorial waters.[41]

The Papua New Guinea Government had made contradictory comments about the desirability of nuclear visiting. However, it allowed six US vessels to visit between 1981 and 1985, including two fitted with ASROC. The Defence Secretary has remarked that ships will only be excluded if he is advised of the presence of weaponry.[42] The Government was nevertheless critical of the US 'bullying' of New Zealand. Other states pointedly refuted New Zealand's example. Tonga and Western Samoa hosted visits and, in January 1986, a nuclear-attack submarine visited Fiji without prior public announcement.

In fact, the main ripple effect of New Zealand's ban within the region may have been in Fiji. There is no doubt whatsoever that the military coups of 1987 were racially motivated. But nuclear visiting had been a political issue since the early 1980s when the United States targeted Fiji as a pivotal state for cultivating with economic and military support. To undercut anti-nuclear pressure in the run up to the the 1982 elections, Prime Minister Kamisese Mara imposed a ban on US ship visits. After visiting Pacific Fleet HQ in Hawaii, with US Ambassador Fred Eckert, he lifted the ban in 1983 and prohibited visits by Soviet cruise liners. Reagan was fulsome in his praise for this action during Mara's trip to Washington in 1984, and Mara heartily endorsed Reagan's foreign policies, including the invasion of Grenada. In the 1987 election, the opposition parties, led by Dr Timoci Bavadra, proposed to reinstate the ban and adopt a vaguely non-aligned foreign policy. The Fijian Anti-Nuclear Group, an umbrella organization formed in response to Mara's reinstatement of visits, was a significant element in Bavadra's coalition, and it seems probable that the Fijian left was emboldened by New Zealand's policy. Lawyers in New Zealand were reportedly drafting a law for consideration by the Bavadra Opposition.[43]

In partial justification for his coup in May 1987, Lt. Colonel Rabuka said that he had become concerned at the Bavadra Government's anti-nuclear policy.[44] So had the United States. Circumstantial evidence of an American role has led investigators to pose questions relating to: General Vernon Walters, no stranger to CIA operations, who in late 1983 had persuaded the Seychelles and Sri Lanka to lift their visiting bans in return for aid, and who was in Fiji just before the coup; alleged CIA agents seen by Fijian officials with Rabuka; the reported presence throughout the crisis of General John Singlaub, fund raiser for the Contras; the activities of officials who administered $US3 million a year in US aid from an office in Suva (the Bavadra Government had begun investigations into the funding of the extremist Taukei nationalist gangs); Mara's alleged visit to CINCPAC HQ before the coup, and his comment to the Council of Chiefs that Shultz had sent a message offering support for a post-coup administration; and finally the presence in the vicinity of the USS *Belleau Wood*, a 39,000 ton amphibious assault vessel, and of three USAF Hercules transports at Nadi airport a month after the coup. Speculation led US officials to say that it was distressing for the US Government to be continually implicated.[45] What one can assume is that the prospect of a nuclear visit ban in Fiji added to alarm in Washington and Hawaii about naval visits in the South Pacific.

It would be ironic if, instead of the US continuing to rely on the Anzacs as proposed in 1978 by the Pacific Office in the State Department, New Zealand's bid for strategic denial actually increased the US naval presence in the region. Pentagon planners were already casting around for possible substitutes for Subic Bay and Clark Field in the event that turmoil in the Philippines rendered them untenable. Belau is a favourite choice, but accommodation is limited. In the South-West Pacific, islands such as Fiji may have been considered as fall-back positions. They are 'soft' targets which could be bought off relatively cheaply. US aid to the South Pacific is currently less than that provided by the Anzacs, about $US15 million a year. But with Lehman's departure and the advent of Gramm-Rudman economic constraints, a policy of relying on allies like Japan and Australia to police sea lanes, is perhaps a more likely development than major expenditures on new bases in marginal areas. The problems of overreach will increase rather than diminish.

THE TREATY OF RAROTONGA

As Kiste and Herr have remarked, it would be extremely naïve to expect the United States 'to jeopardize global positions to achieve localized regional accommodations in the South Pacific'.[46] But endorsement of the SPNFZ would have made no difference to US strategic power, except by challenging the belief system of seamless nuclearism. Albinski suggested that Washington's endorsement would help defuse unfavourable criticism of American handling of New Zealand.[47] On the contrary, however, the New Zealand ban made it more difficult for Washington to accept the zone. It also complicated matters for the Hawke Government, which saw in the SPNFZ a resolution of its dilemma of having to answer ALP demands for arms control whilst preserving US security links.

Hawke took the initiative for a zone at the 1983 SPF meeting with a proposal similar to the Treaty of Tlatelolco. He was determined to avoid a repetition of the US hostility towards the Whitlam–Rowling attempt of 1975–6. Forum states had no difficulty agreeing about a ban on radioactive waste dumping and testing, and Japan had already been pressured to abort dumping in the Marianas Trench just outside the proposed zone. But Vanuatu, Papua New Guinea and the Solomons wanted tight restrictions on the deployment of nuclear warships. As Greg Fry points out, the Melanesians have been more radical about the issue than the Polynesians, and at one extreme, Tonga, a major recipient of US aid, prefers to allow the US the option of a nuclear base in the zone.[48]

The Anzacs insisted that the Treaty would conform rigorously to US criteria as laid down at the UN General Assembly in 1982. The SPNFZ would not, therefore, disturb existing security arrangements, restrict rights under international law, particularly rights of innocent passage, nor affect existing rights and privileges to grant or deny transit, including port calls and overflights. The Forum also decided that stationing of nuclear weapons in ports could not be qualified by a time limit and would be left to individual states. Vanuatu considered the failure to curb warship deployment a major weakness and refused to sign, but a major purpose of the Treaty was to put pressure on France to stop tests and oblige the allies of France to consider their relations with the South Pacific. The protocols are open to signature by nuclear states which undertake not to: (1) station, deploy or store nuclear weapons in their territories within the region; (2) use or threaten to use nuclear weapons against states in the region (reinforcing negative security guarantees); and (3) test nuclear weapons in the zone. Signed in Rarotonga on 6 August 1985, the Treaty came into effect when Australia became the eighth state to ratify in December 1986.

Anti-nuclear critics pointed out that the SPNFZ did nothing to stop superpower rivalry because it permits transit, visiting and the firing of nuclear weapons from within the zone. Protocol 2 expects the Soviet Union not to target the Australian facilities with nuclear weapons. Buried beneath the official rhetoric about complementing the NPT and taking steps to make the entire southern hemisphere nuclear free, cynics detected a Hawke stratagem to 'protect US naval access to friendly regional ports'.[49]

Yet for the zone to gain any international standing it had to attract the signature of the dominant nuclear power in the region. Transit prohibitions could never be enforced anyway, and even dissenters had to acknowledge that the zone might inhibit homeporting and any future territorial basing of nuclear weapons. Indeed these restrictions worried the right-wing opposition in Australia. The SPNFZ would close off the option of storing nuclear weapons on Australian soil in the event of a radically changed security environment. It also sought to constrain the United States without a reciprocal measure in Moscow's sphere of influence.[50]

Initially, however, both Admirals Crowe and Ronald Hays recognized that the SPNFZ did not infringe US rights under international law or interfere with naval operations. Hays urged immediate endorsement. US officials also denied that they had any interest in

167

establishing nuclear bases in the zone, and a faction in the State Department thought endorsement would demonstrate sensitivity to opinion in the region. The US Ambassador in Fiji reported that America's main supporter among the smaller states, Mara, considered it a moderate document.[51]

Although the Reagan Administration had ratified protocol 1 of the Treaty of Tlatelolco in 1981, attitudes in Washington had hardened. The Pacific commanders were silenced, allegedly by Shultz, who wanted to avoid antagonizing France, and by Weinberger, who was anxious about nuclear-free inkblots and a potential spread of the zone to Micronesia. Above all, ideologues in the Administration believed that endorsing the SPNFZ would reinforce the notion that nuclear weapons were a curse and lend credibility to New Zealand's stance. They restated the arguments advanced by a writer for the Reaganite Heritage Foundation who dismissed the zone as the product of leftist trade unions, pacifists and a few church groups openly encouraged by Moscow. To sign any of the protocols would 'legitimize a generally anti-US campaign for unilateral nuclear disarmament' and threaten NATO.[52] French officials lobbied strongly on the basis that continued nuclear testing greatly enhanced NATO's security. In February 1987, within days of the French refusal to endorse the protocols, the Reagan Administration conveyed to the Forum states that although US practices were not incompatible with the zone, its global security interest precluded endorsement. A congressional committee meeting in June, chaired by Solarz, criticized the decision, and it is possible that a new administration in 1989 will take a more positive view of the protocols.[53]

The Thatcher Government acknowledged that it had deferred to its nuclear allies in deciding that to sign would not serve national interests. But Britain would abide by the protocols and not store nuclear materials on its remaining South Pacific territory, Pitcairn. Whitehall left the door open for a future review of the position. This would take account of the implications of the Soviet statement which accompanied Moscow's signature, in December 1986, of protocols 2 and 3.[54]

The Soviet propaganda advantage in endorsing the SPNFZ was, in fact, somewhat diminished by a reservation which stated that transit of, and port calls with, nuclear weapons would be incompatible with the nuclear-free status of the zone. In the event of states calling at or transiting the territory of signatories with nuclear weapons 'the Soviet Union will have the right to consider itself free from the commitments undertaken under Protocol Two to the treaty'.[55] This was subsequently dropped after representations from countries such as New Zealand which were annoyed that the reservation made it more difficult to gain British and American approval. But, compared to ideological considerations, the caveat probably made only a marginal difference to the negative responses of the Western nuclear powers. In signing protocols 2 and 3 in February 1987, China also reserved its position in the event of the signatories or other nuclear states taking any action in gross violation of the Treaty and protocols. But New Zealand welcomed China's adherence as a stark contrast to the attitudes of the nuclear allies.

The Anzacs, then, expressed regret that Britain and the US had disappointed the legitimate aspirations of the Pacific peoples. In a reportedly vigorous exchange with Ambassador Walters, Hawke argued that the decision made alliance management more problematic.[56] Whilst it might be the case that the refusal of the allies to sign the protocols would usefully demonstrate to nuclear protestors that the Treaty must be worthwhile, it seems that Hawke and Hayden sensed that Australia would find increasing difficulty in moderating the SPF's distrust of Western security objectives. The US could have softened the adverse political effect of its nuclear policies, demonstrated Washington's seriousness about arms control and retained the support of the islands. Instead, as was hardly surprising and as noted in a *Canberra Times* editorial (8 January 1987), Washington's standing in the area had diminished.

Finally, if New Zealand's nuclear policy had made the US more reluctant to sign the protocols, Washington's refusal to sign also made it more difficult for New Zealand to drop its visit ban and reactivate ANZUS. The last, but not least important, regional issue to be considered is whether ANZUS can survive.

ANZUS DEFUNCT?

Technically ANZUS has not lapsed, and in theory the dislocation is reversible. The United States and Australia left the way open for resumption of trilateral operations. Also, it might be argued, collective security arrangements are increasingly relevant given the heightened awareness of the Pacific's importance in superpower strategies. It is debatable, however, whether reversion is likely within, say, the next five years.

In considering the future of ANZUS one has to remember that prominent personalities involved in the crisis have either moved on or are likely to lose their grip on power. By 1988, for example, many

169

senior Reaganites, including Weinberger, Lehman and Perle, had left office, and Lehman's successor, James Webb, has been significantly less confrontationalist. The Lange Cabinet's economic policies have alienated traditional supporters and the NZLP will have difficulty staying in power. A change of government in Wellington could allow for a declaratory formula similar to that adopted by Beijing in July 1985, whereby China permitted an RN frigate and destroyer to visit Shanghai on condition that Britain stated that it was aware of China's non-nuclear policy. When this idea was floated as a solution to the ANZUS row it was turned down by the US, ostensibly on the grounds that an ally could not expect concessions in the way that a non-ally could.[57] Now that New Zealand is a non-ally it could presumably claim similar consideration. Modification of NCND by the US is an option and will be discussed further in the next chapter.

Two contrasting scenarios could lead to New Zealand's re-incorporation. Confrontation at sea or on the northern rim might lead to a crisis in which there would be no room for qualified alignment. Tense political and economic competition in the South Pacific might also prompt New Zealanders to reinstate nuclear visiting. Alternatively New Zealanders might be lulled into accepting visits by a superpower arms control agreement which reduced anxiety about maritime nuclear deployments. Arms control in Europe would certainly defuse concern about global nuclear war. But one ramification of the December 1987 INF agreement, for example, might be further investment in nuclear weapons at sea which would not allay such fears. At the very least, some appeasement of regional anxieties, specifically the abandonment of French nuclear testing and adherence by all three Western nuclear states to the SPNFZ protocols, would be necessary before New Zealand re-established nuclear connections. Moreover, if trilateral co-operation resumes it will almost certainly do so in a different form. Civilian watchdogs may not allow defence co-operation to be resumed as before.

The non-reversionary view maintains that long-term developments are likely to be independent of either personality or party. The San Francisco suspension of August 1986, which formally ended US–New Zealand security obligations, also killed the spirit. To say that the trilateral alliance is technically alive is, in the words of one commentator, like saying that the descendants of King Zog are still the rulers of Albania.[58] Reversion is unlikely because ANZUS has been deflowered by an experience which tested assumptions about extended nuclear deterrence and the conduct of inter-allied relations.

The National Party leader, Jim McLay, pointed to the difficulties confronting any future pro-alliance government in Wellington, not least a resistance among US officials to trusting New Zealand again.[59] Further, as discussed above anti-nuclearism not only captured the middle ground in New Zealand but defiance became a matter of national identity. If New Zealand is now defenceless, as alleged by opponents of the policy then, according to polls, few people seem to care about it.[60] Inevitably the intensity of debate about national security has diminished, but it is unlikely that the public will readily relinquish the right to be consulted about fundamental security issues. External events, including the Chernobyl disaster, have probably reinforced anti-nuclear sentiment, and resumption of visits could lead to widespread direct action by those who hold anti-nuclear principles.

The prospect of a Pacific conflict undermining qualified alignment may also be overdrawn. And those who predict Soviet attempts to control not only the dynamic North Pacific economies and the SLOCs, but also, through proxies and subversion, the mineral resources of Australia, display an alarmism which is not shared even by officials for whom worst-case analysis is an occupational hazard.[61]

Consequently ANZUS remains defunct until the United States recognizes that New Zealand will not budge. Defining US-New Zealand relations has vexed the Americans. They could neither allow business as usual nor treat New Zealand as a pariah. Yet Washington has little choice but to live with the anomaly. For in the longer term, as noted by the arch-conservative *New Zealand Herald* (4 May 1987), the weakening of traditional friendships is, 'in the light of geography, divergence of interests and some deepening political maturity, perhaps inevitable.' A new equilibrium with separate bilateral relations and different levels of security engagement is already becoming established.

Australia has become correspondingly more significant to the US, and in Australia support for the idea of alliance with the US has not yet diminished appreciably. Extrapolating from social trends, Coral Bell argues that Australia will become more conservative as the age structure of the population changes.[62] But as we have seen, Australian youth may become increasingly 'dovish' and in any case conservatism across the Tasman was no proof against Gaullism. Official statements emanating from Canberra to the effect that US-Australian strategic relations are enhanced by the crisis perhaps understate the shift which has occurred in Australian policy. Some commentators argue that there is a greater recognition that US interests frequently and seriously diverge from Australian interests, and the relationship will never be as it was even in Fraser's time.[63] In the military sphere, commitment is

171

tempered by increased questioning of the terms of mutual support. This has happened without the degree of friction which characterized the Whitlam period, and has therefore had less of a polarizing effect on Australian opinion. Thus any future right-wing government is likely to follow the gradual path towards self-reliance.

This does not mean the same track as New Zealand. Disengagement is unlikely in Australia's case on account of the base facilities. Although these could be reduced significantly, and Nurrungar closed in 1989 on grounds of obsolescence, the irreducible minimum remains Pine Gap. Consequently, as Joseph Camilleri argues, Australian foreign policy cannot stray too far from the direction set by the nuclear rationale of the alliance.[64]

There is no prospect, either, that New Zealand will divorce itself from Australian security interests. For the foreseeable future then, the likely position is friendly but non-military relations between the United States and New Zealand; strong military-defence links between US and Australia with the latter striving for greater national autonomy in strategic decisions; and increasingly important defence links between the Anzacs. In this sense New Zealand has become more meaningfully aligned than in the past. In view of the increasing complexity and foreign policy divergences anticipated in the South Pacific and the undiminished strength of island concern on nuclear issues, New Zealand continues to play a significant role in the region.

To shore up US security interests in the Pacific, Tow and Feeney offer an integrationalist approach which has the merit of disregarding the rule that in international relations precision is often the enemy of consensus. They suggest, for example, the explicit designation of SLOCs for allies to patrol, a stronger definition of ASEAN security involvements and the spelling out of political and economic functions of alliances.[65] But the fact that South Pacific countries have discovered that their national interests do not coincide with the global interests of the US is testimony to the balkanization of the international system, and the limited scope for Washington to assert definitions of security. Even strategic fundamentalists concede that a more differentiated alliance centred on Australia, interlocking with other Pacific bilateral arrangements and moulded to different needs and capabilities of partners, would be more appropriate to the new situation.[66]

The ANZUS crisis had an impact beyond the security concerns of the South Pacific because it challenged the nuclear deterrence model of alliance cohesion – the seamless web. The concluding chapter, therefore, addresses the broader international implications of the dispute.

9 THE ANZUS CRISIS, NUCLEAR VISITING AND THE WESTERN ALLIANCE

The crisis in the ANZUS relationship had far-reaching importance because it was seen as a challenge to the concept of extended nuclear deterrence as the critical variable in Western security. New Zealand's ban on warships affected the kind of military deployment which is considered by some as a symbol and trigger of commitment, and by others as an aspect of domination. This chapter surveys the visit policies of 'non-nuclear' countries in alliance with the United States, and also suggests that New Zealand's defiance had only a limited demonstration effect. Compartmentalization in the alliance system probably ensured this rather than American attempts to make New Zealand an object lesson.

US reprisals, in fact, drew attention to the problem of instilling centralized discipline. As an editorial in *The Times* (14 August 1986) put it: 'No one who values amity among the nations of the Free World could have watched American action being taken against New Zealand without alarm.' In an increasingly fragmented international system it is, by definition, more difficult to sustain the stability which one would expect to derive from the hegemonic imposition of policy. In such circumstances alliance leaders will tend to regard military collaboration and access to allied facilities as all the more important. But it is a moot point whether the Western Alliance would have been any worse off had the US tolerated untidiness and idiosyncrasy, and not viewed New Zealand's policy as a global threat.

In other cases the United States had put up with selective decoupling, or threats to withdraw from nuclear co-operation. In 1959 France had required the removal of nuclear weapons stored at five bases and some 200 nuclear-configured aircraft. After initially exerting pressure on France, the US worked to develop the remaining ties. The Karamanlis and Papandreou Governments in Greece retaliated for NATO's perceived indifference to the Turkish threat by reducing military co-operation. All the same, the US has made some allowance for

Greek sensitivity about Turkey. After Greece cancelled a NATO exercise and threatened to close bases, Shultz told the Senate Foreign Relations Committee in 1985 that the US should go ahead with a $US500 million loan to Greece. 'We don't want to have some pique of annoyance to throw us off,' he said, 'from having a strong alliance with them.'[1] The US has also complied with Norway's unilaterally imposed restrictions on force deployments in its area, with the exception, perhaps, of nuclear weapons on visiting ships.

Flexibility and differentiation with respect to port calls has been deemed impossible because the doctrine of NCND allows no exceptions. This chapter therefore considers the importance of the doctrine and its future survival. The arrangements for warship visits and the preservation of NCND have been criticized by commentators in several states as a widely-practised deceit in alliance management. To justify it by the 'higher morality' of ensuring successful nuclear deterrence has become more problematic as the validity of nuclear strategies has come under scrutiny. Whether allied governments can adhere to non-disclosure policies is open to question in the light of technological as well as political developments.

COMPARATIVE POLICIES

Allied policies on nuclear visiting have usually derived from security treaties or basing arrangements. In other instances, executive ambiguity about hosting nuclear weapons was preferred to any attempt at legal precision. Nevertheless, the number of parliamentary resolutions and debates on nuclear policy indicates that in some states executive discretion has not entirely met the demands of elected assemblies.

Notes attached to US treaties with Spain, Japan and Iceland provided foundations of a kind for nuclear policies to suit national and alliance interests. Perhaps the least ambiguous provisions, as a consequence of the Palomares accident, were those in the 1976 Treaty with Spain. They required the withdrawal of the US nuclear submarine squadron at Rota, the strict control of visits by nuclear-powered submarines and bound the United States not to install or store nuclear devices or their components on Spanish territory. The provisions were reaffirmed in the second supplementary convention which came into effect in May 1983. Although they contained no specific reference to nuclear-armed vessels, a note of 1983, addressed to the US Ambassador in Madrid, reminded the United States that: 'no aircraft carrying arms or nuclear materials may overfly Spain and that

174

any change in this practice requires the consent of the Government of Spain'. The non-nuclearization of Spain was also adopted, virtually unanimously, by the Cortes.[2] This did not preclude Spain's adherence to NATO. Nor did the policy of the González Government in 1987–8 (requiring removal of 72 USAF F-16 fighter aircraft from the Torrejón base) lead to security reprisals by the United States.

In Japan's case, a note attached to the Treaty of 1960 allowed greater flexibility in interpreting visiting rights. It required the US to seek prior consultation before introducing major changes in equipment deployed in Japan. The US has never publicly sought consultation, and a Japanese negotiator of the Treaty has stated that it was never intended to affect the temporary docking of vessels. The former US Ambassador in Tokyo, Edwin Reischauer, revealed in 1981 that the US and Japan reached a secret verbal agreement in 1960 that platforms carrying nuclear weapons could use military facilities. They regularly did so, said Reischauer, because transit did not amount to 'deployment into Japan'.[3]

Consequently, in Glenn Hook's view, frequent visits by nuclear-capable ships gradually desensitized Japanese opinion to the idea of nuclear weapons in ports. In October 1966 the visit of the USS *Enterprise* had sparked massive demonstrations. When it returned in 1983 the demonstrations were much smaller.[4] The Tanaka Government came under intense pressure after La Rocque's testimony in 1974 that nuclear-capable vessels on operations did not leave nuclear weapons behind when entering ports in Japan or other countries.[5] The Governors of Nagasaki and Kanagawa threatened to reject warship visits to Sasebo and Yokosuka, and the police had to cope with massive demonstrations against the carrier USS *Midway*. But the Government issued denials and rode out the storm. The *Washington Post* (22 May 1981) reported that a landing ship, moored off Iwakuni in 1964, had been used for some months as a kind of nuclear left-luggage locker. The furore over this past occurrence died down. Nuclear visiting continued, and it is widely believed by Japanese defence experts that cruise missiles enter Sasebo and Yokosuka harbours. In any event the three principles prohibiting the manufacture, possession or introduction of nuclear weapons, elaborated by Prime Minister Sato in 1967, were not intended to conflict with nuclear deterrence. They were supplemented by the principles of nuclear disarmament, dependence on nuclear deterrence through the Treaty of Mutual Security and high priority for the peaceful use of nuclear energy.[6]

The Iceland–US agreement of May 1951, revised in 1974, specified that the US was not permitted to make a unilateral change to the nature of the weapon systems at the Keflavík naval base. This has been supplemented by statements from successive governments since 1964 stipulating no nuclear weapons in Icelandic territory. Although a prime concern was the potentially devastating effects on fishing stocks from a nuclear accident, the question of warship visits appears not to have been debated nationally until after the New Zealand ban, perhaps because nuclear-capable and propelled vessels were infrequent visitors.[7]

In other European states, nuclear policies derive from the period in the late 1950s when dual-capable Nike and Honest John missiles were being deployed. The Netherlands, for example, made an agreement with the US in May 1959 under which the Government allowed stationing of nuclear weapons. Parliament was not informed, but when pressed, in 1960, the Government acknowledged their existence though refused to disclose the numbers and locations.[8] As in Britain, warship visiting has not been a national issue in the Netherlands.

Norway accepted only conventionally-armed missiles in 1957, and the Defence Ministry's recommendation for nuclear stockpiling and the acquisition of tactical nuclear weapons was rejected by the Labour Government in the Storting in 1961, bringing nuclear policy into line with existing bans on foreign bases and 'provocative' military activity. In 1963 the Government also announced that nuclear naval forces would not be permitted to 'establish' themselves in Norwegian territorial waters. Elaborating on this in response to questions about an ASROC-fitted American cruiser visiting Oslo in 1975, the Prime Minister, Trygve Bratteli, pointed out that it would be no 'juridical deviation' from established policy if a foreign naval vessel on 'a normal visit' to a Norwegian harbour carried nuclear weapons. Nevertheless, said Bratteli, Norway sought to avoid this happening, and it remained a condition when foreign naval vessels made port calls that nuclear weapons were not carried on board. The Norwegian authorities 'assume that both our allies and other nuclear powers respect this condition'.[9] Defence Minister Anders Sjaastad stretched the policy in 1982 to mean that ships possibly carrying nuclear weapons would only breach the policy if they stayed in a Norwegian harbour for a longer period than normal for visits. Nevertheless Bratteli's statement was reiterated by the Storting Foreign Policy Committee in the spring of 1984, and Norway's nuclear policy remains no nuclear weapons in Norwegian territory during peacetime.

Similarly, Danish visit policy derives from decisions in 1957 not to accept nuclear warheads. The non-nuclear stance was reinforced by the B-52 crash near Thule in 1968, and nuclear weapons remain excluded from Danish soil, harbours and air space by the executive policies of successive governments. The Greenland Parliament adopted its own resolution, on 16 November 1984, declaring the country a denuclearized zone in peace and war. Its validity is in doubt, however, because Denmark retains control of defence. The United States has refrained from issuing any statement of compliance that nuclear weapons are not at Thule and Søndre Strømfjord, but experts consider that the bases are virtually certain to accord with the policy. Denmark has strict regulations governing visits by nuclear-powered vessels, and none has visited since 1964. Like Norway, Denmark deals with other warships on a case by case basis and on the assumption that they will not be nuclear armed.[10] As in Norway, the assumption was challenged by Danish left-wing politicians on several occasions before New Zealand rejected the USS *Buchanan*. A typical exchange occurred in the Folketing in June 1983 when the Foreign Minister was asked: 'How has the Government ensured that the British ship, HMS *Invincible*, would not be armed with atomic weapons during her visit to Denmark?' The response was a model of its kind. Danish policy was clear, the NATO countries were aware of it and it would be extremely discourteous if Denmark expressed mistrust of her allies.[11]

One of the features of the ANZUS crisis was the prominence of localism, both in spoiling visits and exerting pressure for a national NFZ in New Zealand. As a rule, local NFZs have little practical effect unless the central government requires co-operation in conducting civil defence exercises. Central government overrides local authorities on defence matters and is responsible for visit and homeporting policy. But local resistance to warship visits can disturb this by virtue of the fact that vessels require the assistance of port authorities and dock labour, and local dignatories can deny the hospitality which protocol expects. The clash was particularly acute in Japan where national law gives municipal assemblies full control over harbours, except where there are naval bases. In 1975 the City of Kobe imposed a requirement that a ship's master declare that his vessel is not carrying nuclear weapons. Between 1960 and 1975 Kobe had hosted many US warships, but none thereafter. Hakodate followed suit.[12]

In Britain, the NFZ movement originated in 1980 in controversy over municipal responsibilities for civil defence against nuclear attack. Port cities were among the 160 local and regional authorities which declared NFZs, though these have no legal standing. After Southampton was proclaimed a NFZ in 1984, the Council attempted to raise public consciousness about nuclearism by writing to the Captains of HMS *Southampton* and *Amazon* asking them to indicate that the vessels would not be carrying nuclear weapons when they visited the city. Whether or not the vessels were capable of carrying nuclear weapons in peacetime, they did not visit, but the Council backed down two years later.[13]

The 1980s also saw the NFZ movement affect port cities in the United States. Although many ordinances, including Boston's in 1983, have legal status, port visiting is under the jurisdiction of the federal government and according to US officials no planned visits have been cancelled. Resisters were primarily concerned about weapons rather than propulsion, and less about being targeted than accidents. New York State allegedly boasts the Army's largest store at Seneca and, said Rep. Weiss, 1,900 nuclear weapons. One would have imagined that a few more on the USS *Iowa* and its support vessels berthed at Staten Island would make little difference. But opponents in the metropolis, and in San Francisco, objected to the siting of weapons in heavily populated areas. As noted earlier, opposition was overcome by federal legal powers. Nevertheless, US defence researchers argue that the homeporting programme in the United States offered anti-nuclearists 'a rare opportunity to use local political mechanisms to influence, if only indirectly, a US defense program involving nuclear weapons'.[14]

Municipal resistance in Europe reached a highpoint in 1985, a truly bad year for port calls. A visit to Zeebrugge in July by the nuclear-powered submarine USS *Sea Devil* was cancelled at the request of the local authority when protests threatened to disrupt a major festival. Later in the year large demonstrations were triggered by port calls to Copenhagen, Århus and Oslo at the end of NATO's *Ocean Safari* exercise, and the USS *Iowa* cancelled calls to Amsterdam and Rotterdam where civic authorities were known to be hostile. In Tromsø, headquarters of an international anti-nuclear Ports Watch Group, demonstrations greeted the frigates, USS *Groves* and HMS *Battleaxe*. In December the Göteborg authorities boycotted a visit by the type 22 frigate, HMS *Brazen*, and it had to be welcomed by national officials.[15]

It is tempting to attribute this upsurge of hostility to ripples from the ANZUS crisis. But the ripples had also come from Kobe, New York and Sydney in the first instance, and anti-nuclear parties and pressure groups were likely to have continued challenging state policies of 'constructive ambiguity' in any event. Only in one or two instances around the world did New Zealand's example appear to have direct influence on state policy.

RIPPLES FROM THE SOUTH PACIFIC

It frequently happens in politics that advocates of ideo-logically-opposed prescriptions make a similar diagnosis of events. During the ANZUS crisis policy-makers in the Western Alliance feared that the ban on nuclear visiting would spread, or at least declared that it threatened alliance unity. Officials tended to use the neutral phrase 'ripple effect'. They considered that Japan and certain NATO countries were particularly at risk. Publicists and commentators employed the term 'Kiwi disease' to suggest that nuclear weapons were normal and harmless and opposition abnormal. Like 'Hollanditis', used by Walter Laqueur to characterize opposition to nuclear modernization, the notion of a disease suggested a propensity to spread dangerously.[16]

For their part, anti-nuclearists welcomed and promoted the potential which they discerned for inspiring others. Far from imposing penalties of uniqueness, New Zealand's size and geographical position presented opportunities to set trends and show other states how to resist nuclear policies which exhibited, in a favourite metaphor, signs of insanity. New Zealand activists made themselves known abroad and, in 1986 for example, attended international anti-nuclear conferences in Moscow, Perugia and Athens. A leading campaigner, Sonja Davies, reported that the UN Secretary-General had spoken of New Zealand as 'a shining light'. There is little doubt that New Zealand's unilateral nuclear disengagement was noted abroad. To take a tangential example, 3,000 Swedes enquired about emigrating to New Zealand in 1986 after the Chernobyl disaster, compared to the usual hundred a year. According to *Svenska Dagbladet*, New Zealand's reputation had been enhanced by its anti-nuclear policies.[17]

In politics the powerless seek inspiration from every source. Anti-nuclear activism has also become internationalized, and New Zealand's stance was quickly incorporated into the battle honours of anti-nuclear campaigning around the world. A Nuclear-Free North Atlantic group has drawn inspiration from the NFIP movement. In 1987 the Greenpeace organization attempted to capitalize on the potential for a ripple effect by launching a campaign to harass nuclear vessels entering ports in Australia, the United States, Britain and Europe.[18] But there is a distinction to be made between inspiration and execution. The effectiveness of New Zealand peace movements could not easily be replicated elsewhere because of New Zealand's particular domestic situation. The evidence suggests that New Zealand has not had much direct effect on changing state policy on nuclear visiting.

The ruling parties in Australia, Japan, Norway and Denmark distanced themselves from New Zealand's approach in order to maintain the existing ambiguities. As we have seen, the Hawke Government pointedly refused to be a domino. The Nakasone Government not only accepted a port call by the USS *Buchanan*, but was sufficiently alarmed about 'Kiwi disease' that, according to US officials, a trip to Japan by Lange was postponed.[19]

By contrast, it seemed that the People's Republic of China would adopt New Zealand's visit policy. Hu Yaobang, the Communist Party General Secretary, said in April 1985 that ships carrying nuclear weapons would not be allowed in China's territorial waters. The new ban affected a planned visit by USN destroyers to Shanghai, though many warships from other Western countries had called there previously. It was suggested in some reports that the dispute reflected internal divisions in China about how far the country should be seen to align with the United States after visits to Beijing by Weinberger in 1983 and Lehman in 1984. It is also possible that Hu Yaobang's statement represented a device, inspired by New Zealand's ban, for displaying annoyance at the Reagan Administration's increased arms supplies to Taiwan.[20] As we have noted, however, a form of words was found which enabled HMS *Amazon* and HMS *Winchester* to visit in July 1986.

More worrying for the United States have been anti-nuclear moves in the Philippines. They are probably attributable to a spirit of independence in the post-Marcos era rather than 'Kiwi disease'. The proposed constitution of 1986 incorporated a statement that the country 'adopts and pursues a policy of freedom from nuclear weapons in its territory'. This was still awaiting ratification when senators in the Philippines Congress introduced a Bill to ban nuclear weapons, 'whether in transit or disembarkation', from Philippines air space, soil and territorial waters. The device of a law may have been inspired by New Zealand, but it seems that senators have used it as a lever to improve the terms of the bases agreement with the United States, rather than to eject the Americans altogether. Washington's response to the pressure in 1988 was to offer a huge aid package. But acceptance of a non-nuclear formula may be an additional price which the US has to pay.[21]

Outside the Pacific area, the only evidence of a direct policy impact, attributable to the New Zealand ban, is found in Iceland. Citing New Zealand, the left-wing Icelandic politician, Steingrímur Sigfússon, sought clarification of state policy. In April 1985 he asked whether the ban applied to warships in Icelandic ports or transiting territorial waters, 'except in the case where it is quite clear that they are not carrying nuclear weapons?' Foreign Minister Geir Hallgrímsson replied that Iceland's policy clearly extended to ports and territorial waters and he would disallow warships carrying nuclear weapons. He added that there was no need to concretize the policy further because there was no ambiguity about it on the part of Iceland or other NATO members.[22] Hallgrímsson, a leading supporter of the NATO connection, later explained that Iceland's policy was the same as Norway's. This was not regarded by critics as particularly rigorous, and for the first time, on 23 May 1985, the Althing adopted a resolution reaffirming the country's nuclear-free status. It might be regarded as an elaboration and underpinning of existing policy, though without the status of a law.

Whether by coincidence or design, no nuclear-capable or powered vessels visited Iceland for at least a year after the 'clarification'. With the exception of a US Coast Guard vessel, the task force warships on the NATO exercise *Ocean Safari* in the autumn of 1985 did not enter the twelve mile limit, though merchant vessels in the convoy did. However, USN and RN vessels are not believed to be seriously inconvenienced, for Iceland is normally only paid courtesy visits by NATO's Standing Naval Force Atlantic (a multinational flag-showing group). Although obviously important for surveillance of the North Atlantic gap, Iceland is not relied upon for refuelling or as a first line of defence.[23]

Certainly, the perception of a heroic New Zealand resisting US blandishments added to the confidence of Nordic pressure groups when vessels from *Ocean Safari* reached Scandinavian ports. The Norwegian CND (Nei Til Atomvåpen) and demonstrators in Oslo referred to New Zealand's stance. In fact anti-nuclear groups and governments alike frequently misunderstood New Zealand's policy as requiring guarantees of non-nuclear status from the visiting power. Arent Henriksen of the opposition Socialist Left Party asked the Norwegian Government to follow New Zealand's prohibition against nuclear-armed visitors. The Minister of Defence, Anders Sjaastad, replied that it was vital to maintain an allied naval presence in Norwegian waters to demonstrate the capability to secure lines of communication in a crisis. Therefore the Government believed it was 'not timely to make any Norwegian declaration that would make it more difficult or impossible to maintain regular contacts with and support from allied naval forces'. Henriksen asked whether this meant that Norway accepted nuclear weapons if the alternative was that ships would not visit. Sjaastad responded that the allies knew Norway's policy and 'arranged themselves accordingly'.[24]

The Danish left-wing parties also assumed that New Zealand expected guarantees from the USN, a policy which the Schlüter minority Government firmly rejected.[25] Although the Danish left looked forward to Denmark adopting New Zealand's stand, its successful Folketing resolution of 14 April 1988 simply required visiting vessels to be issued with an official statement of Danish policy.

Given the evolution of ANZUS and its unique strategic configuration, it was always unlikely that New Zealand's disengagement would influence other governments in the system. There is no substitute for domestic unrest, and only minority groups have translated the New Zealand situation to their own. The ban on visiting seems to have had little political impact in Britain, for example. It drew a comment from Neil Kinnock that the unfortunate publicity of US bullying would make the Americans wary of doing the same to a future British Labour government. But nuclear disengagement by Britain would be a far more difficult proposition and Labour's unilateralism was in the process of being bullied by the electorate. Even in the programmes of pressure groups like CND nuclear visiting was well down the list of priorities. Anti-nuclearism in various countries might have been reinforced indirectly by the distant example of New Zealand, but it was only one among many external influences. It is more accurate to say that opinion in Australia and New Zealand was influenced by the INF debate in Europe, translating it to a maritime environment. And, while some Danes looked to New Zealand as a model, Lange was telling Shultz that Denmark was the country he wished to emulate.[26]

THE FUTURE OF NCND

There is no question that the hosting of nuclear-armed warships will continue by allies, though the pattern could well change, depending in part on the future of NCND. Thirty years after the US established the non-disclosure policy, its continued existence in the current form cannot be assumed. On land, of course, nuclear weapon stores are readily identifiable and have been recorded in W. M. Arkin and R. W. Fieldhouse, *Nuclear Battlefields* (1985). Indeed, as reported in *The Guardian* (11 July 1986), the DoD provided congressmen with a list of some 20 proposed hardened aircraft shelters in Europe and South Korea, which could store nuclear weapons for quick transfer to aircraft on alert standby.

Actually, New Zealand anti-nuclearists censured the Lange Government for respecting NCND and colluding in its preservation.

Self-assessment was not, however, a model for protecting NCND which appealed to the United States. One might conjecture that an ally's judgement is likely to be better-informed than an adversary's and if the judgement became public the adversary would benefit. Information regarding the alert status of US forces and whether a particular crew included units certified for dealing with nuclear weapons, might be more accessible to an ally. Walter Stoessel conceded that if an Australian Prime Minister made an inquiry as to whether or not US warships were nuclear armed, 'we would be prepared to consult with him on a very frank and very confidential basis as appropriate between allies'.[27] However, according to Desmond Ball, US vessels with nuclear weapons in the Pacific might make daily radio reports to Hawaii on the status of the weapons.[28] The Soviet Union could conceivably gather SIGINT, depending on cryptanalytical capabilities, which is denied to allies unless they are willing and able to spy on the United States.

It is sometimes argued that verification technology will undermine the doctrine. Yet the manifold practical difficulties gave Lehman confidence that distant or ill-equipped observers had no chance of verifying naval nuclear weapons.[29] Protestors in Australia and Denmark who smuggled geiger counters aboard visiting US warships and claimed that they detected the presence of nuclear weapons presumably used ultra-sensitive equipment. Materials in nuclear warheads are less spontaneously radioactive than those used in the civilian fuel cycle and are heavily shielded to safeguard the crew. When the Swedes had a rare opportunity to investigate the grounded Soviet submarine in October 1981, a passive gamma ray detector was pressed against the hull for four hours to check emissions. It detected about 22 pounds of $U238$, which is used as a jacket or reflector in Soviet nuclear explosives. But highly enriched $U235$ is difficult to discriminate from background radiation. Active detectors, which induce emissions from radioactive material, are employable up to a metre away. But the neutron signals can be attenuated by the vessel's hull and the proximity of fuel tanks. Furthermore, stirring up reactions from a weapon is liable to annoy the crew.[30]

Sweden has probably made significant signal enhancements to detectors since 1981, and the Australian researcher Gary Brown argues that it would be surprising if the superpowers had not rivalled Swedish technology. US research into detection has proceeded since at least 1978. The DoD budget provided funds specifically directed at Soviet naval nuclear capabilities, initially through the Technical Sensor Collection Program. Brown surmises that an array of detectors

183

might be placed around shipping choke points, and there are reports that during the 1973 Middle East War a Soviet freighter was detected as it passed through the Bosphorous carrying nuclear warheads to Egypt.[31]

However, no tangible progress appears to have been forthcoming to substitute for intrusive inspection in the arms control context. At the superpower summit of December 1987 the communiqué mentioned the desirability of verification to facilitate a future agreement limiting long-range SLCMs. Apparently the negotiators talked about detection and the Russians offered to produce a national technical means, involving satellites or helicopters hovering over submarines in port. But most commentators are sceptical of the claims.[32]

Problems could arise for NCND if the Soviet Union accepted a disclosure policy. The Danish communist daily, *Land og Folk* (2 November 1985), reported that General Igor Mikhailov had told a communist delegation in Moscow that the Soviet Union would specify, if the Danish Government so requested, that visiting warships were not nuclear armed. Foreign Minister Engell dismissed this as mischief-making, for no Soviet visits were contemplated. But if, in the context of SLCM arms control, the Soviet Union were to back away from insistence on verification and accept the American preference for assurances, there could be consequences for NCND in relation to port visits.

Failing maritime arms control agreements, the proliferation of nuclear warheads in the USN also makes non-disclosure a less credible posture. Not only will adversaries equate 'capable' with 'armed' but, as a forceful American advocate of SLCMs admitted, if every US warship became a potential nuclear platform then visits to friendly ports would become contentious.[33]

It is also a significant issue in the delineation of prospective nuclear weapon-free zones. Idealists would prefer controls on transit and deployment, and some proponents recommend boarding vessels for spot checks. But the viability of any NFZ as a confidence-building measure has to satisfy the major powers, and it was noted above that the SPNFZ endeavoured to do so. In adhering to protocol 2 of the Treaty of Tlatelolco, the United States and France insisted on transit rights, particularly through the Panama Canal. Similarly, in any Balkan zone the Soviet Union would insist on free access for nuclear weapons through the straits. In a Nordic zone, Denmark and Norway would need to continue exercises with nuclear-armed US vessels. Since nuclear powers are unlikely to accept intrusive inspection, their co-operation in limiting deployments at sea would be essential. Even so, this would involve assurances, which would have to be acceptable to adversaries and which would weaken NCND.[34]

US officials regarded New Zealand's policy as akin to treachery perhaps because, in effect, it drew attention to possible assumptions by allied governments that warships do arrive with nuclear weapons on board in contravention of local principles. In the view of US experts, the challenges to NCND are likely to resurface from time to time and pose new headaches for naval and civilian authorities.[35] If the political value of ambiguity is outweighed by disruptive political demands, the doctrine might have to be reviewed. As shown in table 4.1, many national 'prohibitions' relating to nuclear weapons are in the nature of executive decisions which are readily reversed or interpreted to assist nuclear deployment. But a number of parliamentary resolutions, enshrined in New Zealand's case by a law, indicates politicization of the issue in some countries.

It is possible that incidents such as the 1988 Folketing affair could prompt reassessments of NCND policy in Washington and London. As suggested in chapter 1, the UK has no nuclear-tipped tactical missiles at sea. Off-loading any nuclear depth-charges and bombs deployed on surface vessels, except in periods of tension, might be feasible, though at the cost of operational readiness. Britain could not abandon NCND, of course, without creating a precedent which would hardly enthrall the United States. There is, nevertheless, already an aircraft precedent for the B-52s operating at Darwin, and disclosure is provided for in the event of nuclear weapon accidents. Given the variety of national stances and conditions attached to the acceptability of warship and aircraft visits, and given the variety of forms in which provisions are made, there might be at least a case for flexibility about the doctrine.

Full-blooded revisionists propose declarations from each ship on each visit, with or without inspections by the host. An alternative would require hosts to commit themselves one way or the other. If Shultz let the cat out of the bag at Manila, to the effect that allies must expect nuclear weapons to visit from time to time, it might seem as though he was expressing impatience with sensitivities. Visits by nuclear-capable vessels might be based on the assumption that, without distinction, they are nuclear armed. Host states would then have to devise a policy for such visits, perhaps involving conditions relating to frequency and suitable ports. This is roughly the position adopted by Australia which accepts nuclear weapons at the dockside. Allies which disapproved would either forfeit visits altogether, or might be offered courtesy visits only, accompanied by a 'we are aware of your policy' declaration.

There would be practical and political difficulties in such a revision. It would be more problematic for vessels to combine exercises and flag-waving visits involving more than one host country. It would encourage debates about nuclear policy in various countries. Strategic conservatives would regard revision as a weakness, pandering to those wishing to harm alliance cohesion or who are said to exaggerate environmental dangers. Perhaps only a few states, Iceland, Spain and Denmark, for example, would reject nuclear-armed warships outright. The Netherlands and Japan might be willing to accept, and the British Labour Party leaders have said that in office they would not ban US visits. In other instances, denials could lead to strategic instability, for example if Norway and Japan opted out of nuclear visiting.

Less radical solutions which might preserve the sensitivities of visitor and host are China's request that visitors indicate their awareness of the nuclear policy and the Danish Folketing's resolution that clearances are accompanied by a written reminder that nuclear weapons are barred. However, the reactions of the United States and Britain to the latter were entirely negative. Although the Danish Social Democratic Party denied that notification challenged NCND, the nuclear allies argued that visitors crossing into Danish territorial waters after receiving the reminder would be signalling to the Soviet Union that they were nuclear free. Alternatively, if the Danes suspected a vessel of ignoring the policy a more direct challenge might ensue. Britain warned that if vessels were interrogated, Denmark could not expect to receive British reinforcements in time of crisis. As a consequence of another election which the resolution precipitated, a reconstructed Schlüter Government adopted a compromise. When arranging naval visits, embassies would be informed about Danish regulations.[36]

The greatest challenge in moving to an open policy, then, is not to devise a formula but to consider distinctions between support for collective security and particular deployments, between alliance loyalty and nuclear visiting. This, at present, the nuclear allies are not prepared to do and they have fixed nuclear visiting as the point beyond which deviance cannot be tolerated. However, various factors may make it increasingly difficult to resist national pressures for differentiation in nuclear co-operation, including a growing confidence among militarily weak states about the validity of qualified alignment.

CONCLUSION

When a major SIPRI-Pugwash study, *Nuclear Disengagement in Europe*, was published in 1983 the international environment was not auspicious for denuclearization. Since then a lessening of confrontation between the superpowers has generated confidence building between East and West and led to the removal of land-based INF weapons. The Soviet Union is likely to continue pressing for maritime arms control, though this is an area in which the West is reluctant to concede its advantages.[37] Meanwhile domestic anti-nuclear agitation, including demonstrations against nuclear visiting, is unlikely to die down completely. A courtesy visit to Amsterdam by HMS *Illustrious* in June 1987 caused little disturbance. However, in mid-1988 an RN task group was held up by protests which closed docks in Malta, a US destroyer was denied entry to the Danish harbour of Ålborg for several hours, and Australian protestors were active during visits in connection with Australia's bicentenary celebrations. Nuclear issues in general have become politicized, to the extent that élites are perhaps more wary of negative attitudes towards nuclear deployments. Also in so far as anti-nuclearism reflects concerns about accident risks, a tightening up of safety regulations for continued access of nuclear-capable and nuclear-powered platforms might be expected.

As forward-based nuclear weapons become obsolete, opportunities arise for debating nuclear collaboration and redefining national interests. Canada was one of the first allies to undertake a measure of denuclearization when, in the late 1960s, the Trudeau Government abandoned a nuclear role for Canada's new fighter-aircraft, though the last American nuclear missile did not leave until the summer of 1984. By then, the Liberal Party opposition and the New Democratic Party (which had always rejected nuclear proliferation) were opposing tests of air-launched cruise missiles over Canada and demanding ironclad guarantees that Canada would not host nuclear arms.[38] In Greece, the Papandreou Government has refused US requests to renovate ageing nuclear weapons and threatened to close bases. The Greek Prime Minister's anti-bloc rhetoric has been more radical than his actions, and anti-Americanism plays a part in domestic politics. However, the possibility of further base and missile reductions after 1988 prompted the Pentagon to make contingency relocation plans.[39]

In 1987 the Belgian Government decided not to replace ageing Nikes with Patriot nuclear missiles, and since the INF debate, the Netherlands has decided to reduce its nuclear tasks and not to deploy nuclear depth-charges or nuclear bombs for its F-16 fighters. Norway's Labour

Government, elected in May 1986, has pressed for a reappraisal of NATO's nuclear strategy. The Danish Folketing had already resolved in 1984 'to work in NATO and other international bodies in order that Denmark remains free of nuclear weapons in times of peace, crisis and war by furthering the plans which aim at making the Nordic region a nuclear weapons free zone in a larger European context'.[40] Denmark shed nuclear tasks allotted to its forces and, after the 1987 general election strengthened the representation of left-wing parties and environmentalists, anti-nuclear pressures increased. Yet the April 1988 resolution of the Social Democrats and their allies may have been designed to irritate the Schlüter Government rather than undermine nuclear deterrence, let alone jeopardize membership of NATO. There is, of course, little risk in Danes and Norwegians voting for a Nordic NFZ on conditions which are unlikely to be fulfilled. Their caveats signal a desire to preserve alliance membership.

National denuclearization policies do not necessarily denote New Zealand-style disengagement from nuclear deterrence, so much as a recoil from nuclear war-fighting strategies. Canadians broadly support their country's role in protecting the US nuclear deterrent. Yet in their effect on perceptions, unilateral denuclearization measures are bound to challenge the paradigm of nuclear security. The outlooks of small powers may shift further towards an emphasis on East-West reassurance policies and what the Palme Commission referred to as 'common security'.

The notion that developments on the European continent indicate that neutralism has penetrated the political establishments is inaccurate. As Nils Ørvik and Harto Hakovirta point out, the fact that smaller allies have preferred qualified alignment does not mean that their loyalty is at stake. States cannot be assumed to fall into established polar categories such as neutral or aligned. Nor are there models for the grey area in the middle, though Norway is depicted as a textbook case of 'semi-alignment', any more than there are rules for correct alliance behaviour.[41] On the contrary, as opinion polls in NATO countries indicate, the appeal of alignment grew alongside disquiet about particular alliance policies.[42] The parallel with ANZUS is clear. Allied states which refuse nuclear deployments, or restrict their military commitments in some way, do not equate their policies with neutralism or non-alignment.

Ørvik postulates that the origins and motivations for the phenomenon lie in the leading role of social democratic parties in promoting policies akin to the traditional neutralities which were squeezed out of the European system by the two World Wars (and, one might add, the

Cold War).[43] Threat perception and strategic location are other variables. New Zealand conforms to the profile in some respects, such as low threat perception, but dents the central hypothesis that qualified alignment is a modern version of traditional neutrality; New Zealand had a highly partisan tradition. And although a Labour Government effected the visiting ban, ideology had limited relevance. Nor does the factor of proximity to an adversary, which engenders non-provocative policies, fit the New Zealand case. The growing phenomenon of qualified alignment is perhaps more appropriately considered as an aspect of the continuous redefinition of national interests as security dependence upon the United States diminishes. Critics of the Reagan Administration's foreign policy noted its striking illustrations of unilateral action which, ironically, may have stimulated the kind of decentralizing trends so deplored by high priests of globalism. Economic constraints in the United States could result in a further impetus to decentralization, and for some American revisionists, not only was a pact with the Anzacs unnecessary, but the crisis was a golden opportunity for the US to start re-examining the assumptions of collective security.[44]

A re-examination of the seamless web model might be in order. Rather than representing a contagious threat, New Zealand's policy was symptomatic of separatist trends in the Western Alliance as a whole. Writing in the 1960s, Hans Morgenthau found a 'shocking picture of disintegration' in the Western Alliance.[45] A case can be made for saying that the problem is no worse now than in the past, and that disintegration has been stalled by structural divisions in the system. It would seem counter-productive to reduce that element of resilience by insisting on a holistic model of threat containment.

Moreover, the fluctuation in aggregate Western power is unlikely to be tidy. For example, shrinkage in US overseas deployment since the Vietnam War has been uneven. An air base in Spain has been lost, but Sigonella in Sicily, the fastest growing USN base outside the United States, will provide significant logistic and submarine support for linking US forces in Europe and the Indian Ocean. In this connection, Egypt's ban on nuclear propulsion, the outcome of concern about accidents, had greatly hindered reinforcement of the RDF from the Mediterranean. The US was able to claim a major victory when Egypt allowed a nuclear-powered cruiser, the USS *Arkansas*, to pass through the Suez Canal in 1984.[46] In Europe, French governments have encouraged closer operational integration with NATO and have supported a nuclear defence of Europe more enthusiastically than some full members. In the Pacific, Japan has not only become a defence client of the United States, but in 1985 the Prime Minister Yasuhiro Nakasone said the US would be allowed to use nuclear weapons for the defence of Japan if it was faced with annihilation. There has also been academic analysis of the strategic value of Japan acquiring its own nuclear warheads, though the political obstacles are formidable.[47]

It is quite usual for states to live with the kind of untidy dislocation displayed by ANZUS. Obviously, when the alliance commitments of a state fall below the level decided upon by the collectivity, albeit dominated by a superpower, then national interests may no longer prove compatible with the security of the whole. However, the management and shape of the Alliance will need to continue adapting to a world which has moved on from the hey-day of US omnipotence. Failure to do so risks accentuating the difficulties of management in the future. Disciplinarians might wish the United States to use its power in a ruthless way to limit the choices of states which fail to live up to expectations but, as the Reagan Administration discovered, this is no easy matter. An Australian admirer of Reaganism despairingly commented: 'If the U.S. can no longer successfully maintain a long-standing alliance with the region's only stable democracies, the question will arise: What can the U.S. do?'[48] The perceptions of the superpowers are no longer so readily accepted by clients and allies, and coping with initiatives of the kind which emerged in the South-West Pacific will tax the post-Reagan Administration, especially if it adheres to a monolithic conception of Western security. In reality the Alliance moves in discrete ways its wonders to perform.

Nor is it just a question of recognizing the crucial importance and moral strength of democratic pluralism. A major issue at stake in inter-allied relations is the extent to which the United States places a greater value on nuclearism than the political goals which nuclear deterrence is said to safeguard. Either out of conviction or for tactical reasons New Zealand leaders avoided condemning nuclear deterrence as a belief system, especially whilst on visits to Europe. Nevertheless, the ANZUS crisis suggests that both as an explanatory and prescriptive paradigm the identification of an alliance with nuclearism has weaknesses, not least in managing political relationships. The issue of nuclear visiting lays bare the very principles of morality, democracy and the exercise of autonomy which are said to govern a Western Alliance in which military defence is a major, though not the sole, arbiter of both inter-ally and ally–adversary relations.

THE TEXT OF THE ANZUS TREATY

SECURITY TREATY

Between Australia, New Zealand, and the United States of America

The Parties of this Treaty,

Reaffirming their faith in the purposes and principles of the Charter of the United Nations and their desire to live in peace with all peoples and all Governments, and desiring to strengthen the fabric of peace in the Pacific Area, Noting that the United States already has arrangements pursuant to which its armed forces are stationed in the Philippines, and has armed forces and administrative responsibilities in the Ryukyus, and upon the coming into force of the Japanese Peace Treaty may also station armed forces in and about Japan to assist in the preservation of peace and security in the Japan Area.

Recognizing that Australia and New Zealand as members of the British Commonwealth of Nations have military obligations outside as well as within the Pacific Area,

Desiring to declare publicly and formally their sense of unity, so that no potential aggressor could be under the illusion that any of them stand alone in the Pacific Area, and

Desiring further to co-ordinate their efforts for collective defence for the preservation of peace and security pending the development of a more comprehensive system of regional security in the Pacific Area,

Therefore declare and agree as follows:

ARTICLE I

The Parties undertake, as set forth in the Charter of the United Nations, to settle any international disputes in which they may be involved by peaceful means in such a manner that international peace and security and justice are not endangered and to refrain in their international relations from the threat or use of force in any manner inconsistent with the purposes of the United Nations.

191

ARTICLE II

In order more effectively to achieve the objective of this Treaty the Parties separately and jointly by means of continuous and effective self-help and mutual aid will maintain and develop their individual and collective capacity to resist armed attack.

ARTICLE III

The Parties will consult together whenever in the opinion of any of them the territorial integrity, political independence or security of any of the Parties is threatened in the Pacific.

ARTICLE IV

Each Party recognizes that an armed attack in the Pacific Area on any of the Parties would be dangerous to its own peace and safety and declares that it would act to meet the common danger in accordance with its constitutional processes.

Any such armed attack and all measures taken as a result thereof shall be immediately reported to the Security Council of the United Nations. Such measures shall be terminated when the Security Council has taken the measures necessary to restore and maintain international peace and security.

ARTICLE V

For the purpose of Article IV, an armed attack on any of the Parties is deemed to include an armed attack on the metropolitan territory of any of the Parties, or on the island territories under its jurisdiction in the Pacific or on its armed forces, public vessels or aircraft in the Pacific.

ARTICLE VI

This Treaty does not affect and shall not be interpreted as affecting in any way the rights and obligations of the Parties under the Charter of the United Nations or the responsibility of the United Nations for the maintenance of international peace and security.

ARTICLE VII

The Parties hereby establish a Council consisting of their Foreign Ministers or their Deputies, to consider matters concerning the implementation of this Treaty. The Council should be so organized as to be able to meet at any time.

ARTICLE VIII

Pending the development of a more comprehensive system of regional security in the Pacific Area and the development by the United Nations of more effective means to maintain international peace and security, the Council, established by Article VII, is authorized to maintain a consultative relationship with States, Regional Organizations, Associations of States or other authorities in the Pacific Area in a position to further the purposes of this Treaty and to contribute to the security of that Area.

ARTICLE IX

This Treaty shall be ratified by the Parties in accordance with their respective constitutional processes. The instruments of ratification shall be deposited as soon as possible with the Government of Australia, which will notify each of the other signatories of such deposit. The Treaty shall enter into force as soon as the ratifications of the signatories have been deposited.

ARTICLE X

This Treaty shall remain in force indefinitely. Any Party may cease to be a member of the Council established by Article VII one year after notice has been given to the Government of Australia, which will inform the Governments of the other Parties of the deposit of such notice.

ARTICLE XI

This Treaty in the English language shall be deposited in the archives of the Government of Australia. Duly certified copies thereof will be transmitted by that Government to the Governments of each of the other signatories.

TABLES OF USN NUCLEAR DEPLOYMENTS

Table A2.1. *USN surface combatants (excluding carriers) capable of firing Terrier, ASROC and TLAM/N*

Type/class/number (planned)	Terrier	ASROC	TLAM/N
battleships			
Iowa (BB-61) 2 (4)			X
cruisers			
Ticonderoga (CG-47) 4 (27)		X	X
Virginia (CGN-38) 4		X	X
California (CGN-36) 2		X	X
Truxtun (CGN-35) 1	X	X	
Belknap (CG-26) 9	X	X	
Leahy (CG-16) 9	X	X	
Bainbridge (CGN-25) 1	X	X	
Long Beach (CGN-9) 1	X	X	X
destroyers			
Arleigh Burke (DDG-51) 0 (29)		X	X
Kidd (DDG-993) 4		X	
Spruance (DD-963) 31		X	X
C. F. Adams (DDG-2) 23		X	
Farragut (DDG-37) 10	X	X	
frigates			
Knox (FF-1052) 46		X	
Brooke (FFG-1) 6		X	
Glover (FF-1098) 1		X	
Garcia (FF-1040) 10		X	
Bronstein (FF-1037) 2		X	

Source: adapted from Ronald O'Rourke, 'Nuclear-Powered and Nuclear-Weapons-Capable Ships In The U.S. Navy: An Aid To Identification', Congressional Research Service, Library of Congress, Report No. 86–659F, Washington, DC, 1986, p. 9.

Table A2.2. *US naval nuclear weapons, 1987*

Type	Number	Year deployed	Yield, kt.
SLBMs			
Poseidon (C-3)	2,560	1971	40–50
Trident I (C-4)	3,072	1979	100
SLCMs			
TLAM/N	125	1984	200
ASW			
ASROC	575	1961	1
SUBROC	285	1965	1–5
B-57 depth charge (P-3/S-3/SH-3)	895	1964	1–20
SAM			
Terrier	290	1956	1
Carrier Aircraft Bombs (A-7/A-6/F/A 18)	1,530		1–1,000
Total	9,332		

Source: Center for Defense Information, 'First Strike Weapons at Sea: the Trident II and the Sea-Launched Cruise Missile', *Defense Monitor*, vol. 16, no. 6, Washington, DC, 1987, p. 7.

TABLES OF SOVIET
DIPLOMATIC PORT VISITS

Table A3.1. *Soviet diplomatic port visits, 1953–1976 (countries visited 4 times or more, excluding Warsaw Pact)*

		1953–66	1967–76
Developed Countries	(All)	(21)	(30)
Denmark		3	3
Finland		5	6
France		1	7
Norway		3	2
Sweden		4	3
United Kingdom		4	1
Others		1	8
Developing Countries	(All)	(16)	(140)
Algeria		2	4
Cuba		–	17
Egypt		1	4
Ethiopia		2	7
India		–	5
Iran		–	6
Iraq		–	9
Mauritius		–	8
Morocco		–	4
Somalia		–	14
South Yemen		–	4
Sri Lanka		–	4
Syria		1	5
Tunisia		–	5
Yugoslavia		5	13
Others		5	31

Source: adapted and printed with the permission of Pergamon Books Ltd., from Charles C. Petersen, 'Showing the Flag', in Bradford Dismukes and James McConnell (eds.), *Soviet Naval Diplomacy*, New York, 1979, pp. 88–90.

Table A3.2 *Soviet diplomatic port visits by region, 1967–1976*

	Atlantic	Mediterranean	Indian Ocean	Pacific
1967	0	4	1	0
1968	2	2	12	0
1969	4	1	17	1
1970	9	2	7	0
1971	6	2	5	1
1972	5	1	9	0
1973	3	6	7	2
1974	9	7	5	1
1975	4	7	2	0
1976	6	3	4	1
Totals	48	35	69	6

Source: reprinted with the permission of Pergamon Books Ltd., from Charles C. Petersen, 'Showing the Flag', in Bradford Dismukes and James McConnell (eds.), *Soviet Naval Diplomacy*, New York, 1979, p. 92.

THE ANZUS REVIEW, ANZUS COUNCIL COMMUNIQUÉ, JUNE 1983

After the Secretary of State welcomed the ANZUS Delegations, the Council Members reviewed the ANZUS Alliance. It was the first such review since the ANZUS Treaty was signed in 1951. They noted that, although international political and strategic circumstances which prevailed at that time had changed, it is a sign of the resilience of the Treaty that it remains relevant and vitally important to the shared security concerns and strategic interests of the three partner governments.

The Council Members affirmed that the Alliance is firmly based on the partners' common traditions and concern to protect democratic values. They value highly the co-operative defence arrangements, facilitated by the treaty since its conclusion, which have served their government's mutual security interests and promoted a strengthening of each other's defence capability. In the spirit of the ANZUS Alliance, they noted that beyond the activities of defence co-operation, the various efforts, individual and collective, by the partners to promote both regional and global development and stability have also served the cause of mutual security.

The Council acknowledged that the ANZUS Treaty does not absolve each government from the primary responsibility to provide for its own security to the extent which its resources allow. It is for this reason that Article II of the Treaty provides that the parties will 'by means of continuous and effective self-help and mutual aid maintain and develop their individual and collective capacity to resist armed attack'. The Council Members also noted that the ability of each country to defend itself is substantially enhanced by their common commitments under the Treaty. A range of responses is available to the parties to act to meet a common danger in accordance with their constitutional processes.

The Council also reaffirmed that the ANZUS Treaty is an agreement between sovereign and equal states committed to the democratic tradition. In accordance with that tradition, the respective states would at times have varying views and perspectives on various international political and economic issues. Such diversity does not affect their solidarity under the ANZUS Treaty, the maintenance of which reflects the fundamental interests of the three partners.

In order to strengthen the Alliance further and recognising that national security cannot be assured by military strength alone, the Council Members considered a number of practical co-operative measures:

They agreed that ANZUS consultative processes could be strengthened through further periodic ANZUS Officials Talks. These talks, which were revived this year, would rotate between the three capitals and address issues or areas of common concern. Participants would include mid-level and senior officials expert on the issues or areas to be addressed.

They also agreed that the framework of ANZUS and bilateral defence co-operation requires a standardisation of privileges and immunities and of jurisdictional and other matters for military service personnel and their families serving in each other's countries. The members therefore agreed to give priority to early conclusion of a reciprocal ANZUS Status of Forces Agreement.

They expressed satisfaction with the continuing programs of exchanges, combined exercises and visits among the Treaty partners. They also reaffirmed the importance of these programs, of ongoing efforts to modernise and to assure supply of equipment, and of continuing to strengthen alliance defensive capabilities and thus deterrence of conflict.

Source: *APD*, HR, vol. 132, 33(1) 2, 15 September 1983, pp. 899–900.

STATEMENT BY THE UNITED KINGDOM GOVERNMENT: 'OPERATION OF NUCLEAR-POWERED WARSHIPS IN FOREIGN PORTS'

1. The UK Government certifies that reactor safety aspects of design, crew training and operating procedures of the nuclear propulsion plants of UK nuclear-powered warships are reviewed by the UK Nuclear-Powered Warships Safety Committee and other appropriate UK authorities, and are as defined in officially approved manuals. The UK Government also certifies that all safety precautions and procedures followed in connection with operations in UK ports will be strictly observed in foreign ports.

2. In connection with the operation of UK nuclear-powered warships in foreign ports:

    (a) No effluent or other waste will be discharged from the ship which would cause a measurable increase in the general background radioactivity of the environment; waste disposal standards are consistent with the recommendations of the International Commission on Radiological Protection.

    (b) During the period of the visit, the personnel of the nuclear-powered warship will be responsible for radiological control on board the ship and for environmental monitoring in its immediate vicinity. The host Government may, of course, take such surveys as it desires, in the vicinity of the warship, to assure itself that the visiting ship is not creating a radioactive contamination hazard.

    (c) The appropriate authorities of the host Government will be notified immediately in the event of an accident involving the reactor of the warship during a port visit.

    (d) The UK Government assumes the responsibility to salvage or otherwise make safe any nuclear-powered warships that might be incapacitated in a foreign port.

    (e) The UK Government does not make technical information on the design or operation of the nuclear-powered warships available to host Governments in connection with port entry. The UK Government cannot, therefore, permit the boarding of its nuclear-powered warships for the purposes of obtaining technical information concerning their propulsion plants or operating instructions.

(f) The Royal Navy will inform the appropriate host Government authorities as early as practicable, but normally at least 24 hours in advance, as to the estimated time of arrival and pursuant to prior consultation with the host Government, the intended location of mooring or anchoring of its nuclear-powered warships.

(g) The United Kingdom will, of course, welcome the customary protocol visits to its nuclear-powered warships by representatives of the host government.

3. Claims arising out of a nuclear incident involving a nuclear-powered warship will be dealt with through diplomatic channels in accordance with customary procedures for the settlement of international claims under generally accepted principles of law and equity.

Source: reproduced with permission of the Defence Arms Control Unit, Ministry of Defence, London.

AUSTRALIAN AND NEW ZEALAND OPINION POLLS

All poll responses are percentages, and rounding off of figures sometimes means that the total falls short of 100 per cent.

Australian polls

11 November 1966 (Morgan-Gallup):
'Should nuclear weapons be kept out of Australia – or should we ask America and England to base nuclear weapons here?'

keep out	31.1
base here	58.3
undecided	10.6

June 1982:
'For, or against, letting America base nuclear weapons here?'

in favour	47
against	44
undecided	9

6–13 March 1976 (Morgan-Gallup):
'It's been suggested that the American Navy, including nuclear submarines, should be allowed to use that naval base [near Perth]. Are you for – or against – their using it?'

for	53.6
against	26.7
undecided	19.7

19–26 July 1980 (Morgan-Gallup):
'It's been suggested that the United States station some of their planes in Northern Australia. Do you favor or oppose that suggestion?'

approve	55.6
disapprove	27.3
can't say	17.1

29 June 1981 (Age Poll):
[The Australian Government has recently allowed the US to use Darwin as a landing base for its B-52 reconnaissance aircraft.] 'Do you agree with this decision; disagree with it; or do you have no view on it?'

agree	58
disagree	29
no opinion/don't know	13

29 June 1981 (Age Poll):
[Name any of the US communications bases in Australia and their locations.]

unable to name any	47
identified Pine Gap	35
identified North West Cape	18
identified Smithfield	2
identified Nurrungar	1

'Do you favor or oppose the presence of such bases in Australia?'

favor	60
oppose	22
don't know	18

October 1982 (Age Poll):
'We should allow US naval ships to visit our ports'

Even if they may be carrying nuclear weapons	58
Only if they are not carrying nuclear weapons	39
Don't know	3

19–26 June 1982 (Morgan-Gallup):
'Are you for or against visits to Australian ports by American warships carrying nuclear weapons?'

for	47.4
against	43.9
other	8.7

1985 (Age Poll):
'In the light of US policy not to disclose whether its ships are carrying nuclear weapons, should we allow US navy ships to visit our ports; exclude US navy ships from our ports; or don't know?'

allow	65
exclude	27
don't know	8

'Do you agree with nuclear-powered ships coming into Australian ports?'

date	agree	disagree	other
*1976	74	20	6
*1976	62	19	19
1978	59	18	23
*1982	60	30	10
1982	53	40	7
1984	49	39	12
1984	44	46	10
1985	46	44	10

(* The 1976 questions, and one 1982 question, referred to US nuclear-powered ships).

12 July 1983 (Morgan-Gallup):
'If Australia's security is threatened by some other country, how much trust do you feel Australia can have in the United States?'

a great deal	28
a fair amount	44
not very much	18
none at all	4
don't know	6

1985 (Morgan-Gallup):
'If New Zealand is no longer in ANZUS, do you favour or oppose the same kind of mutual defence alliance between Australia and the United States?'

favour	75
oppose	17
other	8

'Do you believe that the New Zealand Government's ban on US nuclear ship visits is a wise or unwise move for New Zealand?'

date	wise	unwise	don't know
1984	32	55	13
1985	33	59	8

1985 (Spectrum Research):
'Do you believe the New Zealand Government's recent actions have damaged the ANZUS alliance?'

greatly damaged	39
partly damaged	37
no effect	14
don't know	10

1985 (Age Poll):

'In the current argument between the United States and New Zealand, should we:

(a) Support the US position and try to influence
    New Zealand to change its policy? 35
(b) Support the New Zealand position and try to
    influence the US to change its position? 22
(c) Remain neutral in the argument? 37
(d) Don't know' 5

New Zealand polls

20 February 1984 (Heylen):

    approved ban on nuclear visits 73

4 August 1984 (Heylen):

approved nuclear-armed ban	76.4
disapproved	18.4
approved nuclear-powered ban	45.5
disapproved	45.9
approved a New Zealand Nuclear Free Zone	69
approved Labour's policy of renegotiating ANZUS	60

9 February 1985 (Heylen):

approved nuclear-armed ban	73.4
disapproved	18.5
approved nuclear-powered ban	52.3
disapproved	37.2

18 February 1985 (*Dominion*):

against visits	56
favoured visits	29
approved ban on nuclear-powered vessels	47
against the ban	42
favoured ANZUS membership	78
against	12
satisfied with Government's handling of the dispute	51
dissatisfied	41

23 March 1985 (Heylen):

approved nuclear-armed ban	76.6
disapproved	18.6
approved nuclear-powered ban	51.8

disapproved	40.9
preferred breaking defence ties rather than visits	44.8
preferred visits to breaking defence ties	45.3

September 1985 (*Herald*-NRB):

favoured ban on armed and propelled visitors	59
against	30
favoured remaining in ANZUS	71
against	14

April–May 1986 (Defence Committee of Enquiry polls, NRB):

Nuclear ship visits:

ban nuclear power only	3
ban nuclear armed only	28
ban both	38
ban neither	28
don't know	3

ANZUS and ship visits:

New Zealand in ANZUS and allow visits by nuclear ships	37
New Zealand in ANZUS and no visits by nuclear ships	44
New Zealand out of ANZUS and no nuclear ships	16
don't know	3

Preferred defence option:

allied to the United States and Australia including the nuclear capability	24
allied to the United States and Australia but New Zealand being separated from all nuclear aspects	42
allied to Australia only	4
allied to some other country	2
no alliances but friendly relations with the United States and Australia in a conventional defence capacity	13
armed neutrality	8
unarmed neutrality, no armed forces	4
don't know	3

Preferred policy option for preventing nuclear war:

fully support our Western Allies and their nuclear capability	9
go along with our Western Allies and their nuclear capability but work for nuclear disarmament	29

reject nuclear weapons for the defence of New Zealand
but contribute to conventional defence with our
Western Allies and work for nuclear disarmament   38
withdraw from all military alliances with nuclear powers
and vigorously promote nuclear disarmament   20
don't know   4

Sources: Australian Parliamentary Joint Committee on Foreign Affairs and Defence, *The ANZUS Alliance, Australian–United States' Relations*, Canberra, 1982, annex C; David Campbell, 'Australian Public Opinion on National Security Issues', working paper no. 16, Peace Research Centre, RSPS, ANU, Canberra, 1986, p. 25–56; Defence Committee of Enquiry, *Defence and Security: What New Zealanders Want, Public Opinion Poll Annex*, Wellington, 1986.

EXTRACTS FROM THE NEW ZEALAND NUCLEAR FREE ZONE, DISARMAMENT, AND ARMS CONTROL ACT

5. Prohibition on acquisition of nuclear explosive devices –
   (1) No person ordinarily resident in New Zealand shall, within the New Zealand Nuclear Free Zone, –
   [and]
   (2) No person, who is a New Zealand Citizen or a person ordinarily resident in New Zealand, and who is a servant or agent of the Crown, shall, beyond the New Zealand Nuclear Free Zone, –
      (a) Manufacture, acquire, or possess, or have control over, any nuclear explosive device; or
      (b) Aid, abet, incite, counsel, or procure any person to manufacture, acquire, possess, or have control over any nuclear explosive device.

6. Prohibition on stationing of nuclear explosive devices – No person shall emplant, emplace, transport on land or inland water or internal water, stockpile, store, install, or deploy any nuclear explosive device in the New Zealand Nuclear Free Zone.

7. Prohibition on testing of nuclear explosive devices – No person shall test any nuclear explosive device in the New Zealand Nuclear Free Zone . . .

9. Entry into internal waters of New Zealand –
   (1) When the Prime Minister is considering whether to grant approval to the entry of foreign warships into the internal waters of New Zealand, the Prime Minister shall have regard to all relevant information and advice that may be available to the Prime Minister including information and advice concerning the strategic and security interests of New Zealand.
   (2) The Prime Minister may only grant approval for the entry into the internal waters of New Zealand by foreign warships if the Prime Minister is satisfied that the warships will not be

carrying any nuclear explosive device upon their entry into the internal waters of New Zealand.

10. Landing in New Zealand –

(1) When the Prime Minister is considering whether to grant approval to the landing in New Zealand of foreign military aircraft, the Prime Minister shall have regard to all relevant information and advice that may be available to the Prime Minister including information and advice concerning the strategic and security interests of New Zealand.

(2) The Prime Minister may only grant approval to the landing in New Zealand by any foreign military aircraft if the Prime Minister is satisfied that the foreign military aircraft will not be carrying any nuclear explosive device when it lands in New Zealand.

(3) Any such approval may relate to a category or class of foreign military aircraft and may be given for such period as is specified in the approval.

11. Visits by nuclear powered ships – Entry into the internal waters of New Zealand by any ship whose propulsion is wholly or partly dependent on nuclear power is prohibited.

12. Passage through territorial sea and straits – Nothing in this Act shall apply to or be interpreted as limiting the freedom of –

(a) Any ship exercising the right of innocent passage . . . or

(b) Any ship or aircraft exercising the right of transit passage . . . or

(c) Any ship or aircraft in distress.

13. Immunities – Nothing in this Act shall be interpreted as limiting the immunities of –

(a) Any foreign warship or other government ship operated for non-commercial purposes; or

(b) Any foreign military aircraft; or

(c) Members of the crew of any ship or aircraft . . .

14. Offences and penalties –

(2) Every person who commits an offence against this Act is liable on conviction on indictment to imprisonment for a term not exceeding 10 years.

15. Consent of Attorney-General to proceedings in relation to offences –

(1) No information shall be laid against any person . . . except with the consent of the Attorney-General:

Provided that a person alleged to have committed any offence mentioned in this subsection may be arrested, or a warrant for any such person's arrest may be issued and executed, and any such person may be remanded in custody or on bail, notwithstanding that the consent of the Attorney-General to the laying of an information for the offence has not been obtained, but no further or other proceedings shall be taken until that consent has been obtained.

NOTES

ANU   Australian National University
APD   *Australian Parliamentary Debates*
CR   *Congressional Record*
FY   Fiscal Year
HR   House of Representatives
IISS   International Institute for Strategic Studies
NZIIA   New Zealand Institute of International Affairs
NZIR   *New Zealand International Review*
NZPD   *New Zealand Parliamentary Debates*
RIIA   Royal Institute of International Affairs
RSPS   Research School of Pacific Studies
RUSI   Royal United Services Institution
SIPRI   Stockholm International Peace Research Institute
USIA/S   United States Information Agency/Service
VPD   *Victoria Parliamentary Debates*

Chapter 1 Introduction: the revolt of an underling

1 *New Zealand Herald*, 1 March 1985, p. 20.
2 Phil Williams, 'The Limits of American Power: from Nixon to Reagan', *International Affairs*, vol. 63, no. 3, autumn 1987, p. 581.
3 Andrew Mack, 'Crisis in the Other Alliance: ANZUS in the 1980s', *World Policy Journal*, vol. 3, no. 3, summer 1986, pp. 466–8.
4 e.g., F. A. Mediansky, 'Nuclear Weapons and Security in the South Pacific', *Washington Quarterly*, vol. 9, no. 1, winter 1986, pp. 33–4.
5 Williams, 'American Power', p. 582. The term 'strategic fundamentalism' occurs in the typology devised by Stuart Croft, in 'The United States and Ballistic Missile Defence: ABM and SDI', Faraday discussion paper, Council for Arms Control, September 1987, pp. 1–2.
6 'Stationing' is defined in the Treaty of Rarotonga and the New Zealand Act as the emplacement, transportation on land or inland waters, stockpiling, storage, installation and deployment of nuclear devices. Although stationing is prohibited in the SPNFZ, an exception is made when it occurs in the context of visiting.
7 Maire Leadbeater (ed.), *Non-alignment and a New National Security*, Auckland, October 1976, p. 5.

211

8 US Congress, 99(1), House Armed Services Committee (Subcommittee on Procurement and Military Nuclear Systems), *Hearing on HR 1873, Department of Energy National Security Programs and Authorization Act for FY 1986 and 1987*, 20 February 1985, Washington, DC, 1985, p. 69. See also, William M. Arkin and David Chappell, 'Forward Offensive Strategy: Raising the Stakes in the Pacific', *World Policy Journal*, vol. 2, no. 3, summer 1985, p. 495. Desmond Ball contends that the tactical nuclear warheads have never had a coherent doctrine for their use, that the USN has not taken escalation control seriously, and that its reasons for refusing to allow permissive action links as electro-mechanical safety locks on naval nuclear weapons are unpersuasive, 'Nuclear War at Sea', *International Security*, vol. 10, no. 3, winter 1985–6, p. 3–31. Norman Polmar and Donald M. Kerr advocate nuclear torpedo warheads to cope with a large number of Soviet submarines in war, 'Nuclear Torpedoes', *Proceedings/Naval Review*, vol. 112, August 1986, p. 68.

9 As well as six dedicated SSBN support auxiliaries which carry nuclear missiles, amphibious landing ships may carry nuclear bombs, shells and mines for the Marines, and ammunition replenishment vessels and tenders may also store nuclear weapons. See, Ronald O'Rourke, 'Nuclear-Powered and Nuclear-Weapon-Capable Ships In The U.S. Navy: An Aid to Identification', Congressional Research Service, Library of Congress, Report No. 86–659F, Washington, DC, 1986; Center for Defense Information, 'First Strike Nuclear Weapons at Sea: the Trident II and the Sea-launched Cruise Missile', *Defense Monitor*, vol. 14, no. 6, 1987, pp. 6–7.

10 Joshua Handler and William Arkin, 'Nuclear Warships and Naval Nuclear Weapons: A Complete Inventory', Greenpeace/Institute for Policy Studies Neptune paper no. 2, Washington, DC, May 1988, pp. 2, 25–7. It has been suggested that nuclear depth bombs were taken as far as Ascension Island during the Falklands War, though they may have been practice rounds, Duncan Campbell, 'Too Few Bombs to go Round', *New Statesman*, 23 November 1985, pp. 10–12.

11 Soviet ships are said to be unable to distil sea water and so to rely on tankers which need port visits to stock up, Peter Tsouras, 'Port Visits', in B. W. and S. M. Watson (eds), *The Soviet Navy, Strengths and Liabilities*, Boulder, Colorado, 1986, pp. 265–75, 285; Charles C. Petersen, 'Showing the Flag', in Bradford Dismukes and James McConnell (eds.), *Soviet Naval Diplomacy*, New York, 1979, pp. 99–108.

12 In 1974 Yugoslavia pioneered the commercialization of Soviet submarine servicing. Greek shipyards have also made commercial arrangements. See, Richard B. Remmek, 'The Politics of Soviet Access to Naval Support Facilities in the Mediterranean', in Dismukes and McConnell, *Soviet Naval Diplomacy*, pp. 357–94; Michael MccGwire, Ken Booth and John McDonnell (eds.), *Soviet Naval Policy, Objectives and Constraints*, New York, 1975, pp. 387–418.

13 Donald C. F. Daniel, 'The Soviet Navy and Tactical Nuclear War at Sea', *Survival*, July–August 1987, pp. 318–19, 324.

14 Tsouras, 'Port Visits', p. 284; Worth H. Bagley, *Sea Power and Western Security: The Next Decade*, Adelphi Paper 139, winter 1977, pp. 28–9.

15 Ken Booth, *Law, Force and Diplomacy at Sea*, London, 1985, p. 209; Barry Buzan, *A Sea of Troubles? Sources of Dispute in the New Ocean Regime*, Adelphi Paper 143, spring 1978, p. 47; Hedley Bull, 'Sea Power and Political Influence', in *Power at Sea, I. The New Environment*, Adelphi Paper 122, spring 1976, pp. 8–9.

16 Peter Nailor, 'The Utility of Maritime Power: Today and Tomorrow', *RUSI Journal*, vol. 131, no. 3, September 1986, p. 18.

17 Dora Alves, 'U.S. and New Zealand: Trouble Down Under', Asian Studies Center Backgrounder no. 18, Heritage Foundation, Washington, DC, 14 November 1984, p. 9.

18 Ian Clark, 'The Western Security System: Programme and Politics', in Brian Hocking (ed.), *ANZUS and the Western Alliance*, London, 1986, pp. 5–23.

19 US Congress, 99(1), Senate Foreign Relations Committee, *Hearings on Commitments, Consensus and U.S. Foreign Policy*, 31 January 1985, Washington, DC, 1985, p. 83.

20 *Ibid.*, pp. 47–51, 198.

21 Joël Bonnemaison, 'Là-Bas, à l'ouest de l'Occident: l'Australie et la Nouvelle-Zélande', *Hérodote*, no. 40, 1 tr., 1986, pp. 132–3.

22 Joint Committee on Foreign Affairs and Defence, *The Australian Defence Force: Its Structure and Capabilities*, Canberra, 1984, xiv; *Disarmament and Arms Control in the Nuclear Age*, Canberra, 1986, p. 654.

23 Stanley Hoffman, 'The Uses of American Power', *Foreign Affairs*, vol. 56, no. 1, 1977, pp. 31–5, 42, 46–7.

24 Worth H. Bagley, 'The Pacific Connection. Strategic Burden or Strategic Opportunity?', *Navy International*, vol. 83, no. 5, May 1978, p. 13.

25 US Congress, 96(2), Joint Economic Committee, *Pacific Region Interdependencies*, compendium of papers, Washington, DC, 1981, pp. 101–5.

26 Raimo Väyrynen, 'Regional Conflict Formations: An Intractable Problem of International Relations', *Journal of Peace Research*, vol. 21, no. 4, 1984, p. 342.

27 R. A. Herr, 'Organizations and Issues in South Pacific Regionalism', in Roderic Alley (ed.), *New Zealand and the Pacific*, Boulder, Colorado, 1984, p. 155.

28 William T. Tow, testimony, US Congress, 99(1), House Foreign Affairs Committee (Subcommittee on Asian and Pacific Affairs), *Hearing on the Security Treaty Between Australia, New Zealand, and the United States*, 18 March 1985, Washington, DC, 1985, pp. 84–5.

29 See, generally, Peter Hayes, Lyuba Zarsky and Walden Bello, *American Lake: Nuclear Peril in the Pacific*, Penguin Australia, 1986.

30 David DeVoss, 'So Says Adm. James A. Lyons Jr.', *Los Angeles Times Magazine*, 10 August 1986, p. 17.

31 Michael McKinley, 'Labour and ANZUS: Heroic Stand or Ascetic Self-indulgence?', *NZIR*, vol. 10, no. 6, November-December 1985, pp. 8–11.

32 Jean Chesneaux, 'France in the Pacific: Global Approach or Respect for Regional Agendas?', *Bulletin of Concerned Asian Scholars*, vol. 18, no. 2, April–June 1986, p. 77; Adam Roberts, 'The Critique of Nuclear Deterrence', in *Defence and Consensus: The Domestic Aspects of Western Security*, Adelphi Paper 183, part 2, 1983, p. 11.

33 See, Christopher Coker, 'The Peace Movement and Its Impact on Public Opinion', *Washington Quarterly*, vol. 8, no. 1, winter 1985, pp. 92–104; Philip A. Sabin, *The Third World War Scare in Britain: A Critical Analysis*, London, 1986, *passim*.

34 Air Vice-Marshal Ian Morrison, in *The Press*, 11 December 1985, p. 8.

35 Robert Chapman, 'No Land is an Island; Twentieth Century Politics', in Keith Sinclair (ed.), *Distance Looks Our Way*, Hamilton, 1961, p. 62.

36 Daniel Mulhall, 'The Foreign Policy Leanings of Small Powers', *NZIR*, September–October 1986, p. 13; Maurice A. East, 'Size and Foreign Policy Behavior; A Test of Two Models', *World Politics*, vol. 25, 1973, pp. 576–7. See also, Mack, 'Defending Australia, is Non-alignment the Answer?', *Current Affairs Bulletin*, September 1982, p. 25.

37 David Lange, speech to UN General Assembly, 26 September 1984, in *Foreign Affairs Record*, vol. 34, no. 3, July–September 1984, p. 8.

38 Richard Falk, 'Nuclearism and National Interest: The Situation of a Non-Nuclear Ally', New Zealand Foundation for Peace Studies lecture, Auckland, 1986, pp. 10–11; Graham T. Allison, *Essence of Decision: Explaining the Cuban Missile Crisis*, Boston, 1971.

39 Steve Smith, Theories of Foreign Policy: An Historical Overview', *Review of International Studies*, vol. 12, no. 1, 1986, p. 25.

40 Barry Buzan, 'Peace, Power, and Security: Contending Concepts in the Study of International Relations', *Journal of Peace Research*, vol. 21, no. 2, 1984, p. 112.

Chapter 2 The ANZUS Treaty and strategic developments

1 M. P. Lissington, *New Zealand and the United States, 1840–1944*, Wellington, 1972, p. 2.

2 *Ibid.*, pp. 19–23.

3 *Ibid.*, pp. 47–9, 79–80; Robin Kay (ed.), *Documents on New Zealand External Relations*, 3 vols, doc. 42, paper on post-war security prepared by the War Cabinet Secretariat, January 1944, vol. 1, Wellington, 1972, p. 61.

4 Kay (ed.), *Documents*, doc. 53, the Australian–New Zealand Agreement, 21 January 1944, vol. 1, Wellington, 1972, pp. 140ff. The Agreement also addressed the problem of island welfare and development, and led to the establishment in 1947 of the South Pacific Commission by Australia, New Zealand, the United States, Britain and the Netherlands. The Commission was supplemented by the South Pacific Forum in 1971, comprising Australia, New Zealand, Cook Is, Fiji, Kiribati, Nauru, Niue, Papua New Guinea, Solomon Is, Tonga, Tuvalu, Vanuatu and W. Samoa. The Federated States of Micronesia has observer status.

5 Lissington, *New Zealand and the United States*, pp. 86, 94–5.

6 Cited by J. G. Starke, *The ANZUS Treaty Alliance*, Melbourne, 1965, pp. 62–3.

7 Cited in Joint Committee on Foreign Affairs and Defence, *The ANZUS Alliance*, Canberra, 1982, pp. 2–3.

8 Kay (ed.), *Documents*, doc. 198, Berendsen to Minister of External Affairs, 14 March 1950, vol. 3, Wellington, 1985, pp. 522–36.

9 *Ibid.*, doc. 199, New Zealand Chiefs of Staff paper, 19 April 1950, pp. 544ff.
10 *Ibid.*, doc. 208, Department of External Affairs, notes on defence aspects of the Japanese Peace Settlement, 30 January 1951, pp. 558–61; doc. 222, Fraser to Doidge, 10 February 1987, pp. 587–8; doc. 226, notes on the Canberra talks, 15–17 February 1951, pp. 593–612; Robert O'Neill, *Australia in the Korean War, 1950–53*, vol. 1, Canberra, 1981, pp. 185–7. New Zealand's overriding concern was Asian expansionism according to Malcolm McKinnon. 'The Richest Prize?', *NZIR*, vol. 11, no. 3, May–June 1986, pp. 10–13. See also, Glen St J. Barclay, *Friends in High Places: Australian–American Diplomatic Relations Since 1945*, Melbourne, 1985, p. 34.
11 Starke, *ANZUS Treaty*, pp. 64–7.
12 Malcolm Templeton, *Defence and Security: What New Zealand Needs*, Wellington, 1986, pp. 14–15.
13 Kay (ed.), *Documents*, doc. 226, notes on the tripartite talks in Canberra, 15–17 February 1951, p. 607. Australia tried unsuccessfully to exclude the proviso in the SEATO negotiations. Implications of the US 1973 War Powers Act are discussed by T. B. Millar in *The ANZUS Alliance*, p. 11.
14 Alan Watt, *The Evolution of Australian Foreign Policy, 1938–1965*, Cambridge, 1968, pp. 120–8.
15 William T. Tow, submission, US Congress 99(1), House Foreign Affairs Committee (Subcommittee on Asian and Pacific Affairs), *Hearing on the Security Treaty Between Australia, New Zealand, and the United States*, 18 March 1985, Washington, DC, 1985, pp. 127–8.
16 US Congress, 90(2), House Armed Services Committee (Special Subcommittee on National Defense Posture), *Review of U.S. Military Commitments Abroad*, Phase III – Rio and ANZUS Pacts, 31 December 1968, Washington, DC, 1968, p. 2.
17 Ross Babbage, *Rethinking Australia's Defence*, St Lucia, Queensland, 1980, pp. 10–11; Joint Committee on Foreign Affairs and Defence, *The Australian Defence Force: Its Structure and Capabilities*, Canberra, 1984, p. 36; *The ANZUS Alliance*, p. 30. A discussion of assistance scenarios was expunged from the *Review of U.S. Military Commitments Abroad*, 1968, pp. 13–14.
18 Templeton, *What New Zealand Needs*, pp. 17–18.
19 Barclay, *Friends in High Places*, p. 152. For a Reaganite view of the scope of the Treaty see, John Dorrance, 'ANZUS: Misperceptions, Mythology and Reality', *Australian Quarterly*, vol. 57, no. 3, 1985, p. 222. For a regional view see, Templeton, *What New Zealand Needs*, p. 16.
20 Kay (ed.), *Documents*, doc. 238, Spender to Gordon Walker, 22 March 1951, p. 670. Dulles explained to General MacArthur in March 1951 that 'the United States can discharge its obligations by action against the common enemy in any way and in any area that it sees fit', *Foreign Relations of the United States 1951*, vol. 6, Washington, DC, 1977, p. 177.
21 *The ANZUS Alliance*, pp. 13–15, 23–4, 27. However, Barclay indicates that the US threatened Indonesia with ANZUS. By leaning on Sukarno, the Johnson Administration could make it easier for the British and the Anzacs to assist in Vietnam, *Friends in High Places*, pp. 140–1.
22 Kay (ed.), *Documents*, doc. 226, notes on the tripartite talks in Canberra, 15–17 February 1951, p. 608.

23 *Ibid.*, doc. 215, UK Political Representative in Japan to the Foreign Office, report of a conversation with Dulles, 2 February 1951, pp. 575–7; doc. 308, New Zealand Minister of External Affairs to the Prime Minister, 7 April 1952, pp. 782–3; *Keesing's Contemporary Archives*, 10–17 January 1953, p. 12677.

24 Terry L. Deibel, 'Alliances and Security Relationships: A Dialogue with Kennan and his Critics', in Deibel and John Lewis Gaddis (eds.), *Containment, Concept and Policy*, 2 vols, Washington, DC, 1986, vol. 1, p. 202; US Dept. of State, 'United States Objectives and Programs for National Security, 14 April 1950', *Foreign Relations of the United States: 1950*, vol. 1, Washington, DC, p. 240.

25 US Congress, 82(1), *Executive Series of the Senate Foreign Relations Committee, 1951 (Historical Series)*, vol. 3, part 1, Washington, DC, 1976, pp. 283–4; *Keesing's*, 16–23 August 1952, p. 12399 and 10–17 January 1953, p.12677; O'Neill, *Australia in the Korean War*, pp. 190–2. Dulles, of course, exceeded the intentions of George Kennan, the architect of 'containment', who by 1951 dissented from all three Pacific alliances on the grounds that what had been conceived as an instrument had become an end in itself, Deibel, 'Alliances and Security Relationships', p. 197.

26 Kay (ed.), *Documents*, doc. 218, Fraser to Doidge, 8 February 1951, vol. 1, Wellington, 1972, p. 584; Starke, *ANZUS Treaty*, pp. 70, 74–5; *APD*, HR, 20(1) 3, vol. 216, 28 February 1952 (Beazley), pp. 609–10.

27 Cited by Richard Kennaway, *New Zealand Foreign Policy, 1951–1971*, Wellington, 1972, p. 54.

28 W. J. Hudson, *Casey*, Melbourne, 1986, pp. 266–8.

29 See, Barclay, *Friends in High Places*, pp.140–9; Keith Jackson, 'New Zealand and the Vietnam War: A Retrospective Analysis', in John Henderson, Keith Jackson and Richard Kennaway (eds.), *Beyond New Zealand: The Foreign Policy of a Small State*, Auckland, 1980, pp. 56–61; W. D. McIntyre, 'The Future of the New Zealand System of Alliances', *Landfall*, December 1967, p. 342.

30 MoD, *Report*, 31 March 1968, Wellington, p. 5; Keith Sinclair, 'New Zealand's Future Foreign Policy: A New Pacific Post', *Political Science*, Wellington, vol. 18, no. 2, September 1966, pp. 75ff; W. D. McIntyre, *Neutralism, Non-Alignment and New Zealand*, Wellington, 1969; Kennaway, *New Zealand Foreign Policy*, chapter 9.

31 O'Neill, cited in *The ANZUS Alliance*, p. 53; Peter Winsley, 'New Zealand's Military Relationship with Singapore', research paper, Peace and Justice Forum, Wellington, 1986, p. 9; T. B. Millar, *Australia's Defence*, London, 1965, p. 76.

32 Cited in *The ANZUS Alliance*, p. 36.

33 Ian Bellany, *Australia in the Nuclear Age*, Sydney, 1972, pp. 61–86; 'The Strategic Basis Papers', *National Times*, 30 March–5 April 1984, pp. 23–30.

34 US Congress, 94(2), House Armed Services Committee, *Report of the Ad Hoc Subcommittee on the Pacific*, May 1976, Washington, DC, 1976, pp. 12–13, and Senate Foreign Relations Committee, *The South West Pacific: Report of a Special Delegation*, February 1976, Washington, DC, 1976, p. 2; Ministry of

Foreign Affairs, *Report*, 31 March 1974, Wellington, pp. 3, 12, 22–3; MoD, *Report*, 31 March 1974, Wellington, p. 6

35 MoD, *Report*, 31 March 1979, Wellington, pp. 3–5; *The ANZUS Alliance*, p. 34; Henry S. Albinski, 'American Perspectives on the ANZUS Alliance', *Australian Outlook*, vol. 32, no. 2, August 1978, p. 150.

36 John Henderson, 'New Zealand in a Changing World: The Talboys Speeches', *NZIR*, vol. 3, no. 1, January–February 1978, p. 8; *APD, HR*, 30(1) 1, vol. 99, 1 June 1976 (Fraser), p. 2738. See, Millar, 'From Whitlam to Fraser', *Foreign Affairs*, vol. 55, no. 4, July 1977, pp. 854–72; Richard A. Herr, 'The American Impact on Australian Defence Relations with the South Pacific Islands', *Australian Outlook*, vol. 38, no. 3, December 1984, pp. 187–8.

37 R. Babbage, 'The Future of the Australian-New Zealand Defence Relationship', Strategic and Defence Studies Centre, working paper no. 113, RSPS, ANU, Canberra, December 1986, pp. 2–9; Hedley Bull, 'Australia–New Zealand Defence Co-operation', paper, University of Otago Foreign Policy School, May 1972, p. 13; Alan Robinson, 'Some Political Problems of Closer Trans-Tasman Defence Co-operation', in T. B. Millar (ed.), *Australian–New Zealand Defence Co-operation*, pp. 91–104.

38 J. Henderson, 'The 1980s – A Time for Commitment', *NZIR*, vol. 5, no. 1, January–February 1980, pp. 5–6; Muldoon, in *Foreign Affairs Review*, no. 27, January–March 1977, pp. 23–4; Ministry of Foreign Affairs, *Report*, Wellington, 31 March 1979, pp. 4, 12; 1982, p. 4; 1983, p. 4.

39 *The ANZUS Alliance*, p. 35. Evidence of US penetration of the islands is in Ralph Premdas and Michael C. Howard, 'Vanuatu's Foreign Policy: Contradictions and Constraints', *Australian Outlook*, vol. 39, no. 3, December 1985, p. 180.

40 R. M. Muldoon, 'Interview. Our foreign policy is trade', *NZIR*, vol. 5, no. 1, January–February 1980, pp. 2–3.

41 GAO, 'The United States Security Consultations and Joint Defence planning with East Asian and Western Pacific Allies', Washington, DC, June 1981, released to Peter Hayes under the US Freedom of Information Act, extracts in *The Press*, 13 May 1987, p. 38.

42 J. Henderson, 'The Burdens of ANZUS', *NZIR*, vol. 5, no. 3, May–June 1980, p. 3; MoD, *Report*, 31 March 1980, Wellington, p. 3.

43 *The ANZUS Alliance*, p. 60.

44 Ministry of Foreign Affairs, *Report*, 31 March 1981, Wellington, pp. 3–4, 15; MoD, *Report*, Wellington, 31 March 1981, pp. 3–5; 1983, pp. 3–5.

45 MoD, *Report*, 31 March 1984, Wellington, pp. 5–6.

46 R. A. Herr, 'Jimmy Carter and American Foreign Policy in the Pacific Islands', *Australian Outlook*, vol. 32, no. 2, August 1978, p. 224.

47 For example, Dorrance, 'ANZUS Misperceptions', pp. 216–17; James Kelly, testimony, US Congress, 99(1), House Foreign Affairs Committee (Subcommittee on Asian and Pacific Affairs), *Hearing on the Security Treaty Between Australia, New Zealand, and the United States*, 18 March 1985, Washington, DC, 1985, text from USIS. See the assessment of the value of ANZUS to the US by Owen Harries, 'Crisis in the Pacific', *Commentary*, vol. 79, no. 6, June 1985, p. 53.

48 W. Tow, 'The JANZUS Option: A Key to Asian/Pacific Security', *Asian Survey*, no. 18, December 1978, pp. 1221–43; 'Australian–Japanese Security Co-operation: Present Barriers and Future Prospects', *Australian Outlook*, vol. 38, no. 3, December 1984, p. 205. See also, Malcolm McIntosh, *Japan Re-Armed*, London, 1986.

49 Michael H. Armacost, 'The Asia–Pacific Region: A Forward Look', *Atlantic Quarterly*, vol. 22, no. 4, winter 1984–5, p. 344; Phil Gramm, testimony, US Congress, 99(1), Senate Foreign Relations Committee, *Hearings on the Philippine Presidential Election*, 23 January 1986, Washington, DC, 1986, appendix, p. 78.

50 Paul Dibb, 'The Interests of the Soviet Union in the Region', in Millar (ed.), *International Security in the Southeast Asian and Southwest Pacific Region*, St Lucia 1983, p. 53. See also, NZ External Intelligence Bureau, in Helen Clark, *Disarmament and Arms Control, Report of the Select Committee on Foreign Affairs and Defence*, Wellington, 1985, p. 47.

51 Millar, *Australia's Defence*, p. 67; Hugh Templeton, 'New Zealand and Southeast Asia', in Terence Wesley-Smith (ed.), *New Zealand and its Southeast Asian Neighbours*, Wellington, 1980, pp. 23–7.

52 Dibb, 'World Political and Strategic Trends: Their Relevance to Australia', in Dibb (ed.), *Australia's External Relations in the 1980s*, Canberra, 1984, pp. 38–9. See also, Henry S. Albinski, 'The U.S. Security Alliance System in the Southwest Pacific', in William T. Tow and William R. Feeney (eds.), *U.S. Foreign Policy and Asian–Pacific Security*, Boulder, Colorado, 1982, pp. 146–8.

53 O'Neill, ANU seminar, May 1982, cited in, H. G. Gelber, 'Australia and East Asia', in Dibb (ed.) *Australia's External Relations in the 1980s*, p. 113; 'Concluding Remarks', in Brian Hocking (ed.), *ANZUS and the Western Alliance*, London, 1986, pp. 77–85.

54 Kelly, testimony, US Congress, 99(1), House Foreign Affairs Committee (Subcommittee on Asian and Pacific Affairs), *Hearing on the Security Treaty Between Australia, New Zealand, and the United States*, 18 March 1985, Washington, DC, 1985, USIS text. Walter J. Stoessel, Deputy Secretary of State, argued that Australia and New Zealand stood guard over the line of communication between the Pacific and Indian Oceans, US Congress, 97(2), Senate Foreign Relations Committee, *Hearings on East–West Relations: Focus on the Pacific*, 10 June 1982, Washington, DC, 1982, pp. 3–4.

55 Cited by Michael McKinley, 'Labour, Lange and Logic: An Analysis of New Zealand's ANZUS Policy', *Australian Outlook*, vol. 39, no. 3, December 1985, p. 133.

56 Kelly, testimony, *Hearing on the Security Treaty*.

57 See, Ken Booth and Phil Williams, 'Fact and Fiction in U.S. Foreign Policy', *World Policy Journal*, vol. 2, no. 3, summer 1985, pp. 501–32; Daniel Yankelovich and John Doble, 'The Public Mood: Nuclear Weapons and the U.S.S.R.', *Foreign Affairs*, fall 1984, pp. 33–46.

58 Roderic Alley, 'The Alternatives to ANZUS: A Commentary', in Alley (ed.), *Alternatives to ANZUS*, Auckland, 1984, p. 21.

59 William G. Hayden, *Uranium, The Joint Facilities, Disarmament and Peace*, Canberra, 1984, pp. 11–13; Joint Committee on Foreign Affairs and

Defence, *Disarmament and Arms Control in the Nuclear Age*, Canberra, 1986, pp. 700–5 (minority report).

60 *APD*, HR, 33(1) 2, vol. 132, 15 September 1983 (Hayden), pp. 898–901.

61 See, S. P. Seth, *Asia Pacific Community*, no. 29, summer 1985, pp. 109–30; Robert Kaylor, 'Why Australia Grows Uneasy with Washington', *US News and World Report*, 29 June 1983, pp. 54–6.

62 Paul Wolfowitz, testimony, US Congress, 99(1), House Foreign Affairs Committee (Subcommittee on Asian and Pacific Affairs), *Hearing on the Security Treaty Between Australia, New Zealand, and the United States*, 18 March 1985, Washington, DC, 1985, p. 166.

63 Deibel, 'Alliances and Security Relationships', p. 190.

64 Ted Galen Carpenter, 'Pursuing a Strategic Divorce: the U.S. and the ANZUS alliance', Cato Institute policy analysis, no. 67, Washington, DC, 27 February 1986. See also, Henderson, 'The 1980s – A Time for Commitment', p. 5; Kennaway, 'Changing views of ANZUS', *NZIR*, vol. 9, no. 6, November–December 1984, p. 3. The ANZUS belief system is discussed by Jim Falk, 'The ANZUS Alliance: A View from Australia', in Harford (ed.), *Beyond ANZUS*, p. 88. By contrast, F. A. Mediansky emphasizes the breakdown resulting from a coincidence of a hawkish administration in Washington and an anti-nuclear one in Wellington, 'Nuclear Weapons and Security in the South Pacific', *Washington Quarterly*, winter 1986, p. 31. David McIntyre has a forthcoming history of ANZUS.

65 Paul M. Cleveland, 'The Benefits of Collective Security', address to NZIIA, 15 April 1986; see also, Kim Beazley, 'After ANZUS: Australia's Future Security Arrangements', in *Australian Foreign Affairs Record*, vol. 56, no. 7, July 1985, p. 605; MoD, *Report*, 31 March 1984, Wellington, p. 5.

66 Steve Hoadley, 'The Future of New Zealand's Alliances', *NZIR*, vol. 9, no. 6, November–December 1984, p. 8.

67 Hedley Bull, 'Australia, New Zealand, and Nuclear Weapons', in Millar (ed.), *Australian–New Zealand Defence Co-operation*, p. 86; Bruce Brown, 'A View from Wellington', in Brown (ed.), *Asia and the Pacific in the 1970s, the Roles of the United States, Australia, and New Zealand*, Wellington, 1971, p. 130. Richard Casey, Australian Minister of External Affairs in the 1950s, found the US military planners anything but helpful or reassuring, Hudson, *Casey*, p. 242. Alan Renouf argues that under Nixon and Kissinger, Australian access to US knowledge and thinking was reduced to virtually nothing, *The Frightened Country*, Melbourne, 1979, p. 111.

68 Coral Bell, 'Australian Defence and Regional Security: The American Effect and the Future', *Australian Outlook*, vol. 38, no. 3, December 1984, p. 207.

69 Daniel Mulhall, 'Australia and Disarmament Diplomacy 1983–1985: Rhetoric or Achievement?', *Australian Outlook*, vol. 49, no. 1, April 1986, p. 32; New Zealand Government, *The Defence Question: A Discussion Paper*, Wellington, 1985, p. 12.

70 Merwyn Norrish, 'The Changing Context of New Zealand's Foreign Policy', address to Takapuna Rotary Club, Auckland, 29 April 1986, mimeo. See also, Steve Chan, 'Growth with Equity: A Test of Olson's Theory for the Asian Pacific-Rim', *Journal of Peace Research*, vol. 24, no. 2, 1987, pp. 135–49; Kennaway, 'Changing views of ANZUS', p 5; US

Ambassador to Wellington, Paul Cleveland, made wide economic claims in 'The Benefits of Collective Security', address to NZIIA, 15 April 1986. Albinski argues that the US State Department found it easier to represent Australia's economic interests after Fraser's supportive actions over Afghanistan, 'The U.S. Position in Asia and the Pacific', in Ramon H. Myers (ed.), *A U.S. Foreign Policy for Asia. The 1980s and Beyond*, Stanford, 1982, p. 95.

Chapter 3 Defence co-operation and nuclear connections

1 Geoff Kitney, 'Ministerial Moves to Cool the ANZUS Debate', *National Times*, 8–14 March 1985, pp. 5, 7; *APD*, HR, 33 (1)2, vol. 132, 15 September 1983 (Hayden), pp. 898ff.
2 Desmond Ball, 'The Security Relationship between Australia and New Zealand', in Ball (ed.), *The Anzac Connection*, Sydney, 1985, pp. 34–52.
3 MoD, *Report*, 31 March 1970, p. 25; 31 March 1984, pp. 9–10, Wellington.
4 Ball, cited in F. A. Mediansky, 'ANZUS: An Alliance Beyond the Treaty', *Australian Outlook*, vol. 38, no. 3, December 1984, p. 178.
5 Keith Burgess, 'The List', *Peace Researcher* (Christchurch), no. 9, 1986, pp. 1–4.
6 Thomas-Durell Young, 'What hope for ANZUS now?', *Jane's Defence Weekly*, 22 November 1986, p. 1228.
7 Named after Vice-Admiral Sir John Collins (Chief of Australian Naval Staff) and Admiral Radford (CINCPAC), its existence was revealed in *National Times*, 20 March–5 April 1984, p. 24. Australia's responsibility runs to the mid-Indian Ocean. New Zealand's area is a band 170°E to 160°W, from the Equator to the Antarctic. *The Press*, 11 April 1987, p. 3; 'New Zealand/United States Secret Agreement', *Peace Researcher*, no. 11, 1986, p. 2.
8 Dennis Small, 'New Zealand's Doomsday Commitment; Anti-submarine Warfare', *Peace Researcher*, no. 6, 1984, pp. 2–9.
9 Burgess, 'The 1982 US/NZ Logistic Support Agreement – and Host Nation Support', *Peace Researcher*, no. 4, 1984, p. 12; Steve Hoadley, 'New Zealand–American Logistics Co-operation', *NZIR*, vol. 13, no. 1, January–February 1988, pp. 23–7.
10 The material concerned strategic facilities in New Zealand and aerial photographs of Pacific islands. Director, New Zealand Joint Intelligence Bureau, memorandum, 26 July 1954, New Zealand National Archives, Wellington, Acc. 1784 EA 59/5/17 (58/9/23).
11 Jeffrey T. Richelson and Desmond Ball, *The Ties that Bind, Intelligence Cooperation between the UKUSA Countries*, Sydney, 1985, p. 150. The NSA controls more personnel than all the other US intelligence agencies combined, but is not itself controlled by any law, established or defined by any statute, James Bamford, *The Puzzle Palace: A Report on NSA, America's Most Secret Agency*, UK edn, 1983, pp. xiv–xvi, 2–4.
12 Peter Winsley, 'New Zealand's Military Relationship with Singapore', research paper, Peace and Justice Forum, Wellington, 1986, p. 13.
13 *Report of the Royal Commission into British Nuclear Tests in Australia, Conclu-*

sions and Recommendations, Canberra, 1985, pp. 7–32. See also, Robert Milliken, *No Conceivable Injury*, Penguin Australia, 1986.

14 Ranger Uranium Environmental Inquiry, *First Report*, Parliamentary Paper no. 309, vol. 15, Canberra, 1976, pp. 115, 148, 185. For a concise critique of uranium sales see, Jim Falk, *Taking Australia Off the Map*, Penguin Australia, 1983, pp. 187–92.

15 'Report of the Anti-Uranium Committee', ALP Victorian Branch State Conference, 25–6 October 1986; *Canberra Times*, 27 October 1986, p. 1; Geoff Kitney, 'Uranium Sales Decision Weakens Hawke's Grip on Caucus', *National Times*, 14 September 1986, p. 2.

16 US Congress, 99(1), House Armed Services Committee (Subcommittee on Military Installations and Facilities), *Hearing on Base Closures and Realignments*, 12 June 1985, Washington, DC, 1985, p. 2; *The Australian*, 16 January 87, p. 3. As of 31 March 1986 there were 741 US servicemen in Australia and 66 in New Zealand, US Navy League, *Sea Power*, vol. 30, no. 2, January 1987, p. 112.

17 Desmond Ball, *A Suitable Piece of Real Estate: American Installations in Australia*, Sydney, 1980, pp. 19–26.

18 On 2 November Whitlam had also said that the CIA was funding the National-Country Party. Ball reproduces a cable from the Australian Security and Intelligence Organization, dated 10 November 1975, reporting CIA alarm, in *Real Estate*, pp. 169–71. CIA sources now admit their links with other agencies over Whitlam, and admit that the US counter-intelligence system could not stand idly by, *The Observer*, 24 January 1988, p. 5. The far left alleges Sir John Kerr, had worked for a secret Australian intelligence unit in the Second World War and was a member of the US-sponsored Australian branch of the Congress for Cultural Freedom. See, Joan Coxsedge and Gerry Harant, *Security Threat; The Case For Abolition of Secret Agencies*, Melbourne, 1984, p. 8; Coxsedge, Harant and Ken Coldicutt, *Rooted in Secrecy, The Clandestine Element in Australian Politics*, Melbourne, 1982, p. 104.

19 'Ministerial Statement on Arms Control and Disarmament', *APD*, HR, 33(1) 3, vol. 137, 6 June 1984 (Hawke), pp. 2987–9; Hayden's speech of 7 August 1984 at the Geneva Conference on Disarmament, in Department of Foreign Affairs, Backgrounder no. 442.

20 Mediansky, 'Beyond the Treaty', pp. 178–9.

21 The Australian Government agreed to acquire land for the exclusive use and occupancy of the United States at a peppercorn rent for 25 years. The lease was due to expire in June 1988. The text of the agreement and subsequent notes are in T. B. Millar, *Australia in Peace and War*, Canberra, 1978, pp. 472–9.

22 Ball, *Real Estate*, pp. 56–7.

23 William G. Hayden, *Uranium, The Joint Facilities, Disarmament and Peace*, Canberra, 1984, p. 18.

24 Richard Bolt, 'Active Peacemaker or Passive Warmonger? The Future of Australia's Links to Global War', Melbourne, 1986, pp. 13–14.

25 Cited by Mediansky, 'Nuclear Weapons and Security in the South Pacific', *Washington Quarterly*, winter 1986, p. 38.

26 Geoff Kitney, 'We Still Have No Control', *National Times*, 25–31 May 1984, pp. 3–4; Bolt, p. 29.

27 S. P. Seth, 'ANZUS in Crisis', *Asia Pacific Community*, no. 29, summer 1985, p. 119; D. Ball, *Pine Gap, Australia and the US Geostationary Signals Intelligence Satellite Program*, Sydney, 1988; interview with Senator Jo Vallentine, 24 March 1987, Canberra.

28 There was an allegation, firmly denied by Hawke, that Australia had intercepted New Zealand cables during the crisis, Brian Toohey, 'Lifestyles of the Super-rich and Famous', *New Zealand Listener*, 14 November 1987, pp. 22–5. Bamford, *The Puzzle Palace*, pp. 205–9, 332–3; Ball, *Real Estate*, pp. 45, 73; Bolt, 'Active Peacemaker', pp. 16–17. Beazley denied that any illegal tapping occurred. *Transcript*, 37th Biennial National Conference of the ALP, Hobart, 7–11 July 1986, pp. 473–6.

29 Andrew Mack, 'Arms Control and the Joint US–Australian Defence Facilities: the Case of Nurrungar', in D. Ball and A. Mack, *The Future of Arms Control*, Sydney, 1987, pp. 183–205; Bolt, 'Active Peacemaker', p. 20.

30 Damien Kingsbury, 'Why Melbourne may be Nuclear Target', *National Times*, 19 April–4 March 1985, p. 10; Bolt, 'Active Peacemaker', p. 22.

31 Interview with Des Ball, 25 March 1987, Canberra. Tangimoana had no official costings or accountability, Burgess, 'The Secrecy Surrounding Signals Intelligence; Operations in New Zealand', *Peace Researcher*, no. 4, 1984, pp. 9–10; Owen Wilkes, 'Tangimoana: Our Most Important Foreign Base', *Peacelink*, no. 18, April 1984, pp. 10–14; Richelson and Ball, *Ties that Bind*, p. 199.

32 Owen Wilkes and Nils Petter Gleditsch, *Loran-C and Omega: A Study of the Military Importance of Radio Navigation Aids*, Oslo, 1986, p. 5; Ball, *Real Estate*, p. 93; Bolt, 'Active Peacemaker', p. 26.

33 Interview with Owen Wilkes, 7 April 1987, Wellington; Wilkes, 'Why the US Military Needs Another Mountain', *New Zealand Monthly Review*, August 1981, p. 8; Bob Leonard, 'U.S. Naval Observatory Nears Completion', *Peace Researcher*, no. 4, 1984, pp. 6–7. The chairman of the authorizing congressional committee confirmed that Black Birch would not have been funded from military construction funds if it did not have military value, Peter Wills, 26 September 1984, submission, Parliamentary Select Committee on Foreign Affairs and Defence, General Assembly Library, Wellington. See also, the MoD submission, in Helen Clark, *Disarmament and Arms Control, Report of the Select Committee on Foreign Affairs and Defence*, Wellington, 1985, p. 66.

34 D. Ball, *Targeting for Strategic Deterrence*, Adelphi Paper 185, summer 1983, pp. 24, 36; *Real Estate*, p. 138; testimony, Joint Committee on Foreign Affairs and Defence, *Threats to Australia's Security*, Canberra, 1981, p. 18.

35 *APD*, HR, 32(1) 2, vol. 122, 5 May 1981 (Killen), pp. 1946–7; Hayden, speech to National Press Club, 14 April 1981, cited in *The ANZUS Alliance*, p. 61; Hayden, *Uranium*, pp. 15–16.

36 *Sydney Morning Herald*, 23 March 1987, p. 1; *The Australian*, 24 March 1987, p. 4.

37 *APD*, HR., 33(1) 2, vol. 132, 15 September 1983 (Hayden), pp. 901–2; *The Age*, 8 August 1984, p. 1.

38 Mediansky, *Washington Quarterly*, pp. 38–9; Daniel Mulhall, 'Australia and Disarmament Diplomacy 1983–1985: Rhetoric or Achievement?', *Australian Outlook*, vol. 40, no. 1, April 1986, pp. 32–8.

39 They were disappointed; the money had been spent earlier, in more exciting places. *TPD*, Assembly, 30 September 1986 (Pearsall), p. 2869. However, US visits were worth $A16.7 million to the WA economy in 1984.

40 *New Zealand Herald*, 29 March 1976, p. 1; 8 April 1976, p. 1; Ian Bradley, in *New Zealand Herald*, 29 October 1985, p. 8.

41 R. K. Thomas, DoD testimony, Senate Committee on Foreign Affairs and Defence, 'Enquiry into Safety Procedures Relating to Nuclear Powered or Armed Vessels in Australian Waters', 16 December 1986, Canberra, pp. 229, 232; Australian DoD and AAEC, *Environmental Considerations of Visits of Nuclear Powered Warships to Australia*, Canberra, 1976, p. 3; Annabelle Newbury, 'Nuclear Warship Visits: A Western Australia Perspective', in Barbara Harford (ed.), *Beyond ANZUS*, Wellington, 1984, p. 108.

42 CINCPAC Instruction 3128.3B 313, 'Port visits in PACOM', mimeo, Camp H. H. Smith, Hawaii, 14 October 1983, cited in Harford (ed.), *Beyond ANZUS*, p. 57.

43 James Kelly, testimony, US Congress, 99(1), House Foreign Affairs Committee (Subcommittee on Asian and Pacific Affairs), *Hearing on the Security Treaty Between Australia, New Zealand, and the United States*, 18 March 1985, Washington, DC, 1985, text from USIS.

44 US Legation in Wellington to Minister of External Affairs, 5 November 1945, New Zealand National Archives, Wellington, Acc. 1784 EA 59/5/17 (58/9/23); *The Dominion*, 2 February 1946, p. 4.

45 Berendsen to Peter Fraser (Prime Minister), 18 October 1946; Secretary of State for Dominion Affairs, Immediate Personal Telegram, 5 December 1946; Sir Patrick Duff (UK High Commission in Wellington) to Fraser, Memorandum, 6 December 1946, and reply, 14 December 1946, New Zealand National Archives, Wellington, Acc. 1784 EA 59/5/17 (58/9/23). See also, Simon Duke, *US Defence Bases in the United Kingdom; A Matter for Joint Direction?*, Oxford, 1987, pp. 16–25.

46 A. D. M. McIntosh (Dept. External Affairs), note, 10 March 1954; Air Vice Marshal W. H. Merton to Minister of Defence, Memorandum, 30 March 1954, New Zealand National Archives, Wellington, Acc. 1784 EA 59/5/17 (58/9/23). B-29 Superfortress bombers arrived in June, the first of annual visits known as *Handclasp*.

47 F. H. Corner (New Zealand High Commission in London), to Secretary of External Affairs, 8 March 1957 with enclosures; Secretary of External Affairs to First Secretaries in Canberra, London and Ottawa, 7 February 1957; ERG [?], to McIntosh and D. Dunlop (Prime Minister's Dept.), note, 15 March 1957; Minister of External Affairs to Dunlop, 15 February 1957; Dunlop to S. O. Merlo (Navy Office), 6 March 1957, New Zealand National Archives, Wellington, Acc. 1784, EA 59/5/17 (58/9/23).

48 Dunlop, note, 29 October 1957, New Zealand National Archives, Wellington, Acc. 1784, EA 59/5/17 (58/9/23).

49 J. Dorrance, 'ANZUS: Misperceptions, Mythology and Reality', *Australian*

Quarterly, vol. 57, no. 3, spring 1985, p. 225; William T. Tow, 'ANZUS and American Security', *Survival*, vol. 23, no. 6, November–December 1981, p. 264.

50 *APD*, HR, 32(1) 5, vol. 128, 7 September 1982 (Beazley), pp. 1122–5.

51 Glen St J. Barclay, *Friends in High Places: Australian–American Diplomatic Relations Since 1945*, Melbourne, 1985, p. 205.

52 *Transcript*, 35th Biennial National Conference, ALP, Canberra, 5–9 July 1982, 554–560, 573–4; Gary Brown, 'Detection of Nuclear Weapons and the US Non-Disclosure Policy', Canberra, 1986, p. 3.

53 *APD*, HR 32(1) 5, vol. 128, 7 September 1982, pp. 488–9.

54 Barclay, *Friends in High Places*, pp. 208–9; *APD*, HR, 33(1) 1, vol. 131, 17 May 1983 (Hawke), p. 595.

55 Correspondence was cited in parliament as evidence that he had requested a nuclear-powered warship visit in 1979, but Muldoon would only say that he had told the Embassy that all visits were welcome. *NZPD* 1(3), vol. 422, 7 June 1979 (Rodger, Muldoon), pp. 504–5; 2(40), vol. 451, 3 August 1983 (Rowling), p. 995; (Waring), p. 1001.

56 MoD assessment, 30 May 1984, in Clark, *Disarmament and Arms Control*, pp. 65–70.

57 Text of notes 11 March 1981, 16 October 1982, in Alister Barry, submission FA/86/1244, 1220W, Parliamentary Select Committee on Foreign Affairs and Defence, General Assembly Library, Wellington. See also, Brown, 'Detection of Nuclear Weapons', p. 1; Henry S. Albinski, 'The U.S. Security Alliance System in the Southwest Pacific', in Tow and William R. Feeney (eds.), *U.S. Foreign Policy and Asian–Pacific Security. A Transregional Approach*, Boulder, Colorado, 1982, 149–51.

58 e.g., Robert G. Sutter, Foreign Affairs and National Defense Division, 'Oceania and the United States: A Primer', CRS report no. 85–218F, 25 November 1985, Washington, DC, p. 5; Albinski, 'The U.S. Position in Asia and the Pacific', in Ramon H. Myers (ed.), *A U.S. Foreign Policy for Asia. The 1980s and Beyond*, Stanford, 1982, p. 102.

59 The Antarctic Treaty permits the use of military, non-combatant logistics support. Harewood employs about 30 civilians who sign an oath of allegiance to the United States. They were long forbidden to join a union, which partly explains why there has been contention over pay and pension schemes, *Off Base*, no. 4, August 1985, p. 4; Wilkes, *Protest: Demonstrations Against the American Military Presence in New Zealand*, Wellington, 1973, pp. 50–1.

60 *The Press*, 10 April 1987, p. 8.

61 *Sunday Star* (Auckland), 14 June 1987, pp. A1, A3; *Peace Researcher*, December 1983, pp. 2–3; *Peacelink*, no. 17, March 1984, p. 6; Bob Leonard, 'United States Military Bases and Projects in New Zealand', in Harford (ed.), *Beyond ANZUS*, pp. 77–8. A communications section at Harewood is part of the US DoD global network using Automatic Digital Network for classified messages, but the US denies that it has the capacity to back up North West Cape.

62 Wilkes, *Protest*, pp. 50–1; *Off Base*, no. 4, August 1985, p. 3. Although ski-fitted Hercules cargo planes were transferred from the USN to the NSF

in the 1970s, the costs were exceptionally low and the NSF granted the designated military commander the right to use them for military missions, Bob Leonard, 'Deep Freeze Ski Planes a Bargain', *Peace Researcher*, no. 11, 1986, pp. 3–4.

63 US Congress, 94(2), House Armed Services Committee, *Report of the Ad Hoc Subcommittee on the Pacific*, 25 May 1976, Washington, DC, 1976, pp. 7–11.

64 O'Neill, 'The Development of Operational Doctrines for the Australian Defence Force', in O'Neill (ed.), *The Defence of Australia: Fundamental New aspects*, Canberra, 1977, pp. 133–4; Ball, testimony, *The ANZUS Alliance*, Canberra, 1982, p. 63.

65 Renouf, cited by Seth, 'ANZUS in Crisis', pp. 114–15; Burgess, 'Policing the State', in Harford (ed.), *Beyond ANZUS*, p. 87.

66 Kim Beazley, 'After ANZUS: Australia's Future Security Arrangements', *Australian Foreign Affairs Record*, vol. 56, no. 7, July 1985, pp. 607–8; *Transcript*, 37th Biennial National Conference, ALP, Hobart, 7–11 July 1986, pp. 456–7.

67 Joint Committee on Foreign Affairs and Defence, *Threats*, p. 23.

68 Andrew Mack, 'Crisis in the Other Alliance: ANZUS in the 1980s', *World Policy Journal*, vol. 3, summer 1986, pp. 457–8.

69 Wilkes, *Protest*, pp. 45–7.

Chapter 4 Warship access and the Anzac liability suspensions

1 'Rules for Navigation and Sojourn of Foreign Warships in the Territorial Waters (Territorial Sea) of the USSR and the Internal Waters and Ports of the USSR', Moscow, 1984, in *International Legal Materials*, vol. 24, 1985, pp. 1715–22. See also, legislation of Denmark, Sweden and Spain, *UN St/Leg/Ser.* vols. B/15–18, New York, 1980.

2 J. C. Woodliffe, 'Port Visits By Nuclear-Armed Naval Vessels: Recent State Practice', *International and Comparative Law Quarterly*, vol. 35, July 1986, p. 732.

3 Ceylon [Sri Lanka], *Parliamentary Debates*, Senate, vol. 19, no. 26, 23 January 1964 (Bandaranaike), pp. 2402–3.

4 US Congress, 96(1), Senate Foreign Relations Committee, *Hearings on Overseas Military Presence*, April 1979, Washington, DC, p. 99.

5 *New York Times*, 12 August 1984, p. 4; *Newark Star-Ledger*, 19 August 1984, p. 2.

6 Ronald O'Rourke, 'Nuclear-Powered and Nuclear-Weapons-Capable Ships In The U.S. Navy: An Aid To Identification', Congressional Research Service, Library of Congress, Report No. 86–659F, Washington, DC, 1986, p. 6.

7 US Commander-in-Chief Pacific, 'Release of Information on Nuclear Weapons', CINCPAC Instruction 5720.2D, 20 January 1982, released to Peter Wills, University of Auckland, under the US Freedom of Information Act.

8 Interview with Lt. Col. John Williams, DoD, 10 March 1987, Washington, DC.

9 Public Law 703, *US Statutes*, vol. 68, 30 August 1954, p. 941; *US Code*, vol. 42, pp. 2011ff.

10 William M. Arkin, 'Confirm or Deny', *Bulletin of the Atomic Scientists*, vol. 41, no. 11, December 1985, p. 4; EO 10501, Eisenhower, 5 November 1952, Safeguarding Official Information, 3 *CFR (1949-53) Comp.*, pp. 979-86; EO 11652, Nixon, 8 March 1972, Classification and Declassification of National Security Information and Material, 3 *CFR (1971-75) Comp.*, pp. 678-90; EO 12065, Carter, 28 June 1978, National Security Information, 3 *CFR (1978-79) Comp.*, pp. 190-205.

11 Gary Brown, 'Detection of Nuclear Weapons and the US Non-disclosure Policy', Strategic and Defence Studies Centre, working paper no. 107, RSPS, ANU, Canberra, November 1986, pp. 12-13.

12 James Kelly, testimony, US Congress, 99(1), House Foreign Affairs Committee (Subcommittee on Asian and Pacific Affairs), *Hearing on the Security Treaty Between Australia, New Zealand, and the United States*, 18 March 1985, Washington, DC, 1985, pp. 169-70.

13 Robert O'Neill, 'Concluding Remarks', in Brian Hocking (ed.), *ANZUS and the Western Alliance*, Australian Studies Centre, Institute of Commonwealth Studies, University of London, 1986.

14 Robert G. Sutter, 'Crisis in U.S.-New Zealand Relations: Issues for Congress', Congressional Research Service, Library of Congress, Report no. 85-92F, 26 February 1985, Washington, DC, p. 5; Interviews with Gene La Rocque and Eugene Carroll, 25 February 1987, Center for Defense Information, Washington, DC.

15 US Congress, 94(1), Joint Atomic Energy Committee, *Development, Use and Control of Nuclear Energy for the Common Defense and Security and for Peaceful Purposes*, Annual Report to Congress, 30 June 1975, Washington, DC, p. 19.

16 Halperin, testimony, US Congress, 93(2), Senate Foreign Relations Committee, *Hearings on Nuclear Weapons in Europe*, March-April 1974, p. 236. Stanley Hoffman also considered that the composition of the deterrent was kept secret for 'fear of political repercussions in Europe . . . if the Europeans should suddenly wake up and discover through an American report that there are nuclear weapons stored on their soil'. US Congress, 93(2), Senate Foreign Relations Committee (Subcommittees on Security Agreements and Commitments Abroad, and Arms Control, International Law and Organization), *Hearings on Nuclear Weapons and Foreign Policy*, 14 March 1974, Washington, DC, 1974, p. 43.

17 US Congress, 99(2), House Armed Services Committee (Military Installations and Facilities Subcommittee), *Hearings on HR 4181 to Authorize Certain Construction at Military Installations for FY 1987*, February-March 1986, Washington, DC, 1986, pp. 136-7. Signatories included Solarz, *New York Post*, 9 August 1984, p. 14.

18 In US Court of Appeals, *Weinberger v. Catholic Action of Hawaii*, 9th circuit, no. 80-1377, 1981, pp. 140, 146.

19 Donald C. F. Daniel, 'The Soviet Navy and Tactical Nuclear War at Sea', *Survival*, vol. 29, no. 4, July-August 1984, pp. 318-35; Michael MccGwire, *Military Objectives in Soviet Foreign Policy*, Washington, DC, 1987, p. 421.

20 Cited by Arkin, 'Confirm or Deny', p. 4.
21 Norman Friedman, 'Soviet Naval Command and Control', *Signal*, vol. 39, no. 4, December 1984, pp. 27–8.
22 James Bush (USN retd, Associate Director, Center for Defense Information), to Sen. Norman Sanders, 25 September 1986, cited by Richard Bolt, submission 43, Senate Committee on Foreign Affairs and Defence, 'Enquiry into Safety Procedures Relating to Nuclear Powered or Armed Vessels in Australian Waters', Canberra, 1987, p. 23; interviews with Gene La Rocque and Eugene Carroll, CDI, Washington, DC, 25 February 1987; Carroll, testimony, US Congress, 99(2), House Armed Services Committee (Military Installations and Facilities Subcommittee), *Hearings on HR 4181 to Authorize Certain Construction at Military Installations for FY 1987*, February–March 1986, Washington, DC, pp. 144, 151–2.
23 e.g. Ray Galvin, *A Nuclear-Free New Zealand ... Now!*, Auckland, 1984, p. 40.
24 *Guardian Weekly*, 10 May 1975, p. 6. See also, David E. Kaplan, 'When Incidents are Accidents; The Silent Saga of the Nuclear Navy', *Oceans*, July 1983, pp. 29–30; H. P. Metzger, *The Atomic Establishment*, New York, 1972, pp. 218–19; US Congress, 93(2), Joint Atomic Energy Committee, *Selected Materials on Atomic Energy Indemnity and Insurance Legislation*, Washington, DC, 1974, pp. 258ff; OECD Nuclear Energy Authority, *Nuclear Legislation: analytical study*, vol. 2, Paris, 1983–4, pp. 160ff.
25 US Congress, 94(1), Joint Atomic Energy Committee (Subcommittee on Legislation), *Hearings on Naval Nuclear Propulsion Program, 1975*, 5 March 1975, Washington, DC, 1975, pp. 12–13.
26 German Federal Republic, 'Act Concerning the Peaceful Use of Nuclear Energy ... 31 October 1976', art. 25a, in *UN St/Leg/Ser*, vol. B/18, New York, 1980, p. 283; Brussels Convention on the Liability of Operators of Nuclear Ships, 25 May 1962, *American Journal of International Law*, vol. 57, 1963, pp. 268–78.
27 US Congress, 92(1), Joint Atomic Energy Committee (Subcommittee on Military Applications), *Hearings and Subsequent Inquiry on Nuclear Propulsion for Naval Warships*, 5 May 1971, Washington, DC, 1972, pp. 8–25, 36ff., appendices 1 and 2; 93(2), Joint Atomic Energy Committee, *Hearing on the Naval Nuclear Propulsion Program, 1974*, 25 February 1974, Washington, DC, 1975, pp. 3–11. See also, N. Polmar and T. P. Allen, *Rickover, Controversy and Genius: A Biography*, New York, 1984; R. G. Hewlett and F. Duncan, *Nuclear Navy*, Chicago, 1974.
28 Much of the evidence remains classified. US Congress, 97(1), House Armed Services Committee (Subcommittee on Procurement and Military Nuclear Systems), *Hearing on HR 2969, Dept. of Energy, Authorization of Naval Nuclear Propulsion Program, 1981*, 9 March 1981, Washington, DC, 1981, p. 180.
29 O'Rourke, 'Nuclear-Powered and Nuclear-Weapons-Capable Ships In The U.S. Navy', pp. 3–4.
30 McCloskey to Price, 17 September 1974, US Congress, 93(2), *Code Congressional and Administrative News*, Washington, DC, 1974, appendix B, p. 6369. Treaty of Friendship and Cooperation Between Spain and the United

States, agreement implementing art. V, 31 January 1976, and supplementary agreement on facilities no. 6, art. I, 24 January 1976, in *US Treaty Series*, vol. 27, pp. 3107, 3034–5; Dina Hecht (prod./dir.), 'Broken Arrow 29', IBT Production, Channel 4, London, 1987.

31 Interview with Lt. Col. J. Williams, 10 March 1987, Washington, DC; DoD and AAEC, *Environmental Considerations of Visits of Nuclear Powered Warships to Australia*, Canberra, 1976, p. 3. US Congress, 93(2), *CR*, Senate, 21 November 1974, pp. 36883–4, S. J. Res. 248. See, George Munster and Richard Walsh, *Secrets of State*, Sydney, 1982, p. 31.

32 Munster and Walsh, *Secrets of State*, pp. 31–2; *APD*, HR, 30(1) 1, vol. 99, 4 June 1976 (Fraser), p. 3042.

33 Interviews with Hon. R. J. Prebble MP and Hon. J. K. McLay MP, 7–8 April 1987, Wellington; Robert Mann *et al.*, *A Nuclear New Zealand?*, A CND *Report*, Auckland, 1975, p. 13; Helen Clark, *Disarmament and Arms Control*, *Report of the Select Committee on Foreign Affairs and Defence*, Wellington, 1985, pp. 119–20.

34 Cited in Mann, *CND Report*, p. 13.

35 US Congress, 94(2), Senate Foreign Relations Committee, *The South West Pacific: Report of a Special Delegation*, February 1976, Washington, DC, 1976, pp. 1–2.

36 *CR*, Senate, 21 November 1974, p. 36884, S. J. Res. 248.

37 Mann, *CND Report*, p. 2; *NZPD*, 1(38), vol. 404, 5 August 1976 (Finlay), p. 1325; Sen. Jo Vallentine, submission no. 56, p. 25, and Michael Lynch, submission no. 10, appendix C, Senate Committee on Foreign Affairs and Defence, 'Enquiry into Safety Procedures Relating to Nuclear-Powered or Armed Vessels in Australian Waters', Canberra, 1987.

38 *Parliamentary Debates*, Commons, 5s., vol. 913, written answers, 17 June 1976 (Rodgers), cols. 98–9.

39 Schlesinger to Price, 4 September 1974, US Congress, 93(2), *Code Congressional and Administrative News*, Washington, DC, 1974, appendix A, p. 6368; *CR*, Senate, 21 November 1974, p. 36884, S. J. Res. 248; Robert J. McCloskey, 24 January 1976, Treaty of Friendship and Cooperation Between Spain and the United States.

40 Greg Fry, 'Australia, New Zealand and Arms Control in the Pacific Region', in Desmond Ball (ed.), *The Anzac Connection*, Sydney, 1985, pp. 101–3; *New Outlook*, January–February 1985, p. 13.

41 *Auckland Star*, editorial, 15 April 1975; 10 July 1975, p. 1; *NZPD*, 1(38), vol. 404, 5 August 1976 (McCready), p. 1320; A. Selden, testimony, US Congress, 99(1), House Foreign Affairs Committee (Subcommittee on Asian and Pacific Affairs), *Hearing on the Security Treaty Between Australia, New Zealand, and the United States*, 18 March 1985, Washington, DC, 1985, p. 30.

42 *Auckland Star*, 16 May 1975, p. 1; 9 June 1987, p. A8. Jim McLay argued that Rowling gave the ANZUS Council meeting of 1975 a private assurance that he would reconsider visits after the November election, 'Disarmament and Security: An Alternative Viewpoint', *NZIR*, vol. 10, no. 3, May–June 1985, p. 21.

43 US Congress, 94(2), House Armed Services Committee, *Report of the Ad Hoc Subcommittee on the Pacific*, May 1976, Washington, DC, 1976, pp. 9–10; US

Congress, 94(2), Senate Foreign Relations Committee, *The South West Pacific: Report of a Special Delegation*, February 1976, Washington, DC, 1976, pp. 1–2.

44 US Congress, 94(2) House Armed Services Committee, *Report of the Ad Hoc Subcommittee*, pp. 6–7, 13; *APD*, HR, 30(1) 1, vol. 99, 4 June 1976 (Fraser), p. 3042.

45 The *aide-mémoire* provided to New Zealand remains classified but a covering letter was released to Peter Wills, University of Auckland, under the New Zealand Official Information Act; *NZPD*, 1(38), vol. 404, 5 August 1976 (Finlay), p. 1325; R. K. Thomas, testimony, Senate Committee, 'Safety Procedures', Canberra, 16 December 1986, pp.207–8, confirmed by the Minister for Defence, Kim Beazley, *Canberra Times*, 9 July 1987, pp. 1, 15.

46 *APD* Senate, 33(1) 2, vol. S101, 15 December 1983 (Evans), p. 3829.

47 Interview with Hon. Wallace Rowling, New Zealand Ambassador, 2 March 1987, Washington, DC; Munster and Walsh, *Secrets of State*, pp. 33–4.

48 US Congress, 93(2), Joint Atomic Energy Committee (Subcommittee on Military Applications), *Hearing on Proliferation of Nuclear Weapons*, 10 September 1974, Washington, DC, 1975, pp. 15–25.

49 *NZPD*, 3(38), vol. 416, 9 December 1977 (Courtney), p. 5245.

50 Mann, *CND Report*, p. 5; Maire Leadbeater, *Non-Alignment And A New National Security*, CND pamphlet, Auckland, 1976, p. 4; Robert Aldridge, *From ANZUS to a Nuclear Free Pacific*, Peace Office pamphlet, Christchurch, 1978; Tom Newnham, *Peace Squadron: The Sharp End of Nuclear Protest in New Zealand*, Auckland, 1986, p. 53.

51 Dr R. Walker, cited by Newnham, p. 32; 'News', *Peacelink*, no. 13, September 1983, p. 6.

52 *NZPD*, 1(38), vol. 404, 5 August 1976 (Prebble), pp. 1313ff.

53 *Ibid*. (McLay), p.1406.

54 Mann, *CND Report*, p. 12.

Chapter 5 Nuclear hazards and environmental safety: issues of the 1980s

1 *APD*, HR, 32 (1) 5, vol. 128, 7 September 1982 (Viner citing Cain) p. 1133; *VPD*, Council, 49 (1), vol. 365, 16 June 1982 (Wright citing Fraser), pp. 1260–1

2 *Australian Financial Review*, 16 June 1982.

3 Coxsedge to Cain, 13 June 1986; to Race Mathews, Victorian Minister for Police and Emergency Services, 16 June 1986, and reply, 26 November 1986 (courtesy Joan Coxsedge, MP); *APD*, HR, 32 (1) 5, vol. 128, 7 September 1982 (Scholes), pp. 1118–20; 32 (1) 5, vol. 128, 18 August 1982, (Sinclair), pp. 488–90; *VPD*, Assembly, 49 (1), vol. 365, 22 June 1982 (Cain), p. 1572; *VPD*, Council, 1982–3 s., vol. 368, 9 December 1982 (White), pp. 1348–76.

4 *The Press*, 25 October 1983, p. 1. Keith Speed, Undersecretary of the Admiralty, was quoted as saying that he would be angry if the ships sent to the Falklands were not carrying nuclear weapons as they would have

needed them 8,000 miles from home if war had broken out. See, Duncan Campbell and Patricia Forbes, 'What's the Royal Navy doing in the Pacific', *New Statesman*, 21 February 1986, p. 8; Owen Wilkes, 'The "Invincible" Task Force', *Peacelink*, no. 15, November-December 1983, pp. 14–15; Keith Burgess, 'Identifying Nuclear Weapons on Board the Invincible Task Force', *Peace Researcher*, December 1983, pp. 4–5.

5 *APD*, Senate, 33 (1) 2, vol. S101, 13 December 1983 (Evans), p. 3640; 14 December 1983, 3742–3; 33 (1) 3, vol. S102, 28 February 1984 (Evans), pp. 100–1.

6 Interview with Derek Woolmer and Gary Brown, Defence Group, Parliamentary Library, 25 March 1987, Canberra; *APD*, Senate, 33 (1) 2, vol. S101, 14 December 1983 (Evans), pp. 3742–3; 13 December 1983 (Hamer, Evans), p. 3640; 15 December 1983 (Carrick), p. 3835.

7 *APD*, Senate, 33 (1) 2, vol. S101, 15 December 1983 (Evans), p. 3829, 14 December 1983, pp. 3745–6.

8 *Ibid.*, 13 December 1983 (Evans), p. 3639; 14 December (Evans), pp. 3745–6; 15 December (Durack), p. 3828.

9 Glen St J. Barclay, *Friends in High Places: Australian-American Diplomatic Relations Since 1945*, Melbourne, 1985, p. 209.

10 *APD*, HR, 33 (1) 3, vol. S102, 2 March 1984 (Evans), p. 330.

11 Tom Newnham, *Peace Squadron: The Sharp End of Nuclear Protest in New Zealand*, Auckland, 1986, pp. 5, 9. See also, Ray Galvin, *The Peace of Christ in a Nuclear Age*, Auckland, 1983, p. 141; 'NZers back Greenpeace', *New Zealand News UK*, 18 February 1987, p. 2.

12 *APD*, HR, 30 (1), vol. 99, 4 June 1976 (Whitlam), pp. 3039–42; *VPD*, Assembly, 49 (1), vol. 365, 17 June 1982 (Cain, Mathews), pp. 1455–65; *VPD*, Council, 1982–3, vol. 366, 21 September 1982 (Coxsedge), p. 178.

13 *APD*, Senate, 33 (1) 2, vol. S101, 15 December 1983 (Mason), pp. 3833–4. At various times governments have been under pressure to close the Garden Island naval base and ammunition store, which is within a mile of the Opera House in Sydney.

14 Information supplied by the US authorities, Helen Clark, *Disarmament and Arms Control, Report of the Select Committee on Foreign Affairs and Defence*, Wellington, 1985, p. 137.

15 David E. Kaplan, 'When Incidents are Accidents; The Silent Saga of the Nuclear Navy', *Oceans*, July 1983, p. 28.

16 Documents released to Peter Wills, University of Auckland, upon declassification under the US Freedom of Information Act: Commander in Chief Pacific, 'Nuclear Safety', Enclosure (4) to 'CINCPAC Peacetime Nuclear Weapon Operations, Logistics, Protection and Safety', CINCPAC Instruction S8110.4C (8 May 1984); Commander in Chief Europe, 'CONPLAN 4367-87 – Response to Nuclear Accidents/Incidents within the Theater', 30 January 1987; Mark Urban, 'US Seizes Nuclear Accident Control', *The Independent*, 25 September 1987, p. 1.

17 Jo Vallentine, submission 56, Senate Committee on Foreign Affairs and Defence, 'Enquiry into Safety Procedures Relating to Nuclear-Powered or Armed Vessels in Australian Waters', Canberra, 1987, p. 33.

18 Interviews with Richard Bolt, 20 March 1987, Melbourne and Sen. Jo

Vallentine, 24 March 1987, Canberra; Scientists Against Nuclear Arms, submission FA/86/813, 787W, Parliamentary Select Committee on Foreign Affairs and Defence, General Assembly Library, Wellington.

19 DoD, submission 80, Senate Committee, 'Safety Procedures', p. 11; Richard Bolt, submission 43, p. 9.

20 *Ibid.*, Hearing, Canberra, 16 December 1986, p. 222.

21 US Congress, 93 (1), Joint Atomic Energy Committee, *Hearings on Nuclear Reactor Safety*, part 1, phase IIa, 23 January–1 October 1973, Washington, DC, 1973, pp. 122ff; Nuclear Regulatory Commission, *Calculation of Reactor Accident Consequences. Reactor Safety Study*, WASH-1400 (NUREG 75–014), Washington, DC, 1975. See also, Elizabeth S. Rolphe, *Nuclear Power and the Public Safety. A Study in Regulation*, Lexington, Mass., 1979, pp. 24–6, 153.

22 US Congress, 93 (2), Joint Atomic Energy Committee, *Hearing on Naval Nuclear Propulsion Program, 1974*, 25 February 1974, Washington, DC, 1975, p. 29 and USN, 'Environmental Monitoring and Disposal of Radioactive Wastes from U.S. Naval Nuclear-Powered Ships and their Support Facilities', appendix 2.

23 Hearing, Senate Committee, 'Safety Regulations', Canberra, 27 March 1987; AAEC, submission 70, pp. 6–7, 11; DoD, submission 80, pp. 11–12; *Disarmament and Arms Control*, pp. 139–43. A graphite fire which caused the Windscale (1957) and Chernobyl (1986) disasters could not occur in the USNs pressurized water reactors.

24 The Soviet icebreaker *Lenin* is believed to have had a reactor casualty shortly after refuelling in 1966; it did not return to service until 1970. A Soviet Alpha submarine sank off Spain in 1970, and an H2 Hotel class submarine had to be taken in tow after loss of propulsion in 1982. Another sank in the North Pacific in the summer of 1983.

25 *The Observer*, 14 February 1988, p. 1; *The Guardian*, 3 March 1988, p. 1. Of reported minor incidents analysed by the various researches, some were caused by mechanical problems, some by operator error and some by electrical faults.

26 *The Guardian*, 3 October 1987, p. 2; Kaplan, pp. 29–32.

27 AAEC, submission 70, Senate Committee, 'Safety Procedures', pp. 12–14.

28 US Congress, 93 (2), Joint Atomic Energy Committee, *Hearing on Naval Nuclear Propulsion Program 1974*, 25 February 1974, Washington, DC, 1975, pp. 27, 30; 98 (2), House Armed Services Committee (Subcommittee on Procurement and Military Nuclear Systems), *Hearing on HR 5263, Dept. of Energy, National Security Programs and Authorization Act. FY 1985*, 28 February 1984, Washington, DC, 1984, pp. 212ff.

29 AAEC, submission 70, Senate Committee, 'Safety Procedures', p. 5 and attachment 1, pp. 1–4, and addendum. NZAEC 500, *Code for Nuclear Powered Shipping*, Wellington, 1976, annex 3, p. 4 assumes rupture of the containment vessel would occur as the result of external force.

30 Australian DoD and AAEC, *Environmental Considerations*, p. 25.

31. Scientists Against Nuclear Arms, submission DAC/83/124, 124, Parliamentary Select Committee on Disarmament and Arms Control, General Assembly Library, Wellington.

32 W. Jackson Davis, submission 92, Senate Committee, 'Safety Procedures',

p. 79; Richard Bolt, submission 43, p. 7. Davis calculated that a nuclear reactor accident involving exposure to 15 radionuclides released over 4 hours in Fremantle/Perth would lead to short term casualties in a range of 4 to 914.

33 Scientists Against Nuclear Arms, submissions, DAC/83/124, 124, FA/86/813, 787W, Parliamentary Select Committees on Disarmament and Arms Control/Foreign Affairs and Defence, General Assembly Library, Wellington.

34 Sen. J. Carrick, Senate Committee, 'Safety Procedures', hearings, Canberra, 16 December 1986, 27 March 1987.

35 Michael Lynch (former Command Ops Officer, WA Area and RAN representative on the WA Visits Co-ordinating Committee, Port Nuclear Safety Panel and Naval Nuclear Ships Safety Organisation), submission 10, Senate Committee, 'Safety Procedures', p. 2; Hon. J. Bannon to Sen. G. McIntosh, 4 November 1986, submission 59; Vallentine, submission 56, p. 14; Western Australia Port Safety Scheme for the Visits of Nuclear-Powered Warships to Fremantle and Cockburn Sound, State Emergency Service, WA, 1986, submission 86.

36 US Congress, 99 (2), House Armed Services Committee (Subcommittee on Military Installations and Facilities), *Hearings on HR 4181 to Authorize Certain Construction at Military Installations for FY 1987*, February–March 1986, Washington, DC, 1986, p. 66; Shaun Gregory and Alistair Edwards, 'A Handbook of Nuclear Weapons Accidents', Peace Research Report, no. 20, School of Peace Studies, University of Bradford, January 1988.

37 *The Dominion*, 3 April 1987, p. 2; MacDougall, testimony, Senate Committee, 'Safety Procedures', p. 215; American Friends Service Committee, *News Release*, 10 January 1986, cited by Bolt, submission 43, p. 16.

38 When La Rocque was in command of half of the 6th Fleet Task Group 62 in the Mediterranean, a merchant ship ran into a destroyer at anchor in Valetta harbour, hitting a nuclear weapons store. La Rocque alleged that such incidents happened all the time. US Congress, 93 (2), Joint Atomic Energy Committee (Subcommittee on Military Applications), *Hearing on Proliferation of Nuclear Weapons*, 10 September 1974, Washington, DC, 1974, pp. 18–19.

39 Dan Caldwell, 'Permissive action links; a description and proposal', *Survival*, vol. 29, no. 3, May–June 1987, p. 225; Gregory and Edwards, p. 49.

40 Davis, submission 92, Senate Committee, 'Safety Procedures', pp. 9, 16. US tests reportedly indicate that under normal weather conditions a radioactive plume could spread 28 miles downwind and 2.5 miles wide, *The Independent*, 15 July 1987, p. 2.

41 DoD, submission 80, Senate Committee, 'Safety Procedures', pp. 23–6.

42 Hearing, Senate Committee, 'Safety Procedures', Canberra, 27 March 1987. Officially, what Martin (Flag Officer, Naval Support Command) 'intended to say and what he thought he had said was that it was not inevitable that some of the ships would be carrying nuclear weapons'. However, Martin is also reported to have said: 'I blew it. Any member of the media who can help me clarify this without getting me any deeper in the ——, I'd be grateful', *The Age*, 25 September 1986, p. 1; *Sydney Morning*

Herald, 25 September 1986, p. 2; Nic Maclellan, 'Speak No Evil: The "Neither Confirm Nor Deny" Policy', *Peace Magazine Australia*, February–March 1987, p. 18.

43 Capt. T. Bush (USN retd) cited by, Bolt submission 43, Senate Committee, 'Safety Procedures', pp. 15–16.

44 *Canberra Times*, 9 July 1987, pp. 1, 15; DoD, submission 80, Senate Committee, 'Safety Procedures', pp. 26–8 and hearings, 16 December 1986, 27 March 1987; Marian Wilkinson, 'After the big blast: the disturbing reality of nuclear accidents', *National Times*, 22–8 March 1985, pp. 11–12.

45 *Parliamentary Debates*, Commons, 6s., vol. 112, no.77, written answer, 20 March 1987 (Stanley), col. 635. The British government has contingency plans, reassessed after the Chernobyl catastrophe, for a submarine reactor accident in British waters. The Naval Emergency Monitoring Organisation has units at Rhu (Scotland), Plymouth and Portsmouth. According to an Australian official, the Royal Navy conducted an exercise in June 1986 to bring a vessel with a damaged reactor back to port from the North Atlantic, Commodore Ian MacDougall, Director-General Joint Operations and Plans and Chairman of Visiting Ships Panel (Nuclear), DoD, testimony, Senate Committee, 'Safety Procedures', Canberra, 16 December 1986, p. 188. The MoD reportedly recognizes that during an accident 'there must always be the chance of an open hatchway or other external venting allowing a small proportion of fission products to escape to the outside atmosphere', *The Independent*, 16 July 1987, p. 5.

46 MacDougall, testimony, Senate Committee, 'Safety Procedures', pp. 223, 228.

47 See n. 16 above.

48 Extracts from the Manual were read at the hearing of 16 December 1987, Senate Committee, 'Safety Procedures', Canberra, p. 232; Defense Nuclear Agency, *Nuclear Weapons Response Procedures Manual*, DNA 5100. 1, Washington, DC, 1984, p. 33, cited in L. Zarsky, P. Hayes and W. Bello, 'Nuclear Accidents', *Current Affairs Bulletin*, June 1986, pp. 4–11.

49 US Defense Nuclear Agency, *NUWAX–83*, p. 46, released to Peter Hayes under the US Freedom of Information Act and cited in Zarsky, Hayes and Bello, 'Nuclear Accidents', pp. 8–9.

50 Bolt, submission 43, Senate Committee, 'Safety Procedures', pp. 12, 25; Davis, submission 92, pp. 85–6. Several submissions pointed out that there was no medical provision to limit damage done by Caesium-137, Strontium-90, or other long-lasting radionucleides.

Chapter 6 Anti-nuclear politics

1 David Harlan, 'New Zealand – The Politics of Identity', *Atlantic Monthly*, September 1986, pp. 14–20.

2 *NZPD*, 3(31), vol. 314, 8 October 1957 (Freer), pp. 2915–25. The RNZAF assisted in the transport of officials, and the RNZN provided two frigates as weather and monitoring ships, one of which reported good views from 50 miles away. In 1988 the surviving witnesses were being given medical checks.

3 *External Affairs Review*, vol. 7, no. 3, March 1957, pp. 5–6; no. 4, April 1957, pp. 18–19; no. 5, May 1957, pp. 17–18. The 1957 Defence Review noted that New Zealand could not afford its own nuclear weapons even if they were available. But the government made provision for university researchers to follow the path blazed by Sir Ernest Rutherford. See, *External Affairs Review*, vol. 7, no. 3, March 1957, pp. 8–9.

4 John Boanas, 'The Campaign for Nuclear Disarmament, Christchurch 1958–66', MA dissertation, University of Bradford, 1980.

5 'The Problem of Nuclear Weapons', in *The Right Honourable Sir Keith Holyoake*, Ministry of Foreign Affairs, Wellington, 1984.

6 This section is based on Owen Wilkes, *Protest: Demonstrations Against the American Military Presence in New Zealand*, Wellington, 1973.

7 Ministry of Foreign Affairs, *Report*, 31 March 1973, Wellington, p. 4. The Government also formally protested to China over the Lop Nor tests, Ministry of Foreign Affairs, *Report*, 31 March 1974, Wellington, p. 30.

8 Interview, private information. Talboys argued that an SPNFZ would be practically difficult or impossible, Ministry of Foreign Affairs, *Report*, 31 March 1976, Wellington, p. 4.

9 *NZPD*, 1(38), vol. 404, 5 August 1976 (Wall), pp. 1316–17. The former US Ambassador Anne Martindell claims that while serving in Wellington from 1979 to mid-1981 she had recommended that no ship visits should occur which might provoke a strong reaction. Her Reaganite replacement, H. Monroe Browne, ended the armistice. But the hiatus may have been a sensitive reaction by the USN to the Three Mile Island accident. Martindell, testimony, US Congress, 99(1), House Foreign Affairs Committee (Subcommittee on Asian and Pacific Affairs), *Hearing on the Security Treaty between Australia, New Zealand and the United States*, 18 March 1985, Washington, DC, p. 51.

10 *NZPD*, 1(40), no. 6, 29 April 1982 (Prebble), pp. 653–4; (Cooper, Wilkinson, Thomson), pp. 655–7, 688; (Waring), p. 662; (Knapp), p. 663.

11 *Disarmament and Arms Control*, Wellington, 1978, p. 39; *Disarmament and Arms Control*, information bulletins, no. 3, Wellington, 1982, p. 9; no. 4, 1983, p. 27; Ministry of Foreign Affairs, *Report*, 31 March 1983, Wellington, p. 4.

12 Editorial, *New Zealand Listener*, 11 January 1986; Ray Galvin, *A Nuclear-Free New Zealand ... Now!*, Auckland, 1984, p. 19; *Living Without ANZUS*, Auckland, 1984, pp. 15–16; Merwyn Norrish, 'The Changing Context of New Zealand's Foreign Policy', speech to Takapuna Rotary Club, 29 April 1986; Jeremy Hammington and Tim Jones, 'ANZUS and the Politics of Insecurity', *Peacelink*, no. 12, August 1983, pp. 10–11.

13 Robert Aldridge, 'From ANZUS to a Nuclear Free Pacific', Christchurch, 1978. Kai Jensen, 'Sea Launched Cruise Missiles', *Peacelink*, no. 27, February 1985, p. 11.

14 Senator Richard Lugar, in *New Zealand Herald*, 29 August 1986, p. 5.

15 Wilkes, 'ANZUS and New Zealand', in Barbara Harford (ed.), *Beyond ANZUS*, Wellington, 1985, p. 73; Sir Jack Hunn, 'The Nuclear Delusion', in Rod Alley (ed.), *Alternatives to ANZUS*, Auckland, 1984, pp. 55–6; Erich Geiringer, *Malice in Blunderland, An Anti-Nuclear Primer*, Auckland, 1985,

pp. 129–31. See also, Dennis Small, 'State Backed Terrorism', *Peacelink*, no. 42, July 1986, pp. 3–7; Allan Cumming, 'Why Grenada?', *Peacelink*, no. 15, November–December 1983, pp. 20–1.

16 Don Turkington, 'The Role of Trade Unions in Foreign Policy', in John Henderson, Keith Jackson and Richard Kennaway (eds.), *Beyond New Zealand: The Foreign Policy of a Small State*, Auckland, 1980, pp. 240–1.

17 An example of a contrary view on the staunch right is the statement by Samuel and Rubenstein in *The Australian*, 27 October 1986, p. 7: 'Events in New Zealand have illustrated graphically what an indigenous pro-Soviet Left, aided by the Soviets themselves, can do in effecting a leftward shift in foreign policy.' See also, Richard D. Fisher, 'Responding to New Zealand's Challenge to Western Security in the South Pacific', Asian Studies Center Backgrounder no. 48, Heritage Foundation, Washington, DC, 24 July 1986, p. 8. The Hoover Institution supported Reagan's bid for power. One of the conference directors was ex-Ambassador H. Monroe Browne, *The Press*, 7 March 1987, p. 5. The Labour Committee on Pacific Affairs, established in Washington in 1983, reportedly received a US government grant and has NZ links, Harford (ed.), *Beyond ANZUS*, p. 14.

18 Nuclear Free Kiwis, 'Destabilisation: USIS, SIS, CIA and ASIO', *Peace Researcher*, no. 11, 1986, p. 7.

19 Larry Jones, editorial, *Peace Movement New Zealand Newsletter*, no. 3, September 1982, pp. 2–3. A video of the Springbok tour protest was used to illustrate lessons for anti-nuclear campaigning, Tim Jones, 'Dimensions of Peace', *Peacelink*, no. 14, October 1983, p. 4. George Armstrong, 'An Ideology and Theology of an Independent and Nuclear-Free Pacific', *Social Alternatives*, vol. 5, no. 1, 1985, pp. 12–13.

20 Helen Clark, 'Reviewing New Zealand's Defence and Security Policies During IYP', *Peacelink*, no. 39, March 1986, p. 6.

21 Roger Foley, 'Inside the peace movement', *New Zealand Times*, 2 March 1986, pp. 10–13.

22 *Auckland Star*, 7 January 1987, p. A8; Defence Committee of Enquiry, *Defence and Security: What New Zealanders Want*, Wellington, 1986, pp. 62–3.

23 Wilkes, editorial, *Peace Movement New Zealand Newsletter*, no. 4, November 1982, p. 2; 'Peace Movement Aotearoa (NZ)', *Peacelink*, no. 40, May 1986, pp. 6–7. Owen Wilkes, expelled from Sweden, joined PMA in Wellington as a full time researcher in 1983. But its finances were always precarious, and it had a debt of some $NZ1,500 in early 1984.

24 Larry Ross, 'Nuclear Weapons Free Zones in New Zealand', *Peacelink*, no. 14, October 1983, pp. 8–9; 'NZ Nuclear-Free Zone Committee', *Peace Studies* (Australia), November–December 1985, pp. 39–41; NFZ Committee, *Nuclear Free Newsletter*, March 1987, p. 2.

25 Interview with Katie Boanas, Christchurch, 11 April 1987; Sonja Antonsen *et al.*, *Peacelink*, no. 23, September 1984, p. 3; *Defence and Security: What New Zealanders Want*, p. 42.

26 Ann Evans, cited by Peter Matheson, 'Doctors Against Nuclear War', *Peacelink*, no. 8, 1983, p. 8. The Royal Society of New Zealand also took a strong anti-nuclear stance, in *The Threat of Nuclear War: A New Zealand Per-*

spective, miscellaneous series no. 11, Royal Society of New Zealand, Wellington, 1985.

27 Tom Newnham, *Peace Squadron: The Sharp End of Nuclear Protest in New Zealand*, Auckland 1986, passim; Jeremy Hammington and Tim Jones, 'ANZUS and the Politics of Insecurity', *Peacelink*, no. 12, August 1983, p. 10.

28 Submission 1829, Defence Enquiry, box 35, University of Canterbury Library (Clements Papers). In April 1982 the Catholic hierarchy issued a strong appeal against nuclear weapons in general terms, a year before the Catholic Bishops of America issued their pastoral letter, 'The Challenge of Peace'.

29 *RSA Review*, December 1986, p. 2; submissions 21, 38, Defence Enquiry, box 1; Sir Jack Harris, submission unnumbered, box 25; Sir Guy Powles, submission 2454, box 31.

30 Michael Pugh, 'Nuclear Deterrence Theory: The Spectre at the Feast', *NZIR*, vol. 12, no. 3, May–June 1987, pp. 10–13.

31 ANZUS Group, *Newsletter*, Masterton, October 1986; Dennis Small, 'Pro-Nuclear Right Prepared for Election 1987', *Nuclear-Free*, March 1987, p. 9. See also, Sir Richard Bolt, former Chief of Defence Staff, *New Zealand Herald*, 21 February 1985; Frank Corner, in *New Zealand Herald*, 28 February 1987, p. 5. It would be untrue to say that the MoD leaked like a sieve in ways embarrassing to the Government, but see the *Herald*, 28 February 1987, pp. 5–6. When Brigadier Hamilton returned as Head of defence liaison in Washington, Frank O'Flynn said: 'I have long suspected Brigadier Hamilton of being totally opposed to the Government's policy. . . . His policy is one of grovelling to the Americans', *New Zealand Herald*, 28 April 1987, p. 5.

32 Sir Ewan Jamieson argued that South Vietnam had been moving towards 'real democracy' before the US pulled out, 'Anti-Americanism and Defence Policy', paper circulated for Hoover Institution Conference, Washington, DC, 3–4 March 1987.

33 Cited by Lawrence Jones, 'Cracks in the Consensus: Shifting Attitudes to New Zealand Defence', in Alley (ed.), *Alternatives to ANZUS*, pp. 43–4. For papers of the 20th Foreign Policy School, University of Otago, 13–16 May 1983, see, Hyam Gold (ed.), *New Directions in New Zealand's Foreign Policy*, Auckland, 1985.

34 Submissions examined for: Parliamentary Select Committees on Disarmament and Arms Control, 1983, and Foreign Affairs and Defence Committee, 1986, General Assembly Library, Wellington; Defence Committee of Enquiry, 1986, University of Canterbury Library (Clements Papers).

35 Stephen Levine and Paul Spoonley, 'Public Opinion and Foreign Policy', *NZIR*, vol. 5, no. 2, March 1980, pp. 19–21.

36 *NZPD*, 2(40), vol. 451, 3 August 1983 (Knapp), p. 1002; (Beetham), pp. 991–3. Allan Cumming, 'Armed Neutrality', *Peace Movement New Zealand Newsletter*, no. 3, September 1982, pp. 16–17; Dianne Davis, 'Armed Neutrality: An Alternative Defence Policy for New Zealand', in Alley (ed.), *Alternatives to ANZUS*, p. 52; *NZPD*, 1(41), vol. 460, 12 February 1985 (Knapp), pp. 2913–14.

37 New Zealand Party, draft manifesto, 21 August 1983, p. 11; *Peacelink*, no. 21, July 1984, centrefold; Tim Jones, 'Catching the Peace Train', *Peacelink*, no. 13, September 1983, pp. 13–14; 'Bob Jones – A Vote For Peace', *Peacelink*, no. 16, February 1984, pp. 4–7.

38 *NZPD*, 3(31), vol. 311, 11 June 1957 (Gotz), p. 54.

39 Jeremy Hammington, 'Disarming the Critics: National and Nuclear Weapons', *Peacelink*, no. 13, September 1983, pp. 12–13. A Heylen-Eyewitness opinion poll in March 1985 suggested that 54.5 per cent of National supporters approved the Lange Government's policy of banning nuclear-armed ships, *The Press*, 1 April 1985.

40 Marilyn Waring, *Women, Politics and Power*, Wellington, 1985, p. 116; *Otago Daily Times*, 1 August 1983, p. 1; Valmai Shearer, submission 532, Defence Enquiry, box 30.

41 Interview with Hon. Wallace Rowling, Washington, 2 March 1987; *Reports*, NZLP Annual Conferences: 64th, 12–15 May 1980, pp. 52–4; 65th, 11–14 May 1981, p. 56; 66th, 10–13 May 1982, p. 38.

42 *New Zealand Herald*, 26 March 1983, p. 1; 7 July 1983, p. 1; Jones, 'Catching the Peace Train', pp. 13–14.

43 *Report*, 67th Annual Conference, NZLP, Auckland, 2–5 September 1983, p. 25.

44 *NZPD*, 3(40), 1984, vol. 456, 12 June 1984 (Prebble), pp. 255–7; (Clark), pp. 263–5; (Muldoon), pp. 265–6. '"Honest Rob's" Almanac of Pacific Wisdom', *Pacific Islands Monthly*, May 1984, pp. 23–4.

45 Labour Party, *Policy Document*, June 1984, pp. 10, 50–2.

46 Defence Committee of Enquiry, *Defence and Security: What New Zealanders Want*, Annex, Public Opinion Poll, Wellington, 1986, pp. 105–6.

47 'U.S. Leans on Warship Ban', *Peacelink*, no. 27, February 1985, p. 15.

48 Larry Jones, 'Can Labour Keep Their Word?', *Peacelink*, no. 22, August 1984, p. 3; *Peacelink*, no. 21, July 1984, centrefold; Ray Galvin, *A Nuclear-Free New Zealand ... Now!*, Auckland, 1984, pp. 12, 54; Harford (ed.), *Beyond ANZUS*, p. 172; Vernon Wilkinson, *New Zealand Politics in the Nuclear Age*, Christchurch, 1984.

49 *The Dominion*, 7 April 1987, p. 2.

50 *New Zealand Herald*, 6 January 1987, p. 6; *The Dominion*, 7 June 1987, p. 6.

51 Hon. Jim McLay 'Managing the ANZUS Alliance', in Hyam Gold (ed.), *New Directions in New Zealand's Foreign Policy*, Auckland, 1985, p. 94.

52 *New Zealand Herald*, 9 July 1987, p. 1.

53 *Auckland Star*, 11 July 1987, p. 8.

54 Michael Pugh, 'Labour's triumph in New Zealand', *The World Today*, vol. 43, no. 10, October 1987, pp. 168–9. For priority issues see the NRB poll, *New Zealand Herald*, 20 May 1987, p. 1.

55 *Sydney Morning Herald*, 16 April 1984, pp. 1–2; R. Milliken, L. Crisp and J. Hurst, 'The Push for Peace', *National Times*, 4–10 May 1984, pp. 18–23; Malcolm Saunders and Ralph Summy, *The Australian Peace Movement: A Short History*, Canberra, 1986, pp. 35ff.

56 Greenpeace has also protested against uranium shipments from Darwin, *The Australian*, 10 November 1986, p. 30. In 1981 CND and trade unions sponsored a ketch, *Pacific Peacemaker*, to sail for Bangor to protest about the

possible upgrade of HMAS Stirling as a Trident forward base, John Hinchcliff (comp), *Confronting the Nuclear Age – Australian Responses*, Bondi Jn., 1981. See also, Annabelle Newbury, 'Nuclear Warship Visits', in Harford (ed.), *Beyond ANZUS*, pp. 104–8.

57 Peter D. Jones, 'The Australian Peace Movement', *Peacelink*, no. 33, August 1985, pp. 16–17.

58 Australian Coalition for Disarmament and Peace, *Report of the Australian Nuclear Disarmament Conference*, Melbourne, 29 August–1 September 1985.

59 At the pre-election ALP Conference in 1982 the Centre-Unity faction, led by Hawke, Neil Keating and Gareth Evans, pushed through an amendment to the Party's anti-uranium policy. Hawke regarded existing policy as an electoral liability. *Transcript*, 35th Biennial National Conference, ALP, Canberra, 5–9 July 1982, pp. 406–53; Joan Coxsedge, 'An Analysis of the New ALP Uranium Policy', *Labor Star* (Melbourne), August 1982, p. 10.

60 Joan Coxsedge and Gerry Harant, *Security Threat: The Case for Abolition of Secret Agencies*, Melbourne, 1984, pp. 3–4.

61 Keith D. Suter, *Australian Nuclear Free Zones: Some Basic Questions*, Sydney, 1985.

62 Coxsedge, 'Snoops Down Under', in Harford (ed.), *Beyond ANZUS*, p. 117.

63 Andrew Mack, 'Crisis in the Other Alliance: ANZUS in the 1980s', *World Policy Journal*, vol. 3, summer 1986, p. 450; David Campbell, 'The Domestic Sources of New Zealand Security Policy in Comparative Perspective', Peace Research Centre, working paper no. 16, RSPS, ANU, Canberra, 1987, pp. 34–5.

64 Alan Renouf, *The Frightened Country*, Melbourne, 1979, p. 531.

65 PND (NSW), 'PND's Non-alignment Policy', leaflet, December 1986. The NSW branch also launched the Australian Anti-Bases Coalition Campaign to have the bases removed and relocated, focussing on closure of Pine Gap, Canberra Programme for Peace, in *Canberra Times*, 19 November 1986, p. 24. See also, Marian Quigley, 'The Rise and Fall (?) of the Nuclear Disarmament Party', *Current Affairs Bulletin*, April 1986, p. 12; Richard Bolt, 'Active Peacemaker or Passive Warmonger? The Future of Australia's Links to Global War,' Melbourne, 1986, pp. 47–8.

66 Interviews with Bill Lesley, PND convenor, Sydney, 22 April 1987; Jo Vallentine and Peter Jones, Canberra, 24 March 1987. See, Peter J. Boyce, 'The Influence of the United States on the Domestic Debate in Australia', *Australian Outlook*, vol. 38, no. 2, December 1984, p. 160; Mack, 'Crisis in the Other Alliance', p. 450.

67 *Transcript*, 35th Biennial Conference, ALP, Canberra, 5–9 July 1982, pp. 597–603; 37th Biennial Conference, Hobart, 7–11 July 1986, pp. 465–76.

68 For example, Colin Rubenstein, *The Age*, 20 March 1987, p. 24.

69 Australian Waters (Nuclear Weapons Prohibition) Act 1985, a Senate Bill. Another Bill challenged the B-52 agreement on the grounds that it was not verifiable and B-52s were to be fitted to carry cruise and short range nuclear attack missiles. *APD*, Senate, 34(1) 1, weekly no. 10, 30 May 1985 (Chipp), pp. 840–1.

70 Saunders and Summy, *Australian Peace Movement*, p. 53.

71 Quigley, 'The Rise and Fall (?) of the Nuclear Disarmament Party',

pp. 14–19. As of September 1988 the Senate representation was ALP 32, Liberal 28, Democrats 7, National 6, Independent 1 and Independent Nuclear Disarmament 2.

72 Interview with Vallentine; 'The Rise of the New Left', *Weekend Australian*, 15–16 November 1986, p. 10. See also, Drew Hutton (ed.), *Green Politics in Australia*, North Ryde, NSW, 1987.

73 Dennis H. Phillips, *Cold War Two and Australia*, Sydney, 1983, pp. 29, 102; David Martin, *Armed Neutrality for Australia*, Victoria, 1984; 'Armed Neutrality – Australia's Alternative', *Peace Dossier*, no. 10. See also, Mack, 'Defending Australia. Is Non-Alignment the Answer?', *Current Affairs Bulletin*, September 1982, pp. 17–30; Joseph Camilleri, 'Neutrality or Non-Alignment?', *Arena*, no. 67, 1984, pp. 117–24.

74 Bolt, 'Active Peacemaker', p. 42.

75 Andrew Mack, 'Gathering of the Doves', *The Bulletin*, 6 September 1988, pp. 63–4.

76 For example, Commission for the Future, *Future Contingencies: 4, Nuclear Disaster*, Wellington, 1982; French reparations for the *Rainbow Warrior* sinking were put towards nuclear-winter research. It is calculated that if 5,000 mt were detonated in the northern hemisphere, fallout on New Zealand would remain 100 times lower than the lethal dose, but a prolonged drop in temperature of 2°C would have a significant effect on agriculture. There would also be social and economic upheaval and a dearth of medical supplies, Helen Clark, *Disarmament and Arms Control, Report of the Select Committee on Foreign Affairs and Defence*, Wellington, 1985, pp. 150–92; Barrie Pittock, in *Canberra Times*, 29 October 1986, p. 1.

77 Campbell, 'The Domestic Sources of New Zealand Security policy', p. 23.

Chapter 7 From negotiation to legislation

1 *New Zealand Herald*, 1 March 1985, p. 20.

2 House Foreign Affairs Committee, *U.S. Relations With the Pacific Area: report of a study mission to Fiji, New Zealand, Australia, Singapore, Thailand, Hong Kong and Taiwan*, Washington, DC, 1981, pp. 6–7.

3 US Congress, 97(2), Senate Foreign Relations Committee, *Hearing on Nomination of Paul D. Wolfowitz*, 9 December 1982, Washington, DC, 1983, pp. 4–22; Armitage, testimony, US Congress, 97(2), Senate Foreign Relations Committee, *Hearing on U.S. Policies and Programs in Southeast Asia*, 8 June 1982, Washington, DC, 1982, pp. 9–10; Iklé, testimony, Senate Foreign Relations Committee, *Hearing on East–West Relations: Focus on the Pacific*, 10 June 1982, Washington, DC, 1982, p. 29.

4 'Press Conference ANZUS Council Meeting', Wellington, 16–17 July 1984, USIS text.

5 Cited by Tom Newnham, *Peace Squadron: The Sharp End of Nuclear Protest in New Zealand*, Auckland, 1986, p. 48.

6 *Evening Post*, 1 November 1985, p. 1. See Frank Walker, 'Lange's Lone Stand', *National Times*, 1–7 February 1985, pp. 4–5; Anthony Hubbard, 'The Sinking of the *Buchanan*', *Dominion Sunday Times*, 28 March 1987, p. 11; Stuart McMillan, *Neither Confirm Nor Deny*, Wellington, 1987, pp. 79–87.

7 National had denied any question of a nuclear powered or armed unit taking part, 'Ministerial Statement', *NZPD*, 3 (40), vol. 456, 14 June 1984 (Thomson), pp. 384–5; (Lange), p. 387.

8 Admiral William J. Crowe, 'USCINCPAC Press Conference', Port Moresby, 15 October 1984, USIS text; H. Monroe Browne, 'Pacific Basin – Challenges and Opportunities', August–September 1984, USIS text.

9 ' "Disloyal" leaks inquiry', *New Zealand News UK*, 5 February 1986, p. 1; Helen Clark, 'What Price Security?' *New Zealand Listener*, 20 September 1986, pp. 34–5; Denis Warner, 'ANZUS – The New Zealand Defence Department's View', *Pacific Defence Reporter*, vol. 11, no. 9, March 1985, pp. 38–9; *New Zealand Herald*, 28 February 1987, p. 6. See, David Robie, 'Challenging Goliath', *New Internationalist*, September 1986, p. 9, for the suggestion that the *Buchanan* request was a carefully laid plan by the bureaucracy to compromise Labour's policy.

10 Marian Wilkinson, 'Hawke takes Lange to task on ANZUS', *National Times*, 25–31 January 1985, p. 5; Ministry of Foreign Affairs, *Report*, 31 March 1985, Wellington, p. 9.

11 Hubbard, 'The Sinking of the *Buchanan*', p. 11.

12 e.g., Lange attacked Sir Ewan Jamieson and another conservative, Frank Corner, on the assumption that they actually attended the 'Red Orchestra Conference' in March 1987 for which they had accepted invitations, *New Zealand Herald*, 3 March 1987, p. 3.

13 George Shultz, 'On Alliance Responsibility', address at East-West Center, Hawaii, 17 July 1985, US Dept. of State text.

14 *Jane's Defence Weekly*, vol. 3, no. 10, 9 March 1985, p. 387.

15 Karl D. Jackson, 'U.S. ponders new relationship with New Zealand', testimony, House Armed Services Committee (Subcommittee on Asian and Pacific Affairs), 25 September 1986, USIS text.

16 *Auckland Star*, 22 September 1986, p. A7; *The Press*, 7 October 1986, p. 3; *New Statesman*, 21 February 1986, p. 8; interviews with Lt. Col. John Williams, DoD, 10 March 1987, Washington, DC, and Desmond Ball, 25 March 1987, Canberra.

17 *Washington Times*, 8 March 1985, p. 8B. A New Zealand intelligence officer and two NCOs remained to provide information and security at the base, Peter Winsley, New Zealand's Military Relationship with Singapore, Peace and Justice Forum, research paper, Wellington, 1986, pp. 10–11; Geoff Kitney, 'Canberra to be Told: Sever NZ Intelligence Link', *National Times*, 15–21 February 1985, p. 4; *Washington Times*, 20 February 1985, p. 8B; *Evening Post*, 1 July 1986, p. 2.

18 James Kelly, testimony, US Congress, 99(1), House Foreign Affairs Committee (Subcommittee on Asian and Pacific Affairs), *Hearing on the Security Treaty Between Australia, New Zealand, and the United States*, 18 March 1985, Washington, DC, 1985, p. 170.

19 *New Zealand Herald*, 29 October 1985, p. 1; *Auckland Star*, 1 November 1985, p. 3. The US accounted for 15 per cent of New Zealand's total trade, worth $US1.5 billion in 1985.

20 *The Press*, 22 May 1986, p. 4. But the head of TV New Zealand disapproved of such visits and treated USIA Worldnet satellite productions with

caution. See articles by Nuclear-Free Kiwis: 'The USIS and the International Visitor Grant Programme', *New Zealand Monthly Review*, 295, February 1987, pp. 12–14; 'Subverting New Zealand: the USIS programme', *Peacelink*, no. 46, November 1986, p. 8; 'Destabilisation: USIS, SIS, CIA and ASIO', *Peace Researcher*, no. 11, 1986, pp. 5–7.

21 Cline had boasted that in Australia the CIA pumped damaging material to Whitlam's opponents and the intelligence community at a time when renewal of the base leases was uncertain, Marian Wilkinson, 'ANZUS Row: CIA's Grubby Money Trail', *National Times*, 15–21 March 1985, p. 4; David McKnight, 'Spooks, Think-Tanks Join the ANZUS Gold Rush', *National Times*, 1–7 March 1985, pp. 22–3; 'Lange Seen as CIA Target', *Canberra Times*, 16 September 1986, p. 7; *New Zealand Herald*, 24 August 1986, p. 6.

22 See also, Warren Berryman, 'CIA Company for "Cover" Here', *National Business Review*, vol. 16, no. 8, 11 March 1985, pp.1–2; Berryman, 'CIA Accused of Orchestrating Company Entry to NZ', *ibid.*, vol. 16, no. 9, 18 March 1985, pp. 33–34; Owen Wilkes, 'How the CIA Set Up a Front in N.Z.', *New Zealand Monthly Review*, 295, February 1987, pp. 3–7.

23 *New Zealand Herald*, 26 January 1987, p. 3; Owen Wilkes, 'The CIA and the Honolulu Loan Scam', *New Zealand Monthly Review*, 296, March 1987, pp. 6–9. Paul Cleveland came to Wellington from the US mission in South Korea. Before that he had served in Indonesia during the last days of Sukarno's régime. He was reported as saying: 'Sometimes it's more difficult to deal with a messy democracy like New Zealand than with some Asian dictatorships', *The Star*, 16 September 1986, p. 3.

24 *The Press*, 21 October 1986, p. 9; Owen Wilkes, 'Stooging Around the Cook Islands. The Mysterious Case of the Disappearing Submarine', *New Zealand Monthly Review*, 291, October 1986, pp. 3–13.

25 'Joint communiqué after Australian–United States Ministerial talks at San Francisco', 10–11 August 1986, Australian Dept. of Foreign Affairs text.

26 Shultz, 'On Alliance Responsibility'.

27 Kelly, testimony, US Congress, 99(1), House Foreign Affairs Committee (Subcommittee on Asian and Pacific Affairs), *Hearing on the Security Treaty Between Australia, New Zealand, and the United States*, 18 March 1985, Washington, DC, 1985, pp.150ff.

28 For example, editorials, in *Baltimore Sun*, 13 February 1985, p. 6; *New York Post*, 28 February 1985, p. 8; *Atlanta Journal & Constitution*, 2 March 1985, p. 6; *New York Times*, 11 March 1985, p. 8.

29 Steve Hoadley, 'American Views of New Zealand', *NZIR*, vol. 11, no. 2, March–April 1986, p.15; Ramesh Thakur, 'ANZUS and the Nuclear Ships Ban: The American Reaction', in Hyam Gold (ed.), *New Directions in New Zealand Foreign Policy*, Auckland, 1985, pp. 52–60.

30 Frank Cranston, 'New Zealand's Break from Special ANZUS Relationship', *Jane's Defence Weekly*, vol. 3, no. 16, 20 April 1985, p. 669.

31 Press release, 5 March 1987, courtesy Dr Karl Jackson.

32 Dellums said: 'when the military places itself in this kind of situation, it is almost campaigning for office', US Congress, 99(2), House Armed Services Committee (Subcommittee on Military Installations and Facilities), *Hear-*

ings on HR 4181 to Authorize Certain Construction at Military Installations for FY 1987, 26 February 1986, Washington, DC, 1986, p. 14; David Bauman, 'Lobbying for a Ship', *USA Today*, 1 July 1985, p. 3.

33 *CR*, Senate, vol. 131, no. 4, 22 January 1985, p. S441; House, vol. 131, no. 11, 6 February 1985, pp. S1024–5; House, vol. 131, no. 16, 20 February 1985, p. E532.

34 Interview with Dr Lawrence Cavaiola, HASC Subcommittee on Sea Power, Washington, DC, 6 March 1987; Alva M. Bowen and Ronald O'Rourke, 'Ports for the Fleet', *Proceedings/Naval Review*, vol. 112, May 1986, p. 148; *New York Post*, 9 August 1984, p. 14; *Newark Star-Ledger*, 27 November 1984, p. 8; *Washington Post*, 12 August 1984, p. 1; 17 January 1985, p. 3; *Journal of Commerce*, 22 January 1985, p. 1B.

35 Molinari, testimony, US Congress, 99(1), House Foreign Affairs Committee (Subcommittee on Asian and Pacific Affairs), *Hearing on the Security Treaty Between Australia, New Zealand and the United States*, 18 March 1985, Washington, DC, 1985, p. 131. See also *CR*, House, vol. 131, no. 21, 26 February 1985 (Molinari, Gilman, Stratton, Carney, Solomon), pp. H695ff; Molinari, testimony, *Hearings on HR 4181*, p. 84.

36 *CR*, House, vol. 131, no. 21, 26 February 1985 (Weber), p. H697. Also, Senate, vol. 131, no. 25, 5 March 1985 (Pressler), p. S2486. Kasich (Ohio), concerned about casein imports, said that 'America ought not to be walked on, we ought not to be slapped in the face, and we ought not to continue to give, give, give,' *CR*, House, vol. 131, no. 21, 26 February 1985, p. H699.

37 *CR*, House, vol. 131, no. 30, 18 March 1985 (Pressler), pp. S3008–9; (Wallop), p. S3048. Sir Robert Cotton, the Australian Ambassador, explained that Australia was taking a different stand but was also a lifelong friend of New Zealand which was entitled to make its own decisions, *The Australian*, 22–3 November 1986, p. 2.

38 *CR*, House, vol. 131, no. 32, 20 March 1985 (Leach), Res. HR 91; interview with David Addington, Republican Counsel, HFAC, Washington, DC, 2 March 1987.

39 US Congress, 99(2), House Armed Services Committee, *Report of the Delegation to the South Pacific*, February 1986, Washington, DC, 1986, p. 15.

40 US Congress, 99(1), House Foreign Affairs Committee (Subcommittee on Asian and Pacific Affairs), *Hearing on the Security Treaty Between Australia, New Zealand, and the United States*, 18 March 1985, Washington, DC, 1985, Solarz, pp. 186–7; Albinski, pp. 126, 136; Tow, p. 128; see also Martindell, pp. 44–60; Carroll, pp. 61ff; Leach, pp. 131–2; Udall, p. 132; *CR*, Senate, vol. 131, no. 172, 12 December 1985 (Proxmire), p. S17469.

41 *APD*, Senate, no. 10, 11 September 1984 (Evans), p. 784; Michael H. Armacost, 'The Asia–Pacific Region: A Forward Look', *Atlantic Community Quarterly*, vol. 22, no. 4, winter 1984–5, pp. 343–4.

42 Geoff Kitney, 'Why Bob Hawke Will Have to Say No', *National Times*, 1–7 February 1985, pp. 3, 7; Alan Ramsey, 'The Iceberg That Went Unnoticed', *National Times*, 8–14 February 1985, pp. 3, 5; *International Defense Review*, vol. 18, no. 3, 1985, p. 291; Alan Ramsay and Michael Gill, 'The Hawke–Shultz Tango', *National Times*, 8–14 March 1985, pp. 3–4.

43 Stapleton Roy, Deputy Assistant Secretary of State for East Asian and Pacific Affairs, in *New Zealand Herald*, 25 February 1987, p. 12; Ross Babbage, 'The Future of the Australian–New Zealand Defence Relationship', Strategic and Defence Studies Centre, working paper no. 113, RSPS, ANU, Canberra, December 1986, pp. 14–16; Geoff Kitney, 'Canberra to be Told: Sever NZ Intelligence Link', *National Times*, 15–21 February 1985, p. 4.

44 'Visit to New Zealand, Joint Statement', Wellington, 12 December 1986, Australian Dept. of Foreign Affairs news release; *New Zealand Herald*, 15 December 1986, p. 5.

45 'Remarks at the ANZUS Ministerial Session', Canberra, 15 July 1985, USIS text.

46 'Interview Prime Minister Robert J. Hawke', *Journal of Defense and Diplomacy*, vol. 3, no. 8, August 1985, pp. 14–15.

47 Hawke, Earle Page memorial lecture, in *Sydney Morning Herald*, 12 September 1986, p. 12. See also, Colin Rubenstein and Peter Samuel, 'How the US is Losing the Pacific', *Weekend Australian*, 25–6 October 1986, p. 24. See also, *Canberra Times*, 18 March 1987, p. 3; Sam Lipski, 'Friends No More: Why Aussies are Shunning Uncle Sam', *The Bulletin*, 23 September 1986, pp. 64–9; *The Australian*, 9 January 1987, p. 2.

48 David Campbell, 'Australian Public Opinion on National Security Issues', Peace Research Centre, working paper no. 1, RSPS, ANU, Canberra, April 1986, p. 38.

49 *New Zealand Herald*, 19 September 1986, p. 4.

50 'Press Conference', Wellington, 19 February 1986, official text.

51 David Lange, address to Auckland Regional Council, NZLP, 9 May 1986, in *Foreign Affairs Record*, vol. 36, no. 2, April–June 1986, p. 16; *The Press*, 21 October 1986, p. 3. Neil Kinnock and Denis Healey argued that a future Labour Government would resume port visits to New Zealand while respecting the anti-nuclear policy, but would not stop US nuclear-armed ships visiting Britain, *New Zealand Herald*, 12 December 1986, p. 9.

52 Baroness Young, 'Old Friends on Different Paths: The British Viewpoint', *NZIR*, vol. 11, no. 4, July–August 1986, p. 22.

53 Michael Pugh, 'Legal Aspects of the *Rainbow Warrior* Affair', *International and Comparative Law Quarterly*, vol. 36, July 1987, p. 666; Ramesh Thakur, 'A Dispute of Many Colours: France, New Zealand and the "Rainbow Warrior" Affair', *World Today*, vol. 42, no. 12, December 1986, pp. 209–13.

54 *The Guardian*, 28 April 1987, p. 7; *New Zealand Herald*, 5 May 1987, p. 21.

55 Lange, 'Foreign Policy Perspectives', address to NZIIA, 30 April 1987, Dunedin, speech notes; *New Zealand Herald*, 2 May 1987, p. 1.

56 Rita Ricketts, 'How Sir Geoffrey Got Offside', *The Dominion*, 25 May 1987, p. 6; Christopher Hitchen, 'New Zealand Feels the Non-Nuclear Fallout', *BBC Listener*, 18 June 1987, p. 7.

57 Senior official, 'U.S. Holds to Framework of ANZUS Alliance', 11 June 1985, Foreign Press Briefing Center, Washington, DC, USIS text.

58 Lange, speech to Geneva Disarmament Conference, 5 March 1985, in *Foreign Affairs Record*, vol. 35, no. 1, January–March 1985, p. 12; Ministry of

Foreign Affairs, *Report*, 31 March 1986, Wellington, pp. 3–4; New Zealand Embassy, testimony, US Congress 99(1), House Foreign Affairs Committee (Subcommittee on Asian and Pacific Affairs), *Hearing on the Security Treaty Between Australia, New Zealand, and the United States*, 18 March 1985, Washington, DC, 1985, p. 20.

59 Richard Kennaway, 'The New Zealand Non Nuclear Initiative: Out of the Frying Pan, Into the Pressure Cooker...?', paper at the Asian Peace Association Conference, Sydney, August 1986.

60 *Auckland Star*, 27 September 1985, p. 1; *New Zealand Herald*, 2 September 1985, p. 3.

61 Interview with Foreign Affairs and National Defense Division, CRS, 18 February 1987, Washington, DC; *NZPD*, 1 (41), no. 68, 5 December 1985 (Lange), p. 8661.

62 Shultz, 'ANZUS, Shultz–Lange Meeting', press release, 2 July 1986, USIS text; *EveningPost*, 18 September 1985, p. 1.

63 *Evening Post*, 30 June 1986, p. 4; *New Zealand Times*, 6 July 1986, p. 1; *NZPD*, 2(41), no. 32, 12 February 1987 (Lange), p. 6980.

64 *New Zealand Herald*, 9 December 1985, p. 4.

65 Ministry of Foreign Affairs, comments on technical aspects of the Bill, and SANA, submission FA/86/813/787W, Parliamentary Select Committee on Foreign Affairs and Defence, General Assembly Library, Wellington, 1986.

66 *Ibid.*, Dr J. Elkind, submission FA/86/75/42W. An absolutist position on the right under UNCLOS of parties to challenge the 'innocent passage' of nuclear-armed vessels is taken by P. Robert Philp, 'The South Pacific Nuclear-Weapon-Free-Zone, the Law of the Sea, and the ANZUS Alliance: An Exploration of Conflicts, a Step Toward World Peace', *California Western International Law Journal*, vol. 16, no. 1, winter 1986, pp. 138–77.

67 Lange, 'Foreign Policy Perspectives'; interview with Helen Clark and Frank O'Flynn, 3 April 1987, Wellington: Elkind, address to Engineers for Social Responsibility, in *New Zealand Engineering*, 1 April 1986, p. 9.

68 *NZPD*, 1 (40), no. 55, 18 September 1985 (Kidd), pp. 6875–6. On the importance of symbolism, see *Auckland Star*, 9 June 1987, p. A8; *NZPD*, 2 (41), no. 43, 4 June 1987 (O'Flynn), pp. 9380–2

69 Interviews with Hon. Paul Cleveland, 3 April 1987, Wellington; Dr Karl Jackson, 10 March 1987, Washington, DC; *New Zealand Herald*, 8 April 1987, p. 6.

70 *The Dominion*, 30 March 1987, pp. 1–2; 7 April 1987, p. 2; *The Press*, 11 April 1987, p. 3.

71 Interview with David Addington, Republican Counsel, HFAC, 2 March 1987, Washington, DC; *New Zealand Herald*, 25 February 1987, p. 12; 28 February 1987, p. 5.

72 Interviews with Gary Brown and Derek Woolmer, Canberra, 25 March 1987; Warren Thomson, 'Comment: Intelligence and the American Connection', *Peace Researcher*, no. 11, 1986, pp. 9–10; Frank O'Flynn, address to the Diplomatic Corps, 7 May 1985, in *Foreign Affairs Record*, vol. 35, no. 2, April–June 1985, p. 22; Steve Hoadley, 'New Zealand–American Logistics Co-operation', *NZIR*, vol. 13, no. 1, January–February 1988, p. 27;

Thomas-Durell Young, 'New Zealand Defence Policy and Labour', *Naval War College Review*, vol. 39, May–June 1986, p. 26; MoD, *Report*, 31 March 1986, Wellington, p. 7; MoD report leaked in *New Zealand Herald*, 28 February 1987, p. 5.

73 Lange, 'Foreign Policy Perspectives'.
74 *New Zealand News UK*, 24 June 1987, p. 3.
75 Lange, 'New Zealand Security Policy', *Foreign Affairs*, summer 1985, p. 1015.

Chapter 8 Regional security and the future of ANZUS

1 *Just Defence Newsletter*, Wellington, May 1986, p. 1.
2 Department of Foreign Affairs submission, Joint Committee on Foreign Affairs and Defence, *The Australian Defence Force: Its Structure and Capabilities*, Canberra, 1984, p. 36. The DoD argued that the responsibility for a global response to Soviet intentions should come from those most directly affected, pp. 62–3.
3 Ross Babbage, 'Considering Alternative Concepts for Australia's Defence', in *Just Defence: Reviewing Australia's Defence Needs*, ANU, Canberra, 1986, pp. 60–79; *The Australian*, 19 November 1986, special report, pp. 5–8; Andrew Mack, 'Defence Versus Offence: The Dibb Report and its Critics', Peace Research Centre, working paper no. 14, RSPS, ANU, Canberra, September 1986.
4 Air Marshal David Evans (retd) and Vice-Admiral David Leach (retd), in *The Australian*, 19 November 1986, special report, pp. 2, 8.
5 Peter Samuel, 'The Dibb Report and Australia's Defense Vagaries', *Strategic Review*, vol. 14, no. 4, fall 1986, pp. 47–53; Samuel and Colin Rubenstein, 'Flaws in Dibb's Doctrine of Retreat into Isolation', *The Australian*, 27 October 1986, p. 7. Admiral James Lyons, in *Weekend Australian*, 21–2 June 1986, p. 3.
6 More important was the limited capacity, for safety reasons, of the RAN's armament depot at Newington, interview with D. Woolmer and G. Brown, Defence Group, Commonwealth Parliamentary Library, Canberra, 25 March 1987. Aboriginal rights and environmental campaigners fear that Jervis Bay will also be the site for a nuclear research reactor, Peace Squadron, letter, Sydney, 26 March 1987; *Canberra Times*, 9 March 1987, p. 1.
7 Beazley, in *The Age*, 20 March 1987, p. 10; *Canberra Times*, 21 March 1987, pp. 1, 3. The RAN gains an increase from 12 to 17 surface vessels, 8 light patrol frigates and Kockums Type 471 conventionally-powered submarines. Air defence is based on the Tactical Fighter Force and integrated radar. Air bases will be sited across the north and a Hornet squadron based in the Northern Territory. Part of the self-reliance is enhancement of defence industries, *National Times on Sunday*, 9 November 1986, p. 19.
8 Interviews with Desmond Ball and G. Brown, Canberra, 25 March 1987; *Canberra Times*, 21 March 1987, p. 1.
9 Ewan Jamieson, 'Defence Dilemmas of Small Countries in the Nuclear Age', *Pacific Defence Reporter*, vol. 13, no. 5, November 1986, pp. 40–1.

10 Ian Bradley, in *New Zealand Herald*, 29 October 1985, p. 7. Even Jamieson agreed that there had been excessive reliance on the US to get defence on the cheap, *New Zealand Herald*, 27 January 1987, p. 5.

11 Ramesh Thakur, 'New Zealand Defence Review 1985–1987', *Asian Defence Journal*, September 1987, pp. 56–65.

12 Malcolm Templeton, *Defence and Security: What New Zealand Needs*, Wellington, 1986, pp. 8–9.

13 Keith Burgess, 'Report on Select Committee on Disarmament and Arms Control', *Peace Movement New Zealand Newsletter*, no. 7, March 1983, p. 9; Marilyn Waring, *Women, Politics and Power*, Wellington, 1985, pp. 116–17.

14 Kevin Clements, 'What's a Quaker Like You Doing on a Committee Like This?', *Friends Newsletter*, part 1, October 1986. The other two members were General Brian Poananga, Chief of Staff 1978–81, and Diane Hunt, a government scientist. It seems that Lange expected the Committee to disagree, thus giving the Government a relatively free hand to pursue the policy of its choice. If so, he was to be disappointed for at an early stage the Committee agreed to work towards a consensus, interview with Clements, Christchurch, 13 April 1987.

15 Asked which countries, if any, posed a military threat to New Zealand 43 per cent did not know or thought that no country did; 31 per cent named the Soviet Union; followed by the United States (14 per cent) and France (13 per cent). Defence Committee of Enquiry, *Defence and Security*, p. 83 and Addendum III, p. 1.

16 Corner's draft and annotations, Defence Enquiry, box 24, University of Canterbury Library (Clements Papers). For example, Corner suggested (*Defence and Security*, p. 9) that the distrust created by the 1944 Australia–New Zealand Agreement had made it difficult to secure a formal guarantee from the United States and that signing the ANZUS Treaty was the most 'independent' act ever taken by New Zealand. As we have seen, the documents suggest that the 1944 Agreement, itself, was the first independent act and was significantly motivated by Anzac distrust of the major powers.

17 Interview with Clements.

18 Singapore and Malaysia regarded this with equanimity, having significantly enhanced their own forces. New Zealand will continue with the Five Power Defence Arrangements and exercises, *New Zealand Herald*, 24 December 1986, p. 1; *Far Eastern Economic Review*, 8 January 1987, pp. 15–16.

19 Jim Bolger, in *New Zealand Herald*, 28 February 1987, p. 5; Brigadier Hamilton, in *New Zealand Herald*, 23 April 1984, pp. 4–6; *RSA Review*, April 1987, p. 1.

20 Owen Wilkes, 'Alternative Defence and Security Arrangements Aotearoa', in Barbara Harford (ed.), *Beyond ANZUS*, Wellington, 1984, p. 143; Hunn, submission 49, Defence Enquiry, box 1; Scott Thomson, 'New Zealand Defence: Lessons from the South Atlantic', *NZIR*, vol. 10, no. 4, July–August 1985, p. 19; Corner, in *New Zealand Herald*, 28 February 1987, p. 5.

21 Corner, in *New Zealand Herald*, 13 December 1986, p. 5.

22 Templeton, pp. 9–10.

23 *Report*, 67th Annual Conference, NZLP, Auckland, 2–5 September 1983, pp. 39–40. See also, Templeton, p. 24.
24 Cited in Templeton, p. 38.
25 *The Australian*, 21–2 November 1987, p. 3; *The Press*, 7 March 1987, p. 1; DoD, 'Joint Communiqué, Australia and New Zealand Defence Ministers' Meeting, Wellington', 5–6 March 1987.
26 *Auckland Star*, 10 June 1987, p. A12; *New Zealand Herald*, 28 January 1987, p. 16; R. J. Tizard, 'Re-equipping the Navy in New Zealand', *The Australian*, 6 November 1987, defence report, p. 20.
27 Greg Fry, submission, Senate Committee on Foreign Affairs and Defence, *Australia's Defence Co-operation with its Neighbours in the Asian-Pacific Region*, Canberra, 1984, p. 31.
28 Dept. of Foreign Affairs, submission, Joint Committee on Foreign Affairs and Defence, 'Enquiry into Australia's Relations with the South Pacific', Canberra, 1987.
29 Jonathan Alford, 'Security Dilemmas of Small States', *The World Today*, August–September 1984, pp. 363–7.
30 Robert C. Kiste and R. A. Herr, 'The Potential for Soviet Penetration of the South Pacific Islands: An Assessment', *Bulletin of Concerned Asian Scholars*, vol. 18, no. 2, 1986, p. 55; Dept of Foreign Affairs, submission, Joint Committee on Foreign Affairs and Defence, 'Relations with the South Pacific', p. 38; Tom Millar, 'Soviet Aims, Targets and Instruments in the South West Pacific', Hoover Institution conference paper, Washington, DC, 3–4 March 1987; Paul Dibb, 'Soviet Strategy Towards Australia, New Zealand and the South-West Pacific', *Australian Outlook*, vol. 39, no. 2, August 1985, pp. 70, 75; Edward W. Desmond, 'Rivalry in the Pacific', *Time*, 24 November 1986, p. 5.
31 *New Zealand Herald*, 4 May 1987, p. 1; *Dominion Sunday Times*, 3 May 1987, p. 1. For Australia, kicking Libya was cost free, whereas New Zealand made clear it would not jeopardize trade with Libya, Paul Malone, 'Why Hawke Kicked Out Gadaffi's men', *Canberra Times*, 23 May 1987, p. 2.
32 See, Greg Fry, 'Regionalism and International Politics of the South Pacific', *Pacific Affairs*, vol. 54, fall 1981, pp. 468–9; F. A. Mediansky, 'Nuclear Free Security in the South-West Pacific?', *Australian Outlook*, vol. 39, no. 2, August 1985, pp. 77–83; P. Lewis Young, 'New Zealand's Role in Regional Security', *Pacific Defence Reporter*, vol. 12, no. 1, July 1985, pp. 10–11.
33 *The Australian*, 12 January 1987, p. 6. Australian commentators argued that France has long suspected an Anglophone plot to drive it out of the Pacific, *National Times on Sunday*, 18 January 1987, p. 9.
34 Cited by Doug Craig, 'Fighting Against a New Colonialism', *Peacelink*, no. 47, December 1986, p. 6. Vanuatu has been characterized as having the rhetoric of non-alignment but effective integration with the West, Ralph Premdas and Michael C. Howard, 'Vanuatu's Foreign Policy: Contradictions and Constraints', *Australian Outlook*, vol. 39, no. 3, December 1985, p. 177.
35 John Dorrance, *Oceania and the United States: an analysis of U.S. interests and policy in the South Pacific*, Washington, DC, 1980, pp. 55, 67.
36 Alva M. Bowen and Ronald O'Rourke, 'Ports for the Fleet', *Proceedings/*

Naval Review, vol. 112, May 1986, p. 148; Catherine Lutz, 'The Compact of Free Association, Micronesian Non-Independence, and U.S. Policy', *Bulletin of Concerned Asian Scholars*, vol. 18, no. 2, 1986, pp. 21–7; Giff Johnson, 'Collision Course at Kwajalein', *Bulletin of Concerned Asian Scholars*, vol. 18, no. 2, 1986, pp. 28–39.

37 Rawdon Dalrymple, 'The Pacific at a Turning Point. How will We Respond?', to World Affairs Council, San Francisco, 18 February 1986, *Vital Speeches of the Day*, 1 April 1986, vol. 52, no. 12, pp. 356–7.

38 Jean Chesneaux, 'French Involvement in the Pacific', New Zealand Peace Foundation lecture, Auckland, 1986; Bengt and Marie-Thérèse Danielsson, *Poisoned Reign. French Nuclear Colonialism in the Pacific*, Australia, 1986, pp. 303–7.

39 Suliana Siwatibau and B. David Williams, *A Call to a New Exodus*, Suva, 1982, pp. 68–9; Gabrielle Panckhurst, 'Who Controls the Pacific', *Peacelink*, no. 16, February 1984, pp. 10–11. Catholic Action of Hawaii argued that their islands were the most nuclearized in the Pacific, in *The Dark Side of Paradise*. Other classics in the anti-nuclear canon are the Danielssons' *Poisoned Reign*, updating *Moruroa, Mon Amour*, 1977; Peter Hayes, Lyuba Zarsky and Walden Bello, *American Lake: Nuclear Peril in the Pacific*, Australia, 1986.

40 In Helen Clark, *Disarmament and Arms Control. Report of the Select Committee on Foreign Affairs and Defence*, Wellington, 1985, pp. 135–6.

41 *The Bulletin*, 13 March 1984; Robert G. Sutter, 'Oceania and the United States: A Primer', CRS report no. 85–218F, 25 November 1985, Washington, DC, p. 21; Clark, *Disarmament and Arms Control*, p. 134.

42 In Clark, *Disarmament and Arms Control*, pp. 133–4.

43 *New Zealand Herald*, 8 April 1987, p. 6; Jone Daknunla, 'Fijian Anti-Nuclear Movement Revives', *Peacelink*, no. 27, February 1985, p. 10. Interview with Russ Surber, Pacific Islands desk, State Dept., Washington, DC, 10 March 1987.

44 *The Age*, 20 May 1987, p. 6.

45 The presence of the Hercules was explained by a US official as necessary to evacuate an injured sailor from the *Belleau Wood*, which is not without its own medical facilities, *Canberra Times*, 26 May 1987, p. 1; documentary on Australian SBS-TV, 15 November 1987; Colin James, 'CIA plot – or not?', *Sunday Star*, reproduced in, *New Zealand News UK*, pp. 13–14; *The Guardian*, 17 June 1987, p. 6.

46 Kiste and Herr, 'Potential for Soviet Penetration', p. 57.

47 Henry Albinski, testimony, US Congress, 99(1), House Foreign Affairs Committee (Subcommittee on Asian and Pacific Affairs), *Hearing on the Security Treaty Between Australia, New Zealand, and the United States*, 18 March 1985, Washington, DC, 1985, p. 118.

48 Greg Fry, 'Toward a South Pacific Nuclear-Free Zone', *Bulletin of the Atomic Scientists*, vol. 41, no. 6, June-July 1985, p. 18; *The Press*, 9 August 1986, p. 1.

49 *National Times on Sunday*, 18 January 1987, p. 2; Michael Hamel-Green, 'South Pacific: A not-so-Nuclear-Free Zone', *Peace Studies*, November–December 1985, pp. 42–3.

50 Joint Committee on Foreign Affairs and Defence, *Disarmament and Arms*

Control in the Nuclear Age, Canberra, 1986, pp. 704–5; Peter Samuel and Colin Rubenstein, 'How the US is losing the Pacific', *Weekend Australian*, 25–6 October 1986, p. 24.

51 US Congress, 99(2), House Armed Services Committee, *Report of the Delegation to the South Pacific*, Washington, DC, 1986, pp. 3–8, 11; F. A. Mediansky, 'Washington Startled by a Roaring Mouse Down Under', *The Bulletin*, 11 November 1986, p. 119; 'The CINCPAC View', *Pacific Defence Reporter*, December 1985–January 1986, p. 57; Crowe interview, '"Softly, Softly" Will Ease ANZUS Crisis', *Pacific Islands Monthly*, December 1984, p. 17; Robert G. Sutter, 'Australia, New Zealand, and the Pacific Islands: Issues for U.S. Policy', CRS report no. IB86158, 29 January 1987, Washington, DC, p. 6.

52 Richard D. Fisher, 'Why the U.S. must oppose the South Pacific Nuclear Free Zone', Asian Studies Center Backgrounder no. 55, Heritage Foundation, 23 December 1986, p. 11; Peter Watson, in *New Zealand Herald*, 2 April 1987, p. 6.

53 *Canberra Times*, 11 June 1987, p. 4.

54 *Parliamentary Debates*, Commons, 6s., vol. 112, no. 77, written answer, 20 March 1987 (Renton), col. 639.

55 *Soviet News* (London), 17 December 1986, p. 518.

56 *Sydney Morning Herald*, 12 February 1987, p. 9; 23 April 1987, p. 2; *Canberra Times*, 22 April 1987, p. 1; *New Zealand Herald*, 13 February 1987, p. 5; 23 August 1987, p. 10. The Australian Ambassador in Washington, Rawdon Dalrymple, argued that it would be more difficult for countries of the region to continue to support Western security objectives, *Le Monde diplomatique*, November 1985, p. 14.

57 *The Dominion*, 2 May 1986, p. 5.

58 *Canberra Times*, 14 August 1986, p. 4.

59 Jim McLay, 'Managing the ANZUS Alliance', in Hyam Gold (ed.), *New Directions in New Zealand Foreign Policy*, Auckland, 1985, pp. 94–5

60 Helen Clark, 'What Price Security?', *New Zealand Listener*, 20–6 September 1986, p. 34.

61 Dora Alves, 'The submarine's role in Soviet Pacific strategy', *Pacific Defence Reporter*, vol. 11, no. 3, September 1984, pp. 10–14.

62 Coral Bell, 'Australian Defence and Regional Security: The American Effect and the Future', *Australian Outlook*, vol. 38, no. 3, December 1984, pp. 207–8.

63 Gay Davidson, in *Canberra Times*, 13 August 1986, p. 2; 'John Edwards Reports', *The Bulletin*, 19 August 1986, p. 24.

64 Joseph Camilleri, 'Nuclear Disarmament: An Emerging Issue in Australian Politics', Australian Studies Centre, working paper no. 9, Institute of Commonwealth Studies, University of London, May 1986, p. 8.

65 William T. Tow and William R. Feeney (eds.), *U.S. Foreign Policy and Asian–Pacific Security, A Transregional Approach*, Boulder, Colorado, 1982, pp. 233–5.

66 Peter Samuel and F. P. Serong, 'The Troubled Waters of ANZUS', *Strategic Review*, vol. 14, no. 1, winter, 1986, p. 47.

Chapter 9 The ANZUS crisis, nuclear visiting and the Western Alliance

1 *USA Today*, 8 March 1985, p. 5. Senators agreed, and extended favourable interest repayments as well as credits for the purchase of 40 F-16 aircraft, *Washington Post*, 28 March 1985, p. 12.

2 Material supplied by Hon. J. I. Carbajal, Minister, Spanish Embassy, London.

3 *Keesing's Contemporary Archives*, 10 July 1981, p. 30972; David C. Morrison, 'Japanese principles', U.S. policies', *Bulletin of the Atomic Scientists*, June–July 1985, pp. 22–4.

4 Glenn D. Hook, 'The Nuclearization of Language: Nuclear Allergy as Political Metaphor', *Journal of Peace Research*, vol. 21, no. 3, 1984, pp. 268, 272, n. 21.

5 La Rocque, testimony, US Congress, 93(2), Joint Atomic Energy Committee (Subcommittee on Military Applications), *Hearing on the Proliferation of Nuclear Weapons*, 10 September 1974, Washington, DC, p. 18. US officials refused to comment on the testimony but were concerned that it might affect port visits to Japan, *Japan Times*, 7 October 1974, p. 2. La Rocque's career included command of a carrier task group and seven years at the Pentagon.

6 Hook, 'Nuclearization of Language', pp. 271–2, n. 4; Robert Y. Horiguchi, 'Kiwi Disease – Japanese Version', *Pacific Defence Reporter*, vol. 10, no. 12, June 1985, p. 48.

7 At its 1985 conference the strongly pro-NATO Independence Party, which has traditionally had a prominent influence on Icelandic external policy, did not exclude the possibility of nuclear weapons being introduced if 'approved by the Icelandic authorities'. *Ályktanir*, 26 Landsfundar, Sjálf-stæðisflokksins, 11–14 Apríl 1985, Reykjavík, p.24. Controversies about the Keflavík base have originated in fears that it poses a threat of cultural erosion. It is used primarily for maritime surveillance, but hosts a fighter squadron and has the capability to support larger scale air operations and transit traffic. Without Keflavík, Norway or the Færoes would have to be considered as an alternative bridgehead. Thus, Icelandic policy is a prerequisite for the no-base policies of Denmark and Norway, Gunnar Gunnarsson, 'Iceland Security Policy: Context and Trends', *Conflict and Cooperation*, vol. 17, 1982, p. 265.

8 *de Handelingen, Tweede Kamer*, 31 (1960–1), 14 December 1960 (Bakker, Visser), pp. 379–86. See generally, the chapters on the Netherlands, Denmark, Norway and Greece, in Nils Ørvik (ed.), *Semialignment and Western Security*, London, 1986.

9 *Forhandlinger i Stortinget*, 15 (1975–6), 21 October 1975 (Henriksen, Foster-voll, Bratteli), pp. 118–20 (translation by the author and Jon Grepstad); Chris Prebensen, *Norway and Nato*, Oslo, 1974, p. 19.

10 Udenrigsministeriet, *Dansk Sikkerhedspolitik 1948–1966*, Copenhagen, 1968, p. 116; Resolution of Greenland, 16 November 1984, in *Revue de droit international public*, vol. 89, 1985, p. 451; Sverre Lodgaard, 'Nuclear disengagement', in Lodgaard and Marek Thee, *Nuclear Disengagement in Europe*, London, 1983, p. 10.

11 *Fortryk af folketingets forhandlinger* (1982–3), 6 July 1983 (Auken, Engell), skriftligt besvarede spørgsmål, nr. S 1383, col. 13125.

12 Keith D. Suter, *Nuclear Free Zones: Some Basic Questions*, Australian NFZ Secretariat, Sydney, 1985, pp. 11–12; Nic Maclellan, 'Speak No Evil: The "Neither Confirm Nor Deny" Policy', *Peace Magazine*, Australia, February–March 1987, p. 20.

13 Correspondence supplied by Southampton City Secretary and Solicitor's Office.

14 Alva M. Bowen and Ronald O'Rourke, 'Ports for the Fleet', *Proceedings/ Naval Review*, vol. 112, May 1986, p. 148; Democrats letter to *New York Post*, 22 January 1985, New Jersey campaigners were also concerned about storage of nuclear weapons at the Naval Munitions Depot at Leonardo, *Newark Star-Ledger*, 27 November 1984, p. 8; Weiss, testimony, US Congress, 99(2), House Armed Services Committee (Subcommittee on Military Installations and Facilities), *Hearings on HR 4181 to Authorize Certain Construction at Military Installations for FY 1987*, 26 February 1986, Washington, DC, pp. 2–5; Simeon Sahaycachny, *Nuclear Trojan Horse – The Navy's Plan to Base Nuclear Weapons in New York Harbor*, New York, 1985, pp. 44, 51.

15 Sweden reportedly cancelled a visit by two USN ships in October 1985 which would have joined destroyer HMS *Liverpool*, but it is suggested that Sweden was concerned about an unacceptably high NATO presence in the country, *Jane's Defence Weekly*, 5 October 1985, p. 719; *Christian Science Monitor*, 30 July 1985, p. 8; North Atlantic Network, *Newsletter*, November 1985, p. 1.

16 W. Laqueur, ' "Hollanditis": A New Stage in European Neutralism', *Commentary*, vol. 72, no. 2, February 1981, pp. 19–26; Hook, pp. 263–71.

17 *New Zealand News UK*, 18 February 1987, p. 19. See also *Nuclear-Free*, December 1986, pp. 1–2; *Auckland Star*, 7 January 1987, p. A8; *New Zealand Herald*, 23 December 1986, p. 2.

18 *Sydney Morning Herald*, 11 July 1987, p. 19; *The Guardian*, 11 July 1987, p. 2.

19 Interview with Hon. Paul Cleveland, US Ambassador to New Zealand, Wellington, 3 April 1987; *Auckland Star*, 18 February 1985, p. 7.

20 Washington denied that assurances had been given about the status of the ships, *Philadelphia Inquirer*, 12 April 1985, p. 18; *Washington Post*, 8 August 1984, p. 17; 17 August 1984, p. 16; 21 August 1984, p. 1; 11 April 1985, p. 1; 16 April 1985, p. 20; *Christian Science Monitor*, 15 May 1985, p. 11.

21 Constitution adopted by the Constitutional Commission on 15 October 1986, art. 2, Declaration of principles and state policies section 8, *Philippine Law Gazette*, vol. 9, no. 5 (special issue), November 1986, p. 3; *The Guardian*, 21 August 1987, p. 8; 13 May 1988, p. 10.

22 The translation of this reservation was offered by Gunnar Gunnarsson from: 'Ég tel ekki þörf frekar að taka af öll tvímæli í þessum efnum, vegna þess að af hálfu íslenskra stjórnvalda og aðildarríkja Atlantshafsbandalagsins hafa engin tvímæli átt sér stað.' *Alpingistíðindi Umræður*, 22, (1984–5), 16 April 1985 (Sigfússon, Hallgrímsson), sp. nr. 16, cols 4208–10.

23 *Jane's Defence Weekly*, vol. 3, no. 22, 1 June 1985, p. 968; Gunnar Gunnarsson, 'Icelandic Security Policy: Context and Trends', *Cooperation and Conflict*, vol. 17, 1982, p. 262.

24 He strongly implied that if the Government made a statement prohibiting nuclear weapons on warships, the allies would cease to visit, *Forhandlinger i Stortinget* (1984–5), 18 February 1985 (Henriksen, Sjaastad), sp. nr. 24, unofficial translation by Norwegian Embassy, London; Nei Til Atomvåpen, press release 7 February 1985.

25 'New Zealand har stillet krav om, at USA afgiver en erklæring, der fastlår, at et krigskib', *Fortryk af folketingets forhandlinger* (1984–5), 27 February 1985 (Engell) skriftligt besvarede spørgsmål, col. 7247; 2 October 1985 (Albrechtsen), sp. nr. S 1, cols 119–20. The Socialist People's Party prepared a law to keep nuclear weapons out of Denmark, *Land og Folk*, 5 November 1985, p. 3.

26 *Evening Post*, 30 June 1986, p. 4.

27 Joint Committee on Foreign Affairs and Defence, *The ANZUS Alliance*, Canberra, 1982, pp. 48–9.

28 Ball, cited in *Evening Post*, 14 December 1985; Nicky Hager, submission FA/86/1200, 1176, Parliamentary Select Committee on Foreign Affairs and Defence, General Assembly Library, Wellington.

29 See, Stanley R. Sloan, Alva M. Bowen and Ronald O'Rourke, Congressional Research Service, Library of Congress, 'The Implications for Strategic Arms Control of Nuclear Sea Launched Cruise Missiles', Congressional Research Service, Library of Congress, Report no. 86–25, Washington, DC, 1985.

30 A. Gsponer, 'Technical Feasibility of the Detection of Nuclear Weapons', in Lodgaard and Thee (eds.), *Nuclear Disengagement*, pp. 209–19; Milton Leitenberg, 'The Case of the Stranded Sub', *Bulletin of the Atomic Scientists*, vol. 38, no. 3, March 1982, pp. 10–13. It is relatively easy to detect plutonium in aircraft, within a few metres and in a few minutes, using counters. See also, *Ekstra Bladet*, 4 October 1985, p. 7.

31 In addition, specially-equipped US SR-71A Blackbirds flying over Israel were rumoured to have detected nuclear materials being moved during the 1973 Arab-Israeli War, Gary Brown, 'Detection of Nuclear Weapons and the US Non-Disclosure Policy', Canberra, 1986, *passim*; Hoag Levins, *Arab Reach. The Secret War Against Israel*, London, 1983, pp. 50–1; Barry M. Belchman and Douglas M. Hart, 'The Political Utility of Nuclear Weapons: The 1973 Middle East Crisis', *International Security*, vol. 7, no. 1, summer 1982, pp. 132–56.

32 *The Times*, 12 December 1987, p. 5; BBC Radio 4 News, 11 January 1988.

33 Russell Hibbs, 'An Uncontrollable Tomahawk?', *Proceedings/Naval Review*, vol. 111, January 1985, pp. 65–70.

34 Klaus Törnudd, 'Possible Rules Regulating the Transit of Nuclear Weapons Inside and Their Deployment Outside a Nordic NWFZ', in Lodgaard and Thee (eds.), pp. 199–208; Donna J. Klick, 'A Balkan Nuclear Weapons-Free Zone: Viability of the Régime and Implications for Crisis Management', *Journal of Peace Research*, vol. 24, no. 2, 1987, pp. 117–22.

35 Bowen and O'Rourke, 'Ports for the Fleet', p. 151; William Arkin, 'Confirm or deny', *Bulletin of the Atomic Scientists*, vol. 41, no. 11, December 1985, pp. 4–5.

36 *Daily Telegraph*, 18 April 1988, p. 9; *The Guardian*, 28 April 1988, p. 7; Sven Auken, letter, 30 April 1988, p. 18.
37 See, David J. Dunn, 'NATO Navies and Arms Control', in R. B. Byers (ed.), *The Denuclearisation of the Oceans*, London, 1986, pp. 187–96.
38 Canada, *Parliamentary Debates*, House of Commons, 1 (33), vol. 111, 19 March 1985 (Turner), p. 3150. The New Democrats would also disconnect linkages with American nuclear strategies and the North American Aerospace Defense Command, but the defence white paper of 1987, *Challenge and Commitment*, underlined Canada's collaboration in nuclear strategies. Consternation had been caused by revelations at the end of 1984 of a Pentagon contingency plan for the crisis deployment of B–57 depth bombs to Canada, Spain, Iceland, Bermuda and Puerto Rico, unknown to the governments concerned. The Canadian Government played down the issue as a hypothetical contingency, but Iceland's Prime Minister called publicly for an explanation. Leslie H. Gelb, 'US Plan for Deploying A-arms Wasn't Disclosed to Host Nations', *New York Times*, 13 February 1985, p. 1.
39 John M. Goshko, 'Pentagon Making Contingency Plans To Remove Bases From Greece in '88', *Washington Post*, 15 February 1985, p. 14.
40 Unofficial translation from the Danish Embassy, London.
41 Ørvik (ed.), *Semialignment*, pp. 1–7, 197; Harto Hakovirta, 'European "Neutralism" in East–West System change', in Hakovirta (ed.), *Fragmentation and Integration, Aspects of International System Change*, Helsinki, 1986, pp. 37–9. For an alarmist view of 'neutralism' see, Paolo Stoppa-Liebl and Walter Laqueur, 'Europe After INF', *Washington Quarterly*, vol. 8, no. 2, spring 1985, p. 81.
42 See, Gregory Flynn and Hans Rittinger, *The Public and Atlantic Defense*, London, 1985, *passim*; Bertel Heurlin, 'Danish Security Policy', *Cooperation and Conflict*, vol. 17, 1982, pp. 237–55. The attempt by centre and left-wing Nordic parliamentarians to keep the NFZ issue alive in the 1980s, to maintain a low state of tension in the northern seas, conflicted with US naval doctrine which emphasized the importance of throwing the USSR off balance by deploying as far forward as possible. The most promising area for maritime nuclear arms control might be the Baltic, where Soviet submarine capability has been in decline. The Soviet leader, Mikhail Gorbachev, reiterated the USSR's interest in a Baltic agreement in his speech to the 1987 Party Congress.
43 Ørvik (ed.), *Semialignment*, p. 253.
44 Ted Galen Carpenter, 'Pursuing a Strategic Divorce: the U.S. and the ANZUS Alliance', Policy Analysis, no. 67, Cato Institute, Washington, DC, 27 February 1986, pp. 13–14.
45 In Karl H. Czerny and Henry W. Briefs, *Nato in Quest of Cohesion*, New York, 1965, p. 125.
46 *Washington Times*, 25 February 1985, p. 8B.
47 Kunio Muraoka, *Japanese Security and the United States*, Adelphi Paper 95, IISS, London, February 1973, pp. 23–8; *Jane's Defence Weekly*, vol. 3, no. 10, 9 March 1985, p. 397.
48 Owen Harries, 'Crisis in the Pacific', *Commentary*, vol. 79, no. 6, June 1985, p. 53.

BIBLIOGRAPHY

Primary sources

Official papers and publications

All federal printed items are published by the Australian Government Publishing Service, Canberra.

Executive

Australia Official Year Book, 1985.

Australian Science and Technology Council, *Australia's Role in the Nuclear Fuel Cycle*, 1984.

Department of Defence and Australian Atomic Energy Commission, *Environmental Considerations of Nuclear Powered Warships to Australia*, May 1976.

Department of Defence, *Australian Defence*, 1976.

[Department of Defence], Dibb, Paul, *Review of Australia's Defence Capabilities: Report to the Minister for Defence*, March 1986.

Department of Defence, *The Defence of Australia*, 1987.

'Joint Communiqué, Australia and New Zealand Defence Ministers' Meeting, Wellington', 5–6 March 1987.

Department of Foreign Affairs, *Annual Report*.

Australian Foreign Affairs Record.

'Australian Note Concerning Staging of USAF Aircraft Through RAAF Base Darwin, and Supplement', 11 March 1981.

[Department of Foreign Affairs], Hayden, William G., MP, *Uranium, The Joint Facilities, Disarmament and Peace*, 4 July 1984.

Department of Foreign Affairs, 'Joint Communiqué After Australian–United States Ministerial Talks at San Francisco', news release, 12 August 1986.

'New Zealand Visit, Arrival Statement' (Hayden), news release, 10 December 1986.

'Visit to New Zealand, Joint Statement' (Lange and Hayden), news release, 12 December 1986.

Report of the Royal Commission into British Nuclear Tests in Australia, 2 vols, 1985.

254

Parliamentary

Commonwealth of Australia Parliamentary Debates (APD):
  House of Representatives (HR).
  Senate.
Ranger Uranium Environmental Inquiry, *First Report*, Parliamentary Paper no. 309, vol. 15, 1976.
Joint Committee on Foreign Affairs and Defence, *Threats to Australia's Security*, 1981.
  The ANZUS Alliance. Australian–United States' Relations, Parliamentary Paper no. 318, 1982.
  The Australian Defence Force: Its Structure and Capabilities, 1984.
  Disarmament and Arms Control in the Nuclear Age, 1986.
  'Enquiry into Australia's Relations with the South Pacific', unpublished submissions, 1987.
Senate Committee on Foreign Affairs and Defence, *Australia's Defence Co-operation with its Neighbours in the Asia–Pacific Region*, 1984.
  'Enquiry into Safety Procedures Relating to Nuclear Powered or Armed Vessels in Australian Waters', unpublished submissions, 1986–7.
Victoria Parliamentary Debates (VPD), Government Printer, Melbourne: Legislative Assembly.
  Council.
Tasmania Parliamentary Debates (TPD), Government Printer, Tasmania: House of Assembly.

NEW ZEALAND

All printed items are published by the Government Printer, Wellington.

Executive

New Zealand National Archives, Accession 1784, External Affairs, 59/5/17, Warship Visits 1945–57, Wellington.
New Zealand Official Year Book, 1985–7.
Defence Committee of Enquiry on the Future of New Zealand Strategic and Security Policies, unpublished submissions and draft report, 1986, University of Canterbury Library, Christchurch (Clements Papers).
Defence Committee of Enquiry, *Defence and Security: What New Zealanders Want*, and *Public Opinion Poll*, July 1986.
Ministry of Defence, *Annual Report*.
  Defence of New Zealand, Review of Defence Policy, 1987.
Ministry of Foreign Affairs, *New Zealand Foreign Affairs Review* (formerly *External Affairs Review*).
  Annual Report.
  Disarmament and Arms Control (Green Paper), 1978.
  Disarmament and Arms Control, Information Bulletins, 1981–5.
New Zealand Atomic Energy Committee, *New Zealand Code for Nuclear Powered Shipping, AEC 500*, AEC, Wellington, 1976.
[New Zealand Government], *The Defence Question: A Discussion Paper*, 1985.

Kay, Robin (ed.), *Documents on New Zealand External Relation*, 3 vols, Historical Publications Branch, Wellington, 1972–5.

Lange, Rt. Hon. David, 'Questions and Answers on the Anti Nuclear Legislation', mimeo, 1985.

The Shape of the Future, 1987.

'Press Conference', transcript, Wellington, 27 April 1987.

Parliamentary

New Zealand Parliamentary Debates (NZPD).

Select Committee on Disarmament and Arms Control, *Prohibition of Nuclear Vessels and Weapons Bill* (Beetham), unpublished submissions, 1983, General Assembly Library, Wellington.

[Select Committee on Foreign Affairs and Defence], Clark, Helen, MP, *Disarmament and Arms Control, Report of the Select Committee on Foreign Affairs and Defence*, 1985.

Select Committee on Foreign Affairs and Defence, *New Zealand Nuclear Free Zone Disarmament and Arms Control Bill* (Lange), unpublished submissions, 1986, General Assembly Library, Wellington.

UNITED STATES

All printed items are published by the Government Printing Office, Washington, DC.

Executive

Executive Orders, *Title 3 – The President-Code of Federal Regulations*, Compilations, 1949–53; 1971–5; 1978–9 (*CFR Comp.*).

US Court of Appeals, *Weinberger v. Catholic Action of Hawaii*, 9th Circuit, no. 80–1377, 1981, pp. 139–50.

US Code.

US Statutes.

US Treaty Series.

Department of State Bulletin.

'Press Conference ANZUS Council Meeting', Wellington, 16–17 July 1984, USIS text.

Crowe, Admiral William J., 'Press Conference', Port Moresby, 15 October 1984, USIS text, Wellington.

Jackson, Karl D., 'U.S. Ponders New Relationship with New Zealand', testimony House Foreign Affairs Committee (Subcommittee on Asian and Pacific Affairs), 25 September 1986, USIS text.

Lilley, James R., 'New Zealand Remains "A Good Friend"', testimony House Foreign Affairs Committee (Subcommittee on Asian and Pacific Affairs), 25 September 1986, USIS text.

'Remarks at the ANZUS Ministerial Session', Canberra, 15 July 1985, USIS text.

'Shultz–Lange Meeting', Manila, Press Conference 27 June 1986 and clarification of remarks, 2 July 1986, USIS text.

Shultz, George, 'On Alliance Responsibility', address at East-West Center, Hawaii, 17 July 1985, US Dept. of State text.

Congressional Reports

Congressional Record (CR).
Code Congressional and Administrative News.
Executive Series of the Senate Foreign Relations Committee, 1951 (Historical Series), vol. 3, part 1 (1976).
90(2), House Armed Services Committee (Special Subcommittee on National Defense Posture), *Review of U.S. Military Commitments Abroad; Phase III, Rio and ANZUS Pacts*, 31 December 1968 (1968).
93(2), Senate, *Nuclear Incidents – Compensation for Damages – U.S. Warships*, Senate Report 93–1281, 1974 (1974).
94(1), Joint Atomic Energy Committee, *Development, Use and Control of Nuclear Energy for the Common Defense and Security and for Peaceful Purposes*, Annual Report to Congress, 30 June 1975 (1975).
94(2), Senate Foreign Relations Committee, *The South West Pacific: Report of a Special Delegation*, February 1976 (1976).
94(2), House Armed Services Committee, *Report of the Ad Hoc Subcommittee on the Pacific*, 25 May 1976 (1976).
96(2), House Interior and Insular Affairs Committee, *Activities of the Subcommittee on Pacific Affairs Including a Report of the Oversight Inspection Trip of January 3 to 17, 1980* (1981).
96(2), Joint Economic Committee, *Pacific Region Interdependencies*, compendium of papers, 15 June 1981 (1981).
99(2), House Armed Services Committee, *Report of the Delegation to the South Pacific*, February 1986 (1986).
Selected Materials on Atomic Energy Indemnity and Insurance Legislation, printed for the use of the Joint Atomic Energy Committee (1974).
House Foreign Affairs Committee, *U.S. Relations with the Pacific Area: Report of a Study Mission to Fiji, New Zealand, Australia, Singapore, 1981* (1981).

Congressional Hearings

92(1–2), Joint Atomic Energy Committee (Subcommittee on Military Applications), *Hearings and Subsequent Inquiry on Nuclear Propulsion for Naval Warships*, 5 May 1971–30 September 1972 (1972).
93(1), Joint Atomic Energy Committee, *Hearings on Nuclear Reactor Safety*, part I, phase IIa, January–October 1973 (1973).
93(1), Senate Foreign Relations Committee, *Hearings on Nuclear Weapons in Europe*, March–April 1974 (1975).
93(2), Joint Atomic Energy Committee, *Hearing To Consider NATO Matters*, 19 February 1974 (1975).
93(2), Joint Atomic Energy Committee, *Hearing on Weapons Program Authorization Request, FY 1975*, 20 February 1974 (1975).
93(2), Joint Atomic Energy Committee, *Hearing on Naval Nuclear Propulsion Program, 1974*, 25 February 1974 (1975).
93(2), Joint Atomic Energy Committee (Subcommittee on Military Applications), *Hearing on Proliferation of Nuclear Weapons*, 10 September 1974 (1975).
94(1), Joint Atomic Energy Committee (Subcommittee on Legislation), *Hearings on Naval Nuclear Propulsion Program, 1975*, 5 March 1975 (1975).

96(1), Senate Foreign Relations Committee, *Hearings on Overseas Military Presence*, April 1979 (1979).

96(1), House Foreign Affairs Committee (Subcommittee on Asian and Pacific Affairs), *Hearings on The Pacific Community Idea*, July–October 1979 (1979)

97(1), House Armed Services Committee (Subcommittee on Procurement and Military Nuclear Systems), *Hearing on HR 2969, Dept. of Energy Authorization of Naval Nuclear Propulsion Program, 1981*, 9 March 1981 (1981).

97(2), Senate Foreign Relations Committee, *Hearings on East-West Relations: Focus on the Pacific*, 10 and 16 June 1982 (1982).

97(2), Senate Foreign Relations Committee, *Hearings on U.S. Policies and Programs in Southeast Asia*, June–July 1982 (1982).

97(2), Senate Foreign Relations Committee, *Hearing on U.S. Strategic Doctrine*, 4 December 1982 (1983).

97(2), Senate Foreign Relations Committee, *Hearing on Nomination of Paul D. Wolfowitz to be Assistant Secretary of State, East Asian and Pacific Affairs*, 9 December 1982 (1983).

98(2), House Armed Services Committee (Subcommittee on Procurement and Military Nuclear Systems), *Hearing on HR 5263, Dept. of Energy, National Security Programs and Authorization Act, FY 1985*, 28 February 1984 (1984).

99(1), Senate Foreign Relations Committee, *Hearings on Commitments, Consensus and U.S. Foreign Policy*, January–November 1985 (1985).

99(1), Senate Foreign Relations Committee, *Hearing on the Philippine Presidential Election*, 23 January 1986 (1986).

99(1), House Foreign Affairs Committee (Subcommittee on Asian and Pacific Affairs), *Hearing on the Security Treaty Between Australia, New Zealand and the United States*, 18 March 1985 (1985).

99(2), House Armed Services Committee (Subcommittee on Military Installations and Facilities), *Hearing on Base Closures and Realignments*, 12 June 1985 (1985).

99(2), House Armed Services Committee (Subcommittee on Military Installations and Facilities), *Hearings on HR 4181 to Authorize Certain Construction at Military Installations for FY 1987*, February–March 1986 (1986).

Congressional Research Service, Foreign Affairs and National Defense Division, Library of Congress

O'Rourke, Ronald, 'Nuclear-Powered and Nuclear-Weapon-Capable Ships in the U.S. Navy: An Aid to Identification', Report no. 86–659 F, 16 April 1986.

Sutter, Robert G., 'Crisis in U.S.–New Zealand Relations: Issues for Congress', Report no. 85–92 F, 26 February 1985.
'Oceania and the United States: A Primer', Report no. 85–218 F, 25 November 1985.
'Australia, New Zealand, and the Pacific Islands: Issues for U.S. Policy', issue brief 1B86158, 29 January 1987.

OTHERS

'Convention on Liability of Operators of Nuclear Ships', Brussels, 25 May 1962, *American Journal of International Law*, vol. 57, 1963, pp. 268–78.

OECD Nuclear Energy Authority, *Nuclear Legislation Analytical Study. Regulatory and Institutional Framework for Nuclear Activities*, 2 vols, Paris, 1983–4.

UN Legislative Series, *National Legislation and Treaties Relating to the Law of the Sea*, vols B/15–19, UN, New York, 1980.

Hansards, parliamentary reports and minutes:

Canada, *Parliamentary Debates*, House of Commons.

Ceylon [Sri Lanka], *Parliamentary Debates*, Senate.

Denmark, *Fortryk af folketingets forhandlinger*.

Iceland, *Alpingistídindi Umrædur*.

Netherlands, *de Handelingen Tweede Kamer*.

Norway, *Forhandlinger i Stortinget*.

United Kingdom, *Parliamentary Debates*, House of Lords, House of Commons.

Greenland, Resolution of Parliament, 16 November 1984, in *Revue général de droit international public*, vol. 89, 1985, p. 451.

Soviet Foreign Ministry, Statement by Soviet Government on the Rarotonga Treaty, *Soviet News*, 17 December 1986.

Union of Soviet Socialist Republics, 'Rules for Navigation and Sojourn of Foreign Warships in the Territorial Waters (Territorial Sea) of the USSR and the Internal Waters and Ports of the USSR', Moscow, 1984.

Pressure group and political material

ANZUS Group/Collective Defence (Wairarapa), *Newsletters*, Masterton, 1986.

Australian Coalition for Disarmament and Peace, *Report of the Australian Nuclear Disarmament Conference*, 29 August–1 September 1985, Melbourne, 1985.

Australian Labor Party, *Transcripts of Biennial National Conferences*, 1982, 1984, 1986.

Australian Nuclear-Free Zones Secretariat, Suter, Keith D., *Nuclear Free Zones: Some Basic Questions*, Sydney, 1985.

Australian Scientists Against Nuclear Arms, *Newsletter*.

Campaign Against Foreign Control in New Zealand, *Congratulations Labour, But . . .*, Christchurch, October 1985.

Christchurch Peace Office:

Aldridge, Robert, *From ANZUS to a Nuclear Free Pacific*, no. 2, Christchurch, 1978.

Jones, Peter D., *The Growing Political, Economic and Strategic Significance of the Pacific Ocean*, no. 3, April 1979.

Citizens for the Demilitarisation of Harewood, *Off Base*, Christchurch.

Committee for the Abolition of Political Police:

Coxsedge, Joan, Coldicutt, Ken and Harant, Gerry, *Rooted in Secrecy. The Clandestine Element in Australian Politics*, Melbourne, 1982.

Coxsedge, Joan and Harant, Gerry, *Security Threat: The Case For Abolition of Secret Agencies*, Melbourne, June 1984.

Heritage Foundation:

Alves, Dora, 'U.S. and New Zealand: Trouble Down Under', Asian Studies Center Backgrounder no. 18, Washington, DC, 4 November 1984.

Fisher, Richard D. Jnr., 'Responding to New Zealand's Challenge to Western Security in the South Pacific', Asian Studies Center Backgrounder no. 48, Washington, DC, 24 July 1986.

'Why The U.S. Must Oppose The South Pacific Nuclear Free Zone', Asian Studies Center Backgrounder no. 55, Washington, DC, 23 December 1986.

Just Defence, *Just Defence Newsletter*, Wellington, 1986.

New Zealand CND:

Leadbeater, Maire (ed.), *Non-Alignment and a New National Security*, Auckland, October 1976.

Mann, Robert *et al.*, *A Nuclear New Zealand??. A Public Report on the US Government's proposal to use NZ ports etc* . . . Auckland, 11 September 1975.

Nei til atomvåpen, *Nuclear Disarmament News*, Oslo.

New Zealand Foundation for Peace Studies:

Falk, Richard, *Nuclearism and National Interest. The Situation of a Non-Nuclear Ally*, Auckland, 1986.

Wills, Peter, 'International Forum of Scientists to Stop Nuclear Testing', Report to the New Zealand Foundation for Peace Studies, Auckland, 13 July 1986.

New Zealand Friends, *Newsletter*, October–December 1986.

New Zealand Labour Party:

Annual Conference Reports, 1980–6, Wellington.

1984 Manifesto, Wellington.

PM Reports, Wellington

The New Nation, Wellington.

Wellington Regional Council, Remit Paper, Masterton, 9–11 May 1986.

Winsley, Peter, 'The Soviet Pacific Fleet', Peace and Justice Forum, Wellington Labour Regional Council, Wellington, December 1985.

'New Zealand's Military Relationship with Singapore', Peace and Justice Forum, Wellington Labour Regional Council, Wellington, January 1986.

New Zealand National Party, *National's 84 Election Policy*, National Party, Wellington, June 1984.

New Zealand Nuclear-Free Zone Committee:

Nuclear-Free, Christchurch.

Peace Researcher, Christchurch.

New Zealand Party:

Freedom and Prosperity: A Manifesto of Recovery, Wellington, 1983.

Jones, Bob, *Manifesto*, Wellington, 1984.

New Zealand Returned Services' Association, *RSA Review*.

Nuclear-Free Zone Local Authorities, 'Transcript of the 1st International Conference of Nuclear-Free Zone Local Authorities', Manchester, 12–15 April 1984.

Peace Movement Aotearoa, *Peacelink* (formerly *Peace Movement New Zealand Newsletter*), Dunedin, Christchurch and Hamilton.

Ports Watch, *Newsletter*, Tromsø, Norway.

Victorian ALP Anti-Uranium Committee, 'Maintain and Strengthen ALP Anti-Uranium Policy', Melbourne, 1982.

Periodicals and Press

The Advertiser (Adelaide)	*National Times* (Sydney)
The Age (Melbourne)	*New York Times*
Auckland Star	*New Zealand Herald* (Auckland)
The Australian (Sydney)	*New Zealand Listener*
The Bulletin (Sydney)	*New Zealand News UK*
Canberra Times	*New Zealand Times*
Christian Science Monitor	*Otago Daily Times*
Daily Telegraph	*Pacific Islands Business*
The Dominion (Wellington)	*Pacific Islands Monthly*
Dominion Sunday Times	*Peace News*
Evening Post (Wellington)	*The Press* (Christchurch)
Far Eastern Economic Review	*Sea Power* (US Navy League)
The Guardian	*The Star* (Christchurch)
IISS, *The Military Balance*	*Sydney Morning Herald*
IISS, *Strategic Survey*	*The Times*
The Independent	*US News and World Report*
Jane's Defence Weekly	*Vital Speeches of the Day*
Jane's Fighting Ships	*Washington Post*
Keesing's Contemporary Archives	*Washington Times*

Secondary sources

Books

Albinski, Henry S., *Australian External Policy Under Labour: Content, Process and the National Debate*, Queensland University Press, St Lucia, Queensland, 1977.

   ANZUS, the United States and Pacific Security, University Press of America, Lanham Maryland, 1987.

Alley, Roderic (ed.), *Alternatives to ANZUS* (rev. edn), New Zealand Foundation for Peace Studies, Auckland, 1984.

   New Zealand and the Pacific, Westview Press, Boulder, Colorado, 1984.

Alves, Dora, *The ANZUS Partners*, Georgetown University Press, Washington, DC, 1984.

   Anti-Nuclear Attitudes in New Zealand and Australia, National Defense University Press, Washington, DC, 1985.

Babbage, Ross, *Rethinking Australia's Defence*, Queensland University Press, St Lucia, Queensland, 1980.

Ball, Desmond, *A Suitable Piece of Real Estate, American Installations in Australia*, Hale and Iremonger, Sydney, 1980.

Ball, Desmond (ed.), *The Anzac Connection*, Allen and Unwin, Sydney, 1985.

Ball, Desmond and Mack, Andrew (eds), *The Future of Arms Control*, ANU Press, Canberra, 1987.

Bamford, James, *The Puzzle Palace: A Report on NSA, America's Most Secret Agency*, Houghton Mifflin, Boston, 1982 (UK edn, 1983).

Barclay, Glen St J., *Friends in High Places: Australian–American Diplomatic Relations Since 1945*, Oxford University Press, Melbourne, 1985.

Bates, Jem, *Nation-hero, Nation-villain – Another Look at the Soviet Threat*, Samizdat, Auckland, 1984.

Bell, C. (ed.), *The Changing Pacific*, Canberra Studies in World Affairs, Canberra, 1987.

Bellany, Ian, *Australia in the Nuclear Age*, Sydney University Press, Sydney, 1972.

Bercovitch, J. (ed,), *ANZUS in Crisis*, Macmillan, London (forthcoming).

Booth, Ken, *Law, Force and Diplomacy at Sea*, Allen and Unwin, London, 1985.

Boston, Jonathan and Holland, Martin (eds), *The Fourth Labour Government*: *Radical Politics in New Zealand*, Oxford University Press, Auckland, 1987.

Boyce, P. J., *Foreign Affairs for Small States*, Queensland University Press, St Lucia, Queensland, 1977.

Brown, Bruce (ed.), *Asia and the Pacific in the 1970s. The Roles of the United States, Australia, and New Zealand*, A. H. and A. W. Reed, Wellington, 1971.

Byers, R. B. (ed.), *The Denuclearisation of the Oceans*, Croom Helm, London, 1986.

Camilleri, J. A., *An Introduction to Australian Foreign Policy* (4th edn), Jacaranda, Queensland, 1979.

Australian–American Relations: The Web of Dependence, Macmillan, Melbourne, 1980.

Danielsson, Bengt and Marie-Thérèse, *Poisoned Reign. French Nuclear Colonialism in the Pacific* (previously *Moruroa, Mon Amour*), Penguin Books, Australia, 1986.

Dibb, Paul (ed.), *Australia's External Relations in the 1980s*, Croom Helm, Canberra, 1984.

Dismukes, Bradford and McConnell, James (eds), *Soviet Naval Diplomacy*, Pergamon Press, New York, 1979.

Dorrance, John C., *Oceania and the United States: An Analysis of U.S. Interests and Policy in the South Pacific*, National Defense University, 1980.

Duke, Simon, *US Defence Bases in the United Kingdom: A Matter for Joint Decision?*, Macmillan Press, Oxford, 1987.

Duncan, J., *Options for New Zealand's Future*, Victoria University Press, Wellington, 1984.

Falk, Jim, *Taking Australia off the Map – Facing the Threat of Nuclear War*, Penguin Books, Australia, 1983 (reprint 1985).

Fieldhouse, Richard and Arkin, William, *Nuclear Battlefields: Global Links in the Arms Race*, Ballinger, Boston, 1985.

Flynn, Gregory and Rattinger, Hans (eds), *The Public and Atlantic Defence*, Croom Helm, London, 1984.

Galvin, Ray, *Living Without ANZUS*, Belmont, Auckland, 1984.

A Nuclear-Free New Zealand . . . Now!, Belmont, Auckland, 1984.

Geiringer, Erich, *Malice in Blunderland, An Anti-Nuclear Primer*, Benton Ross Publishers, Auckland, 1985.

Gidley, I. and Shears, Richard, *The Rainbow Warrior Affair*, Counterpoint Union Paperbacks, London, 1986.

Gold, Hyam (ed.), *New Directions in New Zealand's Foreign Policy*, Benton Ross, Auckland, 1985.

Hakovirta, Harto (ed.), *Fragmentation and Integration, Aspects of International System Change*, Finnish Political Science Association, Helsinki, 1986.

Handel, Michael, *Weak States in the International System*, Frank Cass, London, 1981.

Harford, Barbara, *Beyond ANZUS: Alternatives for Australia, New Zealand and the Pacific*, Beyond ANZUS Committee, Wellington 1985.

Hayes, Peter, Zarsky, Lyuba and Bello, Walden, *American Lake, Nuclear Peril in the Pacific*, Penguin Books, Australia, 1986.

Henderson, J., Jackson, K. and Kennaway, R. (eds), *Beyond New Zealand. The Foreign Policy of a Small State*, Methuen Publications, Auckland, 1980.

Hewlett, R. G. and Duncan, F., *Nuclear Navy*, Chicago University Press, Chicago, 1974.

Hinchcliff, John (comp.), *Confronting the Nuclear Age – Australian Responses*, Pacific Peacemaker, Bondi Junction, 1981.

Hocking, Brian (ed.), *ANZUS and the Western Alliance*, Australian Studies Centre, Institute of Commonwealth Studies, University of London, 1986.

Hudson, W. J., *Casey*, Oxford University Press, Melbourne, 1986.

Hudson, William (ed.)., *Australia in World Affairs 1971–1975*, Allen and Unwin, Sydney, 1980.

Hutton, Drew (ed.), *Green Politics in Australia*, Angus and Robertson, N. Ryde, NSW, 1987.

IDOC International, *Militarisation in Asia and Pacific 1*, nos 1–2, Rome, 1984.

Kennaway, Richard, *New Zealand Foreign Policy 1951–1971*, Hicks, Smith and Sons, Wellington, 1972.

L'Association France-Nouvelle-Zélande, *Où en est la Nouvelle-Zélande?*, Éditions L'Harmattan, Paris, 1986.

Lissington, M. P., *New Zealand and the United States 1840–1944*, Government Printer, Wellington, 1972.

Lodgaard, Sverre and Thee, Marek, *Nuclear Disengagement in Europe*, SIPRI/ Taylor and Francis, London, 1983.

McDonald, Geoff, *The Kiwis Fight Back*, Chaston Publishers, Christchurch, 1986.

MccGwire, Michael, *Military Objectives in Soviet Foreign Policy*, The Brookings Institution, Washington, DC, 1987.

MccGwire, Michael and Booth, Ken, *Soviet Naval Policy. Objectives and Constraints*, Praeger, New York, 1975.

McIntyre, W. David, *Neutralism, Non Alignment and New Zealand*, New Zealand University Press, Wellington, 1969.

McMillan, Stuart, *Neither Confirm Nor Deny, The Nuclear Ships Dispute between New Zealand and the United States*, Allen and Unwin, Wellington, 1987.

Martin, David, *Armed Neutrality for Australia*, Dove Communications, Blackburn, Victoria, 1984.

Metzger, H. P., *The Atomic Establishment*, Simon and Schuster, New York, 1972.

Millar, T. B., *Australia's Defence*, Melbourne University Press, London, 1965.
Australia in Peace and War, ANU Press, Canberra, 1978.

Millar, T. B. (ed.), *Australian – New Zealand Defence Co-operation*, ANU Press, Canberra, 1968

263

Milliken, Robert, *No Conceivable Injury. The Story of Britain and Australia's Atomic Cover-Up*, Penguin Books, Australia, 1986.

Munster, George and Walsh, Richard, *Secrets of State*, Angus and Robertson, Australia, 1982.

Myers, Ramon H. (ed.), *A U.S. Foreign Policy for Asia*, Hoover Press, Stanford, 1982.

Newnham, Tom, *Peace Squadron: The Sharp End of Nuclear Protest in New Zealand*, Graphic Publications, Auckland, 1986.

O'Connor, Michael, *To Live in Peace, Australia's Defence Policy*, Melbourne University Press, Melbourne, 1985.

O'Neill, Robert, *Australia in the Korean War, 1950–53, vol. I. Strategy and Diplomacy*, Australian Government Publishing Service, Canberra, 1981.

O'Neill, Robert (ed.), *The Defence of Australia: Fundamental New Aspects*, ANU Press, Canberra, 1977.

Insecurity! The Spread of Weapons in the Indian and Pacific Oceans, ANU Press, Canberra, 1978.

O'Neill, Robert and Horner, D. M. (eds.), *Australian Defence Policy for the 1980s*, Queensland University Press, St Lucia, Queensland, 1982.

Ørvik, Nils (ed.), *Semialignment and Western Security*, Croom Helm, London, 1986.

Paul, R. A., *American Military Commitments Abroad*, Rutgers University Press, New Brunswick, New Jersey, 1973.

Phillips, Dennis H., *Cold War Two and Australia*, Allen and Unwin, Sydney, 1983.

Polmar, N. and Allen, T. P., *Rickover, Controversy and Genius: A Biography*, Simon and Schuster, New York, 1984.

Preddey, George, *Nuclear Disaster: A New Way of Thinking Down Under*, Asia Pacific Books Wellington, 1985.

Renouf, Alan, *The Frightened Country*, Macmillan, Melbourne, 1979.

Richelson, Jeffrey T. and Ball, Desmond, *The Ties That Bind, Intelligence Cooperation between the UKUSA Countries*, Allen and Unwin, Sydney, 1985.

Rolphe, Elizabeth S., *Nuclear Power and the Public Safety*, Lexington Books, Mass., 1979.

Ross, Anthony Clunies and King, G. Peter, *Australia and Nuclear Weapons: The Case for a Non-Nuclear Region in South East Asia*, Sydney University Press, Sydney, 1966.

Saunders, Malcolm and Summy, Ralph, *The Australian Peace Movement: A Short History*, Peace Research Centre, ANU, Canberra, 1986.

Savigear, Peter, *Cold War or Detente in the 1980s: The International Politics of American–Soviet Relations*, Wheatsheaf, London, 1987.

Sinclair, Keith (ed.), *Distance Looks Our Way: The Effects of Remoteness on New Zealand*, Paul's, Hamilton, 1961.

Siwatibau, Suliana and Williams, B. David, *A Call to a New Exodus: An Anti-Nuclear Primer for Pacific People*, Pacific Conference of Churches, Lotu Pasifika Productions, Suva, 1982.

Starke, J.G., *The ANZUS Treaty Alliance*, Melbourne University Press, Melbourne, 1965.

Templeton, Malcolm, *Defence and Security: What New Zealand Needs*, Victoria University Press, Wellington, 1986.

Thakur, Ramesh, *In Defence of New Zealand: Foreign Policy Choices in the Nuclear Age*, Westview Press, Boulder, Colorado, 1986.

Tow, William T. and Feeney, William R. (eds), *U.S. Foreign Policy and Asian–Pacific Security. A Transregional Approach*, Westview Press, Boulder, Colorado, 1982.

Waring, Marilyn, *Women, Politics and Power*, Unwin Paperbacks, Wellington, 1985.

Watson, B. W. and S. M. (eds), *The Soviet Navy: Strengths and Liabilities*, Westview Press, Boulder, Colorado, 1986.

Watt, Alan, *The Evolution of Australian Foreign Policy, 1938–1965*, Cambridge University Press, Cambridge, 1968.

Wesley-Smith, Terence (ed.), *New Zealand and its Southeast Asian Neighbours*, NZIIA, Wellington, 1980.

Wiens, Herold J., *Pacific Island Bastions of the United States*, Greenwood Press, Westport, Connecticut, 1962.

Wilkes, Owen, *Protest: Demonstrations Against the American Military Presence in New Zealand*, Alister Taylor Publishing, Wellington, 1973.

Wilkes, Owen and Gleditsch, Nils Petter, *LORAN–C and OMEGA; A Study of the Military Importance of Radio Navigation Aids*, International Peace Research Institute, Oslo, 1986.

Wilkinson, Vernon, *New Zealand Politics in the Nuclear Age*, V.W. Publishing, Christchurch, 1984.

Articles

Acharya, Amitav, 'The Asia–Pacific Region: Cockpit for Superpower Rivalry', *The World Today*, vol. 43, nos 8–9, August–September 1987, pp. 155–8.

Albinski, Henry S., 'American Perspectives on the ANZUS Alliance', *Australian Outlook*, vol. 32, no. 2, August 1978, pp. 131–52.

'ANZUS. American Foreign Policy and the ANZUS Problem', *Current Affairs Bulletin*, September 1985, pp. 14–24.

'Australia and New Zealand in the 1980s', *Current History*, vol. 85, no. 510, April 1986, pp. 49–54, 182–3.

Alford, Jonathan, 'Security Dilemmas of Small States', *The World Today*, vol. 40, no. 8–9, August–September 1984, pp. 363–9.

Alley, Roderic, 'Alternative Defences for New Zealand', *Social Alternatives*, vol. 5, no. 1, 1985, pp. 28–31.

Alves, Dora, 'The Submarine's Role in Soviet Pacific Strategy', *Pacific Defence Reporter*, vol. 11, no. 3, September 1984, pp. 10–14.

Andrikos, Nikos, 'A Balkan Nuclear-Weapons-Free Zone', *Bulletin of the Atomic Scientists*, vol. 41, no. 6, June–July 1985, pp. 29–31.

Archer, Clive, 'Deterrence and Reassurance in Northern Europe', Centre for Defence Studies, *Centre Piece no. 6*, Aberdeen, winter 1984.

Arkin, William M., 'Nuclear Weapons at Sea', *Bulletin of the Atomic Scientists*, vol. 39, no. 9, October 1983, pp. 6–7.

'Confirm or Deny', *Bulletin of the Atomic Scientists*, vol. 41, no. 11, December 1985, pp. 4–5.

Arkin, William M. and Chappell, David, 'Forward Offensive Strategy: Raising the Stakes in the Pacific', *World Policy Journal*, vol. 2, no. 3, summer 1985, pp. 481–500.

Armacost, Michael H., 'The Asia–Pacific Region: A Forward Look', *Atlantic Community Quarterly*, vol. 22, no. 4, winter 1984–5, pp. 338–44.

Armstrong, George, 'An Ideology and Theology of an Independent and Nuclear-Free Pacific', *Social Alternatives*, vol. 5, no. 1, 1985, pp. 12–13.

Atkinson, Hugh, 'Mururoa Under Scrutiny', *NZIR*, vol. 9, no. 2, March–April 1984, pp. 2–4.

Babbage, Ross, 'Australian Defence Planning, Force Structure and Equipment: the American Effect', *Australian Outlook*, vol. 38, no. 3, December 1984, pp.163–8.

Bagley, Worth H., 'The Pacific Connection. Strategic Burden or Strategic Connection?', *Navy International*, vol. 83, no. 5, May 1978, pp. 10–13.

Ball, Desmond, *Targeting for Strategic Deterrence*, Adelphi Paper 185, IISS, London, summer 1983.

'Nuclear War at Sea', *International Security*, vol. 10, no. 3, winter 1985–6, pp. 3–31.

Beaglehole, J. H., 'New Zealand Wants to Eat Its Cake and Have It, Too', *Pacific Defence Reporter*, vol. 11, no. 3, September 1984, pp. 22 and 62.

'New Zealand. Hard to Port Across the Tasman', *Pacific Defence Reporter*, vol. 11, nos. 6–7, December 1984–January 1985, pp. 3–4.

Bell, Coral, 'Australian Defence and Regional Security: The American Effect and the Future', *Australian Outlook*, vol. 38, no. 3, December 1984, pp. 207–14.

The Unquiet Pacific, Conflict Study 205, Institute for the Study of Conflict, 1987.

Bonnemaison, Joel, 'Là-bas, a l'ouest de l'Occident: l'Australie et la Nouvelle-Zélande', *Hérodote*, no. 40, 1er trimestre, 1986, pp. 126–39.

Booth, Ken and Williams, Phil, 'Fact and Fiction in U.S. Foreign Policy: Reagan's Myths About Detente', *World Policy Journal*, vol. 2, no. 3, summer 1985, pp. 501–32.

Bowen, Alva M. and O'Rourke, Ronald, 'Ports for the Fleet', *Proceedings/Naval Review*, vol. 112, May 1986, pp. 137–51.

Boyce, Peter J., 'The Influence of the United States on the Domestic Debate in Australia', *Australian Outlook*, vol. 38, no. 3, December 1984, pp. 159–62.

Brooks, Linton F., 'Tactical Nuclear Weapons: The Forgotten Facet of Naval Warfare', *Proceedings/Naval Review*, January 1980, pp. 28–33.

Bull, Hedley *et al.*, *Power at Sea*, Adelphi Papers 122–124, IISS (17th Annual Conference Papers, Sweden, 1975), London, spring 1976.

Buzan, Barry, *A Sea of Troubles? Sources of Dispute in the New Ocean Regime*, Adelphi Paper 143, IISS, London, spring 1978.

'Peace, Power, and Security: Contending Concepts in the Study of International Relations', *Journal of Peace Research*, vol. 21, no. 2, 1984, pp. 109–25.

266

Caldwell, Dan, 'Permissive Action Links, a Description and Proposal', *Survival*, vol. 29, no. 3, May–June 1987, pp. 224–37.

Camilleri, Joseph A., 'Neutrality or Non-Alignment', *Arena*, no. 67, 1984, pp. 117–24.

Campbell, Duncan, 'Too Few Bombs to go Round', *New Statesman*, 23 November 1985, pp. 10–12.

Campbell, Duncan and Forbes, Patricia, 'What's the Royal Navy Doing in the Pacific?', *New Statesman*, 21 February 1986, p. 8.

Center for Defense Information, 'The Soviet Navy: Still Second Best', *Defense Monitor*, vol. 14, no. 7, 1985.

'First Strike Weapons at Sea: The Trident II and the Sea-Launched Cruise Missile', *Defense Monitor*, vol. 16, no. 6, 1987.

Chan, Steve, 'Growth with Equity: A Test of Olson's Theory for the Asian Pacific-Rim Countries', *Journal of Peace Research*, vol. 24, no. 2, June 1987, pp. 135–49.

Chesneaux, Jean, 'France in the Pacific: Global Approach or Respect for Regional Agendas?', *Bulletin of Concerned Asian Scholars*, vol. 18, no. 2, 1986, pp. 73–80.

Clements, Kevin, 'Towards a Self-Reliant New Zealand: Beyond Dependence to Independence', *NZIR*, vol. 1, July–August 1976, pp. 13–15.

'New Zealand's Relations with the UK, the US, and the Pacific', *Alternatives*, vol. 10, no. 4, 1985, pp. 591–605.

Collins, Hugh, 'Australia and the United States: Assessing the Relationship', *Australian Outlook*, vol. 32, no. 2, August 1978, pp.153–68.

Crowe, Admiral William J., 'The CINCPAC View. Help Wanted in Protecting Vital Sea Lines', *Pacific Defence Reporter*, vol. 11, nos. 6–7, December 1984–January 1985, pp. 36–9.

'The Armed Forces of the Asia–Pacific Region. No. 17 – The US Cannot, and Should Not, Go It Alone', *Pacific Defence Reporter*, vol. 11, no. 14, August 1985, pp.11–15.

Dahlitz, Julie, 'Security Implications of the US Nuclear Umbrella for America's Allies: An Australian View', *Australian Outlook*, vol. 38, no. 3, December 1984, pp. 169–77.

Daniel, Donald C. F., 'The Soviet Navy and Tactical Nuclear War at Sea', *Survival*, vol. 29, no. 4, July–August 1984, pp. 318–35.

Darby, Phillip, 'Stability Mechanisms in South-East Asia, II. Balance of Power and Neutralization', *International Affairs*, April 1973, pp. 204–18.

Dibb, Paul, 'The Strategic Interrelations of the US, the USSR and China in the East Asia–Pacific Area', *Australian Outlook*, vol. 32, no. 2, August 1978, pp. 169–81.

'Soviet Strategy Towards Australia, New Zealand and the South-West Pacific', *Australian Outlook*, vol. 39, no. 2, August 1985, pp. 69–76.

Din, Allan M., 'Nuclear Test Bans', *Journal of Peace Research*, vol. 24, no. 2, June 1987, pp. 105–10.

Dorrance, John C., 'ANZUS: Misperceptions, Mythology and Reality', *Australian Quarterly*, vol. 57, no. 3, 1985, pp. 215–30.

East, Maurice A., 'Size and Foreign Policy Behaviour: A Test of Two Models', *World Politics*, vol. 25, 1973, pp. 556–76.

Fry, Greg, 'Regionalism and International Politics of the South Pacific', *Pacific Affairs*, vol. 54, fall 1981, pp. 455–84.

'Toward a South Pacific Nuclear-Free Zone', *Bulletin of the Atomic Scientists*, vol. 41, no. 6, June–July 1985, pp. 16–20.

'The South Pacific Nuclear-Free Zone: Significance and Implications', *Bulletin of Concerned Asian Scholars*, vol. 18, no. 2, 1986, pp. 61–71.

Goldblatt, Joseph and Lodgaard, Sverre, 'The South Pacific Nuclear-Free Zone: Variation on a Latin American Theme', *NZIR*, vol. 11, no. 3, May–June 1986, pp. 14–15.

Graham, Ken, 'After Deterrence – What?', *NZIR*, vol. 11, no. 3, May–June 1986, pp. 5–9.

'Common Security – A Link to the Global Age', *NZIR* vol. 11, no. 4, July–August 1986, pp. 12–16.

Green, Harold P., 'Nuclear Power: Risk Liability and Indemnity', *Journal Michigan Law Review*, vol. 71, no. 3, January 1973, pp. 186–271.

Grimsson, Olafur Ragnar, 'Nordic Nuclear-Free Options', *Bulletin of the Atomic Scientists*, vol. 41, no. 6, June–July 1985, pp. 25–8.

Gunnarsson, Gunnar, 'Icelandic Security Policy: Context and Trends', *Cooperation and Conflict*, no. 17, 1982, pp. 257–72.

Hamel-Green, Michael, 'A Future for the South Pacific – Nuclear-Free', *Peace Dossier 8*, Victoria Association for Peace Studies, Fitzroy, Victoria, December 1983.

'South Pacific: A Not-So-Nuclear-Free Zone', *Peace Studies* (Australia), November–December 1985, pp. 42–3.

Harlan, David, 'New Zealand the Politics of Identity', *Atlantic Monthly*, September 1986, pp. 14–20.

Harries, Owen, 'Crisis in the Pacific', *Commentary*, vol. 79, no. 6, June 1985, pp. 47–54.

Hawke, Robert J., 'Interview', *Journal of Defense and Diplomacy*, vol. 3, no. 8, August 1985, pp. 4–15.

Henderson, John, 'New Zealand in a Changing World: The Talboys Speeches', *NZIR*, vol. 3, no. 1, January–February 1978, pp. 8–11.

'The 1980s – A Time for Commitment', *NZIR*, vol. 5, no. 1, January–February 1980, pp. 5–6.

'The Burdens of ANZUS', *NZIR*, vol. 5, no. 3, May–June 1980, pp. 2–3.

Herr, Richard A., 'Jimmy Carter and American Foreign Policy in the Pacific Islands', *Australian Outlook*, vol. 32, no. 2, August 1978, pp. 224–38.

'The American Impact on Australian Defence Relations with the South Pacific Islands', *Australian Outlook*, vol. 38, no. 3, December 1984, pp. 184–91.

Heurlin, Bertel, 'Danish Security Policy', *Cooperation and Conflict*, no. 17, 1982, pp. 237–55.

Hoadley, Steve, 'The Future of New Zealand's Alliances', *NZIR*, vol. 9, no. 6, November–December 1984, pp. 6–11.

'American Views of New Zealand', *NZIR*, vol. 11, no. 2, March–April 1986, pp. 14–15.

'The Price of Neutrality', *NZIR*, vol. 11, no. 3, May–June 1986, pp. 2–4.

'New Zealand–American Logistics Co-operation', *NZIR*, vol. 13, no. 1, January–February 1988, pp. 23–7.

Hocking, Brian and Warhurst, John, 'Australia and Britain: Drifting Apart?', *The World Today*, vol. 42, no. 12, December 1986, pp. 214–17.

Hoffmann, Stanley, 'The Uses of American Power', *Foreign Affairs*, vol. 56, no. 1, October 1977, pp. 27–48.

Holst, Johan Jørgen, 'The Pattern of Nordic Security', *Daedalus*, vol. 113, no. 2, spring 1984, pp. 195–225, 278.

Hook, Glenn D., 'The Nuclearization of Language: Nuclear Allergy as Political Metaphor', *Journal of Peace Research*, vol. 21, no. 3, 1984, pp. 259–75.

Horiguchi, Robert Y., 'Kiwi Disease – Japanese Version', *Pacific Defence Reporter*, vol. 11, no. 12, June 1985, p. 48.

Howard, Michael, 'The Future of Deterrence', *RUSI Journal*, vol. 131, no. 2, June 1986, pp. 3–10.

Huitfeldt, Tonne, *NATO's Northern Security*, Conflict Study 191, Institute for the Study of Conflict, London, September 1986.

Jamieson, Air Marshal Sir Ewan, 'Defence Dilemmas of Small Countries in the Nuclear Age', *Pacific Defence Reporter*, vol. 13, no. 5, November 1986, pp. 40–1.

Janaki, K., 'From "Basic Defence" to "Comprehensive National Security": Japan's Evolving Defence Stance', *NZIR*, vol. 11, no. 3, May–June 1986, pp. 17–20.

Jarratt, Phil *et al.*, 'Gaddafi Stirs the Pacific', *The Bulletin*, 19 May 1987, pp. 16–23.

Jones, Ray, 'Asroc in New Zealand's Gullet', *Pacific Defence Reporter*, vol. 12, no. 3, September 1985, pp. 25, 55.

Kaplan, David E., 'When Incidents Are Accidents. The Silent Saga of the Nuclear Navy', *Oceans*, July 1983, pp. 26–33.

Kennaway, Richard, 'Changing Views of ANZUS', *NZIR*, vol. 9, no. 6, November–December 1984, pp. 2–5.

Kiste, Robert C. and Herr, Richard A., 'The Potential For Soviet Penetration of the South Pacific Islands: An Assessment', *Bulletin of Concerned Asian Scholars*, vol. 18, no. 2, 1986, pp. 42–59.

Klick, Donna J., 'A Balkan Nuclear Weapon-Free Zone: Viability of the Regime and Implications for Crisis Management', *Journal of Peace Research*, vol. 24, no. 2, June 1987, pp. 111–24.

Lange, Rt. Hon. David, 'Disarmament and Security: The Government's Perspective', *NZIR*, vol. 10, no. 3, May–June 1985, pp. 13–15.

'New Zealand Security Policy', *Foreign Affairs*, summer 1985, pp. 1009–19.

Leifer, Michael, 'The Security of Sea-Lanes in South-East Asia', *Survival*, vol. 25, no. 1, January–February 1983, pp. 16–24.

Leitenburg, Milton, 'The Case of the Stranded Sub', *Bulletin of the Atomic Scientists*, vol. 38, no. 3, March 1982, pp. 10–13.

Levine, Stephen and Spoonley, Paul, 'Public Opinion and Foreign Policy', *NZIR*, vol. 5, no. 2, March 1980, pp. 19–21.

Lutz, Catherine, 'The Compact of Free Association, Micronesian Non-Independence, and U.S. Policy', *Bulletin of Concerned Asian Scholars*, vol. 18, no. 2, 1986, pp. 21–7.

269

MccGwire, Michael, 'Deterrence: The problem – Not the Solution', *International Affairs*, vol. 62, no. 3, summer 1986, pp. 55–70.

McIntosh, Malcolm, 'A Nuclear-Free Pacific?', *ADIU Report*, vol. 9, no. 2, March–April 1987, pp. 5–7.

McIntyre, David, 'The Future of the New Zealand System of Alliances', *Landfall*, December 1967, pp. 327–45.

McKinley, Michael, 'Labour, Lange and Logic: An Analysis of New Zealand's ANZUS Policy', *Australian Outlook*, vol. 39, no. 3, December 1985, pp. 133–8.

'Labour and ANZUS: Heroic Stand or Ascetic Self-Indulgence?', *NZIR*, vol. 10, no. 6, November–December 1985, pp. 8–11.

McKinnon, Malcolm, 'The Richest Prize?', *NZIR*, vol. 11, no. 3, May–June 1986, pp. 10–13.

Mack, Andrew, 'Defending Australia. Is Non-Alignment the Answer?', *Current Affairs Bulletin*, September 1982, pp. 17–30.

'Arms Control and the US Bases', *Peace Studies* (Australia), November–December 1985, pp. 11–12.

'Crisis in the Other Alliance: Anzus in the 1980s', *World Policy Journal*, vol. 3, summer 1986, pp. 447–72.

Maclellan, Nic, 'Speak No Evil: The "Neither Confirm Nor Deny" Policy', *Peace Magazine* (Australia), February–March 1987, pp. 18–21.

McLay, Jim, MP, 'Disarmament and Security: An Alternative Viewpoint', *NZIR*, vol. 10, no. 3, May–June 1985, pp. 16–22.

Martin, David, 'Armed Neutrality – Australia's Alternative', *Peace Dossier 10*, Victorian Association for Peace Studies, Fitzroy, August 1984.

Mediansky, F. A., 'Australia's Security and the American Alliance', *Australian Outlook*, vol. 37, no. 2, April 1983, pp. 22–5.

'ANZUS: An Alliance Beyond the Treaty', *Australian Outlook*, vol. 38, no. 3, December 1984, pp. 178–83.

'Nuclear Free Security in the South-West Pacific?', *Australian Outlook*, vol. 39, no. 2, August 1985, pp. 77–83.

'Nuclear Weapons and Security in the South Pacific', *The Washington Quarterly*, vol. 9, no. 1, winter 1986, pp. 31–43.

Miles, Robert, 'The Nuclear Visitors', *NZIR*, vol. 10, no. 1, January–February 1985, pp. 14–17.

Millar, T. B., 'From Whitlam to Fraser', *Foreign Affairs*, vol. 55, no. 4, July 1977, pp. 854–72.

Morrison, David C., 'Japanese Principles, U.S. Policies', *Bulletin of the Atomic Scientists*, vol. 41, no. 6, June-July 1985, pp. 22–4.

Muldoon, R. M., 'Interview: Our Foreign Policy is Trade', *NZIR*, vol. 5, no. 1, January–February 1980, pp. 2–3.

Mulhall, Daniel, 'Australia and Disarmament Diplomacy 1983–1985: Rhetoric or Achievement', *Australian Outlook*, vol. 40, no. 1, April 1986, pp. 32–8.

'The Foreign Policy Leanings of Small Powers', *NZIR*, vol. 11, no. 5, September-October 1986, pp. 11–15.

Nailor, Peter, 'The Utility of Maritime Power: Today and Tomorrow', *RUSI Journal*, vol. 131, no. 3, September 1986, pp. 15–21.

Palmer, Norman D., 'The United States and the Western Pacific: Understand-

270

ing the Future', *Current History*, vol. 85, no. 510, April 1986, pp. 145–48, 179–81.

Perry, Peter, 'Neutrality and New Zealand', *NZIR*, vol. 11, no. 3, May–June 1986, pp. 15–16.

Philp, P. Robert, Jr., 'The South Pacific Nuclear-Weapon-Free-Zone, the Law of the Sea, and the ANZUS Alliance: An Exploration of Conflicts, a Step Toward World Peace', *California Western International Law Journal*, vol. 16, no. 1, winter 1986, pp. 138–77.

Polmar, Norman and Kerr, Donald M., 'Nuclear Torpedoes', *Proceedings/ Naval Review*, August 1986, pp. 62–8.

Premdas, Ralph and Howard, Michael C., 'Vanuatu's Foreign Policy: Contradictions and Constraints', *Australian Outlook*, vol. 39, no. 3, December 1985, pp. 177–86.

Pugh, Michael, 'Australien und Neuseeland: Neue Wege in der Sicherheitspolitik', *Europa-Archiv*, March 1985, pp. 175–84.

'Anzus on the Rocks', *The World Today*, vol. 41, no. 4, April 1985, pp. 79–81.

'Legal Aspects of the "Rainbow Warrior" Affair', *The International and Comparative Law Quarterly*, vol. 36, July 1987, pp. 655–69.

'South Pacific Security: Alarms and Excursions', *The World Today*, vol. 43, no. 7, July 1987, pp. 125–8.

Quigley, Marian, 'The Rise and Fall (?) of the Nuclear Disarmament Party', *Current Affairs Bulletin*, April 1986, pp. 12–19.

Richardson, Michael, 'Labor Under Pressure to Change on ANZUS', *Pacific Defence Reporter*, vol. 13, no. 9, March 1987, pp. 35–6.

Ricketts, Rita, 'The United States, New Zealand, and ANZUS', *Bulletin of Concerned Asian Scholars*, vol. 18, no. 2, 1986, pp. 83–4.

Rolfe, James, 'Securing the South Pacific', *NZIR*, vol. 10, no. 6, November–December 1985, pp. 16–18.

'Strategic Changes in the South West Pacific', *RUSI Journal*, vol. 131, no. 4, December 1986, pp. 41–50.

Rowling, Wallace, 'New Zealand Foreign Policy: Time for a Change', *NZIR*, vol. 9, no. 3, May–June 1984, pp. 7–8.

Royal Society of New Zealand, *The Threat of Nuclear War: A New Zealand Perspective*, miscellaneous series, no 11, Royal Society of New Zealand, Wellington, 1985.

Sabin, Philip A. G., 'Proposals and Propaganda: Arms Control and British Public Opinion in the 1980s', *International Affairs*, vol. 63, no. 1, winter 86–7, pp. 49–63.

Samuel, Peter, 'The Dibb Report, and Australia's Defense Vagaries', *Strategic Review*, vol. 14, no. 4, fall 1986, pp. 47–53.

Samuel, Peter and Serong, F. P., 'The Troubled Waters of ANZUS', *Strategic Review*, vol. 14, no. 1, winter 1986, pp. 39–48.

Scholes, Hon. Gordon, 'Australia's Strategic Outlook and Defence Policy', *Australian Outlook*, vol. 38, no. 3, December 1984, pp. 137–41.

Seth, S. P., 'ANZUS in Crisis', *Asia Pacific Community*, no. 29, summer 1985, pp. 109–30.

Sinclair, Ian, 'Australia's National Security – The Region and the United States,' *Australian Outlook*, vol. 38, no. 3, December 1984, pp. 142–7.

Sinclair, K., 'New Zealand's Future Foreign Policy: A New Pacific Pact', *Political Science*, vol. 18, no. 2, September 1986, p. 71.

Siracusa, Joseph M., and Barclay, Glen St J., 'The Historical Influence of the United States on Australian Strategic Thinking', *Australian Outlook*, vol. 38, no. 3, December 1984, pp. 153–8.

Smith, Steve, 'Theories of Foreign Policy: An Historical Overview', *Review of International Studies*, vol. 12, no. 1, January 1986, pp. 13–29.

Stephenson, Carolyn, 'Interview with Helen Clark', *Bulletin of Concerned Asian Scholars*, vol. 18, no. 2, 1986, pp. 85–7.

Sutherland, William Morrison, 'Microstates and Unequal Trade in the South Pacific: The Sparteca Agreement of 1980', *Journal of World Trade Law*, vol. 20, no. 3, May–June 1986, pp. 313–28.

Synnot, A., 'The Royal Australian Navy: An Assessment', *Navy International*, vol. 84, no. 1, January 1979, pp. 5–12.

Thakur, Ramesh, 'A Dispute of Many Colours: France, New Zealand and the "Rainbow Warrior" Affair', *The World Today*, vol. 42, no. 12, December 1986, pp. 209–13.

'Nuclear Ship Visits: The Nordic Practice', *NZIR*, vol. 12, no. 3, May–June 1987, pp. 16–21.

'New Zealand Defence Review 1985–1987', *Asian Defence Journal*, July 1987, pp. 56–65.

Thomson, Scott, 'New Zealand Defence: Lessons from the South Atlantic', *NZIR*, vol. 10, no. 4, July–August 1985, pp. 18–21.

Till, Geoffrey, 'Naval Power in the Pacific', *Armed Forces* (parts 1–5), vol. 4, nos. 6–10, June, July, August, September, October 1985, pp. 213–17, 253–7, 299–302, 338–42, 373–7.

Tokinoya, Atsushi, *The Japan–US Alliance: A Japanese Perspective*, Adelphi Paper 212, IISS, London, autumn 1986.

Tow, William T., 'ANZUS and American Security', *Survival*, vol. 23, November–December 1981, pp. 261–71.

'Australian–Japanese Security Co-operation: Present Barriers and Future Prospects', *Australian Outlook*, vol. 38, no. 3, December 1984, pp. 200–6.

Trotter, Ann, 'New Zealand and the Pacific Community Concept', *The World Today*, vol. 39, nos. 7–8, July–August 1983, pp. 312–18.

Turner, John, 'Rethinking New Zealand's Defence Policy', *NZIR*, vol. 8, March–April 1983, pp. 15–17.

Van Ness, Peter, 'New Zealand: What is the Problem?', *Bulletin of Concerned Asian Scholars*, vol. 18, no. 2, 1986, pp. 88–9.

Väyrynen, Raimo, 'Regional Conflict Formations: An Intractable Problem of International Relations', *Journal of Peace Research*, vol. 21, no. 4, 1984, pp. 337–59.

Warner, Denis, 'The Importance of Being ANZUS', *Pacific Defence Reporter*, vol. 11, no. 3, September 1984, pp. 19–21.

'US and Australia Must Define Risks and Responsibilities', *Pacific Defence Reporter*, vol. 12, no. 1, July 1985, pp. 11–12.

Weinberger, James M., 'Allies of a Kind: Australia Copes with the Troubles in ANZUS', *Journal of Defense and Diplomacy*, vol. 3, no. 8, August 1985, pp. 38–40, 43.

West, Dalton, 'The 1983 Defence Review: Prospects and Implications', *NZIR*, vol. 9, no. 3, May–June 1984, pp. 2–6.

Wettern, Desmond, 'US Naval Strategy. Problems of Allies – and Enemies', [interview with Lehman], *Navy International*, August 1984, pp. 473–8.

Wilkes, Owen, 'Why the US Military Needs Another NZ Mountain', *New Zealand Monthly Review*, August 1981, pp. 8–9.

'Stooging Around the Cook Islands. The Mysterious Case of the Disappearing Submarine', *New Zealand Monthly Review*, October 1986, pp. 3–13.

'How The CIA Set Up A Front in NZ', *New Zealand Monthly Review*, February 1987, pp. 3–7.

'The CIA And The Honolulu Loan Scam', *New Zealand Monthly Review*, March 1987, pp. 6–8.

Williams, John Allen, 'The U.S. and Soviet Navies: Missions and Forces', *Armed Forces and Society*, vol. 10, no. 4, summer 1984, pp. 507–28.

Williams, Phil, 'The Limits of American Power: From Nixon to Reagan', *International Affairs*, vol. 63, no. 3, autumn 1987, pp. 575–87.

Wolfowitz, Paul D., 'The Anzus Relationship: Alliance Management', *Australian Outlook*, vol. 38, no. 3, December 1984, pp. 148–52.

Woodliffe, J. C., 'Port Visits by Nuclear Armed Naval Vessels: Recent State Practice', *International and Comparative Law Quarterly*, vol. 35, July 1986, pp. 730–6.

Young, P. Lewis, 'New Zealand's Role in Regional Security', *Pacific Defence Reporter*, vol. 12, no. 1, July 1985, pp. 10–11.

Young, Rt. Hon. the Baroness, 'Old Friends on Different Paths: the British Viewpoint', *NZIR*, vol. 11, no. 4, July–August 1986, pp. 20–2.

Young, Thomas–Durell, 'New Zealand's Dilemmas', *Proceeding/Naval Review*, August 1985, pp. 51–6.

'New Zealand Defence Policy under Labour', *Naval War College Review*, vol. 39, May–June 1986, pp. 22–34.

'New Zealand's Defense Arrangements – An Uncertain Period Ahead', *International Defense Review*, 5, 1986, pp. 591–4.

Zarsky, Lyuba, Hayes, Peter and Bello, Walden, 'Nuclear Accidents', *Current Affairs Bulletin*, June 1986, pp. 4–11.

Research reports and papers

Babbage, Ross, 'The Future of the Australian–New Zealand Defence Relationship', Strategic and Defence Studies Centre, working paper no. 113, RSPS, ANU, Canberra, December 1986.

Boanas, John, 'The Campaign for Nuclear Disarmament, Christchurch 1958–66', MA dissertation, School of Peace Studies, Bradford University, Bradford, 1980.

Bolt, Richard, 'Active Peacemaker or Passive Warmonger? The Future of Australia's Links to Global War', Melbourne, 28 July 1986.

Brown, Gary, 'Detection of Nuclear Weapons and the US Non-Disclosure Policy', Strategic and Defence Studies Centre, working paper no. 107, RSPS, ANU, Canberra, November 1986.

Camilleri, Joseph A., 'Nuclear Disarmament: An Emerging Issue in Australian

Politics', Australian Studies Centre, working paper no. 9, Institute of Commonwealth Studies, University of London, May 1986.

Campbell, David, 'Australian Public Opinion on National Security Issues', Peace Research Centre, working paper no. 1, RSPS, ANU, Canberra, April 1986.

'The Domestic Sources of New Zealand Security Policy in Comparative Perspective', Peace Research Centre, working paper no. 16, RSPS, ANU, Canberra, February 1987.

Carpenter, Ted Galen, 'Pursuing a Strategic Divorce: the U.S. and the ANZUS Alliance', policy analysis, no. 67, Cato Institute, Washington, DC, 27 February 1986.

Gregory, Shaun and Edwards, Alistair, 'A Handbook of Nuclear Weapons Accidents', Peace Research Report no. 20, School of Peace Studies, University of Bradford, January 1988.

Handler, Joshua and Arkin, William, 'Nuclear Weapons and Naval Nuclear Weapons: A Complete Inventory', Greenpeace Institute for Policy Studies, Neptune paper no.2, Washington DC, May 1988.

Jamieson, Sir Ewan, 'Anti-Americanism and Defence Policy', prepared for the 'Red Orchestra' Hoover Institution Conference, 3–4 March 1987, Washington, DC.

Just Defence: Reviewing Australia's Defence Needs, Conference Papers, ANU, Canberra, 18–19 October 1986.

Kennaway, R. N., 'The New Zealand Non-Nuclear Initiative: Out of The Frying Pan. Into The Pressure Cooker ...?', Asian Peace Association Conference, Sydney, August 1986.

Mack, Andrew, 'Defence Versus Offence: The Dibb Report and its Critics', Peace Research Centre, working paper no. 14, RSPS, ANU, Canberra, September 1986.

Millar, T. B., 'Soviet Aims, Targets and Instruments in the South West Pacific', paper for the 'Red Orchestra' Hoover Institution Conference, 3–4 March 1987, Washington, DC.

Riley, Philip D., 'ANZUS Impasse – Analysis, Prospects, and Recommendations', unpublished research report, National Defense University, Washington, DC, January 1987.

INDEX